Montana's
Visionary Mayor

Howard— I think you have something in common with Willard so hope you enjoy this

Montana's Visionary Mayor

Willard E. Fraser

Lou Mandler

Lou Mandler

MONTANA HISTORICAL
SOCIETY PRESS

Helena

Front cover: Willard Fraser on his bicycle, which became a symbol of both his vitality and his vision for moving Billings forward into the future, ca. 1971. Courtesy Billings Public Library

Back cover: Willard Fraser at Canyon de Chelly, 1963. Stu Conner, photographer

Cover and book design by Diane Gleba Hall

Typeset in Arno Pro

Printed in the United States of America

Distributed by Farcountry Press, 2750 Broadwater Avenue, Helena, MT 59602. (800) 821-3874, farcountrypress.com

ISBN 978-1-940527-91-8

Library of Congress Cataloging-in-Publication Data

Names: Mandler, Lou, author.

Title: Montana's visionary mayor : Willard E. Fraser / Lou Mandler.

Other titles: Willard E. Fraser

Description: Helena : Montana Historical Society Press, 2022. | Includes bibliographical references and index.

Summary: This book is a biography of Willard E. Fraser (1907–1972), who served as the mayor of Billings, Montana, for four terms between 1963 and 1972. He was legendary for his indefatigable promotion of Montana as a tourist destination, his efforts to curb pollution, and his commitment to progressive social reforms. He was known for his forward-thinking vision, humanitarian spirit, and clever wit.

Identifiers: LCCN 2022023624 | ISBN 9781940527918

Subjects: LCSH: Fraser, Willard. | Mayors—Montana—Billings—Biography. | Billings (Mont.)—Politics and government—20th century. | Montana—Social conditions—20th century. | Billings (Mont.—Biography.

Classification: LCC F739.B5 M36 2022 | DDC 978.6/39092 [B]—dc23/eng/20220525

LC record available at https://lccn.loc.gov/2022023624

He dared new trails, marched to a different drummer; and little mortals cannot deny him his place as a Big Man with big vision and big dreams.

Harold G. "Hal" Stearns,
eulogy for Willard Fraser, 9/23/1972

Contents

Acknowledgments ix

Introduction 1

CHAPTER ONE
"History belongs to those who tell it" 6

CHAPTER TWO
"Have you seen Billings, Montana?" 14

CHAPTER THREE
"I find myself practically up in the air as to
my most important future" 31

CHAPTER FOUR
"A glorious happy time" followed by "those
horribly, helpless weeks" 45

CHAPTER FIVE
"The way to get into politics is to get into politics" 58

CHAPTER SIX
"I am his partisan" 74

CHAPTER SEVEN
"When I helped to win the war" 85

CHAPTER EIGHT
"Old enough to think, young enough to act" 99

Contents

CHAPTER NINE
"Good government is my lifelong interest and pursuit"   117

CHAPTER TEN
"I know we're going to step on some toes . . ."   130

CHAPTER ELEVEN
"Get Billings going"   143

CHAPTER TWELVE
"The Council continues to be obdurate"   164

CHAPTER THIRTEEN
"You haven't been in a fight until you've been in
    a fluoridation fight"   176

CHAPTER FOURTEEN
"All it took was a five-cent stamp"   189

CHAPTER FIFTEEN
"I am not city limited"   207

CHAPTER SIXTEEN
"What is a city without lively youngsters?"   225

CHAPTER SEVENTEEN
"The confusions of the hour are immense"   241

CHAPTER EIGHTEEN
"This has not been one of my better years"   252

CHAPTER NINETEEN
"Tell 'em Willie Boy is here"   269

CHAPTER TWENTY
"I am looking for men who will think 50 years ahead,
    instead of 50 years backward"   288

A RECKONING
"This is your mayor!"   309

Bibliography   317
Notes   321
Index   355
About the Author   365

Acknowledgments

THIS BOOK exists only because of an ever-expanding web of generous people. In the beginning, my longtime friend Lue Ponich arranged for me to meet with Fraser acquaintances and friends, including James (Jim) Thompson, who shared memories of his close relationship with Willard Fraser and arranged for me to meet Stuart Conner, another close Fraser friend. Both Jim and Stu were invaluable in bringing Willard Fraser to life through their vivid anecdotes of life with Willard, and I owe a huge debt to the time and thought they invested to remembering Willard. Stu shared photographs and directed me to archival information that I might have missed. Jim extended my web of Fraser contacts by introducing me to Fraser's secretary, Abby Ferguson; Fran Calton, the wife of his last city attorney; Fraser friends Dr. Donald Harr and John Bohlinger; and Fraser's cousin, Sally Fraser Moskol. Sally directed me to Fraser's nephew, Mac Fraser, who was the cornerstone of my information on the Fraser family. Mac, in turn, led me to additional relatives—Willard's niece Wendy Fraser Augunas, grandson David Hudnut, granddaughter Marjorie Hudnut Renner, and family historian Judy Koonce. As the grandson of B. R. Albin, one of Willard's mentors, Mac facilitated my contact with Albin relatives Jo Albin, Dr. Sean Haling, and Cathy Wiltgen. Marjorie Hudnut Renner arranged for a very valuable interview with her mother (Willard's daughter), Robin Fraser Hudnut. Robin contributed unique memories and photographs that enriched this book beyond measure.

Kevin Kooistra of Billings's Western Heritage Center shared images and pointed me to online resources, and Montana statesman Harrison Fagg provided a first-hand view of Billings politics in the 1960s. Elisabeth

DeGrenier at WHC directed me to Jim Ronquillo, who provided striking memories of Billings's South Side where the Frasers lived for many years. Former *Billings Gazette* editor Darrell Ehrlick, who authored four articles on Mayor Fraser, was a helpful guide and provided many useful pointers.

A project such as this would be much poorer if people had not saved their letters and photographs and if others had not taken the care to collect them. It is impossible to overvalue the importance of private and public archives and the devoted and helpful people who watch over archival collections. Hats off to the MSU–Billings Library; the Montana Historical Society in Helena; the Rauner Library at Dartmouth College, Hanover, New Hampshire; the Jones Library and the Amherst College Library in Amherst, Massachusetts; the Milne Archives at the University of New Hampshire in Durham; the St. Lawrence University Library in Canton, New York; the University of Michigan Library at Ann Arbor; the University of South Dakota Library in Vermillion; and the Gardner Historical Society in Gardner, Kansas. When archives were closed to researchers during the pandemic, several individuals went above and beyond to email materials to me: Scout Noffke at Rauner, Paul Doty and Paul Haggett at St. Lawrence, Margaret Dakin at Amherst, Eileen Wright at MSU–Billings, and Samuel Herley at the USD. Tressa Stone at the Gardner Historical Museum provided generous long-distance information and photographs even before the pandemic.

And then there were readers. Early on, my writers' group—Anne Batterson, Sherry Horton, Sally Terrell, and Chivas Sandage—gave me astute advice and encouragement. News reporter Chuck Johnson's unique knowledge of Montana politics led me to important information and inspired me to dig deeper into specific topics. Marjorie Hudnut Renner made insightful suggestions and provided additional context. Paul Jakab alerted me to my semicolon fetish and offered substantial observations. A conversation with friend and Vietnam War veteran Peter Bordonaro sent me off to consider Mike Mansfield's role in the Vietnam War. Throughout the process, my husband, JP, supported this project in more ways than I can recount—as reader, tech savior, critic, and chef.

In the last act, I had the perfect editor in Laura Ferguson at the Montana Historical Society Press, whose knowledge of Montana history, skill at adjusting narrative flow, and readiness to ask questions that needed answers made this a more readable and informative book.

Introduction

On April 6, 1971, the front page of the *Billings Gazette* featured a photograph of the city's mayor grinning gleefully as he rode a bicycle into the Northern Hotel, where a jubilant crowd of well-wishers surrounded him. Under the headline "Fraser Bikes to Victory," the paper announced that Willard Fraser had just been elected to his fourth term as mayor of Montana's largest city. Such an unorthodox grand entrance was characteristic of this charismatic and complex politician, who was both beloved and ridiculed, passionate and fun-loving, an intellectual and a man of common sense, an advocate for the marginalized and someone comfortable with the famous and powerful.

Dubbed "a newspaper man's delight," Willard Fraser provided great news copy, and his career can be traced in the pages of various newspapers. The *Billings Gazette* often printed as many as three Fraser-based articles per week on the front page during his mayoral tenure, while the *Great Falls Tribune*, *Missoulian*, *Butte Miner*, and *Montana Standard* followed Fraser regularly. Smaller Montana papers in Helena, Harlowton, Havre, and Kalispell also drew attention to Fraser's appearances, quotes, opinions, or initiatives. The *Chicago Tribune* and other national papers published a Willard Fraser story when a comment or action provoked controversy or merited reporting. This flamboyant and city-proud mayor reveled in attention, pomp and ceremony. Addressing Willard's talent for public relations, *Billings Gazette* columnist Roger Clawson once commented, "Willard will go to any opening, even of a can of beans." A friend once warned, "Don't go out of town with Willard or you'll end up in a parade."[1]

Fraser believed that any publicity he garnered ultimately promoted the growth and progress of Billings and Montana.

Interested in politics since his youth, Willard failed in his early attempts to gain public office, being defeated in eleven different elections between 1933 and 1961 before finally finding success. This posed a conundrum for me: Why did such an interesting, committed, intelligent person fail so often? And after rejecting Fraser so many times, why did the people of Billings elect him as their mayor four times? Certainly, the fact that Willard was a progressive in a deeply conservative region of Montana played a role in his many defeats. No doubt, too, his exuberant personality and penchant for unorthodox ideas created the perception that he was not a serious politician. Despite these challenges, Willard, as he was known by his friends, the press, and the public, eventually cultivated bipartisan support for his ideas and earned votes from Democrats and Republicans alike.

I first discovered Willard Fraser after reading a book of vignettes of little-known literary connections on a flight from my home state of Montana to Connecticut. The section about Robert Frost contained a photograph of the poet with his granddaughter, Robin Fraser, at her high school graduation in Billings in 1952. I was surprised and curious, as I had not known Frost had a Montana connection. Back in Connecticut, I brought out my copy of the *Selected Letters of Robert Frost* and checked the index. Yes, there were letters to and from Frost and Robin's father, Willard Fraser. I was instantly intrigued by this connection between the famous poet's family and the former mayor of Billings, Montana. What started as a plan to draw attention to a Robert Frost–Montana connection, however, led to my decision to commemorate a fascinating and forward-thinking personality, whose life and career provide a window into several decades of growth and change in Montana and the nation. Willard Fraser's vision and accomplishments proved to be particularly relevant in the twenty-first century.

WILLARD FRASER (1907–1972) married Marjorie Frost (1905–1934), Elinor and Robert Frost's youngest child, in 1933. He was proud to be part of the Frost family, and he was not shy about mentioning it, referring to Frost as "my father-in-law" even after Marjorie's death in 1934. Frost affirmed the mutual regard between himself and Willard when he wrote in a 1949 letter to Willard: "You are the only son-in-law I ever cared for."[2] While some Frost biographers sought material about Frost from Willard Fraser, I went to the

Frost family correspondence to learn more about this intriguing Montana figure. The Frost family archival collections at Dartmouth College, Amherst College, the University of New Hampshire, and the University of Michigan provided germane information to supplement hundreds of Fraser's letters now archived at Montana State University–Billings (then Eastern Montana College).

In 1970, during the two-year gap before his last mayoral term, Fraser donated his mayoral papers—some fifteen linear feet of files—to Eastern Montana College (EMC) for that institution's newly established archives. The collection contains his personal and mayoral letters, memos, speeches, and personal writings, as well as notes on myriad topics pertaining to city administration and state and national affairs. In an introduction to the collection, former EMC history professor Robert Smith states, "The historical value of the papers cannot be overestimated. The Fraser papers [are] the key to Billings' recent past. No definitive history of Billings, the Yellowstone Valley, or indeed of Montana could be written without consulting them."[3] Far from being the dry bureaucratic record of an elected official, Fraser's mayoral papers document his diverse interests and his dedication to the betterment of Billings and Montana in one of the most entertaining letter collections since that of Mark Twain.

A consummate letter writer—often churning out as many as fifty letters a day—Willard Fraser wrote to scores of people besides his fellow Montanans, including poets, musicians, novelists, philosophers, politicians, and even astronauts. His letters are laced with entertaining stories, audacious opinions, playful jabs, and exhortations that reveal him to be a skillful relationship builder, a master raconteur, and an outspoken progressive with visionary goals.

Fraser's early letters reveal his interest in the wider political scene during the Great Depression, World War II, and the decade following the war. The bulk of his archived letters, however, were written during the decade of conflict and cultural upheaval—between 1963 and 1972—while he was mayor. They serve as a political weathervane for those tumultuous years, when attitudes toward the Vietnam War and the government divided America, and the nation's young people became a cultural force unlike any previous youth bloc. Reading through the fifteen boxes of Fraser's mayoral letters—at once an exhausting, overwhelming, and inspiring experience—I discovered that Willard Fraser merited attention for reasons beyond his identity as a typical small-city mayor and a mysterious Frost relative. As a person, he modeled tolerance, generosity, and fortitude in the face of many

Robin Fraser Hudnut designed the new city seal for Billings after her father was elected mayor. The slogan was written by Mrs. Fred Wilson. Courtesy Robin Fraser Hudnut

challenges. As a politician, his actions and policies were rooted in a firm belief in governing for the wellbeing of the people and the greater good of his city.

Willard believed that history matters, and that belief served as the foundation of his personal and political philosophy. Alert to evolving social and political issues, Mayor Fraser was not focused solely on Billings or even Montana. Rather, he was connected to organizations and political figures beyond the state and frequently became involved in national issues. As a champion of emerging progressive ideals, he promoted ideas that were often ahead of their time. He was aware of and drew attention to issues such as urban decay, water conservation, gun control, the importance of public lands, and the environment. In the 1960s Willard predicted the invention and use of electric cars, and he advocated joining the computer revolution.

In his personal life and in his public career, Willard faced an abundance of difficulties. The tragic death of his young wife, Marjorie Frost Fraser, following the birth of their only child in 1934 left an indelible mark. Willard never remarried, and his mother, Sadie, served as surrogate mother to Robin in the South Side Billings home where Willard lived for the rest of his life and Robin grew up. A lifelong asthmatic, he endured many hospitalizations for this and other physical ailments. After numerous failures to attain office, when Willard finally became mayor, he faced the opposition of conservatives and ultraconservatives who often blocked his proposed reforms. Nonetheless, he proved to be remarkably resilient, maintaining his optimism and energy in the face of tragedy and defeat. Fifty years after Willard's death, his daughter, Robin, commented on his positive outlook, remembering a favorite saying, "Chin up, not out!"[4] Blessed with an abundance of confidence and determination, he appeared unfazed by criticism and persisted in fighting for progressive goals and the betterment of his community. Even when a city council member called him a "goofy buzzard," Willard gleefully turned it into a positive news story.[5]

The most common adjective used to describe Willard Fraser was "colorful," and he was that, but the word masks the substance behind the show. As mayor of Montana's largest city, he strove to bring business to Billings, to address issues connected to urban growth, and to improve the quality of life for its citizens. Billings South Side resident Jim Ronquillo recalled Fraser's devotion to his work, saying, "I have a mental picture of him lying in bed at night thinking about how to make the city better."[6] A creative thinker with a reformist zeal, Willard reveled in ideas and advocated for people and causes that lay outside the cultural mainstream. He banned smoking in the city council chambers in the early 1960s, advocated publicly for Montana's Indians, enthusiastically promoted the arts as well as opportunities for youth, and campaigned for a cleaner, healthier environment at a time when such concerns were often ignored.

As mayor, Willard Fraser proclaimed, "I am not city limited." Indeed, his life and work testify to this statement. Few politicians have exuded more pride in being a Montanan or have exerted more energy in selling the idea of Montana while maintaining an active interest in and connection to the larger world. Recalling Fraser's far-reaching effect and his visionary leadership, Montana newspaperman and history enthusiast Hal Stearns spoke for many Montanans when he said, "He was my mayor, too."[7]

"History belongs to those who tell it"

WILLARD FRASER's interest in history is apparent in the frequent historical references and facts sprinkled throughout his letters. He believed that
local, state, and national history are relevant to understanding the present
and, therefore, essential to good government. That belief later factored
into many of the projects he initiated as mayor of Billings in the 1960s
and is evident in his enthusiasm for politics and public service. At the root
of Willard's devotion to his country, which often found expression in his
political career, was his pride in his family history.

Willard happily touted his Scottish heritage, Kansas roots, and ties to
Montana—all of which reinforced his pride as an American. Wearing a
kilt of Fraser plaid, he regularly attended Miles City's annual Bobby Burns
Dinner put on by the Caledonian Society in honor of the Scottish poet.[1]
His family's Scottish background provided fuel for his love of storytelling
and hyperbole, such as this note to a friend describing his speech at one
Burns celebration: "I told them that, as everyone knows, Scotch was the
language spoken in the Garden of Eden, but not everyone knows that Eve
washed 'that' apple in Scotch Whiskey before handing it to Adam."[2] When
he welcomed visitors to Billings, he often called on the Caledonian Pipes
and Drums Band to perform. Decades after Fraser's death, a colleague
remarked on his Scottish pride, "He thought all racial and ethnic groups
were wonderful, but the Scots were the most wonderful of all."[3]

Willard's Scottish heritage is well documented. His great-great-
grandfather, William Fraser, was born in Inverness, and Willard enjoyed
claiming that William Fraser was descended from Lord Lovat, Simon
Fraser (1667–1747), who was beheaded in the Tower of London in 1747
for supporting the Scottish attempt to put Bonnie Prince Charlie on the
British throne.[4] He was well versed in details of the Jacobite uprising and

Fraser family, ca. 1909. Back row, left to right: Charles C. Fraser, William H. Fraser, James Higgins Fraser, John Brown Fraser (Willard's father). Front row: Marshall Estella M. "Bird" Fraser, William Fraser, Edna L. Tremayne Fraser. Courtesy Judy Koonce

the Battle of Culloden in Inverness, where Charles Stuart's forces lost to the British, but there is no documentation to prove his Fraser ancestors were descendants of Lord Lovat.

William Fraser and his family left Scotland in 1823 and settled near Marietta, Ohio, where he made a down payment on 160 acres of land for himself and his son James, indicating he was not an impoverished immigrant but one with a solid plan in place. James Fraser, Willard's great-grandfather, married Roxanna Fulcher, and their son (another William) was born in 1841. Just six years later, Roxanna Fulcher Fraser was found dead in the family well. After his mother's murder, young William was sent to Iowa to live with his maternal uncle, John Fulcher, the son of a Revolutionary War veteran. James Fraser was tried for his wife's murder and spent nearly twenty-nine years in prison before being pardoned by Ohio's governor in 1876. An unverified family story is that a former servant in the Fraser household declared on his deathbed that James had not been the one who had killed Roxanna. James Fraser lived only two years after his release from prison, and he is buried in Kansas, where William, Willard's grandfather, settled after the Civil War.[5]

Fraser's ancestors' experiences in the Civil War became an important part of family lore and identity. In 1965, Willard wrote about attending a memorial service in Gardner, Kansas: "A group of aunts—all in the upper 80s and 90s—insisted I go to the cemetery for services. An awful lot of our heritage is buried there, and the entire conversation was about 'the war.' For them, 'the war' is still the Civil War, and such little interludes as World War I, World War II, and Korea are simply irritants, but really hardly on a scale to commemorate in family plots."[6] Although Willard's tone here is a teasing one, his aunts' insistence on recounting family history was a lesson he learned well.

Willard delighted in sprinkling his letters with historical references and anecdotes, including stories about his family. His recital of family legends occasionally illustrated his oft-expressed declaimer: "History belongs to those who tell it." For example, in writing about his paternal grandfather, he said, "It's an old family custom of ours to boast about the time that grandpa was in prison in Little Rock . . . He was part of a Union Army outfit that the Confederates captured and imprisoned . . . I can boast though by saying that eventually he got away, and none were fast enough to catch him."[7] Willard's tale was based on fact, albeit with the embellishment of saying "none were fast enough to catch him." In fact, military records indicate his grandfather was part of a prisoner exchange, not an actual escape.

William Fraser enlisted in the Union army in 1861 at age twenty. Perhaps because he was able to supply his own horse, he served with Company I of the Third Iowa Cavalry, for the duration of the war. According to Civil War historians, "federal troopers from the frontier towns and farms of the West were natural horsemen. . . . In the far-flung Western Theater, these rough and ready riders on both sides proved most effective as long-distance raiders. . . . Using surprise as a weapon, they struck hard at lines of communication, capturing or destroying everything in their path."[8] The Third Regiment was involved in the 1862 Confederate Jenkins Raid in West Virginia and Ohio, the 1864 Confederate Price Raid in Missouri, and the 1865 Union Wilson Raid in Alabama and Georgia.[9] William Fraser was promoted to corporal in June 1862 and was reported captured by rebels on May 1, 1863, at LaGrange, Tennessee, near the Arkansas border, one of about thirty soldiers taken prisoner in a skirmish under the command of Union captain J. Q. A. De Huff. Records confirm that Fraser was confined in a post guardhouse in Little Rock until August 21, 1863, then "delivered at the mouth of White River" on August 25, 1863, and on September 1, "Exchanged and sent to field."[10]

The system of prisoner exchange between the Union and Confederate forces existed from the very beginning of the Civil War. The exchange process underwent several changes, and different commanding officers advocated various stipulations. For example, an 1861 stipulation was that only regular soldiers—not home guards or state militia volunteers—could be exchanged. Regular soldiers made up less than 10 percent of the Union forces. In late 1861, the Union Congress called for "systematic measures for exchange of prisoners." Working out such an agreement took until July 1862, when an exchange cartel was signed. The system was beset with problems from the beginning, and on May 25, 1863, the exchange cartel ended—just three weeks after William Fraser was taken prisoner. Fraser's exchange on August 25 must have been a transaction handled by a special agent of exchange. Both the North and the South had such designated agents.[11]

On January 1, 1864, William Fraser reenlisted in the Third Iowa Cavalry for a three-year term as a "Veteran Volunteer." A few days later, the re-enlisted men, numbering in the hundreds, were transported back to Iowa for a thirty-day furlough. Augmented with new recruits, the volunteers reconvened in St. Louis in February 1864. Within a year, William was promoted to sergeant. The Third Iowa Cavalry spent much of the rest of the war in the Missouri campaign against rebel forces under General Sterling Price, "one of the most important campaigns in the history of its service."[12] In March 1865, the Third Iowa Cavalry pursued Confederate forces through Arkansas, and they arrived on April 1 at the battleground of Ebenezer Church, Alabama, where William Fraser suffered a slight hand wound. He was mustered out on June 1, 1865, and officially discharged on August 8 at Atlanta, Georgia. The Third and Fourth Regiments of the Iowa Cavalry were then provided transportation to Davenport, where the regiment was disbanded.[13]

William Fraser married Charlotte Armstrong in 1866, and they moved to Gardner, Kansas, where their ten children—five boys and five girls—were born. Willard Fraser's father, John Brown Fraser, was the ninth. Willard claimed that his Unionist grandfather named John Brown Fraser after the abolitionist John Brown, who led the October 19, 1859, raid at Harper's Ferry, Virginia. It is true that the famous abolitionist and William Fraser had common Ohio roots, but it is more likely that John Brown Fraser and his brother, James Higgins Fraser, were named after their mother's father, John Higgins Brown Armstrong. Willard's grandfather, William Fraser, died in 1921. In his obituary in the *Gardner Gazette*, William was termed "one of the community's pioneers and most highly respected citizens."[14] The Fraser farmhouse south of Gardner still stands.

America's divided loyalties before, during, and after the Civil War existed within Willard Fraser's family history as well. Willard's mother, Sadie Gay Fraser, was the third of five children born to Lorenda Gorseline and Edward Gay, whose families had settled in the Gardner area before the Civil War began. They were there when Kansas was a major battleground of heated clashes between pro- and antislavery forces in the 1850s and 1860s and it came to be known as "Bleeding Kansas." Just thirty miles southwest of Kansas City and twenty-seven miles southeast of Lawrence, Gardner's proximity to the Missouri border put it in the path of violent Civil War fringe bands, both the jayhawkers of the Union and the bushwhackers of the Confederacy. On May 21, 1856, proslavery forces attacked Lawrence, and in retaliation, on May 24, abolitionist John Brown's supporters killed five proslavery men at Pottawatomie Creek in Franklin County.[15]

The Quantrill Raiders, a pro-Confederate guerilla band led by William Clarke Quantrill, were particularly feared for their bloody raids on Lawrence, Olathe, and elsewhere. Especially notorious was the raid on Lawrence on August 21, 1863, when Quantrill's 450 men killed 183 men and boys and burned much of the city, no doubt sending a wave of fear into nearby communities.[16] In one family story about the Kansas border conflicts, Willard wrote that one of his great aunts was caught by the Quantrill raiders.[17] This probably refers to the family legend about an incident when Quantrill and his men stopped at the house of one of Willard's relatives. The man of the household, Thomas Reid, hid in the family drinking well, as the raiders were intent on killing men and boys. The Quantrills demanded that Reid's daughter make tea for them, and a Reid descendant still owns the teapot reputedly used to serve the outlaws.[18]

Willard claimed that his "mother's grandfather was the first man killed in the raid on Lawrence."[19] Henry Gorseline, Sadie's grandfather, did become involved in a border conflict surrounding the proslavery/abolition debate on the night of October 22, 1861. Fourteen proslavery sympathizers entered Gardner using two horse-drawn wagons, one of which had been taken from the Gorseline farm two miles east of Gardner. While the guerilla invaders looted the town, Henry roused the inhabitants and pursued the bandits. In the melee that ensued, he was accidentally shot by his own gun, and he died two weeks later.[20] So while it is true that Gorseline lost his life as a result of the border conflicts, the family story as Willard told it does not take into account that he was not killed by raiders.

While Willard often made it clear that he was a "Union man," he acknowledged that some members of his mother's family "were on the other [Confederate] side." In one letter about his mother's family's experiences during the Civil War, he states that "almost the entire male population over the age of twelve were wiped out at Antietam, Gettysburg, and Shilo [*sic*]."[21] Another anecdote shares a more intimate aspect of their Confederate past:

> There was old Lucy, a negro who had been given to my great grandmother when she was a very small girl. They were of an age, and I have a faint memory of seeing these two old ladies rocking on the porch, for she never left my great grandmother even after she was freed, and in a real sense, I guess, was a part of the family. There was a saying in the family when I was very small that grandmother and Lucy were so close they used the same set of false teeth.[22]

Gay family, ca. 1910. Back row left to right: Stella Gay, Ella Gay, Sidney Clyde Gay, Sadie Irene Gay (Willard's mother). Front row, left to right: Edward Y. Gay, James Edward Gay; Lorinda Goresline Gay. Courtesy Judy Koonce

Willard sometimes used the family's personal stories to exhort others to "get with it." When a cousin seemed to dissolve in self-pity after the death of her husband, Willard wrote to her, "It seems to me that it's time you thought something about the tremendous courage of our mutual great grandmother Whitaker, who, after her husband was killed in the turbulent turmoil of Bleeding Kansas at the John Brown Raid on Lawrence, tied up her skirts, and with a rifle setting always handily by, and small children wailing—went to work and created quite a farm out of that raw

Marvin, Ruth Jeanne, and Willard Fraser, 1915. Courtesy Sally Moskol

Kansas prairie."[23] This anecdote perhaps refers to the Pottawatomie Creek Massacre, but it is difficult to match story with historical fact.

In 1906, twenty-one-year-old John Brown (J. B.) Fraser married nineteen-year-old Sadie Gay and the couple began farming near Gardner, where two sons were born: Willard in 1907 and Marvin in 1910.[24] Despite the Frasers' and the Gays' deep roots in the Gardner area, however, Willard Fraser was not destined to grow up in Kansas.

It is likely that J. B.'s farming venture was not successful, because the *Gardner Gazette* published a notice of a public "closing out" sale in October 1907. It advertised forty-five head of livestock, thirty head of shoats [young pigs], corn and wheat in field, and farm implements on a farm three miles south of Gardner. The sale did not include the land, suggesting that J. B. continued to try his hand at farming for a few more years. A second public sale notice at the same location appeared in November 1913. This time, the list of personal property for sale was prefaced by a statement from Willard's father: "On account of the health of my boys, have decided to [*sic*] Montana and will sell at public auction at my farm."[25]

The statement, "the health of my boys," certainly refers to the chronic asthma that already afflicted six-year-old Willard and the resulting search for a drier climate to mitigate the symptoms of the malady. The humid climate of eastern Kansas would not have been healthful for an asthmatic. That J. B. Fraser's older brother, James, was already established in Billings factored decisively into J. B. and Sadie Fraser's decision to move their young family to that city, where two more children—Ruth (Jeanne) and Robert—were born.[26]

Relocating from Gardner to Billings did not mean the Frasers severed their ties to Kansas. Both Sadie and J. B. returned occasionally to visit family and to attend family funerals. The Gardner community kept track of the Montana Frasers, a fact illustrated by a 1930 article in the *Gardner Gazette* summarizing young Willard's archaeological work in the Southwest. When Sadie Fraser died at the age of eighty-eight in 1975, the *Gardner Gazette* published an obituary with the note: "Mrs. Fraser visited relatives in Spring Hill, Gardner, De Soto, etc. many times in bygone years and is known by older folks in this area."[27] Although Willard was only six when the Frasers moved to Billings, visits and communication with relatives in Kansas cultivated his regard for family history. While not forgetting his family ties to Gardner and his own affection for the Sunflower State, Willard grew up to be a stalwart champion of Billings and one of the most passionate promoters of Montana in the state's history.

CHAPTER TWO

"Have you seen Billings, Montana?"

WILLARD FRASER once wrote that when anyone from Billings reached heaven, the person would look around and then say to St. Peter, "This is nice, but have you seen Billings, Montana?"[1] Although Kansas-born Fraser traveled extensively outside the state as an adult, Montana remained his true love. Many of Willard's interests and policy positions can be traced to his youth spent in Billings, where his determined mother, working-class upbringing, and Montana acquaintances left their mark on his character. It was here that he developed his appreciation for both history and the natural world during his boyhood and adolescence, and where he first aspired to serve the public.[2]

Established in 1882 on land ceded from the Apsáalooke Tribe, Billings began as a Northern Pacific Railroad stop on the banks of the Yellowstone River in southcentral Montana, with plains to the east and mountains to the west and south. The Yellowstone Valley was once a hunting territory used by multiple Indigenous nations but generally regarded as part of the Apsáalooke (Crow) homeland. By the mid-1800s, treaties with the United States redefined tribal territories and created reservations and the valley was included as part of the Crow Reservation. The U.S. government had its eye on the valley, however, and in 1880, the tribe ceded approximately 1.6 million additional acres—including the valley, which had already been overrun by preemptive white settlers.[3] Among the tribal leaders involved in the land cession were Plenty Coups, Pretty Eagle, Medicine Crow, and Spotted Horse.

The city is nestled between two impressive geological features: the Rimrocks, distinctive sandstone formations that curve around the valley, and the Yellowstone River, which flows around its southern edge. The

Rimrocks range from six hundred to fourteen hundred feet in height and provide the city with a unique backdrop. The five-hundred-foot-high Sacrifice Cliff extends the rim southward at the eastern edge of the city and meets the Yellowstone River where it leaves the valley.[4] "We are here because the River is here," Fraser said of the city. The Yellowstone, which the Apsáalooke people called *Iichíilikaashaashe*, or Elk River, flows nearly seven hundred miles from its sources in the Absaroka and Beartooth Mountains, and eventually joins the Missouri near the Montana–North Dakota border.[5] Today, it is the last major free-flowing river in the lower United States, surviving decades of plans to dam it. The river wends along the southern portion of Billings, and the distant Pryor Mountains and spectacular Beartooth Plateau are visible from the Rimrocks.

The city of Billings was named after Northern Pacific Railroad president Frederick Billings, who owned more than four and a half thousand acres in and near the town. In 1882, when the railroad established Billings as its stopping point rather than the little town of Coulson a short distance upstream, Coulson was doomed and it was soon abandoned. Billings, meanwhile, was incorporated with fewer than one thousand residents, but the new town grew seemingly overnight. The Billings family donated money to construct the Congregational Church and the town's first school building. They later invested in many area projects and became involved in city organizations and government.[6] When James Higgins Fraser, Willard's uncle, came to Billings in 1898, the city was on the cusp of remarkable, magical growth that earned Billings its nickname as the "Magic City."[7] A confluence of factors—its location, the railroad, and a unique coalition of talented civic and commercial leaders, as well as Montana's agricultural boom in the early 1900s—contributed to the city's rapid growth after the turn of the century. Between 1900 and 1910, its population grew by an astounding 211 percent to ten thousand, but even so, decades passed before Billings became Montana's largest city.

In 1903 and 1905, banker Preston Moss, farmer and irrigation expert I. D. O'Donnell, and other investors took advantage of the city's location adjacent to the Yellowstone River to initiate irrigation projects such as the Huntley Project, which made it possible to grow sugar beets on several thousand acres. These investors established the Billings Sugar Company in 1906 and began importing laborers from Mexico to harvest the tens of thousands of tons of sugar beets. This was the beginning of the county's sugar beet farming and sugar refining industry, which have become a regional economic mainstay.[8] The Billings Sugar Company became Great West Sugar Company in 1918.

Billings, Montana, 1915. Built on landed ceded form the Apsáalooke Nation in 1882, Billings owes its existence to the Northern Pacific Railroad. Haines Photos, photographer. pan6a13798, Library of Congress, Washington, D.C.

By 1909, Billings was served by three railroad companies: the Northern Pacific, the Great Northern, and the Chicago, Burlington & Quincy. The arrival of the railroads initiated the development of Billings into one of the most important trade centers in the Northern Plains, serving Montana, North Dakota, and Wyoming. St. Vincent's Hospital, founded in 1899, soon became the cornerstone on which Billings would build its future standing as the major medical center of the tristate area. The Yale Oil refinery, processing oil from Stillwater, Big Horn, and Carbon Counties, was established in 1929 and foreshadowed Billings' becoming the oil capital of the state in the 1950s.[9]

In his first years in Billings, Willard's uncle James worked for one of Billings's most prominent civic and political leaders, Albert L. Babcock, in the A. L. Babcock Hardware store, established in 1882.[10] Eventually renamed Billings Hardware, the business was moved in 1956 to a huge warehouse-like building on North Broadway.[11] Babcock went on to build an opera house in 1895 and the Babcock Theater, which still stands on 2nd Avenue North. He served as president of Yellowstone National Bank and represented Yellowstone County for the Republican Party in Montana's house and senate chambers. Historian Lawrence Small commented about Babcock, "Few of the county's early citizens attained greater influence in the community at large."[12] James Fraser worked for Babcock Hardware until the original store burned in 1911, after which he managed the McElroy Plumbing Company. He also worked for the Renwick Implement Company and the Yellowstone National Bank.

Billings seemed a land of opportunity in 1913. As a result of its economic prosperity, the growing town offered many of the conveniences of
major American cities. Electric service came to Billings in 1887, just five
years after it came to New York and London. Telephones were introduced
in 1890, and by 1912, electric street cars were running.[13] Despite their
uncertain financial status, in this city of ten thousand, the Frasers would
have enjoyed many more conveniences than they had known on the farm
in Kansas.

Shortly after Willard's parents, J. B. and Sadie, moved to Billings, the
Gardner Gazette published an article titled "He is Successful" about James
Fraser and his prosperity in Montana. "Everyone in and around Gardner
knows Jim Fraser and likes him," the *Gazette* reported, adding "Jim Fraser is
one of the finest young men who grew up in this community and his success
is truly gratifying." The article went on to announce Fraser's half ownership
of McElroy Plumbing and Engineering, "one of the largest plumbing concerns in eastern Montana."[14] Sadly, Willard's father had only ten years to
share his new city with James, who died in 1923 at age forty-seven from
melanoma after several years of declining health and fortune.[15]

Of Willard's parents, Sadie seems to have wielded the stronger influence on Willard, whom she outlived by three years. Her indomitable spirit
and evenhanded outlook are apparent in his references to her in letters.
In counseling against strict black-and-white judgments, he wrote, "My
mother used to say there is a little bit of good in every bad little boy, and
a little bit of bad in every good little girl, and this is so, and has always
been so."[16] Another Sadie Gay Fraser story that Willard frequently quoted
encouraged persistence in young people: "'Can't' was a dog that embarked
with the Pilgrims on the Mayflower, and halfway across the ocean there

was a terrible, terrible Atlantic storm, and poor 'Can't' was washed over-board and drowned, so 'Can't' never got to America."[17] Willard's fondness for his mother is palpable when he relates her reaction to the 1968 moon landing. As a young woman in the late 1800s, Sadie had climbed Pike's Peak while wearing high-heeled boots, a long skirt, and a sun hat. Hearing of the moon landing, she quipped, "I walked and climbed to the top of Pike's Peak without help from anyone. Sure, astronauts got to the moon, but they had the whole world helping them, and they rode all the way."[18] No doubt

Sadie's strong will and determination nurtured the persistent optimism of her firstborn who, even after numerous defeats, continued to believe he would be elected to a government post.

Robin Fraser cited "Nana" as "extremely important" in both Willard's and Robin's development, both for her strong will and for her intellectual and political interests. According to Robin, J. B.'s nickname for his wife was "Eleanor" because she admired Eleanor Roosevelt so much. Sadie owned a set of Delphian books, an early 20th century correspondence course designed for women who did not go to college but still desired a systematic education.[19] Sadie's firmness of character also stands out in the memory of her great-grandson, David Hudnut. He described her as a woman who could make a mean rhubarb pie but also chop off the head of any rattlesnakes she found in her garden. He assessed her as "very, very capable, someone who made things work," and opined that Willard inherited his problem-solving ability from his mother.[20]

Willard's colleagues described Sadie Fraser as "a nice lady," "marvelous," and "sophisticated."[21] In photographs, she presents as a taller-than-average woman who remained relatively slender throughout her life and who, although not beautiful, fits granddaughter Wendy's description as an "elegant" woman who often dressed in suits and wore her hair up in the back. She was frequently mentioned in the society pages of the *Gazette*, even after the Frasers moved to the less affluent South Side. One of her grandsons, Mac Fraser, spoke of his grandmother as being socially conscious: "I would ride my Schwinn bicycle to the South Side to their house. Nana would have me

Interior of the Babcock-Fraser Company store in Billings. Left to right, A. L. Babcock (president), J. H. Fraser (vice president and manager) and L. C. Babcock (treasurer), ca. 1909. PAc 82-79.8, MHS Photograph Archives, Helena

Sadie Fraser, who was active in civic and political affairs for many decades, undoubtedly influenced her son's views and supported his political aspirations. She is pictured here on her eighty-second birthday. Norm Hill, photographer. *Billings Gazette*, Feb. 9, 1969

put on a clean shirt, and she would serve coffee and tea and make me serve appetizers while she and her friends played bridge."[22]

Beyond participating in the local social scene, Sadie possessed a broader social sense as well as an interest in politics. She pursued a community-oriented life, one more common to women of the upper middle class. When the Frasers arrived in Billings in 1913, the Billings Women's Club had already joined twenty-two other Montana cities to become part of the Montana Federation of Women's Clubs. Nationally, the General Federation of Women's Clubs was established before 1900 and provided women a way to contribute outside the home and an outlet for their political, intellectual, and social interests. Like many other early clubs, one of the first Billings women's clubs focused on literary topics— particularly Shakespeare. As the clubs evolved, their scope broadened to include home improvement, the arts, philanthropy, politics, science, and community improvement. By 1936, the Montana Federation had 151 clubs and 4,500 members.[23]

Sadie Fraser seems to have lost little time in becoming a part of this civic-minded movement, and she participated in several Billings clubs. She chaired committees for the Women's Council of the Christian Church, which gathered to discuss such topics as "Remembering the Past. We Build for the Future" and to plan rummage sales and other events. As a member of the Mothers' Club, she heard from speakers on children's eye and ear problems and other issues. She also belonged to the Current Topic Study Club. At a 1927 meeting, one member spoke on "Prohibition and Our Presidential Candidates," while she herself spoke on "Aviation and Its Future."[24] She was also active in the city's First Congregational Church, the Billings Women's Club, and the local Democratic Party.

Sadie's involvement in the community likely facilitated the alliances the Frasers formed with influential city families in the years the Frasers lived in the thick of Billings' prime residential area north of Montana Avenue. Berthold Richard (B. R.) Albin, cofounder of the city's premier department store, Hart-Albin, was a family friend, later linked to the Frasers by marriage when two of his daughters, Mary Louise and Jane, married Willard's brothers, Marvin and Bob. Ruth Jeanne Fraser, Willard's sister, was married for a time to Russ Hart, son of Ray Hart, B. R. Albin's partner in Hart-Albin. Perhaps through Albin, the Frasers became well enough acquainted with Lewis Penwell, a wealthy Montana rancher and a leader in the Democratic Party, that the family spent a summer at Penwell's cabin on Rattlesnake Creek north of Missoula.[25] Certainly, the Frasers' relationships with these prominent Montanans—Albin, Hart, and Penwell—fostered Willard's future personal and political relationship with Senator Burton K. Wheeler, with whom all three were close. These early associations with powerful politicians—all Democrats except Ray Hart—undoubtedly aided Willard's entrance into Montana politics and influenced his political philosophy. Willard's eventual success in politics would have been a satisfying fulfillment of Sadie's ambitions, and Mac Fraser recalled that Willard's becoming mayor "made her day."[26]

While Willard's high regard for his mother and her influence on his life are apparent, his opinion of his father, J. B., is harder to assess. Although Willard was proud of his Fraser name, Scottish ancestry, and Kansas forebears, his colleagues say that he rarely spoke of his father. J. B. Fraser died four years before Willard penned the bulk of his now-archived letters, and in them he receives scant mention. Photos show J. B. in his later years to be a bald, somewhat heavy man. Mac Fraser remembers a cordial, quick-witted man with a nice smile whom everyone liked.[27] Robin recalls that her "Granddaddy Fraser played a good game of rummy."[28]

Willard's father is also remembered as an inconsistent provider. Public records reveal that J. B. Fraser worked as a salesman for a succession of automobile companies, verifying that no business employed him long-term. In 1917 and 1918, he worked for the F. B. Connelly Company, a Ford and Overland distributor. In 1919, he sold used cars at Windsor Garage, but later that year, a *Billings Gazette* article listed J. B. as one of nearly two dozen men who were employed "on the tipple [a structure used to load coal into cars], in the boiler room, at the generators, in the weigh house, or in the mine yards" of Community Mine #1, a coal mine in Washoe, at the foot of the Beartooth Mountains.[29] Other employment for Willard's father included the Paige-Jewett Auto Company, the Billings Hudson Essex Company, Midland Motors, Rimrock Motors, and Mustang Motors. Correspondence in the 1930s reveals that J. B. unsuccessfully sought funds to invest in the Beartooth Oil Company, which was drilling in Colorado's Dry Creek Basin, and he left certificates of no value from penny stocks bought in the 1940s and 1950s, indications of a failed desire to improve the family finances. When J. B. died of cancer in 1959 at age seventy-four, his obituary in the *Gazette* reported that he had been one of the first Billings residents to enter the automobile business, and "probably taught more Billings early day residents to drive a car than any other man in Billings."[30] The obituary mentions nothing of any long-term employment.

The family's economic state was precarious enough that Willard's brother Marvin quit school in the tenth grade to work. For a time, Marvin and his father were later employed by the same automobile companies, and the family sense is that the son helped employ the father. Two years younger than Willard and a less extroverted Fraser, Marvin seems to have been a steadying influence whose hard work assisted his family at crucial times.

Because of J. B.'s checkered employment history, the Frasers moved many times, living in at least five different houses during Willard's childhood and adolescence. In their first few years in Billings, the family lived in various houses in the residential neighborhoods north of the tracks, where mansions and more modest family homes were interspersed. The first Fraser residence recorded in the Billings City Directory was a modest three-bedroom house on Terry Avenue. Over the next several years, the family moved often, always renting and sometimes being evicted for failing to pay the rent. In 1917, the Frasers were living on North 31st Street, but by 1923, when Willard was sixteen, they had moved to a small house on Clark Street, and four years later they were living on Wyoming Avenue. J. B. Fraser's rollercoaster employment history and the family's unstable housing history must have fed a determination in the younger Frasers to create a different path for themselves.

Those who knew Willard for many years can attest to his intelligence and his inquisitive nature. Willard's interest in ideas inspired his lifelong love of reading, which, in turn, provided the fund of quotes, information, and stories he drew on throughout his life. His delight in reading surfaced early in his life, again likely resulting from Sadie's influence, as she, too, was an avid reader.[31] The library allowed him to check out two books every week, and each Saturday he faithfully returned the two books he had read and replaced them with two new ones. *Huck Finn* and *Tom Sawyer* were favorites, and he also enjoyed reading the popular Edward Stratemeyer's Tom Swift and Rover Boys series, Jack London's novels, books that dealt with the West, all of Ernest Thompson Seton's wildlife books, and "a lot of poetry."[32] His avid, far-ranging reading habits as an adult are documented in the multitude of requests Mayor Fraser made to Billings librarian Ann Whitmack and her successor, Shirley Hake, and in the reading recommendations he made in letters to friends. Throughout his life, Willard wrestled with persistent health problems, and reading provided him a pastime during convalescence.

In spite of his chronic asthma, Willard was an active child who spent time outdoors. The illness would probably have precluded his participation in organized athletics even if he had the aptitude and inclination for it. Instead, Willard raised rabbits, hunted muskrats and ducks, and enjoyed playing outdoors.[33] While mayor, he wrote to a young Billings boy to

recommend "climbing and knowing each and every tree and rock on our Rimrocks. I climbed them all when I was your age."[34] Although he conceded that he learned to swim in the Billings ditch, when he became mayor, he tried to reroute the ditch around the city partially because other Billings children had drowned in it. His job delivering papers also kept Willard active, and he later told a young newspaper carrier:

> I, too, was a newspaper seller, and carrier—and that was back in the days when one really carried papers! My route, beginning at 3:00 in the morning, started at the library on Montana Avenue, went out to Division and then out to Broadwater and 12th Street, then up and down Custer, Terry, Miles, St. John's, and the other streets between Broadwater and the depot. These were in pre-sidewalk days, and when there was snow, bicycles were out. Hoofing those streets when it was 40 below was really something.[35]

By learning as a child to rebound from the limitations that asthma put on him and to thrive in spite of setbacks, Willard became a very resilient adult.

Willard's childhood experiences with life-threatening diseases and his own struggle with asthma undoubtedly fueled his admiration for science.

During the 1916 polio outbreak in Billings, parents tried to protect their children. "When I was in about the second grade, asafoetida was deemed as a sure preventative of polio, and all Billings small fry had to wear bags of asafoetida around our necks. . . . It has an odor somewhat like a dead tomcat that's been too long in the alley, mixed with a very prurient young skunk, and a dozen rotten eggs. Were we the little 'stinkers.' It must have worked, as I am still here."[36] Despite Willard's negative description of this pungent spice, asafoetida is commonly used in Indian curries and other dishes. It is also considered to be useful in combatting flatulence, but there is no evidence that it protects against polio or other infectious diseases.

Polio continued to strike throughout Willard's youth, prompting health officials to limit many community and social activities as the crippling disease spread. The largest outbreak in Montana occurred in 1934, when there were 322 cases. In a later polio epidemic in the early 1950s, more than 3,000 children died nationwide.[37] Closer to home, Marvin's daughter and Willard's niece, Wendelanne, was stricken with a mild case of polio during these years. Not until 1955 did the Salk vaccine begin to erode and eventually eradicate this dread disease in most countries. Until then, Billings' health authorities and the staff of St. Vincent's Hospital sought to control the disease locally. Dr. Louis Allard and the nuns of St. Vincent's served the families of Billings heroically, seeing twenty-five to forty children each day at the hospital and at the public health office during the 1916 epidemic.

Dr. Allard also ministered extraordinarily to Billings residents during the 1918 Spanish flu epidemic when Willard was eleven. The first flu victim in Montana was sixteen-year-old Violet Paus of Scobey, in the northeastern part of the state, on September 27, 1918.[38] By October 11, influenza had spread throughout the state to the point that the state board of health ordered the closing of "all theaters, moving picture houses and churches and prohibiting the meetings of lodges and other public gatherings." On that date, only 40 cases of flu existed in Yellowstone County.[39] However, by Wednesday, October 16, the number of afflicted people in the county had reached 228, and five days later, the number of victims reached approximately 1,000. By Monday, November 25, the *Billings Gazette* optimistically stated that there had been only one death in the last twenty-four hours and only 130 new cases in the past week.[40] By the end of December 1918, 170 people had died in the Billings area, bringing Montana's death toll due to influenza for that year to 2,654.[41]

With close to 5,000 total deaths during the span of the influenza epidemic, Montana was one of the four hardest-hit states in the nation. Butte, the largest city in Montana at the time, suffered more fatalities than any other city in the state. Over 300 citizens died in that densely populated city in November 1918 alone, and nearly 700 more residents of the mining city died throughout the fall.[42] In Billings, Dr. Allard himself nearly died of it. He developed pneumonia and was unconscious for several days but recovered after two weeks.[43] In total, the epidemic claimed the lives of some 675,000 people in the United States.

Willard's future in-laws, Robert and Elinor Frost, were also affected by the influenza. In early October 1918, they arrived in Amherst, Massachusetts, where Robert taught for the fall semester. Elinor reported that doctors and the army commandant did not want the college to open because Boston, one of the first cities to feel the effects of the flu, had experienced 280 deaths, but President Meiklejohn was determined to open. The Frosts traveled from their Franconia, New Hampshire, home to Amherst by car, thinking the risk of infection was less than by train. Despite such precautions, Robert fell ill and did not meet most of his classes that term. In December, Elinor wrote that he "was just beginning to regain strength," and Robert himself wrote to his longtime friend, poet and critic Louis Untermeyer, in early January, "I don't know whether or not I'm strong enough to write a letter yet. The only way I can tell that I haven't died and gone to heaven is by the fact that everything is just the same as it was on earth."[44]

Willard's childhood was shaped by the 1916 polio epidemic and subsequent outbreaks, as well as the influenza epidemic of 1918. "As one who grew up in the age of dreads—of polio epidemics, diphtheria epidemics, death in childbirth, the threat of typhoid, and with small pox just vanishing over the horizon—Dr. Salk of the Salk vaccine was one man whose accomplishments I truly envy."[45] Willard also referred to Dr. Allard as "a hero of my childhood." Given these persistent threats, it is understandable that he developed an admiration for how science improved medical treatment and health care during his lifetime.

Like the influenza and polio pandemics, political events of the times—both local and national—shaped Willard's worldview and lay the foundation for his public policy perspectives. World War I ushered in a wave of often-misguided patriotism and a tendency toward nationalism. Willard, who was an elementary student at McKinley School on North 31st Street at the time, remembered in particular the anti-German sentiment during this troubled time in Montana's history. During the war, President Wilson encouraged states to form councils modeled on the Council of National Defense to promote the war effort. The resulting Montana

Willard Fraser's future inlaws, Elinor and Robert Frost, with their children, Lesley and Irma (middle row), Marjorie and Carol (front row), ca. 1915. Public domain

Council of Defense, formed by Governor Samuel Stewart, went far beyond simply supporting the war effort to fomenting a hysteria that caused much injustice. The council's most active member was *Helena Independent* editor Will Campbell, described by historian Clemens P. Work as "so reactionary as to be almost a cartoon character." Campbell had previously written "venomous, provocative harangues" against the International Workers of the World, commended the murder of union organizer Frank Little, and tangled with district attorney Burton K. Wheeler over Wheeler's opposition to the powerful Anaconda Company.[46] As a young man with an interest in politics, Willard would also encounter Campbell's zealotry.

Frustrated that the council could not bring about more prosecutions of those they perceived to be traitors, its members pressured the governor to hold a special legislative session in February 1918. These legislators passed the Montana Sedition Act, later described as "the most sweeping violation of civil liberties in modern American history."[47] The law made it illegal to criticize the federal government, the armed forces, or even the state government in wartime. Two months later, even speaking the German language, including from the pulpits of German American churches, was banned. Billings pastors, notably Reverend Seil of the German Congregational Church and Reverend Fred Brose of the Congregational Church, adopted "a sly form of disobedience" and continued to use German.[48] Willard remembered, "In my own boyhood in the Billings area, the term 'German' was a name of great opprobrium. The terms 'Kraut' 'Squarehead' and 'Hun' were exceedingly dirty words."[49] Being exposed to such prejudice did not imbue Fraser with a biased attitude. Rather, it taught him the dangers of bigotry and led him, as an adult, to rail against prejudice and call for tolerance.

In subsequent months and years, Montana's German population suffered harassment and even unjust imprisonment for exercising free speech. Seventy-nine Montana citizens were convicted of sedition and more than forty were sent to prison, two of whom were from Billings. Their offenses could be as mild as calling a government decision "a joke." The federal Sedition Act passed in May 1918 was modeled on Montana's radical law. Thomas Walsh, Montana's otherwise noteworthy senator, was instrumental in passing both Montana's and the federal sedition measures. Although the war ended in November 1918, the ban on the German language was not rescinded until April 1920, and anti-German prejudice continued even after Governor Dixon terminated the Council of Defense on May 21, 1921.[50]

The World War I–era fanatical patriotism made some people receptive to the proselytizing of the Ku Klux Klan after the war's end. Membership in the Klan swelled in Montana in the 1920s, as it did elsewhere in the country.[51] On September 22, 1923, Lewis Terwilliger of Livingston organized a meeting that affiliated the Montana Ku Klux Klan with the national organization. Four provinces were created in Montana, with Missoula, Great Falls, Miles City, and Billings designated as their centers.[52] The following year, the Imperial Wizard, Dr. Hiram W. Evans, stopped in Billings on his tour of the Northwest. On November 12, 1924, Dr. Evans spent the day in Billings and spoke to eight hundred people at the Coliseum and over five hundred more at the First Methodist Church.[53] As many as six thousand Montanans were Klan members in the 1920s.[54]

That the white Protestant base of the Klan inveighed against Catholics, immigrants, Jews, and all nonwhite Americans was not always obvious in some of the news coverage at the time, but the *Butte Miner*, a newspaper in Montana's most heavily Catholic city, made a point of shedding light on the purposes of the Klan. The paper republished an article called "Fighting the Ku Klux Klan," originally printed in Ohio's *Toledo News-Bee*, which exposed "this un-American invisible empire."[55] However, the *Billings Gazette* was not as willing to take a stand against the Klan. The evening before Al Smith, a Catholic and the Democratic candidate for president, arrived in Billings on September 24, 1926, a twenty-by-ten-foot cross was burned on the Rimrocks at the head of 26th Street. The *Gazette* reported the burning "was said to have been the work of individuals . . . rather than of a local Klan organization."[56] The conclusion reached by the paper begs the question: who, besides the Klan, would have been burning crosses in Montana?

The Klan itself sought to portray the organization as a positive one with an interest in societal wellbeing. A letter to the editor of the *Missoulian* from the Helena chapter declared, "The Ku Klux Klan is intensely American. It stands for law and order, for good government, for clean citizenship. It is the enemy of tyranny and oppression in every form."[57] A follow-up article the next week reported information that contradicted these claims. During the night of April 12, 1922, the Klan had secretly distributed handbills that declared they were safeguarding American principles, but the notices also stated membership was limited to "native-born, white, Protestant, American Gentiles."[58] By the 1930s, the Klan in Montana was nearly nonexistent. Its demise was probably caused by a combination of factors: the subsiding of World War I unrest, the exposure of the Klan's internal corruption and its violent tactics, and perhaps a preoccupation with drought and the Great Depression in Montana.[59]

Willard attended Lincoln Junior High and Billings High School during the postwar years when ultra-nationalism was popular in Billings and the Klan became active in Montana. The very visible presence of the Klan during Willard Fraser's teenage years probably contributed to his later distrust of the brand of patriotism espoused by Senator Joseph McCarthy, the John Birch Society, and the "extreme flag waving" that he viewed with suspicion. However, Willard was involved in a different form of Americanism after World War I. The experience of the war created a general belief that America must be prepared for another such event. During Willard's teenage years, the Citizens' Military Training Camp (CMTC), created as part of a national defense act in 1920, trained up to thirty-five thousand American boys "in the rudiments of army life, with a view to their usefulness in case of another great emergency."[60] All expenses, including transportation to the camps, were paid by the government. As part of the recruiting efforts in 1924, officers announced that President Coolidge's sons, John and Calvin Jr., would attend the camps. Willard, his brother Marvin, his cousin Harold, and B. R. Albin's son Berthold participated in these thirty-day camps—Willard for at least four summers: 1924, 1925, 1926, and 1928.

The government took care to give the boys special treatment in an effort to reward their patriotism. In 1925, sixty-seven boys from Billings were transported to Salt Lake City in a special train and were met there by an army band, and special streetcars took them to train at Fort Douglas. At the camps they received physical and military training but were also entertained with dances and barbecues. In 1926, camp was held in Missoula and included a trip up the Blackfoot River. When Willard applied for appointment as a reserve officer in 1942, he listed attending these camps as part of his military service.[61]

Family finances probably caused the delay of the beginning of Willard's college career, and it is remarkable that he was able to attend at all. J. B.'s occupation in the 1926 Billings City Directory, the year of Willard's graduation from high school, is listed vaguely as "stockman," suggesting uncertain employment. Marvin went to work as a teenager to help his family and then married young and began a family of his own, remaining in Billings. Jeanne also married soon after she graduated from high school. Neither she, Marvin, nor Robert attended college. Willard, however, aspired to higher education, and in 1928 he applied to the University of Colorado in Boulder, where his friend Evan Price was a second-year student. His experiences there at the start of the Great Depression proved to be a turning point in his life, offering him opportunities to get to know new people and places, although Billings and Montana held first place in his affection and loyalties.

CHAPTER THREE

"I find myself practically up in the air as to my most important future"

MONTANA and the United States plunged into the Great Depression just as Willard Fraser was coming of age and working toward his goal of higher education. In the early 1920s, the homesteading experiment was nearly destroyed by a prolonged drought and coinciding depression. From 1919 to 1925, nearly 20 percent of Montana's farmland passed out of production, and half of the state's farmers lost their land. Between 1920 and 1926, a majority of the state's commercial banks failed, resulting in the highest bankruptcy rate in the nation. An estimated sixty thousand people left the state in the 1920s. Even before the stock market crash on October 29, 1929, Montana was already suffering the damage caused by prolonged drought throughout much of the state. Farmers abandoned their farms, and the mining industry was hit as well. Tens of thousands of Montanans were in desperate need of relief by the early 1930s.[1]

In such an economic climate, many young adults would not have dared to dream of pursuing higher education, but Willard was different. He and his family held fast to a belief in a better future, and they did what they could to achieve it. Willard's potential was recognized by Isabella Price, his high school English teacher, and she encouraged him to attend college. Specifically, she recommended the University of Colorado (CU) in Boulder, where her brother-in-law, Dr. George Reynolds, was a professor and where her nephew, Evan, was enrolled. With this encouragement, Willard and his family set about making it happen. Willard spent a year working at Cook's Clothery, and the family came up with other money-making ventures.

They obtained permission for Willard, Marvin, Sadie, and J. B. to operate a breakfast stand at the state fair in Billings, and all the proceeds went into Willard's college fund. At CU, Willard's job in the college cafeteria helped defray expenses. Although truncated by financial difficulty, Willard's college experiences profoundly affected the course of his life by expanding his world beyond Montana and Kansas and offering him opportunities to engage with people who would broaden his worldview. His intellectual curiosity, engaging personality, and burgeoning ambition opened doors to new opportunities and interests that would shape the rest of his life.

In 1928, Willard enrolled in the College of Arts and Science, and by his junior year, he was concentrating on courses in the humanities and social science, taking classes in political science, sociology, socialism, and English literature, as well as one called "The Intellectual History of the Advance of the Middle Ages." While Willard seems to have done well in these classes, he found the required courses in math more challenging. In the spring of 1932, Willard confessed to a friend, "I am again beset by trigonometry."[2] English professor Dr. George Reynolds and Willard established an enduring relationship. According to Willard's close friend Charlie Borberg, Dr. Reynolds was a force in molding Willard.[3] Dr. Reynolds advised The Players' Club, the drama society in which Willard became active, and Willard and Reynolds stayed in contact for many years.[4]

As seems appropriate for a book-loving youngster and a future prolific letter writer and sought-after public speaker, Willard served as an assistant editor of the *Window*, the college's literature and art publication, in his senior year, and he was active in debate. Fraser's outgoing personality and his leadership ability shone especially in his membership of the Theta Xi fraternity. He pledged in his junior year, and in his senior year, he represented the fraternity on the Interfraternity Council. In a letter to his friend Dwight Morrow Jr., Willard mentioned being president of Theta Xi in 1932 and commented facetiously, "I think that fraternities are harder to please than democrats and thus it is more of an honor to be president of a fraternity than to be president of the U.S."[5] The fraternity had adopted Benjamin Franklin as its patron "saint," and in his political life, Willard often proclaimed himself to be a "Benjamin Franklin Democrat."

The connections Willard made during college opened doors to new opportunities and employment. While working in the university's Marshall Cafeteria during his sophomore year, Willard struck up a conversation with archaeologist Earl Morris, who had for some years been associated with the University of Colorado's Museum of Natural History and who was working there during the winter of 1930. Morris was already nationally recognized for his work in the Southwest, particularly the excavation of Mummy Cave in Arizona's Canyon de Chelly between 1923 and 1929. He had helped found CU's museum, and much of his collection resides there as well as in the American Museum of Natural History in New York City and the Museum of New Mexico in Santa Fe. Esteemed by colleague Dr. Alfred Kidder for his "gentleness, true humility, unfailing readiness to help, utter sincerity, innate appreciation of quality in people and things,"[6] Morris also earned Willard's admiration. "No finer man ever lived," Willard said about Morris.[7]

After Willard "talked his way onto a field expedition" for the summer of 1930, he joined Morris on three later summer expeditions in 1931, 1932, and 1934.[8] During the depth of the Depression, a young man would have been fortunate to obtain employment of any kind. Willard, who had no formal archaeological training, was one of several college students Morris hired to help with sundry tasks at the camp and on the digs. Some, but not all, students went on to careers in archaeology. Willard is mentioned both in the text and the acknowledgments in two archaeology books, *Earl Morris and Southwestern Archaeology* by Florence and Robert Lister and *Digging in the Southwest* by Ann Morris.[9] *Digging in the Southwest* contains a photo of Willard dressed for KP duty.

Funded by the Carnegie Institution for Science, the expedition work was concentrated in the Four Corners area where Utah, Colorado, Arizona, and New Mexico meet. Because Willard's asthma prevented him from working in the dusty digs, Morris hired him as assistant cook for the camp, which was on the west side of the La Plata Mountains and near the New Mexico-Colorado line and Mesa Verde National Park.[10] When his culinary duties were finished in the evenings, Willard assisted Morris in making notes of the day's progress. This evening work involved Willard with the academic aspects of the work and aroused his interest in the human history of the sites being explored. In other summers, Willard must have done some active digging, because nearly forty years later, when he read *Earl Morris and Southwestern Archaeology*, he reported, "The trouble with reading it is that it brings back so doggone many wonderful memories. I wake up with 'shoveler's grip' after reading it."[11]

In Willard's first summer with the Morris expeditions, Dwight Morrow Jr. was part of the crew, and the two young men formed an enduring friendship, which later resulted in Morrow's brokering an introduction for Willard to Marjorie Frost, the youngest daughter of Robert Frost.[12] Morrow had just completed his freshman year at Amherst College, where Frost had served on the faculty for many years and where Morrow's father was on the board of trustees. There, young Dwight saw "a good deal of the Frost family."[13] Robert Frost's take on the Morrows was expressed in a letter to his friend Louis Untermeyer. After stating that Amherst College "belonged" to Dwight Morrow Sr. and that Smith College "belonged" to his wife, Elizabeth (Betty) Morrow, Frost surmised, "They might belong to worse. The Morrows are the kind of rich who take good care of their playthings."[14]

Dwight and Willard spent two summers together on digs in the Southwest.[15] During one of these hot summers, Charles and Anne Lindbergh flew in for a visit. Willard and Dwight met them and then they hiked together to the White House portion of Canyon de Chelly. Anne did not complain about the heat but was interested in and asked questions

Willard Fraser (right) with Roger Johnson (left) and Dwight Morrow Jr., ca. 1931, while Fraser and Morrow served as interns on Earl Morris's archaeological digs in the Southwest. EHM07.33_024.01#45, University of Colorado Museum of Natural History, Boulder

about their work. When they arrived, Anne took off her hiking boots to reveal bloody feet. Willard was impressed by her fortitude, energy, and intelligence.[16]

In the summer of 1931, Willard again served as an assistant cook for Morris's camp, this time in the northeast corner of Arizona, one location being Broken Flute Cave. Willard and Dwight shared a tent with Deric O'Bryan, who later earned recognition for his research on tree-ring dating and excavations at Mesa Verde National Park.[17] O'Bryan remembered, "Every noon Willard would struggle up carrying our hot-to-warm lunch . . . on a Chinese yoke contraption."[18] It was probably this summer that Willard met J. O. [Joe] Brew of Harvard, who was working at Alkali Ridge in southeastern Utah. Dr. Brew later became head of the Peabody Museum at Harvard. Elinor Frost wrote in 1934 about these young men, "His [Willard's] friends in archaeology are very fine, idealistic people."[19] Willard maintained his relationships with Morrow, Brew, and O'Bryan for the rest of his life, as he did with Earl Morris's widow, Lucille.[20]

Throughout his life, Fraser took great pride in his early association with these prominent archaeologists and his involvement in important excavations. "I was in the first groups to work towards restoring Mummy Cave in Canyon de Chelly, Mesa Verde, the Aztec ruins [of New Mexico]," he wrote to Peter Tufts of Glacier National Park.[21] Several years later, he reeled off the names of key figures with whom he had worked: Jess [Deric] Nusbaum O'Bryan, J. O. Brew, Frank Robert, Sylvanus G. Morley.[22] He commented that Dr. Alfred Kidder "often visited our sites, especially Canyon de Chelly, LaPlata and Aztec."[23] Dr. Kidder was arguably the foremost archaeologist of the southwestern United States in the early twentieth century. Stuart Conner, Willard's first city attorney and an amateur archaeologist, recalled how much Willard treasured the months he spent in the Southwest. After he accompanied Fraser on a return trip to Canyon de Chelly in 1963, Conner said, "Willard was just beside himself with joy that he was able to go back."[24] After Willard's death, Conner reminisced, "The archaeological experiences and associations in Willard's life meant a great deal to him and accounted for many of his most happy memories."[25]

The company and friendship of students and young professionals from such schools as Amherst and Harvard awakened in Willard an awareness of a culture different from that of Montana, one where families had fame and influence on a national scale.[26] His exposure to America's Eastern intellectual culture deepened with his evolving relationship with Marjorie Frost, which began in 1931. Other than Dwight Morrow, John and Margaret

Bartlett were the key players in the development of Willard and Marjorie's relationship. The Bartletts had been Robert Frost's friends since they were his students at Pinkerton Academy, where Frost taught from 1906 to 1911. In 1917, because John was afflicted with asthma and Margaret with tuberculosis, the Bartletts moved from New Hampshire to Colorado, trusting that the drier climate would promote improved health for both. Robert Frost encouraged and partly financed this move. By 1930, still in regular touch with Frost, the Bartletts urged their friend "Rob" to participate in the newly established Rocky Mountain Writers Conference at the university in Boulder. Frost declined the 1930 invitation, but he committed to attending the Writers Conference in 1931.

When Frost's twenty-five-year-old daughter, Marjorie, was diagnosed with tuberculosis that year, Margaret Bartlett insisted that she come to Colorado. Marjorie left Baltimore, where she had been training to be a nurse, and entered the Mesa Vista Sanatorium in Boulder. The Bartletts, who lived just three blocks from the sanatorium, visited Marjorie regularly, sometimes bringing their eight-year-old daughter, who later recalled the visits to her as "a pilgrimage to a princess in a castle, rather than a sick call." She wrote later, "I remember Marjorie best framed against a hospital pillow, her dark hair brushed pompadour style away from a cameo-tinted face, her finely sculptured features and enchanting dark eyes."[27]

Coincidentally, young Forrest Bartlett and Willard were fraternity brothers, but it was Dwight Morrow who wrote to Willard to suggest

that he introduce himself to Marjorie. Willard responded from Boulder about the outcome of this suggestion: "Ann [Morris] and I have been to see her a time or two. She is most interesting, and has as fascinating a face as I have ever seen on a young girl."[28] Willard, at five-foot-ten, with brown hair and blue eyes, was described by the Bartlett's daughter, Margaret, as "a slightly built, pink-cheeked college boy, nervous but with a quick, charming smile and a soft voice."[29] The Bartletts were somewhat concerned about the interest this young man showed in Marjorie,

Marjorie Frost as a teenager. Marjorie suffered from tuberculosis, necessitating her treatment in the drier climate of the Rocky Mountains. St. Lawrence, Canton, NY

Marjorie Frost, possibly as a high school senior. Introduced to one another by Dwight Morrow Jr., Willard and Marjorie became engaged in 1932. 2161K, The Frank P. Piskor Collection of Robert Frost, Special Collections, St. Lawrence University, Canton, NY

because Forrest reported that Willard had a reputation in the fraternity as something of a ladies' man.

In March 1932, less than a year after meeting Willard, Marjorie wrote a long letter to her parents announcing that she and Willard were engaged to be married and that she was "supremely happy." She called him "a dear, kind, and considerate man, another real Victorian, Papa, with the beautiful ideals that I had feared no longer existed." She went on to explain they wouldn't be married right away because Willard had "no money of his own, and will have to make his start in the world with absolutely nothing but his own abilities, which, naturally, I think are considerable." As part of this informative letter about their future son-in-law, Marjorie clearly felt she should mention Willard's age: "About his age. I hadn't asked him yet as I never think of it when we are together."[30] He was twenty-five at the time.

Upon hearing of her engagement, Robert Frost wrote to his daughter, "Willard sounds like a good boy in a sad world. Bless you both. Perhaps on our way out in June we'll see him and on our way back see him and you together." Willard then wrote an introductory letter to the Frosts, and less than a month later, Frost replied, "That was a fine letter. . . . What between you and Marj we begin to get quite an idea of you. We ought to reciprocate and describe ourselves to you. But we shall be coming out so soon now where you can see us and save us the necessity. . . . We are very happy in Marj's happiness."[31]

Just before Willard left for Aztec, New Mexico, in the summer of 1932, he wrote to Dwight to express regret that Dwight had decided not to participate in Morris's third expedition and would not be joining the crew. He added, "Marjorie is here now. We have been painting the town red and having a very nice time. . . . I shall have the pleasure of meeting my future in-laws Saturday in Denver. . . . I am quite nervous about it all."[32] The Bartletts accompanied Willard and Marjorie to Denver to meet Robert and Elinor Frost when their train arrived. Elinor had written to her Franconia friend Edith Fobes to express her worry that Marjorie was "going to be swallowed up by a western marriage," but she added, "We are eager to see him, of course."[33] When Frost met his future son-in-law, Willard later reported that the poet declared, "I know about Montana. That's the land of high mountains and low politics."[34] During this visit, Willard introduced Frost to Earl Morris, who presented Frost an inscribed copy of his book *Temple of the Warriors*.[35]

When Robert and Elinor Frost met Willard and Marjorie in Denver, they were on their way to California, where their son, Carol, and his family had moved to seek medical support for Lillian Frost's tuberculosis. Lillian was a childhood friend of Marjorie's, and so, with Willard off on his archaeological summer, Marjorie accompanied her parents to California for the duration of the season.

Deric O'Bryan and Willard spent six weeks on a project in Black Mesa in the Arizona desert, another experience that fed Willard's intellectual appetite for archaeological study. Their charge was to explore the region and identify ruins that would bear further study. A written report concluded that they found eighty-six possible sites as well as tracks of dinosaurs and a few Jurassic bones.[36] O'Bryan appreciated Willard's participation in their fieldwork that summer and said, "[I]f Willard was not an outstanding contributor to the archaeological knowledge of the Southwest, his unstinting help, common sense, and unflagging good humor did a lot."[37] In addition to the six weeks Deric and Willard spent together at Black Mesa, Willard's archaeological work in the summer of 1932 involved participating in the restoration of Mummy Cave in Canyon de Chelly with Earl Morris.

Robert and Elinor Frost at Longs Peak, Colorado, 1932, likely while visiting Marjorie, who was recuperating at the Mesa Vista Sanatorium in Boulder. This was the sum-mer they met Willard. 2346K, The Frank P. Piskor Collection of Robert Frost, Special Collections, St. Lawrence University, Canton, NY

Later, O'Bryan reported that Willard confided some trepidation over the prospect of joining a notable family: "Willard was most hesitant about his engagement and marrying into the Robert Frost family; many a nighttime conversation over our campfire was on that subject."[38] Willard's apprehension is understandable. Frost was already famous by this time. He was sought after for public performances, had received ten honorary degrees, and had published five volumes of poetry and received the Pulitzer Prize for Poetry in 1924. The Fraser family from Billings and the Frost family of American literary fame lived in very different worlds.

Willard Fraser, ca. 1932. Robert Frost Family Collection, Box 2, University of Michigan Library, Ann Arbor

Nonetheless, the poet and the student formed a bond lasting thirty years, a bond sparked by a shared interest in intellectual discussion, an aesthetic sensibility, a humanistic outlook, and an independent take on the world.

The growing regard between Willard and his future father-in-law was promising, but Willard's financial situation remained a concern. Although Willard attended the University of Colorado for four years, he left in June 1932 without a degree—a fact that he did not readily reveal later in life. Friends ascribe his lack of a degree to the financial stresses of the Great Depression, which had exacerbated the Fraser family's difficulties. In acknowledging his financial problems toward the end of his senior year, Willard wrote, "The depression is certainly making its ugly face known here. . . . I find myself practically up in the air as to my most important future."[39] A month later, he admitted that "the Depression is growing more and more oppressive to yours truly."[40] According to one source, Dr. Reynolds cancelled a $135 promissory note when Willard married in 1933, suggesting both the depth of the Frasers' financial troubles as well as Dr. Reynolds's sympathy for Willard's situation.[41]

Clearly, the Frosts did not have an accurate picture of the Fraser family's economic status. During the summer of 1932, Elinor Frost wrote to a friend, "I don't know what Willard will do next year. If no job materializes, his father *may* let him have enough money to go to Harvard, for a year's work in anthropology."[42] Then and in the future, the Frosts expressed the hope that Willard would settle in the East. Instead of entertaining thoughts of a year at Harvard, however, Willard resolved that he and Marjorie would not marry until he was employed. He was thus overjoyed when, by early fall 1932, he received an offer of a teaching job in Billings. He wanted to tell Marjorie the good news in person, so he postponed his departure from the Southwest and arranged for Marjorie to come from California and meet him in New Mexico in October. Marjorie wrote of a "perfect blue Arizona day" when they met and planned a Thanksgiving wedding. It was not to be, and Marjorie shared the sad news with her friend, Helen Lawrie, whom she had met while visiting Lillian and Carol in California, "The result was that when he arrived in Billings the beet crop was being harvested and the high school enrollment had fallen off to such an extent that they did not need an extra teacher after all. . . . He is a very sad boy just now."[43] Thus, in early November, a disappointed Marjorie returned to Amherst to await news of Willard's being employed. It would be six long months of waiting.

From Billings, Willard wrote to Dwight Morrow that he was "somewhat disillusioned but able to smile though without a job."[44] In Amherst,

Marjorie was disappointed again when a planned Christmas visit from Willard did not occur, as he still had not found employment. She wrote to Helen of their "constantly raised and cruelly dashed hopes." To Willard, she voiced her mother's worries, "She is just as anxious that you get a job as either you or I are—or rather, almost as anxious."[45] Throughout these months of waiting, Marjorie clearly struggled to maintain a positive attitude, but not always successfully. She wrote to Helen that, when she sat down to write a letter, the "vision of my own [past] false happiness" arose and the mood to write left her. By this time, Marjorie had begun writing some poetry, but she confessed, "As for my writing, don't ask me. I cannot find the mood or the heart for it. But that will come back some day. I don't worry about it."[46] The waiting time in Amherst also gave Marjorie conflicted feelings about living again with her parents. She wrote to Willard, "As you know, I love to be at home, after so long away, and to have this opportunity to be with my mother, before our marriage. It's just that it's interesting that when human beings are 'lionizing,' how little they notice the cubs beside the door." She compared her role when outsiders came to visit the famous poet and his family to that of a parlor maid.[47]

Through the cloud of disappointments in these months, Marjorie wrote glowingly and confidently of "my Willard." She gushed to Helen:

> Willard is just so dear and good to me as ever, and after all, that's all that really matters. He is trying, trying, trying to find a place for himself in this modern world of upheaval, and I know he will win in the end. . . . I shall do my part to help him attain his ambitions. He is far, far more ambitious than I ever dreamed at first. . . . He is trying now to work his way into politics so far with considerable progress as he is never idle for a single instant . . . [and] he is trying to see what a good man can do for his country.[48]

Marjorie's adoring tone about Willard remains consistent in her letters, and as she realizes how intense his political ambitions are, she voices support for them.

Willard's growing interest in politics at this time is illustrated in his letters to Morrow. Regarding the election of 1932, he expressed relief over the Republican Party's loss and Franklin D. Roosevelt's landslide victory over Herbert Hoover. Roosevelt carried forty-two of the forty-eight states in the election. Willard was optimistic about Roosevelt's triumph: "We are reentering into a revised era of national good will and cooperation with the world. . . . We live. The American People Live. The people as an important part of government shall live. . . . I believe the real leaders and thinkers of the land are in the Democratic ranks for the first time in many, many years."[49] Fraser's excitement over Roosevelt's success would not have been shared by his future mother-in-law, who freely expressed an intense dislike of Roosevelt. Elinor's distaste for Roosevelt was so great that she kept a large box marked "Things Against Roosevelt," in which she collected newspaper clippings, and she wrote letters against him to various politicians.[50]

Willard would have also been interested in Montana's elections that year, when voters sent two Democrats, Roy Ayers and Joseph Monaghan, to Congress to join the two powerful Democratic senators, Burton K. Wheeler and Thomas Walsh. In Montana's Democratic primary earlier in 1932, incumbent governor John Erickson had defeated Fraser family friend Lewis Penwell, the wealthy attorney and rancher who was also Montana's collector of Internal Revenue and a former state representative. An active Democrat, Penwell had hosted a dinner for Senator Thomas Walsh in 1927 at Helena's Montana Club, where guests included Governor Erickson, former governor Sam Stewart, and future judge Lester H. Loble. Undaunted, Penwell remained a political force and helped shape Willard Fraser's early political career.

In January 1933, just months before his marriage, Willard made his first foray into Montana politics. As the vice president of the Young Democrats Club of Billings, he spoke at a banquet at Helena's Placer Hotel, where party members celebrated the victory of Roosevelt and other Democrats. This must have been a heady experience for a young man, but Willard's college debating experience, his innate self-assurance, and the confidence he gained through his associations with people such as Dr. Reynolds, Dwight Morrow, Earl Morris, and others undoubtedly helped him perform convincingly. Also attending the dinner was future secretary to Burton K. Wheeler, R. Bailey Stortz, with whom Fraser would establish a relationship. Willard's exposure to Montana's political figures ignited his political ambition, and he decided to become one of four candidates in a race for mayor of Billings in April 1933—a bold decision for a young, inexperienced politicial hopeful.

Marjorie encouraged Willard in a letter that would certainly bring a knowing smile to those who knew him. She wrote, "Dearest, of course I think you're crazy, but that's nothing new. I've always known you were. However, don't let that worry you. I like crazy people. Safe and sane people don't interest me in the least, and I simply can't endure snobbish, conservative superior minded people, especially men, and if they show any sign of being afraid, they are simply unspeakable. But I love you, so I'm sure you must be crazy, and divinely wise, too."[51] Her next letter ended with the words, "My only regret is that I don't live in Billings, so I could cast my vote for the future Mayor of that lucky city."[52] In the April 3 election, twenty-six-year-old Willard came in last with 299 votes. Incumbent mayor, Fred Tilton, was reelected but died in office in December. City council president Clarence Williams then became mayor.[53]

On the employment front, a letter from Marjorie indicates that Willard had expressed interest in working at a clothing store again, but by May 1933, he was employed at Lewis Penwell's Helena-based newspaper, the *Western Progressive*. The first issue of the paper, published in 1932, announced its purpose as being "to discuss the issues of the day fearlessly but dispassionately. The important thing is the issues and not personalities." It further stated that the paper "is independent and free from corporate domination. It is nonpartisan in politics. It is not a Communist paper in any sense of the word. It is just sanely progressive."[54] At the time and for years after, most Montana newspapers—including Butte's *Montana Standard*, the *Missoulian*, the *Montana Record-Herald* and the *Independent* in Helena, the *Livingston Enterprise*, the *Billings Gazette*, and the *Butte Post*—were all controlled by the Anaconda Copper Company. Described later by a historian as "the most annoying journalistic opponent of the Company since the *Butte Bulletin*," Penwell's *Western Progressive* was the second in a thin chain of newspapers speaking out against the powerful copper company and big business in Montana.[55]

The news that Willard was employed brought an excited letter from Marjorie to Willard's mother, in which Marjorie said she was looking forward "to meeting you all."[56] She planned to arrive in Billings by train on May 19. After more than a year's engagement, Marjorie and Willard would marry in Billings on June 3, 1933. This alliance of love would reinforce Willard's connection to the world beyond Montana.

CHAPTER FOUR

"A glorious happy time" followed by "those horribly helpless weeks"

ROBERT AND ELINOR FROST did not attend Marjorie and Willard's wedding in Billings in June 1933. Robert had been confined to bed for most of May and, given both his health and his general disaffection for ceremonies, the Frosts decided it would be better to stay in Amherst. They had an announcement of the marriage printed in the Springfield, Massachusetts, paper, and shortly before the wedding, Robert wrote to Marjorie and Willard to say, "You mustn't let your happiness be the least diminished by our absence.... The day of the wedding we'll do nothing but think of you."[1] While Marjorie must have missed her parents' presence at the ceremony, Willard's family and the Frasers' wide community of friends embraced his bride. Fortunately, Sadie Fraser and Marjorie Frost got along well from the start. Willard wrote years later, "Marjorie and my mother were instant friends, and solidly wholesomely compatible."[2]

Both the bride and the groom penned long reports of the wedding to the Frosts. Sixty guests attended the late morning ceremony at the Fraser house at 118 South 38th Street on June 3. Marjorie wore a white silk dress and hat, and she had ordered a coat and suit in rose, her favorite color.[3] Marvin Fraser was best man, and his wife, Mary Louise, was matron of honor. Marvin's father-in-law, B. R. Albin, gave the bride away, while Willard's friend Evan Price played violin to accompany his mother on the piano for the "Wedding March."[4] According to Willard, "It was certainly a Fraser-Albin wedding. . . . Mary Louise's sister was flower girl and her mother served at the reception. The house was full of flowers and old women, all of whom came up and kissed me. . . . My brother Bob was so

Willard Fraser and Marjorie Frost Fraser in the yard at 118 S. 39th Street, Billings, on June 3, 1933—their wedding day. This is the only known photograph of Willard and Marjorie together. Courtesy Robin Fraser Hudnut

excited and had been running so many errands that day that he fainted during the ceremony."[5] Marjorie reported that she was "pretty nervous," so her bouquet of white roses and pink sweet peas "insisted on shaking and fluttering like aspen leaves in a gale."[6]

The newlyweds spent their wedding night in Bozeman and moved into their small apartment in the Templeton Apartments in Helena the next day. From their apartment on Last Chance Gulch, Helena's main street, they had a view of downtown with Mount Helena in the background.[7] Marjorie told Helen Lawrie, "Helena is a beautiful little town situated near the foothills of the Montana Rockies."[8]

Established in the 1860s and chosen as the state capital in 1894, Helena was very different from Billings. At a population of about twelve thousand people in 1933, Helena had four thousand fewer citizens than Billings, but because of its importance in state government and its colorful history, power brokers—both political and economic—were drawn to the city near the Continental Divide. The city's central commercial district is compacted along a narrow gulch bound on the west and south by mountains, forcing later growth into the valley to the north and east. On the town's west side, mansions nestle at the base of Mount Helena, testimony to the merchants, mine owners, and cattle ranchers who struck it rich during the late 1800s. The twin spires of the St. Helena Cathedral rise above the surrounding city. This neo-Gothic cathedral, completed in 1914 and built on a hill a block east of Last Chance Gulch, was modeled after the Votive Cathedral of the Sacred Heart in Vienna.[9] Just a few blocks away, the Templeton Apartments in the Iron Front Hotel building, which still stands today, overlook downtown Helena.[10] Marjorie invited Helen to visit their new home, mentioning that both Yellowstone and Glacier National Parks were nearby attractions, but she went on to say, "Personally, I think my Willard is a much greater attraction than all the parks in the world but I suppose I'm prejudiced."[11]

Elinor Frost worried about how Marjorie would fare in a state as cold as Montana and wondered if her daughter's frail health would give way under the stress of housekeeping. In addition to tuberculosis, Marjorie had experienced a variety of other illnesses. In 1925, when she was nineteen, she suffered from appendicitis, "a general nervous listlessness," and a pericardial infection or bronchial pneumonia, depending on the source.[12] Another bout of illness occurred during a trip to France and England in 1928.[13] Robert Frost biographer Lawrance Thompson refers to Marjorie as being "generally unwell" and as an "invalid."[14]

There was no sign that Elinor's fears were justified. Writing to her parents in the months after her marriage, Marjorie sounded rapturous and offered details of the couple's daily life and her growing fondness for Montana. "Willard has a terrific man's appetite and very nearly eats me out of house and home. Really I am enjoying the cooking if you can believe it," she told her parents.[15] "We had dinner one night on [a "real" ranch] owned by Penwell's son, and I saw the inside of a real sheep herders range wagon. It's almost funny the way I like the West."[16] Marjorie seemed to be thriving in Montana. "In some ways I like Montana even better than Colorado," she confessed to Robert and Elinor. "Our first week together has been—what shall I say? Are there any words for happiness such as ours has been? If just one week can foretell the future, then I shall be happy as long as we live."[17]

"It was a glorious happy time, and no two ever had a finer first year," Willard wrote years later.[18] As part of his employment, the young couple traveled the state during much of 1933 and the beginning of 1934. Marjorie wrote to Helen from Red Lodge to say they were "travelling together through the greater part of this enormous state of Montana. Willard has a fine new job with the government in addition to his position on the Western Progressive, which is a splendid advance for him politically and financially."[19] In Willard's letters, he mentions Wolf Point, Glasgow, Plentywood, and Ekalaka as towns they visited. Their travels were full of adventure: they got stuck in a gumbo road near Wolf Point and had to be pulled out by boys with horses; they were marooned in the Powder River and rescued by cowboys with lassos; and, in the fall, they admired the cottonwoods along the river bottoms "at their golden best."[20] Willard told his father-in-law, "Marjorie and I are certainly seeing Montana. We are now on the reservation [Fort Peck] in the northeast corner of the state."[21]

Fort Peck Dam near Wolf Point, the first of six main-stem dams on the Missouri River, was under construction at the time, and it may have inspired Willard's future support for hydroelectric projects. As a major New Deal project, it employed up to ten thousand workers at its peak construction period. Willard mentioned that it would "irrigate thousands of acres of land now useless and will make homes possible to hundreds of needy families."[22] More than ten years later, in 1944, Congress passed the Pick-Sloan Flood Control Act, which ushered in a flurry of dam building throughout the nation. As decades passed, however, enthusiasm for dams waned among many progressives as it became clear that dams also killed fish populations, devastated wild rivers and scenic areas, and obliterated Indigenous cultural sites. But in the 1930s, '40s, and '50s, progressive politicians, including Willard Fraser, supported dams for the affordable power they generated and their irrigation and flood control benefits.

That winter, Marjorie wrote her mother from a hotel in Columbus, Montana, and devoted much of the letter to a sympathetic recounting of Willard's ongoing battle with asthma, for which there was no treatment at the time.[23] His illness seemed to be exacerbated by the dust and smoke they encountered in Montana's small towns:

> I believe the chief cause of his trouble now is that this work he is doing takes him to all these little country towns which are full of cows and horses and cowboys and farmers, all of which are practically fatal to him. Of course, he has to go into all the many, many pool and gambling halls which always have little or no ventilation, are dense with smoke, and crowded with cowboys and farmers, so when he comes out, he is all stuffed up for the next 24 hours or longer. . . . He does take life and his responsibilities so terribly seriously, and it about breaks my heart to see him suffer so almost every night.[24]

Marjorie added that she felt a remedy might be cod liver oil, and she had begun dosing him with it three times a day.

Even with Willard's busy travel schedule and his bouts with asthma, Marjorie discovered that a happy married life in Montana was a dramatic and welcome change. She demonstrated impressive determination, fortitude, and physical stamina that belied her earlier episodes of ill health. In November, she wrote to Helen, "I have never been better in all my born days than I have been since I came to my Willard, and I have been able to accomplish twice as much as I could up until the time since my long illness." Marjorie's contentment inspired her creativity, and she told her friend, "One thing that makes me especially happy is that I believe the coy and elusive muse has decided to honor me with her presence for a little while, at last after this long absence. In fact, I have nearly finished a sonnet which Willard (a very good and plenty severe critic by the way) thinks is the finest thing I ever wrote."[25] Willard reported Marjorie had found inspiration for her new poem while waiting for their car to be pulled out of

Marjorie Frost sporting a warm fur coat, likely in Montana, ca. 1933–1934. The young couple lived in Helena after their wedding. Robert Frost Family Collection, Box 2, University of Michigan, Ann Arbor

the mud near Wolf Point. While listening to the meadowlarks "roaring out their spring songs," she conceived her poem, which she titled "America."[26] She was eager to share it with her parents. Offering her sonnet in exchange for a little book of poetry from her father, Marjorie wrote, "I am sending you and mama . . . the sonnet I told you about. Willard likes it so much, that I can't help hoping you will like it too, as it would please him more than anything else I could do if I got to writing some again. He really believes in me, which is a stimulus, and makes me want to justify his belief."[27] Frost's response to her sonnet was in a postscript to a letter to Willard: "Has Marj written any more poetry lately? Tell her to send another as good as the last. I like my country written about that way."[28] Scores of years later, Robin Fraser Hudnut averred that the poem is "a concrete manifestation" of the things that gave Willard major direction.[29]

Several of Frost's biographers state that Marjorie, the youngest of the Frost children, was her father's favorite child. William Pritchard wrote, "It was the fourth child, Marjorie, whose spirit was most truly a poetic one."[30] Her letters display a generous and empathic sensibility as well as a knack for verbal expression. Willard's perspective was that she had a "closer kinship" with her father than the other Frost children did. He ascribes this partially to the fact that she arrived after Frost's "bitter struggle" to be recognized as a poet, but he also credits her "softness," which was allied with courage and perceptiveness.[31]

For his part, Willard was still thinking and talking politics, and he frequently shared his views with his in-laws. Frost jokingly warned his son Carol in a September 1933 letter that he had to be careful about his political comments because, he said, "I have allied myself by marriage with one of the most interesting if extreme young Progressives in the world and as always with me it is my family right or wrong."[32] Willard apparently sent copies of the *Western Progressive* to Frost, because Frost wrote to him to say, "I haven't known the kind of excitement in the family your politics give us since I was a young democrat campaigning for Grover Cleveland with my father in San Francisco in 1884. We don't get the hang just yet of your Montana affairs, but the *Western Progressive* is a great help."[33]

Frost's "my family right or wrong" statement could have created great conflict in his loyalties, for Elinor frequently expressed her disdain for both Roosevelt and Democrats, saying in one letter, "What a horror of falsity and deceit Roosevelt is proving himself. . . . If he gets his way, I am going to move to Canada."[34] Robert himself was not an ardent New Dealer, yet he willingly listened to Willard's political opinions and aspirations and later encouraged his son-in-law's efforts to gain office. In October 1933, Willard began a long letter by suggesting that Frost run for Congress because, he said, poets, archaeologists, and politicians have things in common: "They all have ideals in mind, and are always after something that is always opening new visions for the common man." In the same letter, Willard expressed his own lofty ambitions: "If all goes as I think it will go the next four years, I intend to run for Congress in 1938."[35]

Willard's job with the *Western Progressive* apparently ended near the beginning of 1934, and it must have been followed by a period of unemployment, because Marjorie wrote to her parents of "trials and tribulations these past months." Soon, however, she was happy to report that Willard was "back on the State payroll again."[36] He had taken a job at the Internal Revenue office in Helena. She confided to her parents that Willard "needs an anchor, and in spite of politics, and the terrible uncertainties of political patronage, and the great gaps which are so apt to occur in political advancement, I am going to drop an anchor and make a home and life for my family."[37] Still, Marjorie's letters exude her unwavering faith in Willard, an abundance of love for him, and her optimism for their future. That winter, Marjorie announced she was pregnant, and by spring she was sensibly ensconced in a new apartment at 244 Burlington Avenue in Billings while waiting for the birth of their baby. She shared with her friend Helen, "I have great hopes that all will go well, though at times I am a little frightened just as all expectant mothers are."[38]

As the time for the birth of the Fraser baby neared, Marjorie's mother was in a quandary. Elinor's letters often express concern for her children's health, their economic stability, and their happiness, but they also detail her husband's frequent bouts with illness.[39] It is clear she acted as a conscientious guardian of his wellbeing. Elinor evidently wanted to come to Billings to be with Marjorie for the birth, but she changed her mind several times because of Robert's health. In February, Marjorie wrote to her mother to suggest she wait until after the baby came, and she implored her mother to "stick to your plan this time." Her letter to Elinor also offers soothing words of reassurance: "It would be very nice if you came to see me before the baby comes, especially if anything should go wrong. But I believe it's best to steadfastly think that everything is going to be all right . . . I have felt all along that Papa needs you more than I do and he has the first right to you always."[40]

In the end, Elinor did come and was present when the baby was born on March 16, 1934. If the baby were a boy, Willard and Marjorie had planned to name him Frost. Since it was a girl, they named her Shirley Robin. They chose the name Robin because she arrived in springtime along with the robins.

At first, the new mother seemed to be recovering well after the birth, and Willard continued working in Helena on weekdays and returning home to Billings on the weekends. "Then," Willard said, "came those horribly helpless weeks."[41] After a short time at home, Marjorie took a turn for the worse and returned to the hospital. Just before her mother left to return to Amherst in April, Marjorie was strong enough to write the last letter of her life, which she wrote to Willard. She spoke of "suffering pain in so many different places" and said about the doctor: "For some reason he wants my mother to stay longer, but she will have to leave tonight or tomorrow I'm afraid. I hate to have her go." Nevertheless, at the end of the letter, Marjorie assured her husband she would be "worlds better tomorrow."[42] What happened next, however, is a blot on the practice and attitude of the doctors in the Billings hospital.[43] According to Willard, the doctors told him he was over-worried and even made fun of his fears when he expressed concern about Marjorie's deteriorating condition. Lillian Frost later wrote that the doctor had Marjorie sitting up on the seventeenth day so she "would snap out of it."[44] However, Marjorie soon began running a steady high temperature, and a few days later a second doctor diagnosed her with puerperal fever. Willard wired Robert and Elinor, who immediately left for Montana and arrived in Billings on April 8.[45] He also contacted John and Margaret Bartlett in Boulder, Colorado, and they took the next train to Billings so they could offer the Frosts the comforting presence of old friends.[46]

Puerperal, or childbed fever, is caused by the streptococcus bacterium invading the reproductive or urinary tract, frequently causing a fatal case of peritonitis or septicemia. During the eighteenth and nineteenth centuries, it was the single most common cause of maternal mortality, and death often came within a week or two of the infection.[47] Ironically, women who chose to give birth in maternity hospitals, thinking they would get better care, were more apt to die from childbed fever than were women who gave birth at home.

As early as the 1840s, pioneering doctors began investigating what seemed to be a causative link between physicians themselves and cases of childbed fever. After learning of several fatal cases of childbed fever, American poet and physician Oliver Wendell Holmes Sr. submitted a paper on the contagiousness of puerperal fever to the *New England Quarterly Journal of Medicine and Surgery* in 1843. Relying on evidence to show that the disease could be transmitted from one patient to the next by careless physicians, Holmes then embarked on a campaign to get doctors to wash their hands before delivering babies. In response, Charles Meigs of the Jefferson Medical College in Philadelphia rebuffed the notion that doctors could be at fault, saying, "Doctors are gentlemen, and gentlemen's hands are clean."[48] Meanwhile, in Europe, Dr. Ignaz Semmelweis, after studying the mortality rates of mothers in Vienna's General Hospital, theorized that doctors who had conducted autopsies and then delivered babies were introducing deadly germs into the bodies of new mothers. He proposed that doctors institute the practice of washing their hands with a disinfectant, and for that he was ridiculed and ostracized. Although a few individual doctors realized that physicians themselves were often responsible for causing the infection, most of them were reluctant to accept that truth.[49]

By 1934, more than ninety years after it was demonstrated that poor physician hygiene had led to cases of infection, Marjorie's attending physicians, Dr. Rathman and Dr. Movius, should have, at the very least, readily recognized the symptoms of puerperal fever and what it would mean for the new mothers they attended. Antibiotics were just emerging and had not yet been used to combat maternal postpartum infections. When Alfred Knopf, Frost's publisher, informed Frost of an article in *Ladies Home Journal* about the promising new sulfa drugs, Frost told Willard to recommend them to Marjorie's doctor.[50] The physician's dismissive reply was simply, "I'll tell my wife to read it."[51] Instead of trying the new medications, the doctor had Marjorie drink twenty glasses of liquid per day and began giving her blood transfusions every other day.

At the time, blood transfusions were given directly from person to person. A number of Willard's friends offered to donate blood to save Marjorie's life. Robert Frost wrote to his son Carol, "Willard's friends have come forward in a host to give their blood for her. I never imagined anything like it for kindness and friendship."[52] Marjorie, unfortunately, had an uncommon blood type, and many who volunteered to give blood were not a match. Only one in six qualified.[53] In an extraordinary outpouring of support, Ernest Eaton, the president of Billings Polytechnic Institute, brought almost the entire student body down for typing and giving.[54]

The twelve blood transfusions Marjorie received likely kept the infection at bay for a time, but she remained critically ill. The Frosts were fully aware that their daughter's condition could have been avoided, and Elinor wrote to Lesley, "Our situation is aggravated by the horror and lack of confidence we have for the doctor who was on the case at the beginning. I feel two or three mistakes on his part caused all this misery."[55] Lillian Frost also attributed fault to the attending doctor and later told Marjorie's friend Helen, "On the 21st day they found by an examination by another doctor that it was childbed fever. If it had been diagnosed even a week sooner, she very probably could have lived."[56]

On April 26, after Marjorie had spent six weeks in the Billings hospital, Willard and the Frosts decided to transfer her to the Mayo Clinic in Rochester, Minnesota. Leaving newborn Robin in Sadie's care, Marjorie and a nurse were flown to the clinic, while Willard, Robert, and Elinor drove more than eight hundred miles from Billings to Rochester. This dusty, nerve-racking trip was made even more tense at one point by skittish police coming at them with sirens on full blast. Police and the FBI were searching for outlaw John Dillinger, who had spent the month of March on a crime spree in St. Paul and then disappeared after a confrontation on April 23 at Little Bohemia Lodge in Wisconsin. Because Elinor had pulled the curtain over the back window to block the sun, the highway patrol thought the car looked suspicious.[57]

At the Mayo Clinic, a bacteriologist concocted a serum that he thought would counteract the infection that had now spread throughout Marjorie's body. Both her parents wrote of the agony of these weeks. "We are going through the valley of the shadow with Marjorie," Robert Frost told Louis Untermeyer, adding, "Marjorie's tenacity and Elinor's devotion and the mercy of God are our hopes."[58] In another letter, he wondered what would become of Elinor and Willard if the worst happened. Elinor, meanwhile, poured out her fears and hopes in several letters, writing to her daughter Lesley:

> I feel an agony of pity, and my limbs tremble with apprehension as to the outcome. . . . She has been delirious for about three weeks, and while she says heartbreaking things, never once has she said anything that revealed other than a pure and steadfast soul. Papa says her courage and nobility will make death seem simpler and easier when it comes.[59]

Marjorie Frost Fraser died at the Mayo Clinic on May 2, 1934. Her body was brought to Billings for her funeral and burial.[60] Afterward, Willard and his newborn daughter accompanied the Frosts on their return to Vermont, where Elinor and Lillian cared for the baby for the remainder of the summer and into the fall. At some point during these days, Willard changed her name from Shirley Robin to Marjorie Robin because, Lillian Frost recalled, "he wanted one Marjorie anyway, though he couldn't call her by it."[61]

As Robert Frost predicted, Marjorie's death was an emotional catastrophe for both Willard and Elinor. In a long letter to the Frosts toward the end of August, Willard mourned his loss and worried about Robin's care and his own future. "I am floundering so completely that nothing seems real or to matter. . . . Every time I see a happy couple in the street, or see an advertisement, or a show, or read a story, or listen to music, or anything, the hurt is torn afresh." He also expressed his love for Robin and his uncertainty about how best to care for her and work at the same time. "I know it isn't fair to leave Robin with you and then take her away but neither do I want my folks to have her; I want her to be mine, and I don't know how to arrange it. . . . The present and the future both seem beyond my ken, but I always live in the past, and it was all too short a past."[62] Equally shocked with grief, Elinor poured out her heart to her friend Edith Forbes, saying, "I long to die myself and be relieved of the pain I feel for her sake. Poor precious darling to have to leave everything in such a cruel and unnecessary way. I cannot bear it, and yet I *must* bear it for the sake of the others here."[63]

Elinor lived four more years before dying of a heart attack in 1938; Robert claimed that her spirit never recovered from Marjorie's death.[64]

Robert Frost dealt with the loss of their daughter differently than Elinor. Nearly two weeks after Marjorie's death, he wrote to Louis Untermeyer, "Well, the blow has fallen. The noblest of us all is dead and taken our hearts out of the world with her."[65] Not surprisingly, he took to literature—of his own creation and that of others—both to express and to control his grief. In his letter to Untermeyer, Frost stated that his favorite poem, Matthew Arnold's "Cadmus and Harmonia," meant more than ever to him after Marjorie's death. In this poem, Cadmus and Harmonia's "dearest jewel" became the source of their "greatest sorrow."[66]

The Frosts also grappled with what to do with Marjorie's poems. To Louis, Robert expressed his initial hesitation at having the poems published, saying, "The poems are good enough for publication . . . though I doubt if we would have the heart to submit them to public criticism."[67] The Frosts decided to have Marjorie's poems published privately in 1936 in the little volume *Franconia*, the title taken from the Frost farm in New Hampshire where Marjorie grew up.[68] Writing to the publisher, Elinor made a special request: "A soft shade of rose was her favorite color, and I should like the cover to be a flowered rose paper."[69] In a contemporary essay on Marjorie's poetry, Montana poet Tami Haaland states that Elinor and Robert Frost arranged her poems "in a chronological and thematic path from isolation to connection that encompasses a vision of the entire country." Haaland pays particular attention to "America," suggesting this poem "perhaps more than any poem in the book reflects Fraser's capacity as an observer and her imaginative vision of the breadth of her homeland."[70]

> *America*
>
> Before my eyes, and yet so far above my praise
> I scarcely notice you for days and days on end,
> And never once commend the million rainbow ways
> You rest my weary heart. Your self-deniers look
> For you from shore to shore; but while they rove
> I find you in some leafy sunny-speckled grove,
> Or in the frozen fields the harvester forsook.
> America—they say you have no native song, –
> Even among the windy pines they hear no tune –
> But far from where the singing river winds along
> I hear it in the stillest hour of burning noon,
> And those who say no one has ever heard the words
> Are leaving out of all account the voice of birds.

Later in life, Willard often referred to two of Frost's poems, "Choose Something Like a Star" and "Never Again Would Birds' Song Be the Same," saying Frost wrote them in response to Marjorie's death. Willard recalled that during the agonizing time they had spent at the Mayo Clinic, "R. F. and myself walked most of the night. It was springtime, and the robins were bursting with song. He used to cry out at them for their thoughtlessness—or so it almost seemed. From those birds, and from the agony of it all, he wrote not too long after, the poem 'Never Would Birds' Song Be the Same' of, about, to, and for her."[71]

As HE EMBARKED on a life as a widower and father of an infant daughter, Willard depended on the Fraser and Frost families as well as his nearest friends for much-needed support. Soon after Marjorie's death, Dwight Morrow's mother, Elizabeth, whose husband had also recently died and who had suffered through the kidnapping and death of her infant grandson, wrote to Willard. She said that though there are difficulties in life, it is important to keep a good spirit and continue with optimism. In his reply, Willard said he hoped he could come to that kind of spirit, energy, and fortitude.

Reaching for something to steady him, Willard sought solace in his last archaeological expedition with Earl Morris, who, he later said, "saved my sanity." While he worked in the Southwest, infant Robin remained under the care of Elinor and Lillian in Vermont. As a child, Robin would spend a portion of her early years with the Frosts, visits encouraged and arranged by Elinor and Lillian. Although Willard often took Robin along with him on his travels, Sadie Fraser became Robin's primary caretaker in Montana. Willard was often absent while working to support himself and his daughter and while pursuing his political ambitions. At one point, Lesley Frost expressed concern over what she termed Robin's "back and forth" early years, but Willard and Robin developed a "deep and abiding love" for each other.[72] Once she was old enough to attend school, Robin remained in Billings during much of the year. Sadie's constancy and school itself contributed a measure of stability during Robin's childhood and teenage years.

Willard never remarried, and his decision made the Frosts his in-laws for life. Many years later, recalling the days before Marjorie's death, he said she knew what the end would be and had "begged me not to ever give Robin a stepmother. . . . Marjorie had a terror of stepmothers. Our children's literature is full of tales of the brutal stepmother." Willard was reluctant

While grieving Marjorie's death, Willard returned to the Southwest to work for Earl Morris. He is pictured here at an archaeological site in Arizona, ca. 1932. EHM07.02_002#016, University of Colorado Museum of Natural History, Boulder

to speak about this request. He said Marjorie was delirious during those final days, and he feared it would reflect badly on her. Decades later, he admitted that sometimes he was lonely and that there were a few occasions when he might have married—once just before World War II broke out and once in California when he was in the army. But, he said, "I just never could bring myself to bring someone in to take Marjorie's place. Even now, there is a girl I've long liked, but she is a strong Christian Scientist—and I just could not face Mary Baker Eddy across the breakfast table, or when I am having an asthma attack."[73] Reminiscing many years later, his longtime friends Charlie Borberg and Frank Cross opined that Willard never got over Marjorie's death, and Charlie reported that Willard kept her clothes in his closet for many years after her death.[74] Mac Fraser remembers that Willard kept a hinged photograph frame with Robin's portrait on one side and Marjorie's on the other on a desk in the Fraser home. As late as 1972, just six months before his own death, Willard wrote to Marjorie's sister Lesley Frost Ballantine and said, "Time heals, but not really, does it?"[75]

"The way to get into politics is to get into politics"

AFTER THE SUMMER of "recovering his sanity" in the Southwest, Willard returned to Billings, still in the stages of grief. Robin was with the Frosts in Vermont, and Willard was struggling to regain his life's equilibrium. Even his fascination with politics and his love for Montana could not lessen his grief. "Just the word Montana lets loose a torrent of thoughts, and trying to get ahold of things," he wrote to his in-laws. "I talk politics, and try to make myself think politics, but in reality, it is just a mean attempt to keep going. I have not honestly any more interest in politics than I have in oyster fishing."[1] He described his emotional state years later in a letter of sympathy: "Having gone through such an experience myself [death of a loved one], I know that one is numb for a long time afterward, and with the letdown comes the real grief, and the need for friends."[2] In the coming months and years, those friends, as well as the Frost family and Willard's own family, would buoy him up with their support and encouragement.

That fall, he was jobless again and took a temporary job as assistant manager of the Montana Liquor Store, a position made possible through his brother Marvin. Fortunately, Willard soon found stable employment as secretary and lobbyist for the Independent Merchants Association of Montana, of which Fraser family friend and Marvin's father-in-law, B. R. Albin, was president. Albin would become Willard's mentor.

Albin was a creative businessman and a force in the community. Described as "one of the best business hustlers and indefatigable workers that ever dropped into the Yellowstone Valley,"[3] Berthold Richard Albin

Billings, ca. 1935. Businessmen B. R. Albin and Ray Hart, proprietors of the Hart-Albin department store, helped develop downtown Billings. Albin later became Willard's employer and mentor. 941-122, MHS Photograph Archives, Helena

was born in Posen, Prussia, and came to America with his family when he was two.[4] Albin arrived in Montana from Minnesota in 1899 at the age of twenty-one, and in 1902 opened the Hart-Albin Store, a Billings department store, with Ray Hart, who had already invested in several small-town stores. Hart served as president and financial director of Hart-Albin, while Albin was in charge of marketing and was the store's hands-on manager.[5] Hart-Albin opened the first bargain basement in Montana, was the first business in Billings to decorate for Christmas, and provided a rest and waiting room furnished with easy chairs, desks with writing material, and reading tables for the comfort of its customers. A wily marketer, Albin hired a violinist to play a series of Saturday night concerts in the store to attract more female shoppers. He also played a role in getting developer A. L. Babcock to build his theater in the downtown location in 1907, and he led the effort to move the Billings post office to a new location near the Babcock Theater as part of an effort to centralize key facilities near Hart-Albin.

The Fraser-Albin-Hart alliance undoubtedly began when the Frasers lived in the area north of Montana Avenue and continued even after the

Frasers moved across the tracks to South 38th Street. The Albin-Fraser connection was strengthened by the marriage of Marvin Fraser to Mary Louise Albin in 1932 and the later marriage of Bob Fraser to Jane Albin. The Hart family was also part of the Fraser social circle. When Russ Hart, son of Ray Hart, served as a pallbearer at Marjorie Fraser's funeral in May 1934, he was dating Willard's sister, Jeanne, whom he married in 1935.[6]

As a businessman and as a Montana Democrat active in state politics, B. R. Albin provided Willard with more than employment. His important connections influenced Willard's nascent political career during a time when the state and national political scene was rife with bitter divisions and controversial movements. Albin was also a significant role model for Willard Fraser for both his accomplishments and his outlook. He made regular buying trips to New York City, traveling cross-country by train. When he returned to Billings after each trip, the *Gazette* ran an article summarizing his take on the latest fashions for the season. Throughout these years, Albin was interested in much more than advertising clothing for his store. In local and national newspapers, he promoted Montana, issued optimistic forecasts about recovering from the Great Depression, and explained why repealing the Eighteenth Amendment (Prohibition) was good for the economy. The *Washington Post* interviewed Albin in 1917 when he attended the U.S. Chamber of Commerce meeting at the historic Willard Hotel in Washington, D.C. The article described Albin as the "leading dry goods merchant of Billings, Mont.," and it quoted him on America: "the greatest, grandest on the globe. . . . The west is a region not equaled in scenic beauty in any foreign land." He went on to specifically praise the glories of the Shoshone River Canyon from Wyoming to Yellowstone.[7]

A brochure commemorating an early Hart-Albin anniversary extols virtues beyond those of the department store. It praises the location and the climate of Billings, saying, "Who wants to spend a life in the torrid heat of the Mississippi lowlands or the everlasting chill of Duluth?" Drawing attention to the state's "unsurpassed" scenery, the brochure enumerates all the characteristics that made Billings, the "biggest city of the third biggest state in the union," such a pleasant place to live.[8] In time, Willard—as Billings's mayor and lead cheerleader—would adopt Albin's style of promotion as well as his unabashed enthusiasm for Billings and Montana. Albin's frequent travel to the East Coast, his active involvement in economic and political affairs, and his optimistic attitude evoke comparison to the mature Willard Fraser, suggesting the impact Albin had on Willard.

In 1933, when Willard wrote to the Frosts about Albin giving Marjorie away at their wedding, he commented that Albin "is a very outspoken and gruff individual," but Willard certainly admired him and corresponded with Albin in a friendly manner.[9] Albin must have had a caustic streak, though, because Fraser commented that both Marjorie and Robert Frost at different times had compared Albin to satirical journalist H. L. Mencken.[10] Frost and Albin certainly met each other because in 1940 Frost wrote to Robin, "Please deal with Mr. Albin in person at his store and give him my regards."[11] Marvin's son Mac Fraser did not remember the caustic side and said about his grandfather Albin, "I liked who he was and he liked who I was." He added approvingly that Albin took care of his seven children and Mary, his first wife, after they divorced. Two granddaughters and a daughter-in-law, however, remember Albin as being very stern and almost cruel at times, whereas Mac used the word "gentle" in describing him. The family consensus was that his second wife, Vada, "softened" him.[12]

Certainly, this complicated and talented figure influenced the future mayor of Billings. Willard wrote in retrospect about the businessman, "We had a great Billings citizen, B. R. Albin, who possessed one of the quickest, finest, most penetrating minds ever to live in the City."[13] Albin's patronage of Willard was likely not just a family favor. The politically savvy and persuasive Albin recognized and encouraged the same qualities in Willard Fraser, and in time he facilitated the ambitious young man's acquaintance with Senator Burton K. Wheeler.

In 1934, correspondence between Albin and Senator Wheeler discussed a political appointment for Albin in the Roosevelt administration.[14] It never materialized, but in 1935, Wheeler arranged the appointment of Albin's colleague Ray Hart to head the Works Progress Administration (WPA) in Montana, a move the Democrats viewed with dismay because Hart, a Republican, appointed other Republicans. Hart's tenure was short-lived and ended with his resignation in February 1936.[15] Among his many community projects, however, he took a leading role in raising funds to buy a site for Eastern Montana Normal School, now Montana State University–Billings. Hart died suddenly in 1939, and his son Russ took his place as president of Hart-Albin.

Albin and Wheeler shared a personal friendship in addition to their political alliance. Albin family archives contain photos of Albin-Wheeler fishing trips and other travels. When Wheeler stopped in Billings on his campaign as Robert LaFollette's running mate on the 1924 Progressive ticket, the *Gazette* described Wheeler as Albin's "warm personal friend."[16] After a decades-long marriage and seven children, Albin divorced his wife, Mary, and in 1935 at age fifty-seven married thirty-three-year-old Vada Keller. He and his bride immediately sailed on a two-month honeymoon

B. R. and Vada Albin with B. K. and Lulu Wheeler in Japan, 1935. As Fraser's employer and longtime acquaintance, Albin had an indelible influence on Fraser's political views and his passion for promoting Billings. Courtesy Cathy Wiltjen

trip to the Philippines and Asia as guests of Senator Wheeler and his wife, Lulu. The congressional party on the tour included North Dakota senator Gerald Nye and his wife, New York congressman Bertrand Snell and his wife, Indiana senator Sherman Minton and his wife, and Massachusetts congressman Allen Treadway.[17] This was a bipartisan group, as both Wheeler and Minton were Democrats. The intent of the trip was to attend the inauguration of President Manuel L. Quezon of the Philippines, but stops in Hong Kong, mainland China, and Japan made it quite a grand tour. Just before embarking on this trip, B. R. and Vada received a Bon Voyage telegram from a young Willard Fraser.[18]

Albin's alliance with Senator Wheeler gave him an occasional national voice. For instance, in 1939, as part of Wheeler's effort to prohibit war profiteering, he released a telegram from Albin. In the three-paragraph telegram, Albin, writing as president of the Independent Merchants Association of Montana, appealed for congressional action "to ban or prohibit war-engendered speculation in the prices of necessities of life." Wheeler would have agreed with Albin's expressed hope that "no millionaires will be made at the expense of the underprivileged."[19]

Beyond being a role model and employer, B. R. Albin facilitated other career opportunities for Willard. As an active member of the Democratic Party and a close friend of Wheeler, B. R. opened the door to Willard's relationship with the senator, which, in turn, drew Willard further into Montana's political arena. Albin was a close ally of both Senator Thomas Walsh and Burton Wheeler. Given Montana's vigorous political environment during Willard's formative years, it is no wonder that he nursed dreams of public office and that he became a committed Democrat in an area of Montana later awash with Republicans. Fraser's political "gods" at the time were Franklin Delano Roosevelt loyalists who were also establishing reputations in Washington as formidable statesmen in their own right. Albin's political cachet in the Democratic Party is demonstrated by his attendance at the Roosevelt inauguration and the previous evening's victory dinner. At the time, Albin was state chairman of National Business Associates of the United States and president of the Independent Merchants Association. The Albin-Wheeler network provided the perfect environment for the development of the future independent mayor of Billings.

As Willard became more settled in his position with the Independent Merchants Association, both the Frosts and the Frasers agreed in the early fall of 1934 that seven-month-old Robin should return to Billings. Elinor wrote to a friend that Willard would almost certainly be "mostly in the West, and Mrs. Fraser and I agreed that Robin ought to be where Willard can see her as often as possible. . . . Robert and I feel we shouldn't keep the baby longer, as we would get so fond of her a break would be very hard. It is hard to part with her even now."[20] Lesley Frost was teaching at a women's college in Rockford, Illinois, so plans were made for Willard and Sadie to meet the Frosts there in October and bring Robin home to Montana.[21] After returning to the Frost's home in Shaftsbury, Vermont, Elinor wrote to Willard about how difficult it had been for her to part with Robin: "After you left [Rockford] last Tuesday, I sort of gave out, and went to bed for two days. . . . How I do miss precious Robin! . . . My arms feel empty without her."[22]

Willard now took steps to ensure that he could provide a stable environment for his daughter. The Frasers were renting the house on South 38th Street where he and Marjorie had married. In early 1935, when Willard purchased it as a permanent home for Robin, Sadie, J. B., and himself. Willard's employment with Albin's Independent Merchants Association contributed to the financial security that enabled the Frasers to buy the house where Willard and Marjorie had wed less than a year earlier.

In moving to South 38th Street, the Frasers joined one of the oldest neighborhoods in Billings. The Fraser house, which still stands today, was located in the northern section of the South Side, the area south of Minnesota Avenue just across the railroad tracks from downtown. The Great Western sugar beet plant, the Billings Meat Company, and the Pierce Packing Company employed several hundred South Side residents, including many Mexican, Chinese, Polish, and African American laborers.[23] The South Side's ethnically diverse population preserved their own cultures through social and religious organizations. Our Lady of Guadalupe Catholic Church was an important bonding force for Mexican Americans. The Chinese community built a temple and community gardens, and they celebrated Chinese festivals. African American women formed the Phyllis Wheatley Colored Women's Club.[24] The result was a lively neighborhood, very different from the more staid communities north of Montana Avenue.

The two-story frame house hosted scores of people throughout the next four decades—writers, politicians, friends, relatives, the Frost family, and visitors from around the world. During the Great Depression, the Fraser house on South 38th was one of the houses marked with chalk by hobos as a sign that the house was a friendly one that would provide food either free or in exchange for work.[25] Grandson David Hudnut remembered the numerous artifacts in the house, the piano that Sadie often played, and the "warm feeling" the house evoked. It was in this modest South Side home—referred to by the Frasers' grandchildren as "the big

Elinor Frost at Rockford, Illinois, ca. 1934, possibly when delivering infant Robin to the Frasers. 1983K, The Frank P. Piskor Collection of Robert Frost, Special Collections, St. Lawrence University, Canton, NY

house"—that Robin grew up.[26] J. B. was present throughout the years of Robin's upbringing, but as grandson Mac Fraser remarked, "Sadie brought everyone up, and Jack [J. B.] just hung in there."[27] By the end of Willard's life, it would be filled with books and mementos—a grandfather's clock from London, a Mexican vase, a pen from Hubert Humphrey—from his connections and his travels.

Although based in Billings, Willard continued to spend time in Helena, where his political involvement began to receive newspaper coverage. He seemed to be following his own advice expressed in 1933 in a long letter to Robert Frost: "The way to get into politics is to get into politics."[28] Because of his previous work for Lewis Penwell at the *Western Progressive* and at the Internal Revenue Service, as well as his current employment by the Independent Merchants Association, Willard was called as a witness in the 1935 Fowler Committee investigation. This legislative committee, named after Chairman C. W. Fowler, a Republican from Billings, probed the relationship between the powerful "twin" companies of Montana Power and Anaconda Copper, on the one hand, and the state's newspapers, on the other, to discern whether the state's 1912 Corrupt Practices Act was being violated through corporate control of newspapers. Because of these companies' history of undue influence on Montana's elections, the Corrupt Practices Act restricted the money that corporations and individuals could donate to politicians and campaigns. Its intention was to prevent and punish illegal practices in elections.

As part of the investigation, the Fowler Committee subpoenaed right-wing editor William Campbell of Helena's *Independent* newspaper to probe whether the Anaconda Company had exerted undue influence over that newspaper. More than a decade earlier, as an influential member of the Montana Council of Defense, Campbell's xenophobic diatribes against Germans in Montana were instrumental in shutting down German newspapers and inflaming public prejudice.[29] The *Western Progressive*'s thorough coverage of the Fowler investigation aroused Campbell's fighting spirit, and in a series of articles in the *Independent*, Campbell tried to divert attention from his own situation by accusing Penwell of corruption. Campbell charged Penwell of, among other things, using the *Western Progressive* to influence legislation on a chain store tax bill promoted by the Independent Merchants Association. After Fraser was called to testify in the Fowler investigation, Campbell claimed that Fraser, Penwell, and Fowler were "buddies" in an attempt to defraud independent merchants. He charged that Penwell worked with Fowler to exempt Penwell-owned Co-op gas stations from the proposed tax. On March 13, the *Independent* claimed that the Independent Merchants of Montana had been betrayed by the "Fowler-Penwell-Fraser" outfit. The Fowler Committee's final judgment found evidence of the "twin" companies "wielding a controlling influence" over several papers. Critics continued to claim the investigation was a partisan effort opposed to the corporations, however, and the committee's recommendations were not adopted by the House.[30]

The chain store tax proposal, which Campbell brought up during the investigative hearings, was indeed a project of the Independent Merchants Association. The proposal became a drawn-out legal and political battle with the IMA leading the push to increase the tax on out-of-state-owned chain stores in an effort to protect independent Montana merchants. Despite their common Democratic Party affiliation, Governor Elmer Holt and B. R. Albin clashed on the proposed tax. The governor accused both Albin and Fraser of "fraud and misrepresentation" in obtaining the signatures to enable the bill to go forward. He claimed, for instance, that signatures from a liquor control petition had been transferred to the petition for the chain store tax.[31] Albin immediately issued a lengthy rebuttal, accusing Holt, who had recently lost his reelection bid, of being "vindictive" and using his closing days in office to "settle fancied political scores."[32] Albin insisted that it was "absolutely false that independent merchants were involved in the liquor measure" and declared that Holt's accusation was a "libel on me and those who drafted the chain store license law."[33] Albin eventually succeeded in his long battle to have an increased chain store tax law passed. After it failed to pass the Montana legislature in 1935, the Merchants Association filed petitions to put the law to referendum in the 1936 election. The Montana Supreme Court ruled it invalid based on the form or wording of the proposed ballot.[34] Finally, the 1937 legislature passed the law, and in March 1937, Holt's successor, Governor Roy Ayers, signed the chain store tax bill and gave the signing pen to Albin.

The chain store tax was not the only proposal Willard worked on during the early 1930s. He was one of three directors of the Montana Initiative, formed in response to the 1933 Liquor Control Act adopted by Montana after the Twenty-first Amendment repealed Prohibition. The act decreed that a state liquor control board would have authority over all liquor sales except those "by [individual] drink" in Montana. Commercial liquor sales would be allowed by state-licensed vendors only. In a move to abolish the state liquor control system, the Montana Initiative collected signatures to authorize a referendum in the November 1936 election to allow private businesses to sell liquor. Willard traveled throughout Montana to gain signatures for the Montana Initiative, but his work was undone when the Montana Commercial League of Great Falls persuaded some signers to withdraw their signatures. Consequently, the Montana Supreme Court ruled that there would be no vote on the issue in the November election because of their withdrawal.[35] Willard later made a campaign issue of ending state-owned liquor stores, but he never succeeded in ending the state monopoly.[36]

Throughout this time, Willard continued to struggle with asthma, which sometimes prevented him from working. "I have not written lately because I have been very busy and also sick," he told the Frosts. "I work for a while, and then I nurse asthma for a while. I am headed into Billings now, and expect to rest up a few days."[37]

The Frosts and Frasers stayed in touch and arranged periodic reunions in Vermont and elsewhere. Elinor wrote in March 1935 that she hoped to go to Billings to see Robin if she were strong enough and "perhaps bring her [Robin] back,"[38] but Robert wrote in July that he was "trying to dissuade Elinor from a melancholy trip to Billings to visit Marjorie's grave and see Robin."[39] He evidently succeeded, because an alternate visit with Robin was arranged. Frost was a guest at the Rocky Mountain Writers Conference in Boulder that August, and Willard, Sadie, and one-year-old Robin met the Frosts in Colorado. The visit involved the John and Margaret Bartlett family, who had hosted Marjorie during the time when she and Willard first met. Elinor was delighted to find that "Robin was delightfully cunning and bright, and Marjorie's friends in Boulder were very glad to have a chance to see her."[40]

After the 1935 summer visit, the Frosts did not see Robin again until December 1936, but the family relationship was maintained through letters. In January 1936, Elinor wrote to a friend, "Robin is perfectly well and jolly, and developing into a very precocious child, judging from what they [the Frasers] write."[41] This followed Willard's report in February that the nearly two-year-old Robin could say "very cold" in Spanish. The 1930s in Montana were notable not only because of the Great Depression's impacts but also for the unremitting drought followed by severe winters. Willard described struggling through Montana's winter weather, with snowdrifts higher than the car near Baker and blocked roads near Ekalaka. Encountering an emaciated coyote along the way, he commented, "A fine country where even a coyote cannot make a living."[42] The *Gazette* provided further details of this meeting with the coyote. According to the newspaper, when a "lean-looking coyote wobbled across the road," Fraser's companion grabbed a shovel and whacked the nearly starved animal to death. They then sold the hide to help pay for the gasoline for their trip.[43] Willard told the Frosts the hide brought a $2 bounty, a much-appreciated sum during the Great Depression.

Although Willard supported his family through his work as a lobbyist and secretary for the Independent Merchants Association through these grim years, he still aspired to public office. In 1936, he began the process to obtain a federal government appointment in the East, a goal in line with the Frosts' desire for Willard and Robin to live closer to them in the East. He wrote to the Frosts to announce, "I had a letter from Washington saying that my qualifications were all right, and that I have been placed on the list 'Eligible for Appointment,' whatever that may prove to mean."[44] Willard was passed over for an appointment that year, but he persevered in his hope for a federal job. In 1939, Lesley Frost wrote to "Papa" commenting about Willard's prospects and suggesting that, if he succeeded in getting his foot in the door, "perhaps he can get a job in Washington later."[45] This was not to be, but Willard was just as committed as the Frosts were in sustaining his own and Robin's relationship with them.

Willard's aspirations and ambition fostered his interest in state and national politics. Throughout the 1930s, he observed and commented on several political movements led by strong personalities intent on blocking President Roosevelt's reelection. These movements came to a head prior to the 1936 election. In one such movement, Dr. Francis Townsend, a physician from California, formulated a plan in 1933 for all senior citizens to be given a $200 monthly pension. He formed more than a thousand "Townsend" clubs with millions of members. In the summer of 1936, Gerald L. K. Smith, a protégé of Louisiana governor Huey Long, and Father Charles Coughlin, a rabid anti-Semite Catholic priest, joined with Townsend to form the Union Party, a populist alternative to Roosevelt and his New Deal. By this time, Coughlin had already attracted a large following through his radio broadcasts.

The Union Party attracted a considerable following in Montana. Four hundred delegates and six hundred other participants met in Butte to elect a Montana member for the national advisory board of the Townsend movement.[46] Certainly, Montana would have been represented at the Union Party's convention in Cleveland in July, where Representative Lemke of North Dakota became the party's candidate for president in their effort to defeat President Roosevelt. Gerald Smith earned much attention with his bombastic rhetoric, declaiming in one convention speech, "If Lemke forgets about the Townsend plan, then I know a country doctor [Townsend] and a Louisiana preacher [Smith] who will chop his dad-gummed head off."[47] Throughout the summer and fall, Townsend urged his followers to defeat President Roosevelt because of "the dictatorship in Washington."[48]

Just before the 1936 election, Townsend launched even more inflammatory charges against Roosevelt, saying, "A vote for Roosevelt is a vote for communism and fascism."[49] The Union Party dissolved after Roosevelt's reelection, and both Coughlin and Smith went their separate ways. Coughlin's attacks on America's participation in World War II and on Judaism became so shrill that his magazine, *Social Justice*, was banned in 1942, and Archbishop Edward A. Mooney of Detroit ordered him to cease his radio broadcast program in the same year. Smith later led a white supremacist movement centered in Louisiana.[50]

Willard's take on the Townsend movement was expressed in an undated letter to Robert Frost: "I am not carrying the Townsend banner. . . . I went to one of their meetings in Lewistown. I was invited to speak but declined. They are quite up on their psychology. . . . The whole is pathetic, cruel, amazing, and full of danger."[51] Willard's assessment of the Townsend Party stance differed significantly from that of his political hero, Burton K. Wheeler. According to a 2019 biography of Wheeler, the senator "paid frequent lip service to the Townsend plan," a plan author Marc Johnson called "political fool's gold."[52] This view of the Townsendites is corroborated by California historian Kevin Starr, who called the movement a "messianic reform movement" and a "panaceatic mass cult."[53] Willard's skeptical reaction to the Townsend movement characterizes his distrust of ideas buttressed more by emotion than by reason, an attitude he expressed later with such statements as "Political slogans are often just substitutes for thinking." That he did not follow Wheeler's quiet cooperation with the movement demonstrates his ability to arrive at his own conclusions rather than simply adopt those of his political mentor.

In another letter before the 1936 election, Willard mused on the Democratic Party in Montana and the wider political scene. He commented casually about political leadership: "This is Lincoln's birthday. . . . I have a theory that real leaders of men must come from the coast, the mountains, or a frontier. Kansas has none of these so Landon [the Republican candidate for president] never would be a leader, even if he were a president." This is an interesting observation coming from a native Kansan. Willard's pride in Kansas was second only to his feeling for Montana, but Alf Landon's affiliation with Republicans perhaps explains Willard's thinking. In the same letter, he noted, "All the chain papers are against F. D. R., even ours in the West."[54] In 1936, Roosevelt won by another landslide, winning all but eight electoral votes. Democrats won in Montana, too: Ray Ayers became governor, and James Murray retained his Senate seat in a decisive victory.

Montana's two senators, Burton K. Wheeler and James Murray, both progressive Democrats from Butte, soon developed a contentious relationship as Wheeler, who had backed Roosevelt in the 1932 and 1936 elections, began to speak out against the president, most notably opposing both FDR's

1937 attempt to pack the U.S. Supreme Court and the 1941 Lend-Lease plan to make American tools of war available to England. Murray, on the other hand, continued to support Roosevelt's measures and increasingly resented Wheeler's powerful influence. The Wheeler-Roosevelt relationship settled into one of permanent distrust and antagonism. The Wheeler-Murray relationship was equally acrimonious. That Fraser maintained a mutually respectful and genuinely good relationship with both Wheeler and Murray for many years attests to his political savvy and personal amiability.

In December 1936, Willard took a brief break from politics so that he and nearly three-year-old Robin could journey to San Antonio, where the entire Frost family, with the exception of Irma, gathered for the Christmas holidays. Writing to Frost's biographer, Lawrance Thompson, Willard related his shock at a minor incident that took place when Robin and he arrived. Elinor was sitting in a rocking chair smoking a cigarette. The Frosts had begun smoking when they lived in England in 1912, and Elinor had become a habitual smoker of Chesterfields. Apparently, she had not realized how smoking affected her asthmatic son-in-law. Willard later described the moment: "Robin walked all the way around her, and then turned to me and in a shocked tone of voice said, 'We don't smoke, do we, Willard?'" Concerned about a less than sympathetic portrait of Elinor in Thompson's first volume, Willard affirmed his own respect for Elinor, saying, "Never again was Robin to see Elinor smoking a cigarette." He concluded his letter to Thompson with the entreaty, "Treat her [Elinor] kindly."[55]

The Frosts and Willard maintained a warm and respectful relationship despite their different political leanings, and the Frosts welcomed him into their family. When Willard departed San Antonio for Montana on New Year's Day, Robin stayed on with the Frosts for a few more weeks. Robert Frost remarked to writer Bernard DeVoto in March, "We are parting with our granddaughter at St. Louis on Sunday. Her father meets us there and regathers her to Montana and his Democratic politics. It comes hard on us to lose her. It amuses me to think of the heresies she is bound to grow up to."[56]

The Frosts had taken to avoiding New England winters on doctors' advice because of Robert's propensity for "grippe" and bronchial conditions. In the fall of 1937, Elinor wrote that she would like to try Arizona the following winter—mostly because it would be easier for Robin to join them.[57] Instead, during the winter of 1938, the elder Frosts and Lillian and Carol went to Gainesville, Florida, and Willard met them there with Robin. For a second year, Robin stayed with the Frosts through the winter. That spring, sixty-five-year-old Elinor Frost suffered several successive heart

Young Robin Fraser with her paternal grandmother, Sadie Fraser. Sadie became Robin's primary caregiver, though Robin also spent time with her Frost grandparents. Courtesy Gardner Historical Society, Gardner, KS

attacks and died on March 18, 1938, two days after Robin's fourth birthday. Robert immediately wired Willard of the sad news: "Another sorrow. Elinor died this morning."[58] Willard wired back: "Springtime is our time of sadness. Wire your immediate plans."[59]

Frost was devastated by Elinor's death. He had relied on her for both emotional and intellectual support, and she had been a steadfast guardian of his physical health. In need of the kind of mooring Elinor had provided,

Frost soon found a supportive anchor in the person of Kay Morrison, wife of Bread Loaf School of English professor Ted Morrison. Kay became his secretary and general "keeper." Toward the end of Frost's life, some of Willard's Frost correspondence was with Kay, and it was Kay who served as hostess when Robin spent summers in Vermont during her teenage years.

Willard's increasing activity in Montana's politics and the support of political leaders close to him provided motivation to act on his longtime dream of securing an elected position, and Frost, like his daughter before him, offered ample encouragement. True to his stated goal, Willard made a run for a seat in the Montana State House as a candidate from Yellowstone County in 1938. As had been true in his college years, relationships he formed during this time gave him confidence and opportunity. He reported to Frost, "Doing the work I am doing enables me to get all over the state, and make acquaintances. I think that I am better known over the district as a whole than any other candidate but of course my youth will be a factor. I am going to try to have others give my speeches so I will not have to show myself too much on the platform."[60] At thirty-one, Willard was the youngest candidate, but his plan to evade the spotlight must not have sent a message of a strong leader.

Frost replied, "We're glad to hear of your progress in politics. . . . Be a Senator when you get round to it." Frost hoped that Willard's pursuit of career politics would eventually enable him and Robin to live closer to the Frost side of the family: "You'll probably have to have her [Robin] out there, though if you get to Congress soon enough you might like to make your headquarters with us and let us help you bring her up."[61] Willard survived the July primary to be one of the five Democrats vying for the five state house seats from Yellowstone County. In the November election, however, Republicans won all five county seats. Beginning that year, the Republican control of Yellowstone County elections became increasingly dominant—a trend that would last for decades.[62] This would be the challenging political climate in which Willard would run for office, many times over, in the years to come.

CHAPTER SIX

"I am his partisan"

IN THE YEARS between 1938 and the beginning of World War II, Willard Fraser's connections with B. R. Albin and Senator Wheeler fed his own ambition and pulled him into the state political scene. Albin and Wheeler each had a foot in both Montana and the nation. Their lives were rooted in Montana, but their interests and abilities made them influential beyond their Montana base. The Albin-Wheeler friendship contributed to Fraser's growing admiration for Senator Wheeler, and soon he became involved in Burton K. Wheeler's campaigns just as political tension in Montana, the nation, and the world was escalating. Willard described Albin's regard for Wheeler in a letter to Robert Frost, saying, "Albin takes every word of Wheeler's as gospel."[1] Although Willard took a more tempered view of both the war and some of the political figures with whom Wheeler was involved, he allied himself with Wheeler in the senator's position against the war and remained permanently loyal to him, writing decades later, "I am his partisan." Willard's relationships with Wheeler and Albin expanded his world in the same way that his exposure to his archaeological East Coast colleagues and his connection to the Frost family enabled him to understand and be comfortable in a world beyond the West and Montana.

During Willard's teen and young adult years, U.S. senators Thomas Walsh (1859–1933) and Burton K. Wheeler (1882–1975) loomed large, in both Montana and the nation, as statesmen of courage and conviction. Both were progressive politicians who opposed corporate control of government and supported government by the people. Elected in 1912, Thomas Walsh became the chief senatorial spokesman for Wilson's Democratic administration. He was a consistent Senate leader during the terms of Republicans

Harding, Coolidge, and Hoover, but he is best known as the persistent and courageous senator who blew the lid off the Teapot Dome scandal, which ended with prison terms for Secretary of the Interior Albert B. Fall and Harry Sinclair of Sinclair Oil for their role in illegally transferring naval oil reserves to private owners while giving and receiving huge kickbacks.[2]

When Franklin Roosevelt won the 1932 election, he selected Walsh to become U.S. attorney general. However, in February 1933, en route to Washington to assume office, Senator Walsh died suddenly of a heart attack, although some speculated that his new young wife poisoned him.[3] Senator Wheeler accompanied Walsh's body to Helena, where a very large and public funeral was held in March 1933. Wheeler later eulogized Walsh at the memorial service in Washington, D.C.

Walsh's death was followed by political maneuverings directed at filling the vacant Senate seat. Senator Wheeler played a major role in this. Butte attorney and national Democratic Party committeeman Bruce Kremer was interested in the office. As a friend of Homer Cummings, Walsh's replacement as attorney general, and a player in the Roosevelt administration, Kremer seemed a likely candidate for the Senate. Both Walsh and Wheeler, however, had heartily disliked Kremer, who also was a lobbyist for the Anaconda Company. In order to prevent Kremer from becoming senator and a rival to Wheeler's political power, Wheeler persuaded Governor John Erickson to resign and to have his successor, Frank Cooney, appoint Erickson to the seat.[4] This political maneuvering aroused much controversy, but Erickson's tenure as senator was short-lived.[5] In the 1934 primary, Butte attorney and millionaire James E. Murray defeated Erickson and went on to win the two-year term in the fall election over Republican Scott Leavitt. Montana's two Democratic senators, Wheeler and Murray, would become powerful politicians and bitter rivals despite being in the same party.

Burton Kendall Wheeler began his political career as a state legislator in 1910, when Willard Fraser was three years old. After Wheeler supported Thomas Walsh in 1912 for the U.S. Senate seat against a copper company candidate, Senator Walsh appointed Wheeler U.S. attorney for the District of Montana, initiating a colorful career for this principled, savvy lawyer and politician. Wheeler was soundly defeated by Joe Dixon in a bitter campaign for governor in 1920, but he rebounded, winning a U.S. Senate seat in 1922. He first earned a name for himself two years later when, after months of persistence, he spearheaded a Senate investigation into corruption in the Justice Department that culminated in Attorney General Harry Daugherty's censure by the Senate and his dismissal by President Coolidge.

Throughout his career, Wheeler was a voice in opposition to the power of corporations and a proponent of the rights of common people.

Wheeler endorsed Franklin Roosevelt in an April 1930 speech at the Hotel Commodore in New York City. Although he was one of the first politicians of national stature to do so, his support for Roosevelt gradually eroded.[6] The two became bitter antagonists when the senator opposed the president's U.S. Supreme Court packing plan in 1937. The clash between Roosevelt and Wheeler, two powerful politicians with strong egos, manifested itself in sundry ways. In the late 1930s, the construction of Fort Peck Dam, the largest earthen dam in the world, epitomized the New Deal in Montana because of the many jobs it contributed to the economy. According to historian Marc Johnson, Wheeler was responsible for Roosevelt's decision to approve the construction of Fort Peck Dam, yet when President Roosevelt visited Fort Peck in 1937, not long after Wheeler stopped his court-packing attempt, Roosevelt failed to invite Wheeler to accompany him, an overt sign of their strained relationship.[7] The rancor between the two intensified when Wheeler took a strong isolationist stance before America entered World War II, delivering emotionally charged speeches against entering the war and promising he would "fight to save your sons from the bloody battlefields of Europe, Asia, and Africa."[8] Nevertheless, after Japan's attack on Pearl Harbor, Wheeler voted to enter the war.

Throughout these events, and for the remainder of his life, Willard Fraser remained Wheeler's friend and partisan. Both men possessed outgoing, engaging personalities, a willingness to diverge from the party line, and a knack for eloquent and persuasive speech. While there were times when Willard's regard for his mentor was tested, his open admiration for Wheeler—while not as blind as Albin's—never waned, and both Albin and Wheeler influenced Willard's progressive political path.

IN 1939, after his failure to gain a seat in the state legislature, Fraser was still working for Albin's Independent Merchants Association. As a way to supplement his income, Willard had decided to build an apartment building in Billings. A permit for a sixteen-unit building to be built on the corner of 8th Avenue North and North 29th Street had been issued in January 1938, but the financing or construction could not have gone smoothly.[9] In April 1939, he wrote to the Frosts, "Between fighting over my building and waiting for the war to break, I have been living a nervous life."[10]

Senator Burton K. Wheeler of Montana, December, 1939, at his office in Washington, D.C. Fraser worked on Wheeler's reelection campaigns and remained a strong supporter of Wheeler even after Wheeler fell out of political favor. Harris & Ewing, photographer. 27844, Library of Congress, Washington, DC

The Albin-Fraser connection must have led to Wheeler's recommending Fraser for appointment as the U.S. Census Bureau's area manager for the 16th Decennial Census in 1940, which provided Willard with a steady, if temporary, income. Willard's area covered thirty-three counties in eastern Montana, and he supervised as many as five hundred census takers. His office gave him an opportunity to hone his speaking and public relations skills, and, as census manager, he was the subject of several news articles. The *Havre Daily News* published the entirety of a radio address Fraser delivered as the three-month census process was about to begin. News articles followed, one of which exhorted farmers to cooperate with the census enumerator so that "a complete record of farm operations can be made."[11] The published list of facts farmers should know was extensive, including such minutiae as "quantity and value of all products including milk, butter, eggs; the number of acres in use for each crop, pasture land, land lying idle or fallow, woodland," and much more. Knowing the importance of census data to the political process, B. R. Albin played a supporting role in this endeavor. In a letter to Montana merchants, he stressed the importance of the census and asked the business community to cooperate.[12]

By this time, the schism between Wheeler and President Roosevelt was permanent, and it affected relationships between Montana's Democrats. As a committed supporter of Wheeler, Willard observed the unfolding political chasm with interest. During his travels for the Independent Merchants Association, he encountered former western Montana representative Jerry O'Connell in the fall of 1939. Afterward, Willard wrote Albin a letter that reflected the tension between the party's factions at the state level. In his campaign before the 1938 election, Representative O'Connell, a fellow Democrat, had publicly criticized Wheeler because of the roadblocks Wheeler had erected in opposition to several of Roosevelt's plans, including the Supreme Court packing. Seeing an opportunity to establish a following among Roosevelt supporters during his campaign, O'Connell called Wheeler a "decoy Democrat," among other inflammatory tags. Wheeler set out to stop O'Connell's ascendancy by mounting a quiet campaign against him. Wheeler's actions contributed to O'Connell losing his seat in the 1938 election, but afterward O'Connell announced he would challenge Wheeler in the 1940 Senate race.[13] Willard's letter to Albin about meeting O'Connell was steeped in scorn and ridicule: "He asked all about you. (OUT OF THE KINDNESS OF HIS HEART, NO DOUBT.)" Fraser went on to say that he laughed at O'Connell when he "spoke of the Senate."[14]

Willard's skepticism at O'Connell's aspirations to election to the Senate proved accurate. Rather than run for the Senate in 1940, O'Connell ran and lost to Republican Jeannette Rankin in the race for Montana's western congressional district. Wheeler had quietly helped deliver Jeannette Rankin's victory.[15] O'Connell never won another election, losing his final race for U.S. representative in 1942 to Mike Mansfield.

Willard became heavily involved in Wheeler's 1940 campaign for election to his fourth Senate term, and his admiration for the senator is easy to understand. Called "the most powerful politician Montana ever produced" by biographer Marc Johnson, a "great showman" by Senator Lee Metcalf, and "the most courageous politician" by Senator Huey Long, Wheeler was a consistent foe of corrupt power and a statesman who believed in principle above party. Willard would have identified with Wheeler's independence, courage, and staunch conviction of his progressive ideals. Twenty-five years later, Willard stated, "[I]f ever Montana fills the second niche we have available to us in the Hall of Fame in Washington, I would say a statue of Senator Wheeler must stand in that niche."[16] Instead, in 1985, Jeannette Rankin's statue joined that of Charles Russell in the National Statuary Hall in Washington.

As part of his participation in Wheeler's 1940 campaign, Willard spoke to the Kiwanis Club in Harlowton one night and then "also managed by driving practically all one night and getting up early the next morning to attend the Jackson Day Banquet [a Democratic fundraiser] in Helena."[17] He also delivered posters, carried pro-Wheeler signs in parades, and prompted Wheeler to write a letter to several Montana merchants Willard knew through his work for the Independent Merchants Association.[18]

Willard didn't hesitate to give the older, experienced statesman advice. In May, he cautioned Wheeler, "It seems to me that there is imminent danger of doing something in the Convention that would arouse F. D. R. antagonism, whereas if it is handled diplomatically, no such danger will be incurred."[19] Wheeler responded, saying he was "in hearty accord with your views."[20] As the election drew near, Willard suggested to Wheeler's campaign manager, R. Bailey Stortz, that "Wheeler needs to come out for Roosevelt if he wants to get a big majority. . . . [There are] stories going around that Wheeler is sulking in his tent, a poor sport, sour grapes, etc."[21] Despite such fears about the effects of the personal and political clash between Wheeler and Roosevelt, Wheeler won reelection in a landslide over E. K. Cheadle of Shelby. Roosevelt, with Henry Wallace as his running mate, also won a solid victory, but Sam Ford, a Republican backed by Wheeler, defeated Democrat Roy Ayers in the gubernatorial race in Montana.

After the 1940 election, the escalating war in Europe became the focus of much of Willard's correspondence with Robert Frost. "Wheeler thinks that FDR is going to get us into the War," Willard wrote. "I am a little afraid he is letting personal feeling carry him away. I do wish my Gods would act like Gods. If you see your friend the Vice-President, tell him to straighten us out."[22] (Vice president-elect Henry Wallace was, at the time, a friend of Robert Frost.) Willard, unlike Albin, did not think every word of Wheeler's was "gospel." Nevertheless, as Wheeler's opposition to America's involvement in the war intensified, Willard took a similar stance, saying in one letter to Frost, "Senator Wheeler says we must keep out at all cost. I agree, for I can see no reason in fighting to save the King." In a more circumspect letter, Willard acknowledged the "wave of terrific intolerance" sweeping through Europe and wondered what role the United States would play if it did enter the war: "I somehow feel that England is headed for a licking, and I wonder if we have the fortitude to allow it, and that seems the dangerous part that would involve us."

While taking an avid interest in national politics, Willard continued to be active in local affairs involving humanitarian causes.[23] In May 1941, Billings mayor Charlie Trott appointed Willard to one of several committees to set goals for improving the administration of city affairs. That fall, Willard was named chairman for the second year of the Billings United Chinese Relief Committee, which was part of a nationwide campaign to raise five million dollars for famine relief for the civilian population in China, a country then engaged in an undeclared war against Japan.[24]

In June 1941, Willard became chairman of Montana's short-lived America First Committee, a noninterventionist group founded September 5, 1940, by Yale students against American participation in World War II. Initial members included future president Gerald Ford, future Peace Corps director Sargent Shriver, and later Republican publisher and pundit William F. Buckley Jr.[25] Ford dropped out fairly early, and Shriver enlisted in the Naval Reserve program in 1940 and later earned a Purple Heart in the Navy.[26] In Billings, Willard's longtime friends B. R. Albin and Charlie Borberg were charter members. Only two chapters of America First were formed in Montana. An opposing organization, the Fight for Freedom Committee, was organized in Billings that October.

Many early Jewish members of America First left when they discerned an anti-Semitic tone to the organization. When Willard gave a radio address to urge residents to join Montana's chapter of America First, he said in part, "Let me assure you that our ranks are not open to membership for Nazis, communists, fascists, [and] bundists."[27] Despite the intent of the national group not to become associated with such groups, however, the committee was infiltrated by pro-Nazi and anti-Semitic individuals. Some of these members, including Henry Ford, were dismissed from the committee. This initial America First Committee disbanded immediately after Pearl Harbor was attacked.[28]

Charles Lindbergh, Dwight Morrow's brother-in-law, became a particularly ardent spokesman for the America First Committee. Knowing of Willard's friendship with Dwight and the Morrow-Lindbergh connection, Albin sent Fraser a telegram asking him to contact the Morrows in the summer of 1941 to get Lindbergh to speak in Montana. Willard demurred but mentioned that Wheeler had already suggested to America First that they send Lindbergh to the state. Fraser went on to say that he knew that Dwight's mother, Elizabeth Cutter Morrow, was a strong supporter of the war effort, and he guessed Dwight was, too. Mrs. Morrow, a writer and philanthropist, had publicly advocated American aid to Britain before the United States' entry into the war in 1941.[29] Furthermore, the Morrow family had stated that they "agreed to disagree" with the Lindberghs about the war.[30] Even without support from the Morrows, Fraser believed the organization "could get a huge crowd for Lindbergh, and that it would do a great deal toward changing people who are now down on Wheeler, and there are a lot of them."[31]

By that time, Lindbergh had already attracted controversy for his fascist sympathies and white supremacist views. In a November 1939 article in *Reader's Digest,* he spoke of "banding together to preserve that most priceless possession, our inheritance of European blood." In a radio address in 1940, Lindbergh suggested that only because of Jews' support for the war was America in danger of joining it.[32] In the summer of 1941, Secretary of the Interior Harold Ickes called him "one of Hitler's stooges."[33] Ickes's accusation gained support when, in September, Lindbergh gave a speech in Des Moines in which he argued against entering the war and named the Roosevelt administration, the British, and the Jews as the groups responsible for advocating for war. His comments about American Jews aroused intense animus and public excoriation by Thomas Dewey, then the district attorney from New York County who had gained fame for prosecuting leaders of organized crime.[34]

A week after the Des Moines speech, Wheeler was heckled during a speech in Billings when he called Lindbergh "a great American." There were reports that a "barrage of eggs" were thrown at Wheeler during the Billings speech, but Willard, who was seated on the platform with the senator and his wife, Lulu, was quoted in a state newspaper saying that the reports were "grossly exaggerated and on the whole absolutely fictitious and false."[35] While Willard was correct that "barrage of eggs" was a gross exaggeration, some egg throwing had occurred, but not enough to disrupt the occasion. Although he concurred with Wheeler's antiwar stance, Willard did not espouse Lindbergh's anti-Semitism.

In the weeks before Pearl Harbor, Wheeler continued to be a major topic in Fraser's letters to Frost. On November 11, 1941, he pondered the rift between Wheeler and the president, acknowledging the bitterness in Wheeler's failed presidential aspirations:

> Yes, I agree that Wheeler has a number of weak spots in his hide, and not the least is his enthusiastic hate for Mr. FDR. I do not follow him in that. It is a little difficult for me to hate anyone like that. But I certainly agree with him in his opposition to our taking on anyone else's war. Wheeler is very sincere in that. . . . Also, back of his mind is always the thought that if it had not been for that SOB (Wheeler's term) accepting a third term, he would have been President.[36]

The notion that Wheeler could have become president was shared by many Americans within and beyond Montana. In 1939, Willard had expressed his own hope that Wheeler would become president, and Lewis Penwell had written to Wheeler to say that one of his motives in purchasing Wild Horse Island in Montana's Flathead Lake was to provide Wheeler with a "summer White House."[37] Several Democratic senators and North Dakota governor John Moses supported Wheeler's presidential aspirations, and he received near-endorsements from United Mine Workers president John L. Lewis, the American Federation of Labor, and the railway unions. Wheeler was also the subject of positive profiles in such publications as *The Nation*, *The New Republic*, *Christian Science Monitor*, and *Time*, which featured him on its cover.[38] Wheeler's presidential ambitions were dashed when Roosevelt decided to run for a third term.

During this time, future Montana senators Mike Mansfield and Lee Metcalf, both Democrats, were poised to replace Wheeler and Murray as powerful Montana politicians. Metcalf served as a state legislator and then as assistant attorney general of Montana from 1937 to 1941.[39] Mansfield became a representative in 1942 and won a Senate seat ten years later in 1952. That year, Metcalf took Mansfield's House seat and in 1960 won Senator James Murray's seat when Murray retired. Both Metcalf and Mansfield became influential nationally, Mansfield as Senate majority leader and Metcalf as president *pro tempore* of the Senate. Unlike Willard Fraser, they were not particular fans of Senator Wheeler. In fact, Metcalf—a strong supporter of Roosevelt—had chastised Wheeler publicly in 1940 when he believed Wheeler intended to run against Roosevelt. He wrote to Senator Murray that he would work to "offset the work the

Wheeler stooges are doing throughout the state."[40] Metcalf must have known Fraser was working for Wheeler and therefore would have considered him one of those "stooges." It was also perhaps true, as Montana journalist Chuck Johnson commented, that "Western Democrats didn't welcome the eastern Montana Democrats. For starters, there weren't many eastern Montana Democrats in those days."[41] Both Mansfield and Metcalf eschewed publicity, so they may have looked askance at attention-loving Willard Fraser.[42] Certainly, Metcalf's quick temper and Mansfield's cool detachment contrasted with Willard's ebullience.

In mid-November 1941, Willard left for the East with Robin and his sister, who had recently divorced Russ Hart.[43] Willard had persuaded Jeanne to seek a new life by moving to Washington, D.C., where she could live for a time with Lesley Frost. After visiting the elder Frosts in Bennington, Vermont, they traveled to Lesley's home in D.C., where they were when Pearl Harbor was bombed on December 7, 1941.[44] According to Robin, Senator Murray arranged for the three Frasers to sit in the balcony to observe Congress declare war on Japan.[45] The *Gazette* obtained a telegram that Willard, as chairman of the Billings chapter of America First, sent almost immediately to the vice president of the group. In it, Willard wholeheartedly expresses his unwavering patriotism: "War, which we have tried so desperately to avoid, is now our nation's lot. Proudly and without reservation we share a common danger to America. . . . This war is our war, and we of America First shall not be found wanting."[46] Wheeler was in Billings when he heard the news of Pearl Harbor, and the attack also changed his stance on U.S. involvement in the war. "The only thing now is to do our best to lick hell out of them," he said.[47]

Although he had expressed doubts about the war and had joined America First's opposition to U.S. engagement in the conflict, Willard had acknowledged to Frost in 1939 his own sense of patriotic obligation if or when America joined the war: "I would go, but neither with enthusiasm nor cursing. Anyone who pretends to be a politician belongs at the front when his country goes to war."[48] As a single father and an asthmatic, thirty-five-year-old Willard could have applied for a deferment from the draft. Instead, knowing that his daughter would continue to receive Sadie's devoted attention, Willard chose to do his part for the war effort.

On December 14, just ten days after the attack on Pearl Harbor, Willard completed an Application for Appointment and Statement of Preference for Reserve Officers, requesting an anointment as lieutenant in the Officers Reserve Corps infantry.[49] However, in February 1942, he wrote to Wheeler's close friend, radio broadcaster Edmund Craney of KGIR in Butte, to announce that he was going through Butte on the noon train en route to the training camp at Fort Lewis, Washington. His words express a powerful commitment to his ideals and his country:

> The draft caught me like a Missouri mule. I think I could have made a fight and gotten deferred because of my daughter but what's the use. Most of the fellows down here that yelled for war have cold feet; so someone that was not built that way has to go, and it might as well be me. . . . Here is something that might make a news story to show that the Wheeler people are supporting the war. Three of us who talked over the radio here in Billings for America First are now in the army. . . so far as I can find out, not one single person of the Fight for Freedom Committee here has gone.[50]

A formal studio photo taken in 1942 of seven-year-old Robin with Willard in his military uniform seems an attempt to capture and freeze their relationship as insurance against possible wartime tragedies. Willard sent a copy to Frost, who wrote to Robin, "And there is your father beside you all dressed up for war. He makes a fine-looking soldier and you make a fine-looking soldier's daughter. I am proud of both of you."[51] It would be nearly five years before father and daughter would live together again.

"When I helped to win the war"

WILLARD FRASER was not a typical U.S. Army soldier. He was thirty-five, college educated, and asthmatic. These factors probably explain why he became a medic in Company A of the Eighth Medical Battalion of the 8th Infantry Division. There is, unfortunately, limited information on the composition and combat actions of the Eighth Medical Battalion, but the battalion's duties included establishing casualty collection points, evacuating casualties to aid stations and field hospitals, and treating battle injuries and general illnesses. After training in the United States, Willard served mainly in the European Theater of Operations (ETO), primarily in Northern Ireland and in France, until he was honorably discharged in May 1946. His letters to the Frost family, the written memories of close friends, Willard's own references to the war in his mayoral letters, and the history of the movement of the 8th Infantry Division provide a general chronology of Willard's military service during World War II.

The few surviving letters Willard wrote during the war register shock at the devastation the war caused, sympathy for the wounded, and in one instance, frustration over missing an opportunity to see his mother and daughter. They offer few descriptions of the day-to-day horrors he undoubtedly witnessed as a medic tending to the wounded in the final years of the war. A disproportionately high number of Montanans enlisted or were drafted, making Montana's per capita loss of life in service second only to New Mexico's.[1] Among these casualties must have been former classmates and friends from Billings. Decades after his military service ended, Willard wrote occasionally of the time "when I helped to win the War." By then, the anecdotes he shared of his military service were laced with humor or pride, such attitudes being easier to adopt from a distance of twenty or more years. A stark contrast exists between these jocular stories and his likely wartime experiences. Throughout the tragedy and devastation that Willard witnessed during nearly five years in the war, he maintained his patriotism, and his service instilled in him a global, humanitarian perspective.

After enlisting, Willard was sent to a series of training camps in California, Missouri, and Tennessee for 1942 and most of 1943. In early May 1942, he wrote to the Frosts from Station Hospital in Camp San Luis Obispo, where he was doing night duty.[2] Later that month, he sent another letter from California, this time the Camp Young Desert Training Center, where his division was ending its third month of training in desert maneuvers.[3] In January 1943, Willard wrote again to Frost from Camp Fort Leonard Wood in Missouri, where the 8th Infantry trained for a few months. In contrast to his exposure to Eastern Ivy League gentry during his summers in the Southwest, Willard was now billeted with a very different slice of American citizens. His cohorts in the 8th Division were "mainly boys from the Bronx and the mountains of South Carolina."[4] In a letter written nearly three years later, he commented that "listening to Tennessee and Bronx Americans with third grade educations explain the workings and wonders of Four Freedoms and democracy was too much for me."[5] After completing his training in Missouri, Willard was sent to Camp Forrest, Tullahoma, Tennessee, where he trained as a medic for the Eighth Medical Battalion. He remained in Tennessee from February 1943 until December, when he was sent overseas.

According to his friend Charlie Borberg, Willard had applied for officer training school, but was sent to train as a medic before he could receive his commission.[6] Lillian Frost reported that while Willard was at Camp Forrest, his Division was "on alert," and he could not go to officer training school as long as his Division was "alerted."[7]

During the months that Willard was in Tennessee, he suggested that his mother and Robin join Lillian Frost and her son, Prescott, in Florida for the winter of 1943–1944. He felt he would see more of them than if they were in Montana, because too much of his furlough time was taken up by travel to and from Montana. Sadie and Robin traveled to Florida in late November, but they arrived too late to see Willard, who was then on his way to Camp Kilmer, New Jersey, before being sent overseas. [8] In a letter dated November 29, 1943, Willard expressed his dismay to Frost that he had missed seeing Robin and Sadie, adding the comment, "Damn Hitler!"[9] The missed visit must have hit his daughter hard as well. Sadie and Robin

Robin and Willard Fraser on eve of his departure for military service, 1942.
Robert Frost Collection, Box 2, University of Michigan, Ann Arbor

Willard Fraser's military registration card. Fraser served nearly four and half years as a medic in the 8th Infantry during World War II. Department of Selective Service, Form 1, "Fraser, Willard E.," Military Personnel Records Center, NARA

departed Florida at the end of January, stopping in Washington, D.C., to visit Jeanne Blackford on the way home. Robin remembers staying with her aunt Jeanne Blackford and watching a plane flying overhead. Jeanne told Robin to wave very hard at the plane, as her dad might be in it as he headed off to war. Robin waved a long time up to that plane in the sky.[10]

The 8th Infantry Division left from New York Harbor on December 5, 1943, and arrived in Belfast, Northern Ireland, on December 12. The entire division, including Companies A and B of the Eighth Medical Battalion, relocated to Drumcose Estate near Enniskillen in County Fermanagh on December 16. Because Northern Ireland had the most westerly ports and aerodromes in the United Kingdom from which to launch air sorties and convoy escorts, the country became an important staging platform for Allied forces preparing for combat in Europe and North Africa. The port at Lisahally, Londonderry County, was key to victory in the Atlantic. At one point, 120,000 American servicemen were stationed in Northern Ireland, and as many as 300,000 soldiers passed through Northern Ireland during the course of the war, in addition to tens of thousands of Irish volunteers. When General Eisenhower visited in May 1944, he expressed his gratitude to the forces stationed there: "Without Northern Ireland I do not see how [else] the American forces could have concentrated to begin the invasion of Europe."[11]

While Willard was in Ulster, he would have been aware of the social tension caused by the size and diversity of the American military population. The U.S. government prepared soldiers by issuing a handbook, "A Pocket Guide to Northern Ireland" which included such advice as not to discuss politics or religion with the locals. The Irish population was not diverse, and some ugly incidents occurred between black servicemen and local civilians.[12] Willard himself became involved in mediating a romantic relationship between a young Navajo soldier and an Irish girl when an Irish priest tried to arrange their marriage.

Probably more troublesome for Willard was Ireland's damp weather, which exacerbated his asthma. Fraser recalled, "Our diet that wet cold winter of 43–44 in Ulster consisted mainly of Spam and powdered eggs. Had it not been for the wonderful Irish bread, we might have even lost the war. . . . At least it gave considerable strength to the 8th Division." He added the facetious comment: "I think that if one of our political parties would insert a plank in the platform of their party favoring homemade bread, they would sweep the votes of the country."[13]

The 8th Infantry was stationed in England during the spring of 1944 in preparation for launching attacks on Normandy, where they witnessed the German Luftwaffe's bombing attacks. Characteristic of Willard, his retelling of the event illustrates his claim that "[s]ervicemen seem to be able to laugh under the greatest of stresses":

> We were camped along an old, old stone bridge in England. It was very dark, very foggy. German planes had come over, headed for the interior on a bombing raid, and then returned. . . . One came late and to lighten his load, dropped a bomb. It fell square in the old bridge and threw shot and shell and stone fragments all over us. . . . In that awful still moment that comes after a bomb explosion, when everyone is still checking to see if his arms and legs are all there, an Italian boy from New Jersey exclaimed in a voice that carried through the area, "Don't ya wished you'd voted for Senator Wheeler, now, boys?"[14]

Willard composed several verses during the war. One poem, titled "Protestant, Catholic, Buddist [*sic*] or Jew," expresses how the wartime sacrifice and suffering unites soldiers form different religions and ethnicities. The poem ends with the lines:

> We've come from America to share the same Hell,
> The battle tomorrow may end in our Death,
> And our mouldering bones will not ask,
> From the same grave we may share,
> Was he Protestant, Catholic, Mormon or Jew?[15]

In another poem, "Should I Ask the Faith of the Boy," Willard mentions "the boy that we buried last night with his leg shot away at the start of the fight"—a rare reference to one of the many casualties he must have witnessed.

Willard wrote one poem after hunkering in a bomb shelter in England in the spring of 1944. The poem's title, "Easter '44," recalls "Easter 1916" by William Butler Yeats, which describes the Easter when ordinary Irish people rebelled against British rule. Willard's meditation on fear, death, and the experiences of regular soldiers in wartime strikes an authentic note, coming from someone who experienced a range of emotions while anticipating an enemy attack.

Easter '44

Perhaps we die that you may live,
And the sacrifice we give,
Little Men have always had to make
Through all of History's pitiless, blood-washed wake.
Today, we die, as overhead black bombers thunder
"Death." . . An echo of some anguished primitive plunder.
We accept your words of evil-ridden hate,
And halt again the foeman at your gate.
Again, we Little Men must die, and lie
In loveless graves beneath an unknown sky,
And hear again the ancient warrior cry,
Of, "Kill! Kill! Kill!" That we be saved.
Kill! Kill! Lest all our world be lost.
With that, you hope to stir a modern host
Of Little Men resigned to die.
"Christ is again betrayed," you lie.
But it's not Him we try to find,
For fear has made us one-God blind
To any single Hope or Monitor,
This . . . this, all your wars have done
To us . . . the Little Men . . . the wars you do condone.
Now, awaiting the attack—with fear—no kin to cowardice,
Pondering the plight of ageless youth in black
    bomb-proofed abyss;
We clear the obscurity of future years,
And pledge our undimmed faith to you, anew . . .
But you . . . America . . . Be honest with us, too.

While expressing an abhorrence of war in general, the poem focuses on what the soldiers—the "Little Men"—are sacrificing. It also offers a reluctant admission that war might be necessary "lest all our world be lost." Fraser ends the poem with a ringing challenge to the United States to ensure that the men who put their lives on the line in the name of patriotism have not done so in vain, echoing the sentiment in Yeats's plea that the Irish heroes not be forgotten.

Shortly after the bombing in England, Willard returned to the States on a medical leave necessitated by the dank Irish climate. Lillian Frost reported to Robert that Willard had come down with bronchitis, pneumonia, and asthma and had been sent to the United States to recover.[16] Writing to B. R. Albin from a hospital train transporting wounded soldiers to California, Willard mentioned he had obtained a copy of a newspaper that discussed the seizing of Montgomery Ward by the government for the war effort. Fraser called Montgomery Ward's chairman, Sewall Avery, a "traitorous damn fool" for his defiant stance against the seizure. Fraser supported this view by saying, "I am voicing the entire opinion of every man in this car, and some of them left legs, hands, and various other parts of their anatomy in Europe. . . . These men are all Westerners and can read and write, and are not fools. . . . You would enjoy the comments of the fellow in the bed above me. He has no fingers or thumbs. But has definite ideas on Avery." Willard expressed his exasperation to Albin, saying, "Wheeler would be better off investigating who is selling powdered eggs to be fed to the soldiers overseas, 75% of which are thrown away."[17]

The 8th Infantry Division was not part of the initial D-Day landings at the Normandy coast in northern France on June 6, 1944, but Willard was back in the United Kingdom in time to join the Division's departure from Belfast on July 1, 1944. A convoy of troopships and transports began disembarking on July 4, 1944, and assembled near Montebourg, some thirty kilometers southeast of Cherbourg. Germany had occupied the important deep-water port of Cherbourg since 1940. Before the war, Cherbourg was used by freighters and passenger liners such as the *Titanic* and the *Queen Mary*. Gaining Cherbourg was a crucial Allied goal, as it would enable American ships to transport troops and supplies directly to mainland Europe. On June 24, Allied forces—primarily American—began the liberation of Cherbourg. German resistance lasted until June 27, and by the time the 8th Infantry landed, the city and port were under Allied control. Before their surrender, however, the Germans had carried out "the most complete, intensive, and best-planned demolition in history" by blocking the harbor with sunken ships and planting mines, essentially making the harbor unusable for several weeks. The Allies took thirty-nine thousand German prisoners during the Cherbourg attack, and the German defeat signaled a shift in the control of France. Two months later Paris would be liberated.[18]

Photos of the Cherbourg attack show German prisoners being marched through the street and medics giving plasma to injured soldiers on the beach. Willard's letters of twenty or more years later do not mention the wounded soldiers he encountered, the prisoners taken, or even the scene he witnessed upon arrival with the 8th Infantry. Rather, he describes some of the attendant difficulties:

> When I went ashore at Cherbourg in 1944, I fell up to my armpits in some of the filthiest mud of France and wallowed in same for about two weeks before finally we got to a place where a portable shower was set up, and we just got thoroughly soaped when the shower broke down and we had to slosh off with cold water from our canteens. The old saying of "cleanliness is next to godliness" is great, and after two weeks in the mud in any army, I think there is no question but that cleanliness comes first.[19]

This is typical of the selective, upbeat memories a sixty-something-year-old Willard shared from his perspective in the 1960s. In truth, what he would have experienced must have been grim. It is typical of Willard's determined optimism to refuse to be overcome by tragedy or failure.

An undated letter to the Frosts describes some of his work as a medic while he was stationed at Mason General Hospital in Brentwood, Long Island, New York—likely for a brief period in the late spring of 1944.[20] The hospital complex treated shell-shocked combat soldiers who suffered from severe psychological trauma inflicted by their war experiences. Willard reported that his work at Mason General was "not a pleasant job. Since I arrived, we have received about two thousand psychoneurotic patients [soldiers] right off the boat. And the place was full before. When I point out to you that most of these left the front not later than August, you will have some idea of what is in store for us from this month's trouble! . . . Mostly they are just tired—so terribly, terribly tired, and in a way no psychiatrist who has not been there [on the battlefield] can ever understand."[21]

Less than a year after Willard went ashore at Cherbourg, the tide turned against Germany and Italy. Mussolini was killed on April 28, 1945, by Italian partisans, and on April 30, Hitler committed suicide. Willard remarked to Frost, "Goodness what a lethal month April has been for "Great Men"—Roosevelt—Mussolini—and now Hitler. . . . The war is grinding to a slow, hideous, and mysterious finish."[22] After VE (Victory in Europe)

Day on May 8, 1945, Willard remained in France with troops waiting to be demobilized. Three months after VE Day, he wrote to Marjorie's friend Helen Lawrie, telling her that he was running the dispensary at nights and commenting that "one would think the war was still on from the shootings, stabbings, fights, etc. It is Yank vs. negro vs. Frog." He added that many of the French soldiers he treated were "filthy" and suffering from scabies. The German POWs, he said, were not as afflicted.[23]

In August 1945, Willard witnessed the full impact of war's devastation on Le Havre, France, a port city north of Cherbourg at the mouth of the Seine River. Before the war, this historic maritime city had contained boulevards lined with mansions and villas overlooking the sea. Even after the Germans lost control of Cherbourg, they had remained in control of Le Havre. To gain possession of Le Havre, the British Royal Air Force carpet-bombed the city in September 1944. As a result, the town center was obliterated and three-fourths of the city's buildings were destroyed, making it the most severely damaged city in France. Five thousand of the city's 160,000 civilians were killed, and half its population was made homeless.[24] Le Havre fell on September 12, 1944, and the United States took possession of this strategic port.

In a three-page typed letter to Frost from Le Havre, Fraser unleashed a passionate discourse on the destructive consequences of war that he had observed in that city as a result of the British and American bombardment. He termed the news that Americans were receiving in the press "lush platitudes" and described what Americans at home did not realize. "Our bombers have laid Europe in political, economic, and cosmetic ruin. When I see the piles of twisted iron, of junk that once made living possible, of furniture blown to bits, of babies' beds twisted and hanging from jagged walls, it makes me feel as though my own fingers were dripping with blood of babies. We call ourselves a Christian country, but you should see the aged and beautiful churches we left in total ruin in our dash across the country. We have done horrible things to Europe and civilization." After expressing his shock and dismay over the destruction caused by the bombing, he concluded, "I am proud of American Mechanical Achievement, but horrified at the use to which we have put a lot of it. I glory in America's ability to produce, but shudder at the ruin it has caused."[25] Willard's revulsion against the war did not abate. Just before he was discharged in the spring of 1946, he admitted to Frost, "I really hate war. . . . It is our international hypocrisy and holyer [*sic*] than thou that gets me down."[26]

Years after the war's end, Fraser's love of a good story influenced his focus on the odd lighthearted moments that occurred rather than the devastation he witnessed in places like Le Havre. One of Willard's favorite stories of his time in Europe concerned a money-making venture with which he occupied some of his time after the fighting in Europe was over and while the 8th Infantry was waiting to be deployed to "the Orient." During the delay, he secured a leave to visit Scotland. Before his departure, he visited a friend in Saint-Germain-Village, and the friend decided to travel with him. While waiting for a boat, they came upon the monastery at Fécamp, noted for developing the herbal liqueur, Benedictine. Willard wrote, "At that time, only small bottles of Benedictine, holding four ounces at most, limited to five a person, were sold for five francs each." He and his friend pooled their two thousand francs each. "When we came out of the monastery, we had small bottles bulging in our shirt fronts, pockets, our knap sacks, and our helmets." Willard's friend thought they could get seventy-five francs for a four-ounce bottle selling to American servicemen still located in France. "Leave it to a 'Howling' Methodist to know how to make a profit out of the whiskey business," Willard commented.

The two soldiers hitchhiked to Le Havre and soon had sold all the Benedictine to soldiers for seventy-five francs each. By this time, the area around Le Havre served as a staging area for troops landing on the coast. Up to three million American troops passed through Le Havre as they entered or left Europe. The thousands of troops domiciled in the camps around Le Havre at any one time were ready customers for scarce luxuries. After selling their stock of Benedictine in Le Havre, Willard and his friend returned to Fécamp and reinvested their money in more Benedictine. When they finally sailed for England, they converted their francs into what totaled roughly four thousand English pounds. At that time, a British pound was equal to four American dollars, so they netted nearly $16,000.[27] Willard's salesmanship was clearly a natural talent.[28]

While he may have held back on recounting his most difficult wartime experiences, Willard readily described the friendships formed during wartime. His experience in the service admitted him into a fraternity of veterans of the 8th Infantry who comprised part of his postwar network. For two and a half decades, these connections remained important to Willard. One war buddy invited Willard to his daughter's Bat Mitzvah in Illinois, and Willard served as godfather to another veteran's child. He kept in touch with acquaintances in France, and several times he visited a fellow veteran, now a Corning Glass designer in Ithaca, New York, who "helped me win the war," a phrase he often used to describe his war years.[29] Decades later, as mayor, he reflected on the bonds formed through shared military service, saying:

> Whenever I make national news as occurs reasonably often, I receive a number of letters from men with whom I served during "my war"—the big one. Recently, a man from Billings stopped by a wayside stand at an orchard in Michigan. The proprietor saw the Montana license and wanted to know if he knew a Willard Fraser. The Billings man said, "Certainly, he's our Mayor." The fellow said, "He is? Well, here. I'd like to send him a gift. Take him this sack of apples. I was in the 8th Division with him."[30]

Willard's penchant for embellishing a story is illustrated by one World War II story about the liberation of Normandy. Although Robin's remembrance of the chance meeting differs from her father's, both versions illustrate the future mayor's humanitarian instincts. While on a college cruise to Europe in the 1950s, Robin Fraser had a serendipitous encounter with a German man who served as the ship's steward. Willard wrote of their meeting: "The second day out of New York, he looked Robin up and said, 'You are Miss Robin Fraser?'

'Yes.'

'Robin Fraser of Billings, Montana?'

'Yes.'

'Your father, is he Willard Fraser of Billings, Montana?'

'Yes.'

'He captured me. I was his prisoner.'"

The steward had been a young boy hiding under a table in a farmhouse when Willard's company searched an area of northern France after the German defeat. Rather than sending Heinz Schumann to a prison camp, the company used him as a kind of valet.[31] Schumann told Robin that Willard had obtained musical instruments for him and some friends so they could play together while they were prisoners of war.[32] Willard claimed that Schumann paid extra attention to Robin as a way to demonstrate his appreciation for his long-ago escape from becoming a prisoner-of-war, but Robin recalls no special favors.

Willard's ability to make connections and strike a deal benefited a fellow soldier in another World War II incident. Guillaume Auger, a young Frenchman in the camp where Willard served as a medic, was suffering from a severe, potentially fatal case of stomach ulcers. In order to perform the operation to save the man's life, a specific medicine was needed, but it could not be located. Willard reached out to his network of contacts, found someone who had the medication, and ensured it arrived in time for the surgeon to operate.

Despite the fact that Willard did not speak French and Guillaume did not speak English, the two formed an enduring friendship. After the war, Robin helped Willard write letters to Guillaume in French, and Guillaume's niece wrote letters to Willard in English. When Auger visited Billings in the 1950s, Willard arranged for him to rent a convertible, probably with the help of his brother Marvin. Decades later, when Willard's grandson, David Hudnut, studied in Bordeaux in 1979–80, he contacted Guillaume Auger, who invited David to his home for Christmas. As they became acquainted, the Frenchman reminisced about the time he spent with Willard during

Sadie and J. B. Fraser with their grandchildren, 1944. Left to right: Mac, John, Robin, and Jerry. The boys are Marvin Fraser's sons. Courtesy Robin Fraser Hudnut

the war. He said that Willard earned the nickname "the priest" in the camp, because he looked sharp every day and spent most of his time visiting soldiers and encouraging them.[33] It seems only fitting that one day the "priest" medic of World War II would evolve into a Billings mayor who made a point of visiting with residents of Skid Row on Thanksgiving Day and who advocated for children, the elderly, and the marginalized.

In December 1945, Willard returned to the States and was admitted to Beaumont General Hospital in El Paso, Texas, where he was "taking a series of inoculations for asthma and fixing an infection in my foot."[34] While convalescing, he wrote Frost to say that he had talked to Robin and was registering her for Smith College and that he had "almost enough bonds laid away to see her through. What's your opinion on that?"[35] Planning ahead, Willard recognized that attending Smith would put Robin in closer proximity to her grandfather, other Frost relatives, and her aunt Jeanne. Willard's choice was probably influenced both by the family benefits and by his friendship with Dwight Morrow, who had brought Willard and Marjorie Frost together in Colorado.[36] Morrow's mother, Elizabeth Cutter Morrow, was a graduate of Smith, president of the Smith College Alumnae Association and a member of the Smith Board of Trustees. She also served as acting president of the college from 1939 to 1940. Willard's own exposure to the cultural and academic world of the Morrows, the Frosts, and others he knew during his college years had offered him new opportunities and a broadened perspective of the world, and he wanted Robin to gain the confidence and possibilities offered by an Eastern education.

During the months he was in El Paso, thoughts of his own future formed the centerpiece in another long letter to Frost. Always thinking of ways to improve society, Willard articulated a seven-point plan for putting Europe together. He suggested a Federal European Union, one European currency, and the elimination of border restrictions such as tariffs.[37] Today, there is the European Union, the euro, and the European Economic Community. Willard's suggestions foreshadowed future policies and corroborate B. K. Wheeler's later comment that Fraser was a man ahead of his time.

Willard was officially discharged in May 1946 with the rank of sergeant. He was awarded an American Theater Service Medal, a Victory Medal, an ETO Medal, and a Good Conduct Medal.[38] He returned to Montana that month to face a new set of unknowns in his personal life. He was eager to reconnect with other family members, friends, political contacts, and civilian life itself. He had been separated for nearly five years from Robin, who was now twelve. The wartime bond between Sadie and Robin now drew in Willard as he and Robin reestablished a day-to-day father-daughter relationship. According to Robin's daughter, Marjorie Renner, the three soon became "a solid bunch."[39]

During Willard's absence, war had brought changes to Montana as well. The farmers who had stuck it out through the years of drought and Depression prospered in the 1940s because the rains returned and wartime prices for crops were high. Demand for Butte's copper, Red Lodge's coal, and Montana's crude oil also brought renewed life to Montana's industries. However, the state lost population during the 1940s because of the lure of well-paying jobs in the defense industry, such as shipbuilding and aircraft construction on the Pacific Coast. Montana's population dropped from 559,456 in 1940 to 470,000 in 1943. Even the construction in 1942 of East Base, which would become Malmstrom Air Force Base in 1955, did not stop the population slide during the war years.[40] The city of Billings, however, gained population, growing from 23,261 residents in 1940 to 31,834 in 1950, largely due to the development of Williston Basin oil, which made Billings the epicenter of Montana's oil industry, and the increased production of the sugar beet fields that made the Great West Sugar Company the largest sugar manufacturer in the United States. The city held promise.

As he set about rebuilding both his personal and professional future, Willard considered how to reenter politics. In a letter to Frost, he explained that, while he still held political aspirations, he was not wholly in step with the Democratic Party. "Thinking more than a little of running for Congress but it looks like a Republican year. Although I'm completely out of sympathy with the present Dems—I'm not a Rep either."[41] Willard's independent thinking and his refusal to follow a prescribed dogma fore-shadowed a future politician who would, in time, appeal to voters across party lines.

"Old enough to think, young enough to act"

WHEN Willard returned to Billings after nearly five years in military service, he was thirty-nine years old and once again faced uncertainty about his future. Rejoining his parents and Robin in the family's South Side home, he became a regular presence in his daughter's life. He resumed his lobbying activities, reinvigorated his real estate ventures, and took additional work with the Census Bureau in order to support the family. Willard threw his hat in the ring for multiple elective offices between 1946 and 1952—losing every race but gaining a foothold in Montana's political sphere. An optimist with a genuine desire to make the world a better place, Willard continued to engage in important civic and political events and cultivated a growing network of acquaintances as he did so. Among the endeavors he was most passionate about at this time was advocating for the Yellowtail Dam, a project to which Willard devoted his attention and energy for over a decade.

In the immediate postwar era, Willard went to work for Burton K. Wheeler's 1946 U.S. Senate reelection campaign. Initially, Willard was confident, writing to Frost, "Wheeler will win handily."[1] As chairman of the Veterans for Wheeler group, Willard was involved in arranging dinners, speaking to the press, writing campaign ads, and otherwise promoting Wheeler to Montana's voters.[2] He reported to Frost that he, often with Robin in tow, "covered the state pretty much" during the campaign.[3] Because Robin was still quite young, Willard had to learn to braid her long hair when they were on the road and invented games associated with what they observed in the passing countryside.[4]

An opposing organization, Veterans Against Wheeler, waged a high-profile counter-campaign against the incumbent senator. Chester Kinsey, spokesman for the group, called Wheeler "a terrific sellout to veterans" and charged he was guilty of "cutting the throat of President Roosevelt's war efforts." The United Auto Workers Union and the National Maritime Union contributed to their cause.[5] Fellow Montana senator and Wheeler archrival James Murray privately supported Wheeler's opponent, Leif Erickson, who had just served six years as an associate justice on the Montana Supreme Court. Murray's son Charles, with whom Fraser would have a friendly relationship in the 1950s, aided his father's efforts to defeat Wheeler.[6]

Wheeler lost in the July 1946 primary to Erickson, a stunning but in some ways not a surprising loss for the four-term senator, who had lost support from Montana's unions. His opposition to the war and to Roosevelt cost him votes, and some of his previous supporters now regarded him a conservative rather than a progressive. Senator Murray was reportedly elated at Wheeler's defeat, but Willard expressed his dismay in a note to Frost: "By now you know the terrible news. Wheeler is to be no longer the champion of American Liberty, and I have newly born respect for PAC [Political Action Committees] and CIO [Congress of Industrial Organizations]. They certainly went to town [against Wheeler] in Montana."[7] Erickson in turn lost to Republican Zales Ecton in the 1946 general election, but he served briefly as the head of the Montana Democratic Party a few years later. Following his loss in the 1946 primary, Burton K. Wheeler withdrew from the political sphere and went on to establish a successful law practice in Washington, D.C., Wheeler and Wheeler, with his son Edward. With the departure of this powerful politician, historians note, "A certain vigor and controversy disappeared from Montana's political life."[8]

Willard was left searching for a new job after Wheeler's defeat. Fortunately, his previous experience as area manager of the 1940 Decennial Census and his political connections landed him a position as supervisor of the federal census in Montana, which took him to Kansas City in November to the national meeting of census officials, where he spoke on public relations.[9] By January 1947, Fraser was working in Choteau as the state's director of the Census Bureau. In this role, he and his work received considerable coverage in the *Choteau Acantha*. The newspaper published a biographical sketch of the new census director, including Fraser's characteristically colorful description of his military training in America before his war service overseas, when he walked with the 8th Infantry Division "through the mud of Missouri, the chiggers of Tennessee, and the

Willard Fraser, ca. 1948. After the war, Fraser worked briefly for the U.S. Census Bureau out of Choteau, but he returned to Billings to complete the construction of an office building that he rented to the Bureau of Indian Affairs.
Robert Frost Collection, Box 2, University of Michigan, Ann Arbor

blistering heat of the desert."[10] The local news covered the radio talks and public speeches Willard delivered during these months. Already an experienced speaker from his involvement in political campaigns, Willard's knack for speaking kept him in the public eye for the rest of his life, whether he held public office or not.

The temporary nature of a census job did not promise a secure future, so Willard resumed developing a real estate venture. Before the war, he had formed the Fraser Realty Company, listing his mother and brother Marvin as principals. With the support of Senator Wheeler, he had secured a loan of $38,000 toward construction of an apartment building on North 29th Street in downtown Billings.[11] He had since received permission to convert the building into offices. Construction had halted during the war, but in July 1947, Willard resigned from the Census Bureau and returned to Billings to finish and manage his "new $100,000 building, which will be leased to the Indian Service."[12] By December 1948, he was receiving regular rental income with the Bureau of Indian Affairs as the primary tenant. Covering the open house for the building, the *Billings Herald* (the *Gazette*'s rival), featured photos of handwoven fabric, pottery, and other American Indian crafts. In one photo, Willard stands beside a table displaying a variety of crafts, proudly promoting Native American cultures.[13] In 1957, after taking out a $125,000 loan, Fraser added a four-story annex to the building, and the next year the Farmers Home Administration, Federal Housing Administration, Bureau of Mines, and Predator and Rodent Control Branch of the U.S. Fish and Wildlife Service moved into the building. A later tenant was the Plant Pest Control Division of the Grasshopper Control Office, U.S. Department of Agriculture.[14] Willard also invested in a three-story apartment building at the corner of 12th Avenue and North 26th Street that contained twenty-nine two-bedroom apartments. The rent from these buildings provided the major source of income for Willard and his family for a number of years.

In the postwar era, Willard also resumed lobbying at the state legislature, mostly on behalf of the Independent Merchants Association but also for Montana Family Security and various other groups. Helena's *Independent Record* cites his frequent stays at Helena's historic Harvey Hotel.[15] Lobbying gave him the opportunity to stay attuned to current political affairs at the state level, and Helena became a regular destination as he participated in the political action at the Capitol. Robin remembers that the *Congressional Record* was delivered to their house weekly, and each evening as they ate supper, the family listened to radio commentator Gabriel Heatter. As background to contemporary news, Willard kept a copy of the *Federalist Papers* beside his bed and referred to it regularly.[16]

Willard certainly also had his eye on his political future, which may have been an additional motivation for him to return to Billings in the summer of 1947. In November, he announced he would run as a Democrat for Congress from Montana's eastern district in the 1948 election. He yearned to secure a position that would give him a state and national voice. Frank Cross, Fraser's friend from Billings High School, served as the secretary-manager of the Fraser for Congress Club before the 1948 summer primaries. Willard's campaign stated he favored a reduction in federal income taxes but opposed both peacetime military conscription and attempts to place public lands into private hands.[17] Robert Frost wrote a note of encouragement to his son-in-law, saying, "I find that anyone I take sides with usually wins . . . though I fear you won't find the climate of Washington D.C. just what you are after for your health. . . . One good thing: it will mean seeing you oftener if you come east to live a spell a year. And you'll have Robin with you."[18] Fraser won the Democratic nomination over Bernice Kingsbury and would face Republican Wesley D'Ewart, an ultraconservative rancher from Park County, in the general election.

Working against Willard were D'Ewart's incumbency and Montana's heavily Republican eastern district. Willard joined a caravan of Democratic candidates touring the vast eastern district. Other candidates on the caravan included incumbent senator James Murray; John Bonner, candidate for governor; Paul Cannon, lieutenant governor candidate; and Arnold Olsen, attorney general candidate. The group appeared at rallies in more than twenty towns, including Bridger, Red Lodge, Hardin, Ryegate, Roundup, Lewistown, Jordan, Glendive, Billings, and Great Falls. State auditor John Holmes and Mary Condon, candidate for state superintendent of schools, joined the group in locations near Billings.

Although Senator Murray and John Bonner garnered more speaking time at rallies, Willard received positive endorsements in several of these small towns. High school students in Miles City, Lewistown, and Billings organized Fraser for Congress and Students for Fraser clubs. Ward Shanahan, president of the Miles City club, stated, "We want a man who has an interest in Montana's future generation."[19] The Roundup local of the United Mine Workers of America endorsed Willard, saying, "We admire your stand on the Taft-Hartley Act and your entire program for the state of Montana and the nation."[20] (Fraser was against the Taft-Hartley Act, which restricted the power of unions.) In Plentywood, James Sparling, a former Montana agriculture commissioner, acknowledged the importance of Willard's lobbying work when he said, "If it weren't for Fraser, we would not have our state fair trade and unfair practice laws."[21]

The concerted campaign efforts resulted in victories for Democrats Mansfield, Murray, Bonner, Cannon, and Olsen. Montana also voted for Harry Truman over Thomas Dewey. Fraser, however, lost by 2,413 votes, earning 58,711 to D'Ewart's 61,124. Feeling his loss, Willard wrote to Robert Frost, "I was a fast horse on a mud track. It was close [but] he finally got his nose over the finish line." His tone was more political in a letter to Mansfield: "Though I did not win, I cannot feel too badly in light of the great general victory." Mansfield responded with a cordial congratulation on Fraser's "splendid race."[22] Mansfield's gracious note gives no hint of a letter he had received that revealed how Willard's love of the spoken word and penchant for attracting publicity sometimes earned him the ire of other politicians. After the 1948 election, a Helena man wrote to Mansfield to complain, "I think Fraser is a light weight and talks too much."[23] Telling Willard Fraser he talked too much would have been pointless. He was an irrepressible, incurable talker.

Willard's loss in his bid for Congress did not dampen his desire to effect change by securing political office. In early 1949, he declared as a

FORWARD With FRASER

Old Enough to Think —
— Young Enough to Act

A Business Man · Property Owner · Parent · Veteran

Fraser's 1949 campaign ad encouraged voters to embrace his forward-thinking agenda. He lost the race to Tom Rowe, owner of a Billings furniture store, and went on to lose three more mayoral races in the next few years. Billings Gazette, *April 3, 1949*

candidate for mayor of Billings. Unlike his first run for mayor in 1933, when he was just twenty-six, he could now claim significant political, military, and employment experience. He campaigned under the slogan "Old Enough to Think, Young Enough to Act."[24] He proposed ambitious plans for the city, such as creating a gravity water system for Billings, constructing a highway overpass connecting the north and south neighborhoods, re-sectioning various city wards, improving the city health program, and expanding recreational land in the city. He promised that, unlike previous mayors, he would be a fulltime mayor.

The field consisted of four candidates: Tom T. Rowe, owner of a Billings furniture store; R. C. Dillavou, city attorney and former state legislator; Forrest H. Crum, a building contractor; and Willard Fraser. Candidates for mayor at this time did not declare a party affiliation. In a close race, Rowe became mayor by winning just two thousand votes out of seven thousand cast, barely nudging out Dillavou. Willard came in fourth with 1,607 votes, just forty votes behind Crum.

Willard's increasing public profile did not translate into a win for him in the July 1950 primary contest for U.S. representative. Among the six Democratic candidates, Fraser came in second to state auditor John Holmes. Not one to sulk in defeat, he campaigned for Holmes in the fall election by giving radio talks and otherwise supporting the Democratic candidate. On June 25, 1950, the Korean War began, and both incumbent representatives, Republican Wesley D'Ewart and Democrat Mike

Mansfield, remained in Washington to attend to war issues instead of campaigning in Montana.[25] Holmes was defeated in the fall election by D'Ewart, who had won a narrow victory over Fraser in 1948.[26]

Soon after the general election, Willard made the newspapers with a public request that the 1951 legislature vote to install voting machines for future state elections, maintaining that "many errors in the recent election count, caused by complete weariness and exhaustion for so many judges" showed the need for machines.[27] The issue received little media attention until 1952, when numerous articles in the *Great Falls Tribune* cited the need for election accuracy. Some of these editorials echoed Willard's earlier complaint that "antiquated voting methods" resulted in a disregard for instructions and led to tabulating mistakes by officials. In 1953, Cascade and Silver Bow Counties, both citing fiscal savings and the need for accurate elections, purchased machines to be used for the first time in the July 1954 primary.[28] Yellowstone County first used voting machines in the July 1956 primary.[29]

Immediately after the 1948 election, Willard had announced he would seek the Democratic nomination for representative again in 1952. Rather than taking a leave from politics until the 1952 congressional contest, however, Willard cast his hat into the ring for the 1951 race for mayor of Billings, declaring, "Good government is my lifelong interest and pursuit." He was one of five candidates attempting to unseat incumbent mayor Tom T. Rowe, who had defeated Fraser and others in the previous mayoral contest. Also running were Harry E. Biddinger, a former mayor; Forrest Crum, a candidate from 1949; and Fletcher Edwards, a World War II Navy veteran. This time, Fraser came in second, just eight hundred votes short of defeating Rowe, who won a majority. Crum came in third, Biddinger fourth, and Edwards last.

Democrat Willard Fraser and incumbent Republican Wesley D'Ewart both ran unopposed for representative in Montana's eastern district in the July 1952 primary. In the period between the primary and the general election, Fraser attended the Democratic National Convention in Chicago as a Montana delegate and, a month later, participated in the Democratic state convention as a member of the Platform and Resolutions Committee, serving alongside Leif Erickson, Lee Metcalf, Arnold Olsen, Mike Mansfield, and Governor John Bonner.

By this time, Willard was on his way to becoming known as a perennial candidate, yet his life consisted of more than running for public office and managing his office building. Yearning to be a mover and shaker, and believing strongly in citizen participation in government, he maintained a public profile through other civic and political activities. As chairman of the American Legion Boys State Committee, he chaperoned young men going to Boys State in July 1949, and as an active Democrat, he spoke at party banquets and fundraiser events. As a member of the Billings American Veterans (AMVETS) post, Willard, with Paul Walters, represented the Yellowstone chapter at a meeting of the national executive committee in Washington, D.C., in March of 1950. The following year, Willard was appointed to the national legislative committee of AMVETS, the first Montanan to serve on such a committee. In this role, he attended their meeting in Boston.[30] He introduced Governor Bonner at an AMVETS function, and his growing reputation for public speaking kept him in the news. When Billings Senior High School sponsored a debate on whether the Democratic Party was tending toward socialism, Willard debated on the opposing side.[31] Most notably during this period, he became a passionate and vocal supporter of the proposed Yellowtail Dam on the Bighorn River.

With Senator James Murray and Murray's son, Charles, Willard devoted more than a decade to the effort to promote the Yellowtail Dam in the spectacular Bighorn Canyon in southeastern Montana. Metcalf and Mansfield later joined in efforts for the approval of the dam by Congress, but Murray had pushed it from the beginning. Fraser's promotion of the dam was coordinated through Murray's office, beginning shortly after the dam was authorized in 1944 and continuing through the many years of negotiations before construction was approved in 1957.[32] Given the animus between Wheeler and Murray, and Willard's loyalty to Wheeler, Willard's work for Murray in the 1950s speaks to Willard's political skill and his ability to assess people without prejudice.

In 1944, the Pick-Sloan Program, named after William G. Sloan of the Bureau of Reclamation in Billings and Colonel Lewis A. Pick of the Corps of Engineers, was initiated as part of a Flood Control Act calling for dams on the Missouri River to provide cost-effective electricity and irrigation opportunities for farmers and to prevent recurrent flooding. Administered by the Bureau of Reclamation and the U.S. Army Corps of Engineers, the federal program built six dams on the Missouri River between 1946 and 1966: Canyon Ferry in Montana, Garrison in North Dakota, and four more in South Dakota. Although Yellowtail Dam on the Bighorn River, a tributary of the Yellowstone, was not part of the Pick-Sloan Program, supporters of the dam applied the same arguments as those used to back Pick-Sloan. In the first of several trips to Washington, D.C., to speak in favor of Yellowtail Dam, in June 1949, Fraser argued to the Senate Appropriations Committee that the ninety-million-dollar dam project would be "an outstanding achievement in the realm of reclamation, soil conservation, irrigation, and power development."[33] Later that month, he spoke to business and professional men in Hardin and predicted that from revenue derived from power alone, the dam would pay for itself in less than fifty years.[34] At the time, lawmakers' objections to dams were based mostly on the cost rather than environmental or other concerns.

Throughout the 1950s, Willard undertook many trips to Washington to use his public relations skills to advocate for the dam's creation and to make a case for federal funding for the Yellowtail project.[35] Robin Fraser Hudnut recalls that on one of those auto trips, she and Willard were accompanied by a lawyer and Chief Robert Yellowtail. On the drive, they couldn't find a hotel in Indianapolis so they drove all night. It was perhaps on this same trip that, as they walked through a park in Washington, D.C., someone pulled a knife on Willard, demanding his wallet. Uncowed, Willard grabbed the knife, cutting his own hand, and ordered the would-be assailant, "Now you go on your way!" Willard's injury must have needed medical attention, because Maureen Mansfield, Senator Mansfield's wife, took Robin into their home that night. Robin tied Willard's necktie and shoelaces for the remainder of the trip.[36]

In 1951, working in conjunction with Senator Murray's office, Fraser wrote a document urging a congressional appropriation for the dam. The document was approved by both houses of the Montana legislature, signed by Governor Bonner, and submitted to the U.S. Congress as part of the request for federal money, or, as Willard put it in a letter to Frost, to "raid the treasury."[37] By the late 1950s, Senator James Murray's effectiveness was diminished by his advanced age—he turned eighty in 1956—and Fraser began to correspond about the dam directly with Charles Murray and the senator's executive assistant, Victor Reinemer.[38]

Citizen Fraser's regular speaking appearances and his activity on behalf of Yellowtail earned him regular coverage in Montana's newspapers. Just before one of Willard's first trips to D.C. to testify in favor of funding, the *Great Falls Tribune* printed an extensive excerpt from his prepared statement, a piece of persuasion in logic, content, and language. In an appeal to national, not merely regional, interests, Willard voiced the common argument, "Yellowtail would be an investment that would return many-fold its original cost to the nation's treasury." He cited the support of agronomists, economists, soil scientists, and engineers, and he referred to the vision of past western congressmen—"some of the soundest and straightest thinking men of the west."[39] The *Billings Herald* published an interview with Fraser in which he argued that funding for the dam

Crow chief Robert Yellowtail accompanied Fraser on a trip to Washington, D.C., to advocate for adequate compensation for the Crow Tribe if a dam were built on the Big Horn River. Fraser was an ardent proponent of the dam.
James Willard Schultz Collection, #89 (cropped), Montana State University–Bozeman

should have equal priority with defense projects in the national budget: "This program of bringing water to thirsty lands, and thereby food to the Nation's tables, . . . is as important as building defenses for those lands." He cited statistics on projected increased population, arguing that more cropland would be needed to produce food.[40]

One article reported on a unique argument Willard used to support the dam. In 1951, he wrote to former president Herbert Hoover to ask him to verify an earlier Hoover statement: "The whole metal resources of the U.S.S.R. do not equal [those of the] State of Montana." Hoover, a mining engineer with knowledge of metal resources, responded, saying the statement "is a fact." Fraser used the Hoover letter often to support his belief that harnessing power was key to developing Montana's vast metal resources, claiming that the "only potential source of that power for this area is Yellowtail Dam."[41] The dam was predicted to produce 584 million kilowatt hours of firm energy.[42]

While Yellowtail Dam held the promise of an abundance of electrical power, irrigation potential, and recreational opportunities, its creation was not without controversy. Fraser and other supporters faced objections by the Crow Tribe, whose lands would be affected, and one of its leaders, Robert Yellowtail, after whom the dam is named. Yellowtail, who had studied law at the University of Chicago, served as superintendent of the Crow Reservation for eleven years and as tribal chairman from 1952 to 1954. Yellowtail had long been an advocate for Apsáalooke legal rights in the face of government exploitation. Initially, the Crows were not entirely opposed to a dam, but they wanted to control the river water and receive just compensation for the value of the flow of the river and the value of the land. With the election of William Wall as tribal chair in 1954, the Crows split, and Yellowtail lost some negotiation power, although he continued to be a forceful spokesman against the evolving decision. He stated that government treaties with the Indians had been "kicked to the winds" by the dam's proponents.[43] A subsequent Crow tribal chairman, Edward Whiteman, wrote to Representative Leroy Anderson in 1958 to argue for five million dollars in compensation, saying, "Remember the Crow Tribe never, at any time, proposed to sell the dam site. The proposal always came from the Bureau of Reclamation under a threat that unless the Crow Tribe sold the dam site the government would force the issue and require it to be sold by condemnation."[44] Despite tribal opposition, plans for the Yellowtail Dam inched forward.

The potential for dams' negative environmental impacts also raised the alarm among citizens concerned about the destruction of riparian landscapes and the erasure of culturally significant sites. In 1946, historian and essayist Bernard DeVoto undertook a three-month tour of the West, and four years later writer Bill Lederer and Montana writer A. B. Guthrie accompanied DeVoto on an extended tour of the Missouri River beginning at Great Falls.[45] Their guide was Brigadier General S. G. Sturgis of the Corps of Engineers. These trips were research for DeVoto's two award-winning books—*The Course of the Empire,* a book covering the Lewis and Clark Expedition, and *Across the Wide Missouri,* about the rise and fall of the Rocky Mountain fur trade.[46] In North Dakota, he witnessed the "boom" precipitated by preparation for the construction of Garrison Dam. The principal conviction DeVoto brought back with him after these tours was opposition to the Pick-Sloan plan for the Missouri River. In creating Lake Oahe, the Garrison Dam would flood over 153,000 acres on the Fort Berthold Indian Reservation—94 percent of the reservation's agricultural land—and force many of its Mandan, Hidatsa, and Arikara residents to relocate. In his subsequent "The Easy Chair" column for *Harper's Magazine,* DeVoto challenged the cost-figure benefits of the Corps of Engineers and Bureau of Reclamation and "the rosy expectation" that dams like Yellowtail would provide water for irrigation.[47] His criticism eventually had an effect, although other conservationists, such as Lee Metcalf and Stewart Udall, supported some dams into the 1960s.[48]

During America's post–World War II energy boom, however, dams were widely viewed as both beneficial and necessary. In 1952, while running for Congress, Willard handed out pamphlets on the proposed dam and predicted that its construction would substantially increase the population of Billings. He said his opponent, incumbent Wesley D'Ewart, had given only lip service to the dam, and proclaimed, "If the people of Eastern Montana want Yellowtail Dam, they must defeat Wesley D'Ewart."[49]

Left to right: Senate candidate Mike Mansfield, Interior Secretary Oscar Chapman, President Harry Truman, Senator James Murray, Margery Cowan, Governor John Bonner, and congressional hopeful Willard Fraser at the dedication of the Tiber Dam, 1952. Mike Mansfield Collection, Mss 065, 98.0831, Mansfield Library, University of Montana–Missoula

Willard himself certainly gave more than lip service to promoting Yellowtail Dam. As the 1952 campaign got under way, Fraser, Representative Mansfield, Governor Bonner, and Senator Murray were part of the Democratic caravan blitzing a major section of the state, during which Fraser's commitment to the project made the news. Early in October, the caravan accompanied President Truman in the Montana section of his whistle-stop tour promoting Adlai Stevenson and other Democratic candidates. Truman's speech at Tiber Dam on the Marias River included the promise, "Fraser won't rest until he gets Yellowtail Dam."[50] Fraser's support of the dam was linked to his interest in developing Montana's natural resources—then a general position of the Democratic Party platform—and he said during a campaign stop in Fort Benton, "The rivers, the land, the forests, the soil and the buried minerals are for us to utilize for the benefit of all mankind, but we must ever remember that we are only stewards of these resources."[51]

The results of the November 1952 election fit an evolving Montana tradition, with conservative eastern Montana voting Republican and the more progressive western area voting Democratic. In a repeat of the 1948 election, Republican D'Ewart won over Fraser in the eastern district, while Democrat Lee Metcalf narrowly won the House seat from the western district over Wellington Rankin, brother of former congresswoman Jeannette Rankin. Votes from the western district secured a Senate seat for Democrat Mike Mansfield over incumbent Zales Ecton. However, the state went for Dwight Eisenhower over Adlai Stevenson, and incumbent Democratic governor John Bonner lost to "the Galloping Swede," Republican J. Hugo Aronson.

Willard continued lobbying in the Montana legislature and working with the Murrays to advance the Yellowtail project. In the interval between bouts of ill health in March and December of 1955, he participated in the first of several float trips down the Bighorn River with the goal of establishing the feasibility of dam construction. Willard's friend Charlie Borberg persuaded him to join the August 1955 trip by assuring him that others would do the rowing for the asthmatic Fraser. Among the people participating in the float were Grant Salisbury, editor of the *U.S. News and World Report*, and Montana attorney and archaeology enthusiast Stuart Conner.[52] That summer, as the project inched through Congress, Senator Murray wrote to Willard to say, "You deserve a lot of credit for what has finally been accomplished."[53]

When funds for the construction were finally approved in Congress in the summer of 1957, Murray announced in a press release, "Montana's three Democrats in Congress worked hard for the finally successful appropriation, but a lot of people back home did spadework." He named five such individuals from Billings and Hardin, one being Willard Fraser.[54]

Construction was held up for years—first through wrangling in Congress; then through President Eisenhower's initial veto of the project; then through legal cases involving the sale, lease, or condemnation of the site; and finally, over the amount of compensation for the tribe. In the end, the Crows received $2.5 million—just half the sum they asked in compensation for twelve thousand acres of their land and the loss of use of a naturally flowing river. Crow displeasure with the dam project is apparent in a letter from Edison Real Bird, chairman of the Crow tribal council, to Senator Lee Metcalf, in which he asked that the name of the dam and the associated reservoir be changed from Yellowtail to Bighorn to avoid associating the dam with the Crows.[55] The letter was written after the dam was completed but before it was dedicated in 1968. Ironically, and perhaps tragically, the name of the dam is still Yellowtail.

The highest dam on the tributary system of the Missouri River, Yellowtail Dam was constructed in the 47-mile-long Bighorn Canyon—the third-longest canyon in the country—on the Montana-Wyoming border. Groundbreaking occurred in 1961, the first concrete was poured on March 15, 1963, and the last in October of 1965.[56] Secretary of the Interior Stewart Udall represented President Johnson at the dedication in 1968. The dam is 525 feet high between canyon walls that in places reach 2,000 feet. It spans 1,450 feet across the canyon and creates a 71-mile-long lake with a 195-mile shoreline. More than a half century later, the dam produces enough electricity to power eighty thousand homes. It has also averted $113 million in potential flood damage, but the promised irrigation benefits never materialized. Instead, water is sold to industrial clients.[57] The Bighorn Canyon National Recreation Area created by the dam offers magnificent scenery and superb hiking, boating, and fishing. According to the Park Service, it is the most fished stream in Montana.[58] The visitor center on the Wyoming side is named after Lovell mayor Cal S. Taggart, who joined Willard and friends on several float trips down the Bighorn River before the dam was built.

Initially at least, Fraser had supported other dam projects in addition to Yellowtail: Tiber Dam on the Marias River, Libby Dam on the Kootenai River, Hungry Horse Dam on the Flathead River, and Paradise Dam on the Clark Fork. Interestingly, when Fraser instituted the Yellowstone River Boat Float during his second mayoral term, he extolled the fact that it was the rare free-flowing river in the state.

By the late 1960s, much of the initial optimism and enthusiasm for large hydroelectric dams had waned, and future dam construction was highly controversial in light of their negative impacts on fisheries and watersheds. In 1968, when the Bureau of Reclamation and the Army Corps of Engineers proposed constructing additional dams on the upper Missouri River between Fort Benton and Fort Peck, the National Park Service objected and advocated preserving the last remaining undisturbed section of the Missouri. The Park Service prevailed, and the *Gazette* reported, "The days of big dam building on the Missouri are over—as is the case increasingly throughout the West."[59] In 2020, ninety thousand dams existed in the United States, and many decades-old, aging dams were in danger of collapse. By then, one thousand dams had already been torn down, and over fifteen

Willard and Robin share a joyful Christmas moment, ca. 1951. Robert Frost Collection, Box 2, University of Michigan, Ann Arbor

thousand were classified as high hazard. Today, dam operators and environmentalists, with input from local communities, are discussing how to retrofit some of the remaining dams to produce more hydroelectric power, which does not generate carbon, in order to make dams less damaging to the environment.[60] Unfortunately, the timber, wildlife habitat, cultural resources, and agricultural and tribal lands already lost to dams cannot be replaced.

Willard traveled frequently to fulfill his official responsibilities with the Census Bureau and to promote Yellowtail and other projects, as well as to campaign for office. In order to spend more time with his daughter, he sometimes took Robin along on his travels. She remembers, "On travels with Willard, he wanted me to know how each state had special treasures." Because Wisconsin's was dairy, they had milk-shakes there and bought big rounds of cheese. In Kansas and Nebraska, the "Breadbasket of America," they purchased homemade bread. Robin recalled a vivid memory of a particularly cold trip to Choteau when Willard was campaigning for Congress. She and Mac Fraser took turns driving so Willard could make notes for his speech. Despite his attention to the speech, Willard pointed out cattle frozen in the snow, reminiscent of Charles Russell's frozen cows.[61]

Because of Willard's frequent travel, however, Sadie was the more consistent parental figure in Robin's life. In addition to raising Robin, Sadie remained actively involved in local civic and political activities. The memories of her grandchildren, Willard's references to her in letters, and glimpses of her in newspaper articles evoke a profile of an intelligent, well-read woman who was interested in the world beyond her household and who believed in acting to influence her world. As Robin recalls, her "Nana" would say, "My hands were in the dishpan, but my thoughts were elsewhere."[62] Sadie was elected president of the Billings Women's Club in

1947 and reelected in 1948. News articles confirm that the club was not just a tea-and-crumpets social organization. In May 1948, part of the meeting's program was a forum on "Universal Military Training." A few years later, Sadie was photographed with a committee of Yellowstone County Democratic women, and she became president of the City Federation of Women's Clubs in 1954.[63] Although Sadie provided much of Robin's day-to-day upbringing Willard remained an involved parent. Just as he had arranged for her education at Smith when she was twelve years old, he offered advice on her education as she entered high school. When Robin was registering for classes at Billings Senior, she balked at signing up for Latin. Willard's response was, "You are a Fraser, and Frasers take Latin." Robin took Latin, and later, as a college student, she admitted to her father that she was glad she had done so.[64]

Robin also continued to spend time with the Frost family, spending the summers of 1949 and 1951 in Vermont with the Frosts. After one of these visits, Willard wrote to Frost of his fifteen-year-old daughter, "Robin had a wonderful time with you this summer. It gave her a new slant on life as it is in the Eastern part of these United States."[65] During this time and for many years, Robert Frost spent summers in a cabin near the Bread Loaf campus of Middlebury College in Vermont and participated in its program. This association led to Willard's acquaintance with writers like poet and editor John Ciardi, who later visited Billings.[66]

In the spring of 1952, the Frasers observed an important family milestone. Robin Fraser graduated from Billings High School, and in response to repeated requests by Willard and a pleading letter from Robin, Robert Frost agreed to speak at the graduation ceremony. For the first time in its history, the school held commencement ceremonies in two parts, with Frost delivering the commencement speech on Monday, May 19, and the students receiving their diplomas at a separate ceremony on June 4. Introducing her famous grandfather to her fellow graduates, Robin shared, "Baseball is his favorite sport. Boston is his team. He played baseball until last year."[67] Frost's love of baseball was evident during his summers at Bread Loaf, when he regularly participated in the annual softball game. It also surfaced when he met fellow poet Carl Sandburg one fall in Chicago, an encounter that Willard witnessed and wrote about later.[68] At the time, the Chicago Cubs and St. Louis Cardinals were in competition for the National League pennant, and the two poets discussed baseball, not poetry. In the battle for the pennant, the victorious Cardinals pitcher Dizzy Dean and fielder Joe "Ducky" Medwick, future Hall of Famers, garnered headlines as part of the "Gaslight Gang."[69] The Cardinals won the subsequent

World Series against the Tigers (4–3). Willard wrote, "R. F. and Sandburg sat up till almost daylight discussing and arguing over just which [team] had played the best game or pitched the best ball—not only of that game but for games going back to the turn of the century."[70]

At her commencement, Robin reflected on the influence Frost had on her life: "Being a real person . . . involves a great deal of responsibility. My grandfather gives me the incentive to push myself as hard as I can."[71] In his

Robert Frost and Robin Fraser at Robin's graduation from Billings Senior High School where Frost gave the 1952 commencement address. Robert Frost Papers, MS1178.B12.F40, Rauner Special Collections Library, Dartmouth University, NH

graduation address, Frost spoke of the value of reading, the importance of individual initiative, and the necessity of finding a permanent anchor. He chose to support this last point with a quote from the poem, "Choose Something Like a Star," the same poem that Willard maintained Frost had composed while recovering from the death of Robin's mother, Marjorie:

> So when at times the moth is swayed, / To carry praise or blame too far, / We may take something like a star, / to stay our mind or be staid.[72]

Frost also spoke at Eastern Montana College of Education (now MSU–Billings) and Rocky Mountain College while he was in Billings. During one of these engagements, he quoted from a poem that would have been especially appreciated in a rural state like Montana: "One has to be versed in country things to understand the deeper things in life."[73]

That fall, Robin left for Smith College as Willard had resolved years earlier, bringing her closer to her grandfather as well as her aunt and uncle, Jeanne and Ben Blackford in Connecticut.[74] In Billings, Willard continued to look ahead to his future, and over the next decade he would work toward finding his role in the public sphere.

CHAPTER NINE

"Good government is my lifelong interest and pursuit"

By 1953, Willard Fraser had lost a total of seven elections, but he persisted in his quest for public office. He continued to lose. While his progressive profile in a conservative section of the state certainly played a significant role in his defeats, other factors contributed. In several contests, his was a lackluster campaign. In one instance he acceded to a draft, and in another, he decided to run just so the incumbent would face opposition. In at least one contest, his health played a significant factor in diminishing his ability to wage a creditable campaign. Often, Willard's colorful personality garnered more attention than his vision, his intelligence, and his sense of civic responsibility. Thus, his public profile perhaps created a sense of an eccentric rather than a serious politician. Of course, a losing record does not command votes, and then there was the matter of his independence. He spoke his mind whether his mind at the time agreed with the Democratic party line or not. These factors had the effect of obscuring Willard's very earnest desire to participate in a sound government for the people.

Fraser wished to gain a political office that would give him a voice in national affairs, but lacking success there, he ran for state and local offices: mayor, representative to the state legislature, governor, and Montana Railroad and Public Service commissioner. As the 1953 race for mayor began in March, Willard was not the most enthusiastic candidate. L. O. England of the Billings Citizens Alliance and Protective Association circulated and filed the petition for Willard's candidacy on March 22 while Willard and his family were on a family trip to Mexico. In announcing his support for Fraser's candidacy, England said, "He is honest and efficient and if elected is capable of transacting the city's business without the assistance of a high-priced city manager." England reported that Fraser had said before he left on vacation that he would run if a petition were circulated.[1]

Mac Fraser, Willard's nephew, speculates that the trip to Mexico was a small "payback" to Sadie for her years of care for Robin. Brother Marvin donated the use of a 1952 Cadillac from his automobile business for the trip. Marvin's sons, Mac and Jerry, accompanied Sadie, J. B., and Willard on their Mexican vacation. Mac remembers that Willard and Mac's parents, Marvin and Mary Louise, felt the experience of such a trip was more important than the weeks of school he missed. Willard ensured that Mac made up his homework and that he kept a diary of the trip. After checking for misspellings, he helped Mac type the diary on Willard's manual Royal typewriter.

Ever intent on improving both the world and those in his inner circle, Willard gave history lessons as they traveled, taught Mac to count in Spanish, and put him in charge of purchases so he could practice his Spanish skills. The fourteen-page diary that twelve-year-old Mac Fraser turned in as a project when he returned to school demonstrates Willard's energy and passions. The report verified that this was not a trip spent lounging on beaches. Rather, the Frasers toured glass, silkworm, pottery, tequila, and sugar factories. They visited prehistoric cliff dwellings, pyramids, museums, and farms. Mac's descriptions of these visits were laced with historical facts that bring to mind a Willard lecture, and Uncle Willard often entered the narrative directly. When describing Guadalajara and its new sewer system, Mac wrote, "My uncle says that is the way we should plan things in Billings." Concluding his travelogue, Mac made a comment that would strike a chord with those who witnessed Willard's passionate opposition to smoking. Mac wrote, "My uncle says this trip was possible because he doesn't waste his money smoking cigarettes." Of course, Mac's own voice is present in the report as well. After witnessing a bullfight, he concluded, "I think I will stick to baseball."[2] The time Willard devoted to this family event may have come at a political cost, but commitment to his family was a core element of his principles.

Back in Billings at the end of March, Willard had only days to solicit votes. His campaign ad in the *Gazette* bore the headline, "Draft Fraser for Mayor!" and was paid for by the Draft Fraser Committee. The late March entry for the early April election did not bode well for success, and Fraser came in third with county clerk and recorder Earle Knight securing the mayoral seat with a rare majority vote and incumbent Tom Rowe coming in second.

Despite his loss, the media continued to cover Fraser because of his activism and his ability to articulate quotable opinions on public issues. A month after the 1953 mayoral race, Fraser made headlines in Montana papers by speaking out against a bill introduced by Republican representative Wesley D'Ewart. The intent of D'Ewart's bill, supported by Montana stockmen, was to extend the grazing regulations of the 1934 Taylor Grazing Act to allow more grazing in national forests. Fraser stated that the so-called land grab act would "give away forest lands, hunting and fishing areas that are owned by the public at large" to private ranching enterprises. As environmentalist and historian Bernard DeVoto had railed against the Pick-Sloan dam proposal, he also spoke out against D'Ewart's bill in his "Easy Chair" column. DeVoto's most notable books concerned Western history, and he held strong opinions about how the "cowboy culture" was bartering away the West's natural resources and beauty. His efforts undoubtedly contributed to the bill's defeat. As a voracious reader and someone with an interest in environmental issues, Willard would have been aware of DeVoto's columns in *Harper's Magazine* and likely knew of the Frost-DeVoto friendship.[3] The use and regulation of public lands, as well as the tension between environmentalists and some cattle ranchers, continues to be a national and Montana political issue.

Willard's interest in environmental issues mainly concerned the impacts of pollutants on public health. As early as 1949, he advocated for clean drinking water in Billings. After years of suffering the ill effects of secondhand smoke, Willard began waging what would be a lifelong, very public battle against cigarette smoking, smog, and pollution in 1953. His ardent opposition to air pollution was partially rooted in its effect on his asthma, but he was also aware of its effect on the health of the general population. Adopting the general cause against pollution, Fraser wrote to Mayor Knight and council members, "For the past several years, there has been an ever-increasing smog menace in our city," and he urged the city to study the problem and take steps to mitigate it. The *Gazette* noted that Willard's letter "was received and placed in file."[4]

In the spring of 1954, Fraser filed for the fourth time for U.S. representative from the eastern district. This time, Willard's health kept him from waging a vigorous campaign. In the weeks before the July primary, he was being treated for a kidney infection in a Denver hospital, where he remained until the primary election.[5] From his hospital bed, he issued campaign

WILLARD E.
FRASER
FOR
CONGRESS

Second Congressional District of Montana

● Willard E. Fraser has never refused a call of assistance from any citizen, regardless of his economic, political, racial, religious, or social status; nor has he ever refused a call to duty by city, state, or nation.

VOTE . . . November 4th. It is one of your great American rights and privileges.

Excerpt from one of Fraser's campaign fliers. As a candidate and as an elected official, Fraser encouraged Montanans to stay politically engaged and to exercise their right to vote. Frost Collection, Ms1178.B12.F40, Rauner Special Collections Library, Dartmouth University, NH

statements, including a promise to work actively for statehood for Alaska and, on the eve of the election, a statement against political witch hunts: "I would like to have the record show I am flatly opposed to McCarthyism, or any other form of intolerance, and I believe Senator McCarthy has been the greatest giver of 'aid and comfort' Communist Russia has had of late in the New World."[6] (Senator Joseph McCarthy was conducting his infamous Army-McCarthy Senate hearings at the time, which ended in his December 2, 1954, censure by the Senate.) Fraser's inability to campaign in person certainly contributed to his loss in the July 20 primary to state senator LeRoy Anderson. Anderson earned a plurality of 17,783 votes to Fraser's 12,305 and Theodore Johnson's 6,097 votes. That Fraser came in second out of three candidates while spending most of the campaign in a hospital indicates he was seen as a viable candidate. Anderson was defeated in the fall election by Republican Orvin Fjare, but in the next election, in

1956, Anderson won the first of two terms as the representative from the eastern district.

Willard's persistence is all the more remarkable considering his recurrent bouts of serious illness. In addition to lifelong asthma, he endured recurrent kidney problems. The kidney ailment that had sidelined him during the 1954 primary campaign brought him in October to the Mayo Clinic in Rochester, Minnesota, where Marjorie had died twenty years earlier. Fraser was back at Mayo in March 1955, when he wrote to Senator Murray's son Charlie, "My insides are kicking up so I am entering Mayo Clinic tomorrow."[7] A week later, again writing from Rochester, he commented, "My bladder is getting to be as public as Grand Central." Nine months later, in December, he was again at Mayo for surgery. This was one of the few years that Willard did not run for political office. However, in a November article in the *Gazette*, he vowed he would be a candidate in 1956—if his health permitted.

True to his stated intention, Fraser ran for office again in 1956—this time for Montana Railroad and Public Service commissioner. By now, his record of losses was fair game in the press. Journalist and future editor of the *Harlowton Times*, Harold G. "Hal" Stearns, wrote in his "Uneasy Chair" column in the *Eastern Montana Clarion*, "Our good personal friend and political foe Willard Fraser is toying with the idea of running for state railroad commission. Someday, mark my words, Willard's philosophy of getting on the ballot every election is going to get him elected in spite of himself."[8] In the June primary, Willard came in second to Lou Boedecker, a former railroad conductor and the first head of the Montana Highway Patrol, who went on to win the fall election. Boedecker died suddenly before he assumed office, and Governor Aronson appointed Republican Ory Armstrong to complete the term.

Shortly after the 1956 June primary, Robin Fraser graduated from Smith College. Willard, his parents, and Robert Frost attended her graduation. The ceremony in Northampton, Massachusetts, was part of an extended trip that included observing a session of Parliament in Ottawa, a stop in Washington, D.C., to see Lesley Frost Ballantine, a side trip to see relatives in Kansas, and a visit with Jeanne and Ben Blackford in Connecticut. The Blackfords had provided a second home for Robin during her four years at Smith, and the close relationship they established endured. Jeanne and Ben supported other Fraser nieces and nephews as well. The Blackfords had no children of their own, so perhaps their nieces and nephews filled a void for them. Marvin's son Mac attended Greenwich High School in 1954–55 while living with Jeanne and Ben, an experience he later said was "like a kick in

Mrs. and Dr. Werner, Robin, Willard, Sadie and J. B. Fraser celebrate Robin's engagement in Billings, 1958. Billings Gazette, *Mar. 30, 1958*

the ass for a kid from Montana." Mac's sister, Wendelanne Fraser, also spent several months with the Blackfords. Both Mac and Wendy felt that the time with their aunt and uncle opened the world for them. Wendy commented that her exposure to the Greenwich community gave her social confidence and enabled her to mix with all kinds of people.[9]

After Robin's graduation from Smith, she divided her time in the summer of 1956 between the Frost home in Ripton, Vermont, and a summer session at the University of Kansas in Lawrence, in the home county of her Fraser grandparents. She then pursued graduate work in art at Montana State University (now the University of Montana) in Missoula, but she married before she was able to complete her degree.

Willard traveled east to attend Robin's April 1958 wedding to David Beecher Hudnut in the Princeton University Chapel, where Jeanne Blackford served in the mother-of-the-bride role. Robin married into a family that her father enjoyed and with whom he kept up a friendly correspondence. Like their distant ancestors, the Beechers of Connecticut, several members of the Hudnut family—David's father, Rev. Dr. William Hudnut, and two of his brothers, Robert and William—were pastors in the Presbyterian Church as well as being active in politics.[10] Willard's son-in-law David Hudnut fit perfectly into the Fraser family, and they came to know him well in the summer after his marriage to Robin when he worked for the Montana Highway Department. David earned his law degree at Cornell after his marriage and subsequently worked as a lawyer in a New York City firm, for Ford Motor Company in Michigan, and finally as senior vice president of U.S. Leasing in California. Willard appreciated David's generous spirit and business savvy, and David became a close friend of Robin's cousin, Mac Fraser. Sadie Fraser often visited both the Hudnuts and the Blackfords at their homes back East. During her extended visits in 1955 and 1959, the *Gazette* reported that Sadie included visits to Robert Frost.[11] In 1961, Robin and David Hudnut and Robert Frost were Christmas dinner guests at the Blackford home.[12]

Willard's battle with health problems hindered his political ambitions during this period. He had missed the Democratic National Convention in August 1956 and indicated in a letter to Frost that it was because he had been ill for much of the summer. He went on to say that his interstitial cystitis was being treated with a weekly injection of clorpactin into the bladder. Fraser wryly commented that he was "more inclined to believe it [clorpactin] is a mixture of moulton [*sic*] lead and melted sulphur. Pretty rugged, and puts me out of commission for three or four days each week but it does seem to be helping."[13] By October, 1956, he reported, "[For] the first time in about four years, I'm feeling reasonably human."[14]

Robin and David Hudnut, pictured here ca. 1970, were married in Princeton University Chapel in 1958. Courtesy Robin Fraser Hudnut

Several *Gazette* articles attest to Willard's renewed energy that fall. He was appointed state finance chairman to assist the state Democratic Central Committee, he campaigned for Democrat LeRoy Anderson in his bid for representative from the eastern district, and in a speech before the Billings Exchange Club he sounded themes that would become identified with him: water usage, smog, use of federal funds, and Yellowtail Dam.[15] In the 1956 national election, Eisenhower carried the state over Stevenson to win his second term. In Montana, incumbent Republican governor Aronson defeated Democrat Arnold Olsen, Democrat Lee Metcalf was reelected to the U.S. House from Montana's western district, and LeRoy Anderson won the eastern district seat. Willard spent the legislative session in the winter of 1957 in Helena, where he continued his lobbying career.[16]

According to Willard, he played an important but unheralded role in history during Montana's 1957 legislative session. Decades later, he wrote

The Fraser family in 1959, the year J. B Fraser died. Standing, left to right: Willard, Marvin, Jeanne, Robert. Seated: Sadie, J. B. Courtesy Gardner Historical Society, Gardner, KS

that during some downtime in the session, he read a newspaper article about the possibility of Alaska becoming a state. He promptly composed a resolution urging that Alaska become a state and cast about for a likely lawmaker to introduce it. He settled on a "nice, decent, quiet human being from Roundup in Musselshell County" and asked him, "Why don't you introduce this?" He did so, both Houses passed it, Governor Aronson signed it, and when it appeared before the U.S. Congress this lawmaker testified. When Alaska became a state, Willard was invited to be in attendance when Eisenhower signed the bill of statehood.[17] His letter contains no names, but it is true that Representatives William J. Glancy of Musselshell County and John R. Devier of Dawson County introduced the Alaska proposal in Montana in 1957, and the U.S. Congress voted on that proposal in March 1959 to admit Alaska as the forty-ninth state.[18] Willard wrote that before Glancy died, he told Willard he had all the letters and resolutions saved in a safety deposit box so his grandchildren and great-grandchildren would know the part he played in Alaska's statehood.

Undaunted by his previous political defeats and health challenges, Willard ran for mayor for the fifth time in 1957. He seemed a tepid candidate. Incumbent Earle Knight announced in February that he would run in the early April election, and no opposing candidate filed until Fraser stepped in on March 15 after returning from the legislative season in Helena. His announcement included the statement: "Providing voters of the city of Billings with a choice between two or more candidates is a basic part of the democratic process."[19] Knight won with 54 percent of the vote: 4,694 to Fraser's 3,874. Given Fraser's late start, his apparent lack of finances, and Knight's incumbency, Fraser's showing was creditable.

Willard's ongoing medical problems explain why he didn't run for office in 1958 or 1959. He suffered from "an awful lot of asthma, which coupled with bladder trouble, makes sleep almost impossible."[20] He spent two weeks in the hospital in January 1959. The following summer, Fraser wrote about "being in the hospital myself, and attending to my dad, who is in the hospital now with a very bad cancer."[21] Fraser had already lost other important figures that decade: family friend B. R. Albin in December 1953 and his archaeologist hero, Earl Morris, in 1956. J. B. Fraser died in August 1959.

Although election losses, medical problems, and the loss of friends and family marred the years from 1946 to 1959, Willard could still celebrate many family milestones, not the least of which was the birth of a grandson, David Beecher Hudnut Jr.—the first of Robin's five children, in February 1959. He could also count among the high points of these years his contributions to making Yellowtail Dam a reality and his growing confidence as an advocate for public reforms.

The 1960s started badly for Willard Fraser, who continued to suffer from health problems. In January, he wrote from the Mayo Clinic to Frost, "I've about had the works here, though they tell me that I shall probably have to come back in a couple of months for surgery again. Rough. I've just had one of the Mayo's famous, painful—and expensive—treatments." He signed off, "The best from the 'Vatican of the Medical World' to coin a phrase."[22]

In spite of his health issues, Willard entered Montana's political fray in a statewide race, announcing on February 18, 1960, that he planned to run for governor, and that as governor he would "do all possible to aid and assist the cultural growth of Montana," because "one part of having a good business climate is to have a good cultural climate."[23] In his official filing statement on April 28, he stated that Montana still labored under the antiquated "oxcart mentality" of the original 1889 state constitution, which Copper King William A. Clark had supervised, and he called for updating it—something that Montanans would do in 1972. Other positions Fraser advocated included merging some sparsely populated counties, taking the state out of the retail liquor store business, developing natural resources, building Yellowtail Dam, and revising the tax system.[24]

Willard's decision to enter the race for governor earned some ink inspired by Billings mayor Carl Clavadetscher, who was managing the gubernatorial campaign of Jack Toole, a Shelby rancher and former Democratic state chairman. At 6'5" and at least 250 pounds, Clavadetscher was physically imposing and known for his bluntly expressed opinions and colorful speech. He had attended a Bighorn float with Fraser and also had a knack for getting ample press coverage, but now this former friend charged that Fraser's campaign was being financed by Republicans. Clavadetscher further claimed that "Sweetwater Willie" (a nickname slapped on Willard because of his advocacy for such water issues as the municipal gravity-flow system and construction of dams) was making promises beyond the realm of executive powers. He also made an issue of Fraser's previous election losses—nine according to Clavadetscher.[25] Fraser had actually lost eleven. Perhaps Clavadetscher was not aware of Willard's run for mayor in 1933 or the legislature in 1938.

Six Democratic candidates entered the primary race for governor in 1960. Governor J. Hugo Aronson could not run for a third term, and his lieutenant governor, Butte native Paul Cannon, became a candidate. Other candidates were Bozeman bricklayer John Nickey, Mike Kuchera, Jack

Toole, Merrill Riddick, and Willard Fraser. This was Nickey's second run for governor; he had been defeated in the 1956 primary by then attorney general Arnold Olsen. Fraser, never shy about proclaiming his connection to Robert Frost, was certainly behind a large *Gazette* ad announcing a local TV spot featuring "the Granddaughter of America's Beloved Poet Robert Frost, Robin Fraser Hudnut."[26] He was one of three candidates noted for their colorful personalities and persistent attempts to gain political office. Fraser's Yellowstone County rival, Mike Kuchera, a Billings furniture store owner, was said to have lost thirteen elections, although Kuchera himself said he had lost only eleven.[27] He campaigned with a polka band, and on his half-hour television shows, he promised to push for gambling sanctioned by individual counties. Merrill Riddick, an early aviator and flight instructor from Phillipsburg, had also waged a number of idiosyncratic campaigns and later even ran a ragtag campaign for president. When he turned to politics, Riddick's actions and proclamations were significantly more outrageous and far less practical than Fraser's. All three lost when Paul Cannon of Butte became the Democratic nominee for governor in the June primary. Of the six candidates, Toole came in second, Kuchera third, Fraser fourth, Nickey fifth, and Riddick last. It would not be the last time the Kuchera/Fraser/Riddick trio would garner public attention, but of the three, only Fraser would eventually gain public office.

A few months later after the election, Fraser and Russell Conklin of Great Falls—former mayor, state representative, and candidate for Congress—formed an organization called "The

Undaunted by past losses, Fraser sought the Democratic nomination for governor in the 1960 primary, but he came in fourth out of a field of six candidates.
Billings Gazette, May 29, 1960

FACE THE FUTURE

WITH

WILLARD E. FRASER

DEMOCRATIC CANDIDATE FOR

GOVERNOR

If it is brains you want in the Governor's office—then you will vote for Willard E. Fraser.

Paid political advertisement. Fraser for Governor Club, Lyman Williams, Secy.

Ben Franklin Democrats of Montana" and continued to advocate for some of the issues of Fraser's campaign, including a constitutional convention, combining Montana's fifty-six counties into twelve districts, and removing state government from retail liquor sales.

In a post-primary letter to the *Gazette*, Willard obliquely acknowledged that some Republicans had supported him. "Why shouldn't they?" he asked. "They know that I have a greater understanding of and appreciation for good government than do most Montana politicians. . . and I appreciate their confidence and the confidence of men of both parties."[28] As admirable as Fraser's bipartisan attitude was, on the practical level, his very ability to appeal to voters across party lines may have played a role in some of his losses, as longtime Montana legislator Harrison Fagg suggested decades later when he called Fraser a "renegade."[29] For instance, when Democrats objected to the firing of a state project engineer on charges of insubordination, Fraser issued a statement saying, "Under the circumstances, I cannot help but feel that my fellow Democrats. . . are in the wrong in coming to the defense of [the engineer]." He went on to say that "no organization could operate with disloyal employees."[30] The Democratic Party may not have been eager to support and fund a candidate who sometimes exerted his independence by publicly disagreeing with the party, just as Wheeler had done decades earlier.

As the fall 1960 elections approached, Senator John F. Kennedy made the third of five trips to Montana when he visited Billings in September to campaign. He had also visited Billings in 1958 and attended the Jefferson-Jackson Day Dinner in Butte in 1959. Willard made sure his nephew, Mac Fraser, came to see Kennedy, as he had done when Hubert Humphrey stopped in Montana in 1959.[31]

In the 1960 election, John F. Kennedy became president over incumbent Nixon without carrying Montana. While his inauguration was being planned, incoming Secretary of the Interior, Stewart Udall, suggested that eighty-seven-year-old Robert Frost read a poem at the event. Udall and Frost had become friendly in 1959 when Frost served as poetry consultant at the Library of Congress.[32] As Robin had represented the Frasers at Frost's eighty-fifth birthday celebration in New York City, so she and David Hudnut traveled in a snowstorm from Ithaca, New York, to attend the inauguration, the presidential balls, and an official dinner.[33] Photos of the inauguration ceremony record Jacqueline Kennedy's and Vice President Lyndon Johnson's concerned expressions as they watched Frost, partially blinded by sunlight, struggle to see the poem, "Dedication," that he had composed for the occasion. Finally, Frost recited "The Gift Outright" from memory.[34]

The 1960s began well for the Democrats at a national level, but in Montana, election results were split between parties. Democrat Lee Metcalf won the Senate seat vacated by James Murray, and Democrat Arnold Olsen became the representative from Montana's western district, while Republican James Battin, a Billings lawyer, was elected to Congress from eastern Montana. Senator Lyndon B. Johnson came to Great Falls to campaign for Paul Cannon for governor, but several newspapers came out against Cannon—including Helena's *Independent Record*, which branded him a "political clown."[35] Republican Donald Nutter of Sidney defeated Cannon to become Montana's governor. Nutter's election illustrated the political power of the state's ultraconservative element, which was rooted in Willard's home district of eastern Montana. After Nutter became governor, some Democrats became concerned about the secret and vigilante aspects of the rightwing Sidney-based John Birch Society, whose statewide coordinator, Math Dasinger, had organized pro-Nutter campaign activities in Montana's largest cities.[36] Nutter died in a plane crash near Helena in 1962, and Lieutenant Governor Tim Babcock replaced him.

Willard Fraser's own aspiration to attain elective office had led to repeated failure for over a decade, but his constant effort and his willingness to engage in important local and statewide issues were attracting favorable notice. In the fall of 1961, John Jarussi from Joliet wrote to the *Gazette* to say that Fraser's "interest in government and local affairs has been unequaled in Yellowstone County" and that he should serve in the next legislature.[37] In March 1962, H. W. White of Billings wrote to the editor of the *Gazette* to suggest that aldermen select Fraser for mayor, saying, "No one man has done more for Montana and been less credited. . . . This is NOT partisan, as I am a registered Republican."[38] If progressive Fraser were to gain elective office in conservative Yellowstone County in the years ahead, he would need to earn the backing of both Democrats and Republicans. In the meantime, he continued to stay in the public eye by sharing entertaining stories and voicing his opinions on public issues.

"I know we're going to step on some toes, but you can't progress and you can't grow without doing some stepping"

UNDAUNTED by his failed attempts to gain elective office, Willard Fraser determined to contribute his ideas as an engaged citizen. His irrepressible desire to effect change, allied with a talent for speaking and writing, kept his name in the media throughout the early 1960s. When the city and county butted heads over how to meet the need for a nursing home in Billings, he represented a chamber of commerce committee that proposed construction of a two-hundred-bed nursing home for the county. Although the proposal received support from Mayor Clavadetscher and County Commissioner Fred Plath, private companies rather than the county received the contracts to build nursing homes. Willard's engagement with state and community issues ensured press coverage of his many opinions and activities and resulted in a multitude of headlines such as "Fraser Advocates State Sales Tax," "Fraser Blasts Critics of Dam," "Fraser Urges City Planning," "Fraser Talks on Indians," and "Fraser Blasts House Action on Sunday Closing." Willard's commitment to public affairs kept him in the spotlight, undoubtedly helping him build a coalition of supporters. Although he entered the 1960s hindered by poor health and saddled with a long history of defeat, he would finally attain a political office that gave him a platform for putting his many ideas into effect and a pulpit from which to wax eloquent on those ideas.

Never one to duck controversy, Willard sometimes voiced unpopular views or took a stance against injustice. He had little tolerance for racism, and he often used the press to express his indignation at actions that he saw as prejudicial or unjust. In early 1962, he voiced an objection to a racist stance taken by Mayor Clavadetscher. The *Gazette* reported on January 31, 1962, that a sick Crow woman, a Billings resident for twelve years, had been refused admittance to Billings' hospitals because the public health service would not pay for her care.[1] Discussing the question of whether the city should be responsible, the *Gazette* stated, "Neither Mayor Carl Clavadetscher or Yellowstone County Commissioners make any secret about being unhappy about the migration of former reservation Indians to Billings. . . . The main plan of attack has been to encourage the Indians to stay on the reservation."[2] In a letter to the editor, Willard referred to the seven thousand American Indian citizens—mostly Northern Cheyennes and Crows—who spent hundreds of thousands of dollars in the city. He asked, "Can we afford to lose the good will and trade of Indians?" Protesting Clavadetscher's wish that Indians be segregated from the city, Willard asserted, "The only thing wrong with the Indian is that he is a member of the human race with exactly the same capacity for making a good citizen or a darn fool of himself as the rest of us."[3]

Later that year, he chastised the *Gazette* editor for writing a headline for a front-page article that announced, "3 Indian Girls Wounded in Fray." The girls, reported the paper, were involved in a fight that sent one young woman to the hospital.[4] Willard asked, "Why was it necessary to proclaim to the world that they were Indian girls?" Referring to another recent incident reported by the paper—one in which a white teenaged boy had damaged the floors of Billings Senior High with fire extinguishers and vandalized the school's walls—Fraser noted that the perpetrator's race had not been noted in the press.[5] He asked, "If you are going to so label every Indian misdoer, then shouldn't you likewise, in all fairness, so label every Kiwanian, Rotarian, Baptist, Catholic, Congregationalist, Lutheran, Mormon, Irish, German and Swede? Wouldn't it have been equally fair to have headlined recently, WHITE BOYS DO GREAT DAMAGE TO SENIOR HIGH?"[6]

While Willard often spoke up on serious matters, sometimes it was simply his flair for drama and love of a good story that gave him space in the local paper. In one letter to the editor of the *Gazette*, for example, he suggested a solution to a reader's plea for humane slaughter of animals. The two-column letter described Fraser's visit to Mexico during which his host decided to cook a turkey dinner. The letter focused on a description of "how to relax a turkey" before its demise. The method involved pouring tequila down the turkey's throat in three doses until the turkey was relaxed enough to endure a "truly painless slaughter" at the hands of the maid's machete.[7] Whether or not such an approach assuaged the concerns of the animal rights reader, Fraser later received requests for permission to reprint the piece.

In another instance, *Gazette* columnist Addison Bragg capitalized on Willard's mastery of the written word to entertain the reading public with an article titled "Bureaucratic Balderdash." Willard and Ben Blackford had decided to send Sadie to Europe for her birthday in the spring of 1962. Bragg described Willard's frustration at his attempt to obtain a passport for his mother. The article began by saying that since Fraser wasn't "running for anything this season . . . it gives us carte blanche to detail the latest tilting session indulged in by Yellowstone County's newest bane of bureaucracy." Besides evoking the image of Don Quixote tilting at windmills, Bragg compared Fraser to a western gunslinger. Willard had sent Sadie's marriage certificate and the page from the family Bible recording her birth to the Kansas Bureau of Vital Statistics as part of his effort to obtain a birth certificate, but initially his efforts were fruitless. Matching Willard's wit and humor stride for stride, Bragg detailed the struggle:

> More concrete evidence that Willard's mother was born was needed, they [the bureau] advised primly . . . Kansas didn't know it, of course, but they were dealing with one of the fastest pens in the west. "Enough is enough," Willard's letter in reply began, "and some things approach the idiotic. Such as your declining to issue a delayed birth certificate to my 76-year-old mother on the evidence I supplied you. Your declining to accept these proofs so that she can obtain a passport to visit Europe approaches the ridiculous, especially the part wherein you ask for letters from people who knew her before she was five years old. . . . Bear in mind that she is 76. Suppose you go out and find people who knew her before she was five."
>
> Here Willard shifted into second. "She only wants to take a trip to Europe and not skip the country. Admittedly, she might try to evade military service; it is true she might drop a bomb on the Vatican or chuck one into the Kremlin or pinch a picture from the Louvre or write her name on St. Paul's, for all things are possible and she is only a great grandmother."
>
> Then into high. "As if being born in Kansas doesn't make one about as American as it is possible to be, she also married a Kansas boy named John Brown Fraser, named after THE John Brown and she also shares the grandparenthood of Robin Fraser Hudnut and the great-grandparenthood of David Beecher Hudnut, Jr, with Robert Frost, all of which should

make her American enough for any Kansas—or other—
bureaucrat. So get busy and send up that certificate. When one
is 76, she doesn't have time to mess around with the type of
nonsense you propose."

The sequel . . . is of course, that Willard's mother is galli-
vanting about Europe, passport and all. And Willard, having
blown the smoke out of his pen-muzzle, is waiting for the next
challenger. He'll even let him draw first.[8]

Ever tenacious, Willard sometimes dogged public officials until he
pushed them to exasperation. In the early 1960s, he became involved in
an issue that inspired *Gazette* reporter Sam Blythe to comment, "When
Fraser embraces a cause, he holds tight."[9] In 1959, the General Services
Administration (GSA) had announced that it planned to build a new
federal building in Billings. Initially, the local population was relatively
quiet about this plan, but Fraser, Forrest Crum, Donald Lee, and George
McKinnon—all owners of buildings with federal tenants—immediately
opposed the idea. Fraser's building leased twenty thousand square feet of
office space to the Bureau of Indian Affairs, and the rent from the still-
mortgaged building was Willard's primary source of income. Knowing he
would lose this important tenant if the new federal office building went
through, Fraser waged a determined campaign against the project.

Although Willard's arguments against the proposed building focused
on what was best for the community, his vested interest certainly played a
role in his opposition. Throughout 1961 and 1962, he unleashed a blizzard of
protest letters to Montana's congressmen, Interior Secretary Stewart Udall,
the Commissioner of Public Buildings Service, and the *Gazette*. He even
sent a telegram to President Kennedy and tried to engage Robert Frost as
an advocate. Frost, who was in Moscow meeting with Russian leader Nikita
Krushchev, declined to get involved. In the press, Fraser argued, "Contrary
to their [proponents'] beliefs that the proposed building will hold business downtown, the contrary is true." He maintained that the government
would open a facility where government employees would buy gasoline,
clothing, household appliances, and food that Billings retail businesses
currently provided, forcing locally owned businesses to close or move out
of the downtown area.[10]

In his efforts to block the new federal building, Willard drew on
out-of-state connections—a tactic that resulted in articles in the *Chicago
Tribune* and the *U.S. News and World Report*. One of these connections was
Grant Salisbury, who had in 1954 become an editor at the *U.S. News and*

World Report and who shared a particular interest in energy and America's natural world. Willard's friendship with Grant Salisbury seems an unlikely alliance between an editor for a conservative magazine and a progressive politician, but by the mid-1950s, they were regular correspondents. Like Fraser, Salisbury was a World War II veteran and a native of Kansas. Stuart Conner assessed Salisbury as "one of the most level-headed, bright guys I ever knew" and acknowledged that "for Willard to become a buddy of his was a real good thing for the state of Montana."[11] The Fraser-Salisbury connection resulted in considerable coverage of Montana issues in *U.S. News*, while Salisbury benefited from knowing Fraser by securing an interview with Robert Frost and meeting Burton K. Wheeler.[12] Certainly, Willard's friendship with Salisbury instigated and influenced the March 26, 1961, *U.S. News* article "City Gets a Federal Building—But Does It Want One?" The *Gazette* coverage discussing the *U.S. News* piece seemed not to be aware of the Fraser-Salisbury friendship.

Willard was neck-deep in the federal building controversy for months, during which Senator Metcalf received a number of letters from Billings citizens and officials supporting the building. Finally, Senator Metcalf responded impatiently to the barrage of Fraser letters of opposition, stating, "Willard, this building will have to be accepted as a *"fait accompli"*—it has been approved, the money appropriated, the proposed site picked. . . . Since many or perhaps even most of the people in Billings are in favor of the construction of this building by the GSA, it would seem that in this case it is the majority against one."[13] After President Kennedy signed a bill containing funding for the building in August 1961, Fraser was quoted as saying, "This is a manifestation of great fiscal irresponsibility."[14] He argued that the government bore some responsibility for the financial woes he suffered because of the loss of his tenants. He explained to Representative Arnold Olsen some years later that the GSA had insisted he put an addition on his building at a cost of $185,000, and he was still carrying a substantial mortgage when the new federal building was completed.[15] Willard likely had a hand in the follow-up article in *U.S. News*, which Salisbury titled "How a City Got a Building It Didn't Ask For."[16]

Local development issues also prompted Willard to put in his two cents' worth. When the *Gazette* announced in 1962 a proposal to widen the road to the airport by blasting 551,600 cubic yards of rock from the top of the Rimrocks, Willard asked, "How crazy can we get?" The project would "tame" the sheer rock wall of one section of the Rims to a 45-degree slope and would cost $1,333,453.[17] In a letter to the editor, he argued, "Some things in life should be permanent, and among these are our Rim Rocks

. . . and to even propose to tear down this handiwork of God approaches the sacrilegious."[18] Willard suggested as an alternative one of his favorite ideas: a tunnel through the Rimrocks in the neighborhood of 15th or 20th Streets. Instead, the new airport road along the rims proceeded despite his objections.

In early October 1962, the *Gazette* announced that Fraser had indicated he would run for mayor in the April 1963 election. In early December, shortly after his sixth campaign for mayor began, a *Gazette* editorial titled "A Spring Breeze From the South" commented on the candidacy of this resident of South Billings: "Whether one agrees or not with Mr. Fraser, who can offer an opinion on numerous subjects, his comments on public matters are often stimulating and his entry into the mayoralty race holds promise of an interesting campaign."[19] Willard's campaign would indeed be interesting, although it would not start in earnest until early March, after he finished lobbying in Helena during the legislative session.

That winter, Willard mourned the death of his father-in-law. On January 29, 1963, Robert Frost died at age eighty-eight in Cambridge,

Willard (upper left), accompanied by Robin and David Hudnut, leaves the private memorial services for Robert Frost, January 29, 1963. Howard G. Schmitt, photographer. PH4-F3331, Robert Frost Collection, Robert Frost Library, Amherst College, Amherst, MA

Massachusetts. Frost's death was a significant loss for Willard, who revered his late wife's father. His connection with Frost had been a major bond for three decades. He attended a private service for family and close friends in a Harvard chapel on January 31. The small group in attendance included Lesley Frost Ballantine and her children and grandchildren; Prescott Frost (Carol and Lillian Frost's son); Willard Fraser with Robin and David Hudnut; Frost's cousin Joseph Frost and his wife; Lawrance Thompson; Louis Untermeyer; longtime friends Kay and Ted Morrison; and critic I. A. Richards.

Even after Robert Frost's death, Willard corresponded frequently with Lesley Frost Ballantine (front). They are pictured here with National Education Association representative Irva Mae Applegate in Billings, Dec. 8, 1965. Billings Gazette, Dec. 8, 1965

Following Frost's death, Willard continued to correspond regularly with Frost's eldest daughter, Lesley, and with Lillian, the widow of Frost's son Carol. He visited them in the East and welcomed them both to Billings. Lillian spent three weeks with the Frasers in the late fall of 1962 and wrote to Frost of an entertaining evening listening to author A. B. Guthrie and artist J. K. Ralston tell stories.[20] When Lesley visited Billings in 1965, the *Gazette* published a photo of her, Sadie Fraser, and Myrtle Mockel, the president of the Montana Women's Press Club, at a reception at the Fraser home.[21]

Willard must have decided to visit his sister in Connecticut and Lesley Frost Ballantine in Washington, D.C., after Robert Frost's funeral, because two weeks later his flight from Newark to D.C. inspired a *Gazette* headline, "Fraser Reports Narrow Escape." Willard recounted his adventure with a characteristic knack for eye-opening detail and a chaser of humor. The article began, "'It was like looking eternity in the face,' Willard Fraser said." During the flight the plane's landing gear malfunctioned, and passengers were told to prepare for a crash landing. They were instructed to keep their heads down so their necks wouldn't snap on impact. Willard recalled, "There was only one encouraging sign. I couldn't spot a hearse" among the fire engines and ambulances waiting on the ground. The plane did not crash, and all thirty passengers slid down the chute and ran to safety.[22]

Home safely, Willard geared up for the upcoming election. The 1963 race for mayor of Billings featured partisan candidates for the first time. In all previous races, mayoral candidates ran as independents, but in 1963, candidate Bill Hagen broke the independent tradition in Billings and ran as a Republican. Although Willard had been described as a "well known Democrat," he went on record early to say that "partisan politics has no place in city elections." He maintained that such partisanship would result in a corrupt "ward-heeler government" in which political operatives would be interested in spoils and jobs, not good government.[23] True to his values, he ran as an independent. The other candidates were Harold Gerke, the incumbent mayor who had replaced Clavadetscher after he resigned; Republican Bill Hagen, a radio announcer and auctioneer; Bernard Lustig, a young businessman; and Dewey Maynard, a veteran city alderman. All candidates but Hagen ran as independents.

This time, Fraser and his supporters waged a campaign unlike any previous one. An early large advertisement paid by the Friends of Fraser lists friends Stuart Conner, Frank Cross, Dr. Jess Schwidde, photographer Denes Istvanffy, Professor Aaron Small of Eastern Montana College, and fifteen other citizens as supporters. The Fraser for Mayor Club published Willard's 17-Point Program for Billings' Progress, which covered topics ranging from

To Willard E Fraser.
a fine friend throughout
these many years. and
one who has both guts
and brains :
Sincerely your friend
Burton K Wheeler

BURTON K. WHEELER speaks about WILLARD FRASER

Pd. Pol. Adv. by Fraser for Mayor Club, Norvell Besinque, Treas.

Among the campaign advertisements run by the Fraser for Mayor Club in 1963 was this handwritten endorsement from former senator Burton K. Wheeler.
Billings Gazette, Mar. 28, 1963

controlling dogs, eliminating nuisance starlings, and building swimming pools to encouraging industry, recreation, and tourism. Numerous ads for "the man with the "KNOW-HOW" urged Billings citizens to "Be Independent, Vote Independent." One ad promised, "No one in Billings has 52,851 friends, but 52,851 people in Billings will have one friend in City Hall when Willard E. Fraser is elected Mayor."[24]

In separate ads, Fraser invited people to send questions and ideas to him at his home address. One paid advertisement by realtor Kenneth Hollar in the *Gazette* stated, "Willard Fraser made many trips to Washington in behalf of Yellowtail Dam."[25] Throughout the campaign, Willard touted his contribution to seeing Yellowtail Dam through, stating that he knew government and the possibility of development of the area. "That is why I worked so hard—and so successfully—to secure construction of Yellowtail Dam," he assured voters.[26] Another ad simply featured a handwritten note that read, "To Willard E. Fraser. A fine friend throughout these many years and one who has both guts and brains. Sincerely your friend, Burton K. Wheeler."[27] It had been seventeen years since Wheeler represented Montana in the Senate, but his voice still resonated with many of the state's residents. Addison Bragg commented in the *Gazette* about the "neatest political gimmick of the campaign": a blank blue button. When asked about it, the wearer would announce it meant "Quietly for Fraser."[28]

In news articles, Fraser stayed true to long-held issues. "In 1949," he said, "I was alone in working to convince some people that city planning was important. The idea was shrugged off then, but no one is laughing now." Billings was well on its way to passing Great Falls as Montana's largest city. In 1963, its population was just under fifty-five thousand, but Willard was aware that a growing city required advance planning. Ten years earlier, he had urged pursuing a gravity-flow water system, but instead the city was still pumping water uphill for miles. "I never realized that any group of men who call themselves intelligent could be ignorant of a basic natural law— that water flows downhill," he said.[29] More than fifty years later, Fraser is still remembered for his advocacy of a gravity water system—which was never implemented.

By and large, candidate rhetoric during the campaign seems to have been mostly civil, but there were a few heated charges and countercharges in the press. When Gerke made a promise to do away with parking meters, Willard called it "an act of hysteria."[30] An informal poll by the *Gazette* put Gerke in the lead. One person who responded to the poll commented about Fraser, "I'm not going to vote for him, but I think he's the smartest one of the bunch."[31] Gerke undoubtedly felt confident. He had the advantage of incumbency, and he discounted Willard because of his long record of losses.

Just days before the April 1 city election, Willard gained two important endorsements. Joe Leone, fourth ward alderman, announced that he backed Fraser, and, even more newsworthy, candidate Bernard Lustig told an audience of chamber of commerce members, "If you don't vote for me, vote for Willard Fraser."[32] Decades later, Harrison Fagg, a Billings architect and state legislator, gave some interesting background on Lustig's announcement. In 1963, Fagg was president of the Billings Jaycees, a civic leadership organization for young adults, of which Lustig was a member. Willard approached Fagg and asked, "Can you help me get Lustig out of the race? If he's out, I can get elected mayor." Fagg, knowing that Lustig had little support in the race, agreed to introduce the two candidates. The three spent an interesting day together, which included Fraser taking Lustig and

Fraser's 17-Point Program for Billings' Progress

1. **Business.** Support private contracting over city if job can be done as well and more economically.

2. **Police.** Courtesy tickets. Make Billings a friendly town.

3. **City Employees**. I would change only one job. Appoint Stuart Conner City Attorney.

4. **Streets.** Maintain best streets possible after storm sewers, drainage, and utilities are in place.

5. **Ditches.** Must be solved for safety and control of seepage damage.

6. **Dogs.** Dogs must be sometimes restricted but I will not be a party to depriving children or adults of pets.

7. **Swimming Pools.** I oppose charging fees from children using the pools.

8. **Recreation.** Develop Indian Caves, the Yellowstone River and the Rimrock areas into attractive parks. City Government should develop these as well as the Art Museum. A road to Yellowtail is a must.

9. **Industry.** By cooperating and utilizing the brain power of industry we can attract new industry.

10. **Programming.** I will bring order to the chaos now existing in Billings planning for community development.

11. **Starlings.** The starling problem can be handled without calling on Federal Government Aid and Money.

12. **Eastern.** City Government should be thrown into the struggle to save the educational status of Eastern Montana College. Eastern is everyone's business as well as Rocky Mountain College.

13. **Friendlier Face.** We need a "friendlier face for Billings" for tourists, visitors and new industry.

14. **Get Billings Going.** End this "Stop and Wait." Fill vacant housing, vacant stores and office buildings.

15. **Out-Of-Town Attractions.** A Billings Mayor Should Think Big and not be just city-limited. Billings can only prosper as the area around it prospers.

16. **Brain Power for Progress.** We need to use the talent and education available through Government Offices, Schools, Business and Labor groups to get Billings going again.

17. **What Do You Want?** The needs and wants of the people should be paramount—not just campaign oratory, but these ideas should go into the office of mayor with the man.

Willard E. Fraser Collection, MSU–Billings Library

Fagg to see a pictograph on the Rimrocks.[33] The day spent together resulted in Lustig's surprise March 29 recommendation to the chamber of commerce to vote for Fraser.

On April 2, 1963, the morning after the city election, the front page of the *Gazette* announced the results. "'They always claimed,' a man outside city hall said, 'that it would be a cold day in Hades before Willard Fraser was ever elected to anything.' . . . for April, it was cold and Fraser is the city's next mayor."[34] In his thirteenth attempt—his sixth for mayor—Willard Fraser had finally won an election. As was usual in a race with multiple candidates, Willard earned a plurality, not a majority. Hagen came in second, incumbent mayor Gerke third, Maynard fourth, and Lustig last. A *Gazette* photo showed a genial transitional handshake between Gerke and Fraser, but Gerke's true feelings about losing to Fraser surfaced in a letter to Senator Mansfield in which he called Fraser "that man."[35] Less than

A victorious Willard Fraser shakes the hand of rival Harold Gerke after becoming the new mayor of Billings in 1963. Ray Pearson, photographer. *Billings Gazette*, Apr. 2, 1963

a year later, Gerke was in charge of the Jefferson-Jackson dinner for Senator Ted Kennedy's visit to Billings. It was notable that among the number of Democrats mentioned or involved, Fraser, the mayor of the host city, was neither mentioned nor given a role.[36]

One can imagine fifty-six-year-old Willard Fraser's joy and excitement knowing that at last he had a platform from which he could promote his vision for Billings and, through this position, champion Montana causes. A victorious Fraser wrote B. K. Wheeler a jubilant note: "You and I have been elected Mayor of Billings."[37] As someone who had "a great deal of experience at losing elections," Willard took time to say, "I have great sympathy and real understanding for those men . . . against whom I have won the election."[38] Willard was optimistic about his administration, expressing immediately his philosophy of governance: "We will have an open mind and an open door to all those who have anything they want to add or incorporate in the body politic, because we think the area has great possibilities and great potential, and we intend to utilize every man, woman and child and every idea in our administration."[39] The *Gazette*'s post-election editorial, however, sounded a wary tone, noting that Fraser had achieved victory by receiving only one-third of the twelve thousand votes cast and warning this did not signify agreement with some of Fraser's previous public positions, such as his opposition to the new federal building and the new airport road.[40] In contrast to the paper, Governor Babcock, a Billings native, wrote to the mayor-elect to say, "Before I congratulate you, first let me say that I didn't vote for you. I do feel, however, that in many instances, your philosophy of local, state, and federal government is very much aligned with mine, so that we may, in many respects, have the pleasure of working together."[41]

In the weeks between the election and Willard's inauguration, Stuart Conner served as a sounding board for Willard's thoughts on mayoral appointments and initiatives. Fraser would break with tradition by not requiring city department heads to attend council meetings and by establishing four advisory committees to begin work immediately on salient city issues: the role of private industry, urban renewal, a single service for utilities, and the swimming pool issue. He appointed up to twenty individuals to each committee. In a public relations masterstroke, he appointed author A. B. Guthrie to the swimming pool committee.

To the new mayor's dismay, the *Gazette* ran an article stating that Fraser could not appoint Bernard Lustig to chair the city's recreation committee, as the committee members themselves had to choose their chairman.[42] Shortly before Fraser's inauguration, a headline announced a "Mayor-Council Fight" over Fraser's desire to appoint his own committee chairmen. "Fraser wants the first and last word on everything," one council member grumbled.[43] Fraser's unabashed response to the critical dismay of his dissenters was, "I know we're going to step on some toes but you can't progress and you can't grow without doing some stepping."[44] True to his word, Willard Fraser would step on various toes throughout his seven-plus years as mayor, and these initial conflicts with the council anticipated others.

On May 7, 1963, an inaugural dinner was held at the Northern Hotel followed by Fraser's swearing in at city hall. Mayor Fraser then immediately presided over his first city council meeting. He was ready with committee appointees and a plethora of ideas that he had long waited to put into action. This mayor would use his public relations skills and his gift for persuasion to combat complacency, small-mindedness, and intolerance and to encourage Billings and its people to work for and embrace progress. Life would not be dull in the city of Billings with Willard Fraser at the helm.

CHAPTER ELEVEN

"Get Billings Going"

THE SUBTITLE of a late summer 1963 *Gazette* article, "Go Get 'Em, Willard," illustrates the delight journalists took in describing the enthusiasm and unconventional words and actions of the city's new mayor.[1] Both the press and local residents relished having such a visible, active mayor, and Willard's availability positively affected his image. No longer was Fraser seen as a perennial loser or a politician who evoked laughter more often than respect. Willard's newfound popularity inspired a reaction in Stuart Conner: "It amused me that all of a sudden—it really was sudden—the attitude in town about Willard changed. He made more sense than anyone did long before that, but it [his positive image] took over in 1963."[2] Willard Fraser had vowed to "Get Billings Going" in his campaign ads, and he immediately focused his considerable energy on promoting projects and events that would improve Billings and draw attention to it.

Gazette staff writers Addison Bragg, Sam Blythe, and Roger Clawson, who replaced Blythe, commented regularly on Fraser's personality, actions, and opinions. In their columns and feature articles, the mayor was often simply "Willard," not the formal "Mayor Fraser." The *Gazette* writers did not always agree with Fraser's actions, and their words sometimes conveyed incredulity at his ideas or positions. Still, there was an undertone of affection in their coverage, and both Bragg and Clawson described themselves as Fraser friends. Willard also forged friendships with small-town Montana newsmen—especially Hal Stearns, editor of the *Harlowton Times* and a fellow history buff, and Mel Ruder, the Pulitzer Prize–winning publisher of the *Hungry Horse News*. Willard's expansive, optimistic personality and

Willard Fraser served four terms as mayor of Billings between 1963 and 1963. Among other works of art, a portrait of his father-in-law, Robert Frost, hung in his office.
Courtesy Western Heritage Center, Billings

the attention he garnered from the press ensured that the people of Billings always knew what their mayor was up to, and he was up to plenty.

Considerable cooperation and sometimes friendly rivalry marked the relationship among the mayors of Montana's larger towns. The same year Willard was elected, Republican Marian Erdmann became mayor of Great Falls, and Republican Howard Dix became mayor of Missoula. A year later, Butte elected Democrat Thomas Powers. All three of these mayors and Fraser were reelected in 1965. Fraser consulted with his fellow mayors in 1964 about the possibility of adopting Daylight Saving Time and visited with Mayor Dix in Missoula to support north–south air service for western Montana, saying he would "work for stronger air ties between Missoula and Billings for the mutual benefit of the two cities."[3] In 1965, a good-natured "feud" between Fraser and Mayor Powers of Butte was sparked by Fraser's public statement welcoming Butte "into the Billings trade area."[4] Naturally, Powers objected to the implication that Butte was a commercial suburb of Billings. When Fraser spoke to the Butte Rotarians soon after, the *Montana Standard* quoted the program chairman as saying that although Powers and Fraser were seated together at the event, they made sure a ring referee sat next to them.[5]

Newspaper articles and letters between Erdmann and Fraser demonstrate a particularly congenial relationship, and the *Great Falls Tribune* tended to give Mayor Fraser plenty of positive coverage. When Erdmann introduced Fraser as a speaker in Great Falls, she ribbed him by calling him the mayor of the state's Number 2 city, although Billings claimed to be Number 1 in population. When Fraser "expanded his Scotch domain to declare today 'Robbie Burns Day' in Great Falls," Mayor Erdmann responded with the quip: "Just think, if he comes in a kilt, the mayors of Montana's two largest cities both will be wearing skirts."[6]

Willard's friendly relationships with the mayors of other Montana cities kept him informed on statewide problems and activities. While he sometimes used such information to suggest Billings' superior progress, he also readily gave his support to such efforts as improved transportation, environmental awareness, and attracting tourism. He participated in the annual Mayors' Snowmobile Race, which attracted mayors ranging from Poplar to Livingston, and he traded ideas with mayors of other towns along the Yellowstone River.[7] In the same vein, he attended the national mayors' conference each year both to air his own ideas and to keep abreast of issues in other cities around the nation.

Mayors were generally expected to issue proclamations, but many of them regarded this tradition as an obligatory but distasteful task. A born promoter, Willard embraced this official act with enthusiasm, using proclamations as a bully platform from which he declared hundreds of special days, weeks, and months during his tenure as mayor. Sometimes his special weeks concurred with national ones—National Crime Prevention Week, National Camp Fire Girls Week, and Fire Prevention Week—but Mayor Fraser often created his own. During his first week in office, he designated the week of May 7 as Be Kind to Animals Week. He declared February 1965 to be American History Month; designated April 6, 1965, as Police Officers Memorial Day; and appointed that same week Barbershop Harmony Week. In 1964, Shakespeare Week marked the bard's birthday in April, and in June there was Teenage Safe Driving Week. Billings residents learned that their mayor had once played the Wall in a performance of *A Midsummer Night's*

Stuart Conner served one year as Mayor Fraser's first city attorney. Conner remained a close friend and trusted advisor to Fraser for the remainder of Fraser's career, and the two shared an abiding interest in archaeology and American Indian cultures.
Courtesy Stu Conner

Dream at the University of Colorado.[8] Willard confessed, "I hate cut and dried proclamations so I always try to put a little life, history, and warmth into mine."[9] Accordingly, in his proclamation for July 4, 1964, he wrote, "I direct and order that at the solemn hour of 11:00 A.M. on the 4th day of July, that all bells, chimes, sirens, whistles, and all other implements capable of glorious noise making, sound out for a full five minutes at that given moment. Let these five minutes fill the air with joyous and lusty confusion, and at this moment, let everyone proudly proclaim, 'I am an American.'"[10] This, like other proclamations, allowed Willard to vocalize his core beliefs without waiting for a formal speech opportunity.

While issuing proclamations drew attention to Fraser's values and interests and certainly added to his media coverage, the new mayor did not lose any time in making more substantive improvements throughout the city. Fraser was an idea man, and he often discussed ideas with close friends and colleagues who could provide support or offer cautionary advice as needed. He found these qualities in his first two city attorneys, Stuart Conner and James Thompson.

Through his past involvement in the Billings Archaeological Society, Willard had become acquainted with Conner, one of the society's founders. Conner moved back to his hometown of Billings in 1955 after a short career as a special agent for the FBI. At that time, the two men did not share a common political view. Conner had run an ad supporting conservative Republican Orvin Fjare in the 1955 congressional race, but he later switched to the Democratic Party. In May 1963, Fraser named Conner his first city attorney. Conner immediately became a trusted advisor whom Willard compared to Earl Morris, saying that Conner had "the same sensitivity and ability to do original thinking."[11] Decades later, Conner admitted that before he knew Willard, he, like others in town, viewed Willard with amusement because of his colorful persona and for the times he took positions vastly different from those of the rest of the community. Working with Mayor Fraser, Conner learned otherwise. "Once I knew the depth of his understanding of people and their needs, I had nothing but admiration for him," Conner recalled. "He was a VERY intelligent guy, and he never met a stranger."[12] Willard consulted Conner on his political appointees, depended on him to write city ordinances, and regularly sought his counsel, calling him "the right arm of this administration."[13] Unfortunately, Conner's private practice suffered because of the time required as city attorney—then a low-paid, part-time job—and he resigned in April 1964. Conner continued to be a lifelong friend and advisor to Willard and became a noted Montana figure on his own merits.[14]

After Conner resigned, Willard selected young James Thompson to replace him. Thompson had graduated from law school in 1962 and met Fraser in 1963, when Stuart Conner recommended him for the assistant city attorney position. As city attorney, Thompson met with Fraser nearly every day and attended to city legal matters. He participated in city council meetings and filled in for Fraser at funerals and other functions when Fraser could not be present. After two years, Thompson also found that the part-time city attorney position interfered with his private practice, and he resigned. Willard's response was, "You may be off the payroll but you're not off the job."[15] He kept Thompson involved politically by appointing him to various boards over the years, writing in one recommendation that Jim was "a man with a great sense of social justice and need without the least being 'soft headed.'"[16]

Fraser sometimes referred to Stu Conner and Jim Thompson as his "legals," and he valued their advice, friendship, and occasional chauffeuring throughout the remaining years of his life. Willard acknowledged his dependence on them in a letter he wrote before a planned stay in Yellowstone Park some years later: "As always, I will bring my two legal beagles and their wives, as it gives us a chance to do a lot of chewing over things that need to be chewed over; so again, hold a room for Stuart Conner and Jim

James Thompson, pictured here with his wife, served as Mayor Fraser's second city attorney and became Fraser's lifelong friend. Billings Gazette, Jun. 27, 1965

Thompson and wives, and myself."[17] Both men worked on Willard's future campaigns and, in a final act of love and respect, both would be pallbearers at his funeral.

Billings' new mayor was not content with maintaining the status quo—particularly when new scientific evidence or best practices justified improvements. He soon applied these principles to the police department. To evaluate applicants for the police force, Fraser added the Minnesota Multiphasic Test to the battery of intelligence tests and other screening measures already in place.[18] The test is a personality inventory used in the diagnosis and treatment of mental illness, but it is also used as a screening instrument for some professions. Commenting decades later, Billings psychiatrist Donald Harr said that the test generated a description of an individual's personality, their integrity, and tendencies toward anger, violence, or paranoia. "It gave a reasonable understanding of the individual's approach to people," Dr. Harr noted.[19] A psychologist would interpret the test results, and then Harr would meet with Fraser to discuss whether the tested individual would be a suitable police hire. Fraser recommended the test to officials in other cities several times over the years, writing to Great Falls mayor Marian Erdmann in 1965, "As a result I promoted a sergeant to Chief over the heads of quite a number of people."[20]

In step with societal changes happening across the nation, Fraser worked to ensure his leadership reflected up-to-date attitudes. During Fraser's first term, the city's police department hired its first woman police officer, Lora Lunnen, who may also have been the first policewoman in Montana, because Fraser said that young women were reluctant to speak to male officers. When Lunnen had to resign because of ill health, Delores McClure replaced her. Chief John Beven called the pioneering act of hiring female police officers "an experiment," but it was an experiment that lasted.[21]

This trend continued in other appointments. When Bernadine Jovanovich was voted in as Billings' first woman council member in 1967, Willard announced that he was pleased that he could now put a woman on a standing committee, saying, "Billings women should now be happy, and when they are happy, I am happy."[22] Later, Fraser appointed Republican Jean Bowman to the Air Pollution Advisory Board and later the Air Pollution Control Board, while selecting Democrat Jean LeBar to serve on the City County Planning Board. By the time Willard entered his third term, he received praise for the number of women he had put on city commissions.[23]

Undoubtedly Fraser's progressive attitude toward women owed quite a lot to his mother. Sadie was committed to the women's suffrage movement in the early twentieth century.[24] Her home state of Kansas had given women the right to vote in 1912, and Montana's women became voters in 1914, the same year the Frasers became Montana residents. Three years later, voters sent Jeannette Rankin to Congress. Sadie Fraser's participation in local politics, her active involvement with Montana's Federation of Women's Clubs, and her own capable character likely inspired Willard's confidence in women's competency. Upon congratulating a colleague on appointing a woman to a local board, Willard wrote, "If it wasn't for the women, we men would still be out in the hills, lying on our backs, watching the clouds go by, spending our hours dreaming on the springtime weather."[25]

In another first, Willard solicited the service of a Spanish translator to facilitate communication between the city's Spanish-speaking residents and police officers. He estimated, conservatively, that about one thousand people of Mexican ancestry lived in Billings at the time he instituted this policy.[26] Most of these citizens would have been residents of the South Side, Willard's home turf. [27]

The mayor did not waste any time setting in motion his major goals of improving Billings' physical appearance and expanding the city's recreational and cultural opportunities. On May 7, 1963, the day of his inauguration, Fraser sent a news release to the *Gazette* announcing an Urban Renewal Committee that would collaborate with a soon-to-be-formed City Planning Committee to revitalize Billings. He was undoubtedly encouraged in this undertaking by hearing of similar efforts from mayors at the U.S. Conference of Mayors he had already attended. Beginning with the Housing Act of 1949, federal loans were available to cities to develop and improve cityscapes. The term "urban renewal" came into use with the Housing Act of 1954. While promoted as way to rejuvenate distressed areas within cities, urban renewal efforts nationwide often resulted in the displacement of entire neighborhoods and the destruction of historic buildings. Between 1950 and 1980, about 7.5 million dwellings were demolished in the United States. Boston lost one-third of its old city buildings.[28] In Montana, Helena alone witnessed the demolition of 228 buildings, including many Victorian-era structures comprising much of the city's historic downtown district.[29] In contrast to such destructive approaches, the best form of urban renewal encouraged renovation and reserved demolition for only truly decrepit buildings that posed a safety hazard. Prioritizing restoration over demolition, Fraser's Urban Renewal Committee worked to halt deterioration of historic neighborhoods and downtown structures. The committee also studied interstate highway programs and considered relocating the Northern Pacific Railway tracks that bisected the town—all in a push to revitalize the city's economy and image.[30]

In conjunction with urban renewal, Fraser was committed to getting rid of rundown properties. Within two months of gaining office, Fraser put city attorney Conner to work drafting an ordinance to establish minimum housing standards, which would include a kitchen sink and a flush toilet in every residence. Fraser declared war on the "horrible messes" found in the city, and condemnations were issued for open privies, dilapidated shacks, junk cars, abandoned refrigerators, and piles of refuse.[31] He applied his aesthetic sense against blight by writing letters to offenders, telling one citizen, "[You] promised me that you would get that shed, and other types of 'crap' removed."[32] Memos to department heads requested action on weeds, potholes, cockroaches, and general "filth." At the end of his first term, Fraser counted such cleanup as one of his greatest accomplishments.[33]

Willard had promised to solve the nuisance of the "pesky, noisy, messy" starlings at the public library, a task that turned out to be more challenging that he anticipated. This seemingly minor problem earned considerable coverage in the press during Fraser's first term, and various methods were tried, including the application of an ammonia and detergent spray, broadcasting high-frequency sound recordings, and placing a mock owl, Oscar, on the building. One resident suggested a bourbon-soaked pea solution, but the mayor finally resorted to poison.[34] The starlings at the library were no more, but they reappeared a few years later.

Simultaneously, Fraser focused on the city park system and city streets to improve Billings' aesthetic appeal and to provide expanded recreational opportunities. He worked with park superintendent Vern Prill to upgrade Swords Park atop the Rimrocks, tried to establish a municipal golf course, and proposed a beginner's ski run at Pioneer Park. The last two endeavors never materialized, but during Mayor Fraser's tenure, the city's designated park acreage doubled. As part of his beautification program, Fraser also embarked on a tree-planting project. Park department employees planted 455 trees of twenty-two varieties—including his favorite, gingkoes—at city parks during the spring of 1964.[35] His plan to replace the aged cottonwoods on Poly Drive along the base of the Rimrocks generated controversy at first, but Fraser persuaded the city that the rotting cottonwoods were "dangerous death traps."[36] In the spring of 1966, in honor of Arbor Day, the mayor was photographed in a mock planting of one of fifteen Norway maples that replaced some of the two hundred cottonwoods.[37]

An avid promoter of the arts, Fraser attended the February 10, 1965, premiere of Gates of Hell, *a film production by Billings resident M. Brooks Fitzgerald. Pictured with Fraser are, left to right: musician Bob Fitzgerald; actor and Cooke City carpenter Milton Sales; Rocky Mountain College's dean of men, Ernest Dibble; and Robley Lawson, RMC's music director.* Dennis Calkin, photographer. PAc 2003-07.75, MHS Photograph Archives, Helena

Recognizing that art and culture enrich a community, Fraser was an enthusiastic supporter of the arts in Billings. He displayed paintings by Montana artists on his office walls, installing new work periodically. At various times, busts of Robert Frost by James Masterson, Chief Plenty Coups by Dolly Felt, and John F. Kennedy by modernist Bill Stockton sat on his desk. Willard counted Western artist J. K. Ralston and cartoonist Stan Lynde among his close friends, and he promoted the art of other Montana artists, such as landscape artist Leroy Greene, watercolorist Jim Haughey, and sculptor Lyndon Pomeroy.[38]

In December 1963, Fraser traveled to Cheyenne, Wyoming, to speak at the unveiling of Ralston's *The Fetterman Fight*, saying it was "an important gesture to show we were cognizant of his ability now because he will rank as one of the great western artists."[39] The painting depicts an 1866 battle in which General William Fetterman and seventy-nine soldiers were killed by a confederation of Lakota, Cheyenne, and Arapaho warriors at the outset of what became known as Red Cloud's War. The Indigenous victory shut down the Bozeman Trail, which had been the main route from the plains states to the goldfields of southern Montana Territory. Later, Fraser used his influence to have another of Ralston's paintings, *Into the Unknown*, which portrays Lewis and Clark embarking on their expedition, installed in the Jefferson Memorial in St. Louis, Missouri.[40]

Mayor Fraser's dedication to the arts extended beyond mere appreciation, and in 1964 he voiced his support for creating the Yellowstone Art Center, now the Yellowstone Art Museum. For many years, Billings-area artists and art enthusiasts had sought to establish a repository and learning center for local artists, including an emerging group of Modernists such as Isabelle Johnson and Bill Stockton, whose avant-garde methods and works pushed the boundaries of authentic "Montana" art.[41] Since 1954, the Billings Art Association (BAA), a Yellowstone County affiliate of the Montana Institute of the Arts, had attempted to secure support and funding to turn the historic Yellowstone County jail into an art center, but city voters repeatedly rejected the bond. In May 1963, the newly elected mayor encouraged the BAA to keep fighting for their cause, telling its members, "The end result of mankind's achievements thru the ages has been exemplified and remembered in its art. My administration intends to honor and extend an understanding and appreciation of the arts in all the many forms that it may take in this—our industrial, atomic age; so, to the artists tried and trying, let me say, 'I am your partisan.'"[42]

Over the next year, Willard worked with BAA members John Self, Walter Woodcock, Bob Fehlberg, Donna Forbes, Virginia Snook, and Isabelle Johnson—among others—to promote the art center. Armed with petitions and offering locally solicited funds as proof of community support, the BAA approached the Yellowstone County commissioners. Fraser lent his support by advocating for the project. "Persuasion by Woodcock, Bob Fehlberg and especially by . . . Mayor Willard Fraser and the promise of an army of volunteer laborers convinced the commissioners of the [project's] viability," a BAA newsletter notes.[43] In 1964, the city and county approved the conversion of the former county jail into an art center.

When a *Chicago Tribune* article stated that in Florida a jail had been turned into an art museum for the first time, Fraser promptly sent a three-page letter to the reporter to detail how the Billings community had come together to create their art museum. He described sitting next to the head of the contractor's union in Billings on a flight to Denver and persuading him to put contractors to work on the old jail during their winter slow time. "Women's organizations, service clubs, labor unions, high school groups, college men and women, architects and artisans—in fact, people from every single walk of life in one way or another added their bit toward our museum," Willard wrote.[44] A year later, he proclaimed a Yellowstone Fine Arts Week and recommended that citizens visit the art museum once a month.[45]

While championing contemporary and regional artists, Fraser also admired the works of nineteenth-century Western masters. Two of the earliest artistic chroniclers of the West—painters George Catlin and Karl Bodmer—attracted Fraser's appreciation for the historical and artistic importance of their work. Both artists had traveled through the upper Missouri River region in the 1830s. Their paintings depict the Indigenous inhabitants and natural landscapes of the northern Plains prior to the general encroachment by EuroAmericans. Inspired perhaps by an April 1965 Catlin show at the Whitney Gallery in Cody, Wyoming, Willard wrote to the Smithsonian in September 1965 inquiring about the possibility of a Catlin display at Billings' new Yellowstone Art Center.[46] Consequently, in July 1966, the center held a show of forty Catlin paintings. A proud Willard wrote to archaeology friend J. O. Brew in Boston telling him of the exhibit and inviting him to visit.[47] A few months later, he wrote to the Joslyn Art Museum in Omaha asking about the possibility of a loan of their Bodmer collection.[48] The Montana Historical Society in Helena had exhibited some of Bodmer's watercolors and sketches in 1964, but there is no record to indicate that Willard succeeded in bringing the Bodmer show to Billings.

Willard's passion for the arts caught the attention of a writer for the White Plains, New York, *Reporter Dispatch*, who wrote an article in 1969 beginning, "Anyone who is not sufficiently persuaded of the possibility that politicians and poets can actually work together should consider the case of Willard E. Fraser." The article went on to detail how Fraser persuaded local contractors to help convert the old jail into an art museum. Fraser told the writer that one of the works on his office walls was of a nude painted by a former police officer, George Cunningham, who took up painting after suffering a heart attack. On the policeman's transformation, Fraser commented, "Today he is known as the Grandma Moses of the Billings Police Department. . . . When I reach the bar of heaven and St. Peter says, 'What accomplishment did you achieve as mayor?' I am going to say, 'I made an artist out of this policeman.'"[49]

While working to make his beloved city safer and more attractive, Fraser employed myriad methods to promote Billings—inviting organizations to hold conventions in town, plugging the city and Montana in local and national publications, fostering projects that brought attention to the area, and enticing noted people to visit. When the Montana Tuberculosis

Association planned a banquet for their fiftieth anniversary, Willard, knowing that astronaut Scott Carpenter was national honorary chairman of the association, led a movement to invite Carpenter to Billings. Fraser declared that it would only be fitting for Carpenter to visit Montana, as many explorers before him had. Carpenter replied, "To date, I have received five letters urging acceptance, and I just can't decline under such pressure."[50] April 22, 1965, declared "Scott Carpenter Day" by Mayor Fraser, seemed the perfect Fraser-orchestrated event. There was a reception with music at the airport; a parade featuring Carpenter and his wife, Governor Babcock, and Mayor Fraser; a talk on the courthouse lawn at which Fraser was master of ceremonies; and the banquet itself.

To entice out-of-town visitors to spend time (and money) in the city, Mayor Fraser aimed to "make Billings a friendly town by issuing courtesy tickets." Just a month into his first mayoral term, Willard worked with the chamber of commerce to issue courtesy parking tickets to convention-goers. The tickets bore the words, "Welcome to Billings. Mayor: Willard E. Fraser." In another gesture, on St. Patrick's Day in 1965, Fraser declared that drivers of green cars could park free while drivers of orange cars had to pay double at parking meters.[51] This tinkering with parking tickets morphed into a wholesale forgiving of tickets for out-of-town visitors as a public relations move that continued into Willard's third term, when the overly generous mayor was reported to have forgiven more than 750 traffic tickets in one year.[52] The city council objected to the lost revenue and what they saw as the mayor's abuse of power, and councilmen eventually took legal steps to halt such generosity. No longer able to honor the stream of requests to forgive tickets, Willard responded to one such request with a one-line letter, "The judge says you have to pay."[53] The city later made allowances for convention-goers, but the matter pointed to simmering tension between the mayor and his councilmen.

Fraser particularly relished welcoming national political figures to Billings. Four months into his tenure, the mayor received the first of many political dignitaries when President John F. Kennedy visited in September. Fraser, who had hoped to put on a parade for the president, initially objected to the "back door" route the Secret Service recommended for the journey from Logan Field to Midland Empire Fairgrounds, where Kennedy would speak. Rather than parading through downtown Billings, the motorcade traveled by Montana Highway 3 and U.S. 10 to reach the fairgrounds, thus avoiding twenty-five intersections and numerous buildings, all of which posed a security problem and took too much time out of the ninety minutes allotted for Kennedy's visit.[54]

Fraser enjoyed welcoming celebrities and visitors to Billings. Among those to visit during Fraser's first term was President John F. Kennedy. Left to right: Tom Kelly, Mayor Willard Fraser, Governor Tim Babcock, Senator Gale McGee (WY), Senator Mike Mansfield (MT), and President Kennedy. Carl Kubo, photographer. *Billings Gazette*, Sept. 26, 1963

Fraser shared the seating on the speaker's platform at the fairgrounds with Secretary of the Interior Stewart Udall, Wyoming senator Gale McGee, Montana senators Lee Metcalf and Mike Mansfield, Representative Arnold Olsen, Governor Tim Babcock, and Billings residents Mrs. Arthur Laney and Thomas Kelley. This was one of several times that Fraser and Udall appeared together in a political ceremony. Udall returned to Billings a few months later when Lady Bird Johnson visited, and both Udall and Fraser participated in the dedications of St. Louis's Gateway Arch and the Yellowtail Dam. Fraser and Udall also corresponded occasionally, and when Fraser was in Washington, D.C., he was apt to visit Udall.[55]

On October 16, 1963, Robin and David Hudnut met President and Mrs. Kennedy at the dedication of the Frost Memorial Library at Amherst College in Massachusetts, where the president delivered a memorial to the great American poet. Just a month later, Kennedy was assassinated in

Dallas. Robin called Willard in tears after the assassination. To an acquaintance Willard recalled the favorable impression the Kennedys had made on his daughter at the Frost Library dedication, writing "At the event, both Jack and Jackie were extremely kind and courteous to Robin and David so his death was more than the death of a President."[56]

Across the nation, a somber hush prevailed on Monday, November 25, as businesses and schools closed for Kennedy's funeral and Americans contemplated the horror of a presidential assassination. Mayor Fraser and city councilmen attended memorial services at the First Congregational Church as a group. On the same day, Willard joined Billings' Mexican American community in mourning at the South Side's Little Flower Church. At both services, Fraser delivered a short eulogy honoring the president. He read Robert Frost's "To a Soldier," which begins, "He is that fallen lance that lies as hurled . . ." and concludes, "But this we know, the obstacle that checked/ And tripped the body, shot the spirit on/ Further than any target ever showed or shown." He spoke to the "travesty of our time . . . for by all the laws of order and nature, young men should bury the old men . . . yet today . . . three aged Presidents are burying a young President." Fraser warned against the destructive power of hate, and said, "There should be no place in our America for those who would rule by the knife and the assassin's bullet." In conclusion, he read "The Gift Outright," which Robert Frost had recited at Kennedy's inauguration. Fraser mentioned at the close of the eulogy that the president had asked the poet to change the last line of the poem from "Such as she was, such as she would become" to "Such as she was, such as she *will* become."[57]

Later, Montana artist Bill Stockton sculpted a bust of John F. Kennedy, which the mayor kept on his desk for a time. Willard sent a photo of it to Jacqueline Kennedy and included the memorial address he had delivered at the Billings memorials. She responded, "Yours will always be the memorial address that means the most to me—yours and Senator Mansfield's will always be the only ones I can bear to remember."[58]

In the summer of 1964, First Lady Lady Bird Johnson visited Billings. As had been true of President Kennedy's visit, the day was carefully scheduled. She arrived at Logan Field on August 14 at noon accompanied by Maureen Mansfield, Senator and Mrs. McGee of Wyoming, and Secretary of the Interior Udall and Mrs. Udall. At the airport, she was greeted by Mayor Fraser and others, including Sadie Fraser and Betty Babcock, the wife of Governor Babcock. Fraser made a brief welcoming address, after which he presented a ceremonial key to the city of Billings to Lady Bird. The key was engraved with the city seal, which had been designed by Robin

Fraser.[59] Following this short reception, Lady Bird was taken for a five-hour tour of Crow Agency and the Custer Battlefield.

What happened next became fodder for national news and caused red faces for Montana's senators, but Fraser, unabashed, turned the awkward moment into positive press coverage. On previous occasions when Fraser had presented the key to other dignitaries—including the ambassadors of Denmark, Korea, and Mexico and the syndicated newspaper columnist Ann Landers—he had engaged in "a little fun and merriment" by saying, "Now you have the city's key in your hands, you must give it back, for I am just an Indian giver at heart."[60] This time, he omitted that reminder, and the First Lady kept the key. According to Fraser, newspaper columnist Addison Bragg heard that the mayor had not gotten the key back, and very soon "Bragg with his 'little black notebook and little black heart' came out in his column to say, 'The Mayor has lost the city's key, and the council's on the war path.' It hit the fan and I started receiving calls, letters, and keys from all over the world."[61] This was exactly the kind of gossip-tinged story that *Washington Post* correspondent Drew Pearson relished, and he covered the flap in his column. The incident was aired on the popular NBC evening news program, the *Huntley-Brinkley Report*, and the Associated Press

Fraser, standing behind the podium, listens as First Lady Lady Bird Johnson addresses a crowd at the Billings airport, 1964. The First Lady's visit made nationwide news when she accidentally kept the key to Billings presented by Mayor Fraser. Associated Press photo

Mayor Fraser reclaims the key to the city, which Lady Bird Johnson sent back to him with a friendly note. Addison Bragg, photographer. *Billings Gazette*, Aug. 30, 1964

distributed it in New York. Soon Montana's senators and the Johnsons were dealing with stories about the First Lady absconding with the key to Billings, Montana.

In a taped conversation between Senator Mansfield, Lady Bird, and President Johnson, the president read from an article titled "First Lady faux pas" in the *Paris Herald*, a newspaper favored by Americans living abroad, which stated that "in Billings, the frugal city fathers give the same key to all visiting dignitaries."[62] At one point in the conversation, the president referred to the "goddam key" that the City of Billings, apparently, wanted back. Mansfield advised the Johnsons to "forget it, to hell with them," and the three had a good laugh.[63] Later, in a public speech, President Johnson joked that he would have brought Lady Bird along, but he was afraid of what she might pick up.[64] Senator Lee Metcalf joined the fray when he wrote to Willard saying he would be "honored to replace the key to your fine city" so that Lady Bird could keep the key given to her.[65]

The story was kept alive when Lady Bird mailed the key back to Willard accompanied by an understanding note saying that she was married to someone who went around the White House turning the lights out. The *Gazette* featured a photo of a smiling Fraser displaying his key, but Fraser didn't let matters rest there. When Johnson retained the presidency by defeating Barry Goldwater three months later, Sadie Fraser attended his inauguration, and Senator Metcalf arranged a meeting during which Sadie presented Lady Bird Johnson and Muriel Humphrey, wife of Vice President Hubert Humphrey, with keys made of Montana agate that they could keep.[66]

Rather than being embarrassed by such national news coverage, Willard reaped the benefits of his and Billings's heightened public profile. The story about the key to Billings was featured on German television, and the mayor of Billings, Germany, interested to know about a twin Billings in America, contacted Mayor Fraser. The resulting correspondence produced an invitation several years later for Willard to speak at the laying of the cornerstone of the new Rathaus (city hall) in Billings, Germany, which he did on October 31, 1970.

During Willard's first term, Montana celebrated its territorial centennial. One central project was a Centennial Train that would travel from Montana to the World's Fair in New York City, stopping at major cities along the way on the thirty-day journey. The twenty-five-car train was loaded with displays to communicate "Montana's magnificence," including seventy horses, three hundred passengers, a stagecoach, paintings by Charles Russell and Frederic Remington, General Custer memorabilia, gold nuggets, and numerous other exhibits. The train departed from Billings on April 5, 1964, but Willard was not a passenger. When he attended a mayors' conference in New York in May, however, he presented Mayor Robert Wagner with Montana Centennial glasses.[67]

Willard Fraser inaugurated the Yellowstone River Boat Float—originally called the Mayors' Float— a 126-mile float from Livingston to Billings, coordinating with mayors along the route and the local Jaycees. In this 1965 photo are (left to right): Bob Gutierrez, Willard Fraser, Richard Glendinning, Russ Fillner, Debbie Canan, and Dick Brown. Courtesy Stuart Conner

Willard had his own plan for celebrating Montana's territorial centennial. A February 19, 1964, *Gazette* article began, "It's Montana's [Territorial] Centennial year and Mayor Willard Fraser has a new thought on how to do it up in a big way." His idea was to organize and lead a three-day boat flotilla procession down the Yellowstone River along a section of river navigated more than a century and a half earlier by members of the Lewis and Clark Expedition.[68] In accordance with his campaign promise that "Billings can only prosper as the area around it prospers," Fraser initiated the event to "bring the river's beauty and history to the attention of Montana residents." He invited his fellow river-city mayors—George Ommundsen of Livingston, Henry Klindt of Big Timber, Harold Nordahl of Columbus, and John Beslanwitch of Laurel—to float 126 miles down the river from Livingston to Billings in July. "There is so much beauty and romance, dating from the age of the Indian through the voyage of Captain Clark, that can enrich the lives of present and future Montanans," he said.[69]

Fraser persuaded local Jaycees to get involved, and with their help the Yellowstone River Boat Float—originally called the Mayors' Float—was launched in July 1964 with two dozen canoes, kayaks, and rubber rafts. Willard floated in a ten-man rubber landing craft from the Korean War, which had been acquired earlier by Willard, reporter Addison Bragg, longtime friend Charlie Borberg, and boyhood friend and future political rival Carl Clavadetscher.[70] His raft held cartoonist Stan Lynde and his wife, Fraser's nephew Mac Fraser, his son-in-law David Hudnut, his godson Ted Cross, and Billings Art Association chair John Self.[71] The Yellowstone offered enough white water to make the float exciting but not dangerous for the participants, who floated under bridges and past ranches, camping areas, historic sites, and side channels.[72] The three-day adventure featured riverbank breakfasts, barbecues at noon, and open-air sleeping. In this first float, Fraser was photographed using a personalized paddle to guide his raft, but this was mostly for show; prior to a later trip, Willard admitted he was the "only gentleman on our float—everyone else rows," because his asthma prevented him from such exertion.[73]

The next year, Stan and Jane Lynde sent a resolution to the "Hon. Willard E Fraser . . . Commander of the Flotilla and First Lord of the Admiralty" acknowledging that the flagship had been "improperly equipt [*sic*]" on its maiden voyage and offering to "rectify the breach of protocol, disregard of tradition, and flaring omission." The Lyndes then presented Fraser with an official "River Rat" flag designed by Stan (the "designer of heraldry and all-around American boy") and hand-sewn by Jane (the "doer

Adding to the pomp and fun of the Yellowstone River Boat Float, Jane and Stan Lynde presented Willard with an official "River Rat" flag in 1965. Dennis Calkin, photographer. *Billings Gazette,* Jul. 3, 1965

of hard work and Betsy Ross of the Big Sky"). Fraser flew the flag proudly, and the "River Rats" nickname stuck.[74]

True to his publicist soul, Fraser sent letters to travel and outdoor writers advertising the float, and he invited everyone he corresponded with—and they were legion—from near and far. One such invitation lauded the Scottish pipe band's "sad and soul-torturing tune" that sent the River Rats off and extolled the float itself. "When you add the piping to the joys and color of our float trip of the Yellowstone River—man, that is living!" Willard exclaimed.[75] His efforts resulted in a Who's Who of participants that included Captain William Clark's great-great grandson, Clark Adreon; Montana author A. B. Guthrie; and Florida writer Richard Glendinning. Fraser bragged that his boat in the 1967 float included a New York lawyer, a medical student from Stockholm, Sweden, a Presbyterian minister from Minneapolis, an authority on Lewis and Clark, Billings city attorney Jim Thompson, and Stan Lynde.[76] After one float, he reported to Salisbury that among the occupants of his boat were "a young fellow who is halfway between altar boy and Pope in his study for the Priesthood and a very voluptuous eighteen-year-old girl, who insisted on taking sun baths in the scantiest of bathing suits. . . . Visions of St. Anthony flashed in my mind, and I suspect it did in the embryo Priest['s] too."[77]

As Willard hoped, the float generated ample local and national media attention, including a full-page spread in the *Chicago Tribune*. Coverage of the float in the *Saturday Evening Post* was provided by journalist Anne Chamberlin, who participated in the 1966 float.[78] Fraser's papers include several letters to Chamberlin and one to A. B. Guthrie in which he relates an incident during the 1966 float. He and Anne had to leave the trip early, so at a bridge west of Columbus, they got off the boat, climbed a fence, and hitched a ride to town on the highway. This detour prompted Anne to say, "This is the first time I've ever gone hitch-hiking with the Mayor of Billings, or with any Mayor for that matter."[79] Apparently, the mayor

Fraser (right) and Sherry R. Fisher, chairman of the Lewis & Clark Trail Commission, at the Yellowstone River Boat Float in 1966. Dorris Whitorn played the part of Sacagawea on that year's commemorative float. Bill Whithorn, photographer. 2006.045.1963, Yellowstone Gateway Museum, Livingston

of Billings nicked himself on the barbed-wire fence, and the wound later became infected. Willard shrugged off his injury, telling Anne, "I'm simply not used to going under bridges with pretty girls in recent years."[80] The next year, when Chamberlin wrote articles on the Custer's Last Stand reenactment and Montana dude ranches, Fraser wrote and admonished her for abbreviating Montana: "It is a musical sounding word, and all the fun is taken out of it when it is abbreviated. Where is the fun in 'Mont.'?"[81]

In conceiving of the Yellowstone River float, Fraser was ahead of his times. Recreational floating was not especially common or popular at the time. The mayor had always promoted Montana as a tourist destination and maintained that the state could do more to encourage people to visit what he believed was the most scenic state in the union, a state that also had a fascinating history. Fraser put all his public relations acumen to work on advertising the float, and its media coverage boosted the economies of river towns, drew attention to Montana, and inspired the development of the state's river recreation industry. Decades later, floating and fishing on Montana's rivers has become a major tourist draw. Today the annual Yellowstone River Boat Float is one of Montana's most popular summertime events—albeit changed quite a lot since Willard's time. Mayors Landing in Livingston, named in honor of Willard and his fellow mayors, remains the launching point.

WILLARD'S zeal for promotion and improvement fueled his vision to get Billings going. During his first term, the energetic mayor began what became an ongoing campaign to clean up urban blight, enhanced the city's aesthetic appeal by planting hundreds of trees, conquered the starling problem at the library, reorganized the police department, directed the passing of bond issues for storm sewers and a new fire station, and facilitated bringing city water to the Heights. He collaborated with local groups to facilitate construction of the Yellowstone Art Center and with other mayors to initiate the Yellowstone River Boat Float. Drawing attention to Yellowstone County's spectacular scenery and rich history, Mayor Fraser put Billings on the map and attracted visitors and businesses. The city's residents, including many Republicans, voted their approval by reelecting Fraser in 1965. Nonetheless, Willard's boundless enthusiasm for progress prompted some aldermen to dig in their heels, and Mayor Fraser would go into his second term facing increased opposition from the city council.

CHAPTER TWELVE

"The Council continues to be obdurate"

BECAUSE of Mayor Fraser's enthusiastic salesmanship, Billings was in the news as it never had been during his second term. He maintained his busy travel schedule, saying it drew trade to Billings by keeping the city in the limelight. He brought conventions to Billings and attracted tourists, well-known politicians, and famous writers to the area. Willard also drew attention to Montana's rivers as key components in the state's emerging outdoor recreation industry by floating the Yellowstone and Bighorn Rivers multiple times and the Missouri River from Fort Benton to Fort Peck in the summer of 1966. In addition, Fraser's election as the president of the Montana Archaeological Society in 1965 and his nomination as Yellowstone Man of the Year in 1966 enhanced his reputation during his second term.[1]

While Mayor Fraser's frequently headstrong approach brought success in many ventures, it did not endear him to some of his city council members. *Gazette* reporter Sam Blythe had described the first year of Fraser's governance with the headline, "Year of Fun and Fight." The article captured Willard's joy in being mayor, but it also detailed the frequently adversarial relationship between the mayor and his council. In saying that Fraser "often did things his own way," Blythe expressed a reason for some of the most heated council objections to Fraser's ideas.[2] Councilmen regularly accused him of overreaching his authority and pushing ahead with an idea despite their objections. An example of their exasperation at Fraser's use of authority was when an alderman, learning that the mayor could perform weddings, exclaimed, "You mean he can marry people too? Oh, good grief!"[3]

Going into his second term, Fraser's central goal as mayor was to further his progressive vision for the city he loved, but once again the conservative makeup of the city council determined the success or failure of many of his planned improvements. His persistence and optimism had been tested by what he called an "obdurate" council throughout his first term, and the council was no more cooperative during his second.

In previous races, Willard had run as an independent, even though he was a known Democrat. However, the general nonpartisan approach began to change in the 1960s. In the 1963 city elections, two aldermen had run as Republicans, the other eight as independents, and one mayoral candidate, Bill Hagen, had run as a Republican. In 1965, other aldermen who had previously run as independents also aligned themselves with a party, and eight Republican and only two Democratic aldermen were voted in. Furthermore, Republicans had hoped to defeat Fraser, and they held a primary election to determine a Republican candidate for mayor, thinking that if Fraser faced only one Republican candidate, he could be defeated. This strategy failed. Fraser beat Republican John Self by 1,436 votes out of 17,413 cast. Perennial candidate Mike Kuchera came in a distant third. Kuchera, who had a checkered partisan history, ran as an independent. Kuchera had once been a Republican, but after he switched to the Democratic Party, he antagonized many Democrats by running against Roland Renne in the 1964 primary race for governor. Fraser was the only independent candidate to win an office in the 1965 city election, and the Republican dominance on the council signaled trouble for the progress-minded mayor.

Mayor Fraser's May 1965 inaugural dinner at the Northern Hotel featured both former senator Burton K. Wheeler and Governor Babcock as speakers. Wheeler spoke of his friendship for Fraser, who "was for me when it took guts to do so." Republican Babcock expressed sympathy for Fraser, noting that the mayor would "have the same problems I had" with party affiliations.[4] Democrats had controlled the Montana Senate in the 1963 legislative session, and Democrats controlled both houses of the 1965 state legislature. Considering the council's partisan leanings, defeated alderman William Jull echoed Babcock's statement: "All I can say is I'm sorry for Willard in the next two years."[5] The council would continue to be dominated by Republicans throughout Willard's next two terms, a situation that set the stage for frequent disagreements and even heated clashes between the mayor and the council.

Joseph Leone and Cornelius Riedl were the lone Democrats on the city council during Willard's first three terms. Leone, who had supported

Fraser in the 1963 election, nonetheless spoke out against Fraser's use of police cars in ferrying visiting movie producers and went on record to oppose city subsidy of the Western Transit bus system, which Fraser supported. However, by Fraser's second term, Leone had become a Fraser supporter and remained so. In the 1967 election, Leone threatened not to run because he felt helpless against the Republican majority.[6] He did run and remained on the council throughout Willard's terms, eventually becoming mayor himself.

That Willard operated in a conservative Republican environment was underscored in the November 1966 state elections when the GOP dominated Yellowstone County: voters sent seventeen Republicans and just one Democrat to the state legislature. Locally, the conservative Yellowstone Taxpayers Association joined the city council in challenging many Fraser-proposed programs and in opposition to most new spending projects. Among the Republican members of the city council, Howard Hultgren, Alvin Wendte, Allen Wharton, and Robert Glennen, later joined by Donald Baker, criticized Fraser continually. The Republican members of the council often dined together before the regular council session and were often unified in partisan opposition to Fraser.[7]

Fraser's asthma woke him to the health dangers of air pollution, but he also recognized it to be an environmental problem that had a negative effect on everyone. He used his mayoral standing to address this most obvious environmental problem of Billings. Even on this issue, he encountered resistance from the council. Years before Willard became mayor, the Montana Power Company had been formulating a plan that would deliver a double-edged result to Billings: locating a coal-fired steam electric plant in the city. While the plant would bring dollars and employment to Billings, it would also worsen the haze and air pollution caused by already-established industries. The Corette plant was formally announced in June 1963 and construction began in 1966. Its location on the river, just west of Sacrifice Cliff, not only detracted from the beauty of the cliff but also made it more likely that emissions from the plant would be trapped in the valley. Willard had no role in bringing the plant to Billings, but it, along with other refineries, became a target of his war against air pollution.[8]

Billings' air quality problem was verified by a 1965 report by an industrial engineer from the State Board of Health. The information that the city had a "significant" air pollution problem—largely due to the three oil refineries located in or near the city—did not move the council toward action to evaluate or address the situation.[9] When Fraser submitted a request to the city council to include $3,100 in the 1965–66 budget for an air

Two smokestacks, an elevated storage structure, and a water tower rise above the Great Western Sugar Company processing plant in Billings, ca. 1940. Mayor Fraser sought to curb the air pollution generated by industrial plants, including the coal-fired Corette power plant, but he faced stiff opposition from the city council. 941-126, MHS Photograph Archives, Helena

pollution study, the council denied it. Willard was "amazed and shocked."[10] He continued to fight for funds and ordinances to attack the air pollution created by the combination of industrial emissions and worsened by the city's location in a valley. In June 1966, Willard sought funds to enable litigation against industrial polluters. He declared that he had used a "soft approach" for three years but was now ready to take court action.[11] Only Alderman Riedl joined Willard in seeking a means to regulate industrial pollution. Reidl uncovered a state statute that allowed cities to take legal action against offending industries, and he urged Fraser to take action.[12]

Fraser apparently was not ready to abandon persuasive techniques. In July, the *Gazette* reported that after the mayor "worked for some time with it," an unnamed industry had installed a $250,000 control device.[13]

In September 1965, the council did approve Willard's request to ban smoking in the council chambers, a vote that must have pleased the mayor, who had banned smoking in his office during his first term. A huge No Smoking sign and an ashtray in the outer office bore a warning about the health effects of smoking. In his antismoking campaign, Willard was again ahead of national trends. Warnings on cigarette packages did not begin to appear until 1966, and not until 1969 were such warnings legislated. In a personal revelation to explain his vehement antismoking stance, he told Salisbury, "[To] die of shortness of breath is horrible. There have been many times when I, fighting for breath, have thought I couldn't survive another hour, but even so, I have never desired to end the struggle."[14]

While Willard's asthma could be life-threatening, he was capable of joking about it at times, such as when he said, "The only one they [medical people] have let me down on so far is asthma—and there is nothing worse than a politician short of wind."[15] More often, he didn't bother with humor when objecting to smoking and its effect on his health. Niece Wendy Fraser Augunas remembers him breaking her mother's cigarettes in half when she smoked in his presence.[16] During a press conference after he had returned to Billings from the "polluted East" in early 1965, he snapped at a reporter, "Put that cigarette out. I've had a hell of a week."[17] His opposition to smoking was justified. Not long after Willard met Stuart Conner, they attended an archaeological meeting where several members were smoking cigars in a closed environment. The next time he saw Willard, Conner was shocked to learn that his friend had spent ten days in the hospital as a result.[18]

Even without support from his council, Fraser continued his individual fight against air pollution. He banned burning tires at the city landfill, spoke to student and civic audiences about the issue, and continued to work for environmental legislation at the local, state, and national levels. He noted publicly that no Montana legislator was scheduled to attend the air pollution conference in D.C. in December of 1966. As a result, state senators Elmer Flynn of Missoula and Jack Rehberg of Billings did attend.[19] Willard did as well. Not until his fourth term was Fraser successful in putting pressure on the major industries in Billings to reduce their air pollutants, and even so, Billings' air quality continued to be a problem for several decades.

Fraser had long advocated creating a tunnel under the Rimrocks to provide expansion to the north. He foresaw that without a convenient link to the area above the Rimrocks, the town would spread farther to the west, creating a population far removed from the main business district. In June 1966, he appointed a Tunnel Committee to study the idea. Committee members concluded that the tunnel and the resulting growth north of town would preserve the downtown area as the "center of gravity" for Billings and would save the cost of new and larger water and sewer mains that would be required for a westward expansion. The committee asked the city council to request a feasibility and cost study from the Montana Highway Department. When the request was brought to the city councilmen, the *Gazette* reported on their response, "Most of the aldermen grinned when the Tunnel Committee report was read—some even snickered."[20] Despite Fraser's confident claim, "Time will see a tunnel under the Rimrocks in the area of North Park," it was not to be, and Billings has continued to expand westward.

More than fifty years later, after the growth of Billings had been concentrated toward the west, Fraser's tunnel proposal is perhaps his best-remembered idea, and the memory is not accompanied by a snicker. Dr. Donald Harr commented retrospectively about the tunnel, "First, it was expensive, and city and county were not willing to consider the cost. It was an idea that costs a lot in the present but could save a lot later on, but most politicians and business people tend to look at the present without contemplating the consequences later on. His ideas for the future were beyond what most people were willing to accept as reasonable, so they were ridiculed."[21] In 2018, South Side councilman Jim Ronquillo said, "When Fraser proposed it, the cost was $20 million. Years later, it was $60 million. Now it is $80 to $100 million and they're still talking about it. If the city had his vision, Billings would be a wonderful place."[22] Harrison Fagg, longtime Yellowstone County architect and politician, agreed that although the tunnel would have been expensive, it "would have made good sense."[23]

When the need for a new library for Billings arose during Fraser's second term, the mayor and the council again disagreed. The Parmly Library on Montana Avenue, built in 1901, was no longer adequate, and the city had to decide whether to build a new library or to renovate the vacated, warehouse-like Billings Hardware Company building. Willard was in favor of funding a new building on the Cobb Field location—a plan the *Gazette* called "grandiose." "We must not let our imaginations be chained in our approaches to our future," the mayor asserted in defense of his position.[24] The library board felt it was "prudent" to purchase the Billings Hardware building because it would cost less to renovate it than to construct a new building. The council sided with the board. Although Fraser finally supported the bond authorizing renovation of the hardware building, his dismay is evident in a letter: "Look at our library deal in Billings as a glaring example of the wrong way, the expensive way, to do a job. We paid $200,000 too much for that warehouse, lost a hundred jobs for Billings, and deprived the County of $57,000 a year in taxes. We could have built a really fine library for what we are going to sink into this warehouse which, of course, will hold books but will always lack an aesthetic touch."[25] The visionary mayor would have been happy with the new library Billings constructed in 2014, which won a library design award from the American Institute of Architecture and American Library Association in 2016.

Fraser's concept of the ideal city included plenty of recreation facilities and city parks. Although Willard himself was not a golfer, he thought that a city should have a municipal golf course. In early 1967, Billings had the opportunity to buy Lake Hills Golf Club for $470,000, to be paid for through revenue bonds. The council felt the financing was "just too risky" and rejected the option to purchase. A week later, Fraser asked the aldermen to reconsider. They stuck by their original decision.[26] Willard refused to let his dream of a municipal golf course die. He later wrote to John McDermott of the Golf Committee, "I'm not going to take the Council's inaction as a final judgment." Despite his avowal to secure a golf course for the city, it wasn't until 1974, two years after Willard's death, that the par 3 Exchange City Course opened near Mountview Cemetery. Today there are two courses open to the public, but no city-owned municipal golf course.

Occasionally, Fraser and the council did work together to achieve necessary improvements, such as when they agreed to install a storm sewer system for Billings in order to prevent flooded basements and streets such as the disastrous flood of 1937 had caused. This time, the project was temporarily stalled by the conservative Yellowstone Taxpayers Association. A bond issue for storm sewers had been approved by voters during Fraser's first term, but a lawsuit initiated by the association delayed it. During Fraser's second term, when the path to installing the storm sewers was cleared, it was necessary to apply for a grant from the Department of Housing and Urban Development to fund the amount added by rising costs. In a rare instance of cooperation, Alderman Allen Wharton and Mayor Fraser both worked with Montana's Senators Mansfield and Metcalf and Representative Jim Battin to secure grant money for the project. Work on the storm sewer system began in 1968.

The press took pleasure in highlighting conflicts between the mayor and the council in such headlines as "Fraser Flays GOP Alderman."[27] Third ward alderman Allen Wharton frequently led attacks on Fraser, as a 1966 headline, "Wharton Hits Mayor's Administrative Policy," suggests.[28]

Wharton was once described in the *Gazette* as a "well-known foe" of Fraser.[29] The newspaper noted in another article that Wharton "criticizes Fraser more frequently" than other aldermen did.[30] At times, Willard privately complained that newspaper coverage exaggerated the contentious relationship between him and his council members. Writing to a friend, he commented, "Sometimes I think that if the ordinary family breakfast conversation was reported as is the council meetings, the line at the divorce courts would reach from here to eternity."[31] His second city attorney, James Thompson, agreed. "I would read the newspaper account of the Council meeting the next morning and wonder if I was at the same meeting," he said.[32] Nevertheless, a fair amount of conflict between the mayor and his council was real.

Generally, Willard knew how to use the press to his advantage, and he rarely complained publicly about newspaper, radio, or television coverage. In a letter to Charlie Borberg near the start of his third term, however, he shared an experience with the media that seemed to merit a public admonishment, but there is no record of such action. Fraser wrote that KGHL had asked him to produce a tape about the city's approach to prostitution, "which I did, as likewise did the Chief, and the Judge. Then later, quite unbeknownst to us, they went and got a prostitute to give a tape. Then they spliced the tapes back and forth; so that when they ran them, it sounded as though the four of us were sitting together around the table in a very cozy coffee clutch discussing 'business opportunities' in Billings. Hardly ethical, I would say."[33]

While the council stymied many of the mayor's plans, Fraser used his position to address unsightly and unsanitary conditions

To publicize his efforts to make Billings cleaner and more attractive, Mayor Fraser rode with the city's sanitation crews once a year. Billings Gazette, Aug. 4, 1965

in the city, continuing his vigorous campaign to rid the city of ugly garbage, decrepit automobiles, ramshackle structures, unsanitary privies, and rampant weeds. He maintained that eliminating "shacks" addressed some social ills. To raise the consciousness of his constituents, Fraser rode on a garbage truck route once a year to inspect alleys for weeds and trash. The

Gazette was notified ahead of time of his planned ride, and a photo would appear in the *Gazette* of Willard emptying a garbage can.[34] In addition, he urged city employees to address substandard conditions by "knocking on doors." Rather than threaten offending property owners with legalities, he tended to write letters to them. Sometimes these letters were direct and unvarnished. Other times, he used a familiar Fraser tactic of establishing a common ground with the offender. For example, in a letter requesting the removal of a dilapidated shed, he told the recipient, "You and I have the interest and welfare of Billings deep in the very marrow of our bones."[35] Fraser never undertook bulldozing entire neighborhoods as happened in some cities, but his cleaning project was not a respecter of persons. In one sweep of the city to remove junk cars in 1967, a clunker belonging to city attorney James Reno was towed away.[36]

Sometimes Fraser's effectiveness derived from taking approaches that did not have to go through the council. For instance, in his effort to eradicate eyesores in the city, he decided that both the Calvary Cemetery of St. Patrick's Parish and the city's Mountview Cemetery needed sprucing up. Rather than bringing the matter before the city council, he wrote to Fr. John Dimke of St. Patrick's and cemetery superintendent Arnold Kautsky to suggest that prisoners from the city jail could clean up the cemeteries. He assured Father Dimke that the prisoners were not criminals, "but only fellows who have had a little more than average difficulty with the law, the bottle, driving, fisticuffs, and things of the general demeanor type. Real criminals go to the county jail." Fraser stated it would be better for them to be doing work than lying on their backs in the city jail, and the community and the church would benefit as well.[37] The *Gazette* noted that city jail prisoners had been used in the past at city parks and had been put to work cleaning up the grounds at Indian Caves, a nearby archaeological site. When Fraser took city officials on a tour of nine city parks, two prisoners were raking leaves and doing other maintenance alongside park employees at Rose Park.[38]

Addressing another environmental situation, Willard wrote a long letter to the secretary of the Montana Livestock Association about the smell of the manure produced at the Billings auction, saying "Good air is everyone's business." He admitted, "Naturally, an operation of this type cannot eliminate all odors, and the Mayor of Billings and the people of Billings are well aware of the biological processes of animals confined in stockyard enclosure." However, he stressed that manure contributed to the fly population, and he asked that a system be created to dispose of the manure as efficiently as possible.[39]

Fraser took a stance on environmental problems caused by livestock outside the city as well. After observing large feedlots along the river west of Billings, he wrote to the director of the Division of Environmental Sanitation in Helena to express concern about the potential of nitrogen from the manure deposits running into the water during a rainfall.[40] Fraser complained he had "only his persuasive power" to clean up properties outside the city's boundaries. He applied this power to a statewide situation when he wrote to Governor Babcock to ask him to nudge the highway department to get rid of a junkyard on the road from Billings to Pryor.[41]

The summer of 1965 offered Willard a brief respite from city politics when he joined the last float trip down the Bighorn River before construction began on Yellowtail Dam. Organized by the National Park Service, the trip began in Lovell, Wyoming, and the group spent four days navigating the sixty-five miles down the Bighorn Canyon. The main purpose of the trip was for representatives from Montana and Wyoming to identify potential recreational opportunities in the area once the dam was constructed and the area opened to visitors. The twenty-nine people in the six boats making the trip included Wallace Iron and Edison Real Bird, representatives of the Crow Tribe; Cal Taggart, the mayor of Lovell; members of the Wyoming Highway Department; and representatives of the Wyoming and Montana Fish and Game Departments.[42]

Initially, only Fraser and Grant Salisbury had been invited as part of the limited number of floaters, but Willard showed up with several additional friends—including Dr. Donald Harr, Stuart Conner, and Charles Borberg and his son, Bob. Conner remembered that the park official tried to tell those who did not have an invitation to go home, but Willard wasn't hearing it. "Willard wouldn't have even the slightest hint of accommodating the government. If he was going somewhere and going to have some fun, he wanted his friends there," Conner recalled. "When you invited Willard, you unknowingly invited a whole bunch of other guys. By God, those were his friends and he was going to take them with him. That was the way it was with everything with Willard."[43] In the end, Fraser's friends stayed. The ferocity of the rapids on the third day, the camaraderie of the three nights camping, and the experience of being helicoptered out of the canyon on the fourth day were highlights of this float. Mayor Fraser's later promotion of the construction of a road to Yellowtail Dam was one result of the trip.

Following the Bighorn float, Willard engineered publicity for another issue close to his heart—pollution in the form of littering. He had observed numerous discarded beer cans along the riverbank, so he wrote to the DuPont Company to ask if, to counter this "growing national problem"

Indian Caves, ca. 1937. Fraser's desire to involve the city in protecting Indian Caves, a significant archae-ological site located a few miles from Billings, and his quest address environmental concerns beyond city limits drew the ire and opposition from city aldermen. PAc 2004-23.10, MHS Photograph Archives, Helena

of littered cans, they could invent a beer can that would decompose in twenty-four hours. His request generated articles in state and national papers as well as editorials in the *Chicago Tribune* and the *Kansas City Star*.[44]

Willard had pledged to be a fulltime mayor, and he lived up to that promise. As his nephew remarked decades later, "He was married to the City of Billings."[45] Like any marriage, this one had its rough spots. Fraser occasionally confessed to the challenges of dealing with those who opposed his ideas, such as when he wrote to a member of the Great Falls Chamber of Commerce to comment on the conflict inherent in governing: "There are so many problems and all of them having forty-seven sides plus your side, my side, and the side of the man next door."[46] But overall, Fraser relished his role as mayor and generally focused more on the "fun" than the "fight" aspect of his position. Remembering the strong opposition Fraser often faced, Dr. Harr commented with a note of admiration, "He could put it aside as if it didn't exist."[47] Rather than brooding over his difficult relationship with his council or the frustrations he faced in his job, Fraser applied his considerable energy to dawn-to-midnight days of activity, an approach captured later by Addison Bragg's article "Run, Don't Walk," which describes a day shadowing the mayor. The day began at 7:30 A.M. with a breakfast meeting and ended at 11 P.M. at a friend's house, where he borrowed a tam o'shanter to wear at a picnic the next day.[48]

Unfortunately for Willard, the city council was not the only group that challenged some of his ambitious goals. The mayor's efforts to make Billings the best city in America in every way did not always meet with cooperation from all his constituents. For example, Fraser knew that Butte and Anaconda had adopted Daylight Saving Time in 1964, and given the confusion wrought by different times in different Montana cities, he explored it for Billings by consulting with other city mayors. When put to referendum during Fraser's second term, however, the citizens of Billings voted against it. Fraser responded to a query with an air of disbelief:

> It is my unhappy duty to advise you that Billings does not enjoy Daylight Saving Time. I think we should, but unfortunately such a tirade was put on the radios when it was up for election last year that it was roundly defeated. Among the many nonsensical letters that I received was [this] one—and it was written in all sincerity—"Mayor Fraser, if you give us one more hour of sunshine, all you will do is burn up our crops, our days are too long now."[49]

This would not be the first time strident or uninformed voices would be a thorn in the mayor's side. Willard Fraser had been in office a mere six months when he optimistically began a crusade that would turn out to be one of the bitterest and longest-lasting battles of his tenure, one that would not be put to rest until the 1967 local elections. This time, the progressive mayor faced opposition from a large group of recalcitrant citizens, not the conservative city council.

"You haven't been in a fight until you've been in a fluoridation fight"

IN JULY 1966, midway through his second term, Mayor Fraser wrote ruefully to a friend, "You haven't been in a fight until you've been in a fluoridation fight. This is one that really brings all the squirrels down out of the trees—but fast."[1] In December 1963, a group of Billings-area dentists had stated publicly that fluoridation is "an invaluable tool in reducing tooth decay." Speaking for the group, Dr. L. L. Dailey and a second, unnamed dentist stressed that their purpose was to "let people know the whole truth" about fluoridation.[2] This well-intentioned move by the town's dentists to educate the public about fluoridated water initiated an intense controversy that stoked emotions and sharply divided Billings' citizens in a verbal and legal battle that lasted nearly four years. Backed by medical evidence and supported by local dentists, Fraser advocated for fluoridation with characteristic passion and humor—only to discover that the public is not always persuaded by scientific proof or the advice of experts. Alarmist warnings, controversial figures, and heightened emotions would play a major role in deciding whether the city of Billings would fluoridate its water.

Once dubbed "America's Longest War," the issue of fluoridating water began in 1945 when Grand Rapids, Michigan, fluoridated its water. Scientists and the medical professions lauded the dental and health benefits of fluoridation, and soon cities throughout the nation adopted fluoridation measures. Such efforts were met with controversy early on. One of the most prominent opponents was the John Birch Society, an ultraconservative advocacy group, which proclaimed it was a Communist plot to begin to take over the United States through mind control.[3] This sentiment was picked up by writer-director Stanley Kubrick in his 1964 satirical film *Dr. Strangelove*, in which General Jack D. Ripper, a paranoid anti-Communist, becomes increasingly deranged as the film progresses.[4] At one point in the film, Ripper explains the evils of the fluoridation "conspiracy" to character Lionel Mandrake:

> Ripper: Mandrake. Mandrake, have you never wondered why I drink only distilled water, or rainwater, and only pure-grain alcohol?
> Mandrake: Well, it did occur to me, Jack, yes.
> Ripper: Have you ever heard of a thing called fluoridation. Fluoridation of water?
> Mandrake: Uh? Yes, I have heard of that, Jack, yes. Yes.
> Ripper: Well, do you know what it is?
> Mandrake: No, no I don't know what it is, no.
> Ripper: Do you realize that fluoridation is the most monstrously conceived and dangerous Communist plot we have ever had to face?[5]

Indeed, such an argument was made by opponents of fluoridation in Billings, who contended that it was a forced medication, a poison, and part of a Communist plot to take over the world.[6] These were just some of the extreme arguments against fluoridation that the Billings-area dentists sought to dispel.

Initially, Fraser did not espouse fluoridation, but he did show his hand when the *Gazette* quoted him saying that an acquaintance of his was raised in one of the first cities to fluoridate its water supply, and that person had no cavities.[7] A few days later, "history buff Fraser," anticipating objections to fluoridation, referred to those Americans who, when refusing to receive a smallpox vaccination in the late 1700s, said it was God's will if people died of smallpox. Fraser was quoted in the newspaper as saying he liked to think it was God's will that provided the remedy for smallpox.[8]

In 1954, a federal bill to prohibit federal, state, or local agencies from treating water with fluoride had been defeated in Congress. The result was that fluoride additions would be decided by local governments.[9] In early 1964, Mayor Fraser appointed an advisory committee composed of doctors, dentists, and pharmacists with the clear hope that the committee would recommend fluoridation. "Can we as a progressive city continue to deny our children this benefit?" he asked.[10] The committee did indeed recommend fluoridation, and Fraser asked the city council to approve fluoridating the city water. As part of his request, he submitted a memo demonstrating that he had "done his fluoridation homework," citing twenty-seven organizations and sixty-eight accredited medical colleges that favored fluoridation. He pointed out that twelve hundred American cities, including thirty-nine in Montana, fluoridated their water.[11] Armed with such information and statistics, Fraser must have felt optimistic about accomplishing his goal of fluoridating city water. Rather than taking action, however, the council decided to poll the electorate on the issue. At the end of February 1964, the city enclosed 16,400 postcards seeking opinions on fluoridation with that month's water bills.

For the next ten days, the *Gazette* was filled with arguments for and against fluoridation, and it became evident that this was a highly contentious issue. Arguments against fluoridation ranged all over the map. Some opponents charged that fluoride would corrode the water pipes, while others contended that putting fluoride in the water violated constitutional rights. They also argued that it would be too expensive and even that it was a form of poison. "No rat poison in my water," wrote one man.[12] Water Department manager Ed Waldo, a proponent of fluoridation, received a letter threatening to poison him.[13] Fluoridation foes also distributed

Mayor Fraser at work, 1967, flanked by educators John Niemi and George Israel.
Fraser pushed for reforms that would safeguard public health and the environment.
Courtesy Western Heritage Center, Billings

literature that claimed fluoridation was a form of socialized medicine and an illegal practice of medicine that violated the pure food laws. State senator Henry Hilling (R) from Yellowstone County came out against fluoridation, saying it violated basic American freedoms.

In response to Hilling's argument, Billings lawyer William Bellingham retorted, "Every court of last resort in this country [that has reviewed the question] has ruled that fluoridation is a legal and proper exercise of governmental power and does not constitute an infringement of individual constitutional rights."[14] The editorial board of the *Gazette* came out in favor of fluoridation, as did the local Jaycee Board. Dr. Merwin Fry, president of the Ninth District Dental Society, comprising Yellowstone, Carbon, Stillwater, and Big Horn Counties, stated that adding fluoride to water was like adding chlorine to water to prevent disease, and he noted that it was approved by the American Dental and Medical Associations, the National Research Council, and state health departments. The Billings Citizens for Fluoridation paid for a huge, fact-filled advertisement in the *Gazette*, "Consider the Facts—Then Say YES to Fluoridation."[15] The ad counteracted claims of opponents with a list of eighteen questions and answers, giving information on statistics on decreased tooth decay, citing the World Health Organization's endorsement of fluoridation, and stating that the American Cancer Society had declared that fluoride does not cause cancer. Furthermore, the ad noted that the American Water Works Association had said it did not corrode water pipes, denied that fluoridation restricted religious freedom, and observed that twelve of the largest thirteen cities in the United States fluoridate their water.

The Billings public was split on fluoridation. Of the 16,400 postcards sent by the city, 9,012 were returned; 4,506 were against fluoridation, 4,063 were in favor, and 443 were neutral. Accordingly, after a sometimes-heated open meeting in early March 1964, the council refused to order fluoridation and "tossed the hot potato into the hands of the electorate" by recommending that the matter be voted on by the public.[16] Opponents to fluoridation circulated a petition to put it on the ballot for the next city election, in April 1965, but it failed to get enough signatures, and the issue was officially quiet for a time. Nevertheless, fluoridation was still on Fraser's mind, sometimes with wry humor. He wrote to a professor at Eastern Montana College, "I can't help noting that almost no one at Eastern knows how to spell 'fluoridation' or 'Fraser.'" He went on to say he forgave the students, but "I have yet to find anyone opposed to it [fluoridation] who can spell it."[17] Despite his light tone, Fraser had fought vigorously for the issue and wasn't about to let it go.

To counteract the arguments of the anti-fluoride group, Fraser waged his own war of words. In a response to an apparent accusation that fluoride was poisonous, he wrote that any substance could be dangerous if taken in too large quantities:

> Sunshine can be deadly. Albumin of an egg injected into your veins would kill you as quickly as rattlesnake venom. Were you to drink a cup of salt, you would be dead in a very short order, and a painful death, too. Yet if you fry that albumin of an egg and sprinkle a little poisonous salt upon it, it makes something that is nourishing to the body. So, too, with fluorides. The body needs a certain amount of fluorides, and when it is in less than required amounts, the body suffers such as in the instance of weaker bones in the aged or poor teeth in the young.[18]

When Willard Fraser ran for his second term as mayor in April 1965, he stood as a strong advocate for fluoridation. He still won decisively in all five wards, beating Republican John Self and perennial candidate Mike Kuchera. Having just been reelected, Fraser may have felt encouraged about his prospects for winning this round of the fluoridation war, but he also felt somewhat battle-scarred. In writing to the mayor of Laurel, he used his river experiences to create a metaphor about politics: "I feel a little bit like the rapids out of Livingston were sort of mild cascades compared to what I have recently been through, and I suppose you feel somewhat the same—but such is the political world. It's the white water though that really makes it interesting."[19] Fraser could not be accused of lacking a fighting spirit.

At the April 27 council meeting, outgoing council members Henry Cox and William Jull, who were in favor of fluoridation, introduced a resolution calling for the introduction of fluorides into the city's water system.[20] Cox thought a council vote would revive the issue and, if the opposition was strong enough, force a referendum. Fraser broke a 5–5 tie to enact an ordinance providing fluoridation of the city water supply, calling the act "a defeat for bigotry and ignorance."[21] With this news, however, the anti-fluoride contingent sprang back into full-throated action. The controversy would last for the duration of Fraser's second term, with vitriol emerging on both sides.

In Fraser's words, the issue did indeed "bring the squirrels down from the trees." As Aldermen Cox and Jull had anticipated, the opposition again circulated a petition with the intent of rescinding the council approval of fluoridation. Charges and defenses immediately flooded the radio talk shows and newspapers. The anti-fluoride forces were led by Francis Deisz, a Billings insurance agent, and his energetic and vocal wife, Leona. Their followers maintained that the council ordinance infringed on people's right to vote on issues. Among their other claims, the Deiszes contended that fluoridation would be a financial burden on the city and taxpayers, and that since fluoride is available in toothpaste and pills, people should not be forced to consume it in water.

Proponents for fluoridation made the point that lower-income families were not as apt to be able to take advantage of fluoride pills. In supporting fluoridation, Alderman Joe Leone reminded the public, "The late President John F. Kennedy, President Lyndon Johnson, and the surgeon general are for it, so who am I to be against it?" Not all fluoridation proponents were as circumspect. Alderman William Jull stated that while he didn't think everyone who was against fluoridated water was a crackpot, he did believe that some of them were "mentally deranged."[22]

Fraser's responses to letters from those against fluoridation could be sharp and impatient, especially when he felt they were ignoring accepted scientific conclusions. The fledging magazine, *Prevention*, received his scorn after an anti-fluoride activist sent him an article from the magazine. An entire Fraser letter to the Bozeman woman consisted of two sentences: "I cannot possibly imagine anyone with an R.N. even reading, let alone taking seriously, such a fantastically nonsensical magazine as *Prevention*. It sounds as though it is a magazine devoted to contraceptives."[23] Several months later, he wrote to a Wyoming woman, "*Prevention* magazine, in

Leona Deisz (left) and her husband, Francis, contended that fluoridation was part of a Communist plot. Right, aldermen Con Riedl and Norman Schoenthal listen skeptically to Deisz's testimony at a 1971 city council meeting when Deisz voiced a similar argument against updating the city building and zoning ordinances. Phil Bell, photographer. *Billings Gazette*, Nov. 30. 1971

my opinion, is one of the most irresponsible magazines ever to be sold on the market place of America, and it has helped fill the cemeteries of America with unnecessary deaths—deaths that could have been prevented by proper medical attention. We must use the intelligence and the brains that God provides to our medical research men, and failure to do so would be to castigate God—and this I'm not prepared to do."[24] Fraser's distrust of *Prevention* was overblown, but his reaction can be understood, given his medical history and in light of the gains medical science had made in his lifetime. As a survivor of the 1918 influenza pandemic and polio epidemics and as a chronic asthmatic, Fraser believed firmly in acknowledging and applying the advances of medicine and science.

Despite the fact that most of the aldermen favored fluoridation, they were ready to let the taxpayers decide the issue, saying they believed that the public should have a voice in a matter that affects all residents. By May 1965, a month after the council passed the fluoridation ordinance, the petition circulated by the Deiszes and other fluoride opponents had acquired the number of signatures—5 percent of eligible voters—to rescind the council's decision and call a referendum on fluoridation at the April 1967 city election.[25] Fraser expressed his frustration at the delay in a poem submitted to a nationwide city health officers' publication and printed in the *Great Falls Tribune*:

> Fools rant and we capitulate
> And drop our plans to fluoridate.
> We're easy to intimidate,
> Like timid souls we hesitate.
> While we sit and procrastinate
> Our children's teeth disintegrate.[26]

For a time, the fluoridation issue was somewhat quiet. In August 1966, fluoridation opponents Ann Roe and Francis Deisz, hoping to run for the state legislature, were defeated in the Republican primary. By this time, Francis Deisz was chairman of a citizen's organization called Billings Council for Free Rights and Pure Water, a group devoted to rightwing conservative positions.[27] Fraser credited voters with "scientific forwardness" for defeating Roe and Deisz, whom he privately called the "unholy opposition."[28] Perhaps emboldened by the voters' rejection of Roe and Deisz, Fraser and other proponents decided it would be preferable to put the fluoridation vote on the November 1966 general election ballot rather than waiting for the April 1967 city election. The general election would bring a larger voter turnout, and waiting until the city election would give the anti-fluorides more time to wage an intensive campaign against it. The Billings Citizens for Fluoridation accordingly circulated a petition to put the issue on the November ballot and garnered over five thousand signatures.

On behalf of the Billings Citizens for Free Choice and Pure Water, Francis Deisz responded by filing suit in district court to block a November vote and to affirm the April 1967 referendum. On October 11, 1966, district court judge Charles B. Sande ruled that the election must be held on the previously scheduled April date. The city appealed that decision, and the case went to the Montana Supreme Court, where Judge Sande's decision was upheld.[29] Over the following six months, a bitter campaign for and against fluoridation resumed in the press, on the radio, in letters to and from Fraser, and in door-to-door distributions of literature.

The debate was heated and sometimes ugly. Using humor, Fraser downplayed some of the personal attacks against him. Describing one such occasion, he wrote to his nephew Prescott Frost: "Somebody called my Mother the other day and informed her they were going to have to kill the Mayor if he insisted on poisoning people with this damned fluoride. . . . When I get such calls, I always say, 'Well, there are thirty-six ahead of you this morning but if you will get in line, I'll give you your chance.'"[30] While Willard himself could poke fun at the incident, it angered him that his mother, who had taken the call, was upset by it.

In his effort to put objective facts and the opinions of knowledgeable authorities before the public, Fraser solicited expert support from all quarters. Fraser himself went to Washington, D.C., to moderate a panel of the National Dental Health Assembly. There he met Harvard Medical School professor Dr. Frederick J. Stare, and within months, the *Gazette* received a letter to the editor from Dr. Stare that stated, "Fluoridation is one of the truly great advances of modern public health." Stare explained that fluoridation also helps retain calcium in bones, a considerable help to older people.[31] Fraser shared with the *Gazette* a letter he received from a Mormon and Public Health official in Brigham City, Utah, who wrote of the "progressive mayor, city council, and enlightened citizenry" who voted for fluoridated water in

VOTE THE AMERICAN WAY! VOTE THE FREE CHOICE PRINCIPLE! VOTE AGAINST FORCED FLUORIDATION

This advertisement paid for by the Citizens Committee for Free Choice and Pure Water. Francis Deisz, Chairman, Rev. C. A. Hallberg, Treasurer. P.O. Box 962, Billings, Montana.

Make Contributions to Rev. C. A. Hallberg

Excerpt from an anti-fluoride advertisement run by Deisz's Citizens Committee for Free Choice and Pure Water, 1967. Billings Gazette, Mar. 22, 1967

Brigham City.[32] Leaving few stones unturned, Fraser even wrote to the Medical Research Section of the Vatican to ask, "In this age of advancement and change, I am wondering if either Pope Paul, or one of the other more recent Popes had issued either directly, or through the Vatican Council, any information dealing with fluoridation."[33] There is no record of a response from the Vatican.

It wasn't just Fraser who spoke up in favor of fluoridation. A *Great Falls Tribune*'s editorial cited statistics of fewer cavities in children from Montana towns that had fluoridated their water, and ended with the statement, "Condition of children's teeth should receive first consideration."[34] Billings dentists and doctors continued to speak up in favor of fluoridation. One local dentist, Dr. Richard Prill, spoke to the local Optimist organization and showed a movie promoting fluoridated water by nationally noted pediatrician Dr. Benjamin Spock. James Reno, chairman of Billings Citizens for Fluoridation, did his best to publicize statements from recognized authorities who favored fluoridation such as Dr. C. W. Mayo of the Mayo Clinic and Dr. Albert Sabin, developer of the oral polio vaccine. Reno, Fraser, and other proponents of fluoridation consistently claimed that opponents were guilty of dispensing misinformation, and they sought to counter these inaccuracies with objective, demonstrable facts. The scientific evidence by reputable sources they presented far exceeded any comparable evidence presented by opponents, who tended to rely on anecdotal evidence, outdated information, and unsubstantiated, negative predictions.

At times, those leading the fight for fluoridation were overwhelmed by the frustration of trying to combat emotionally charged claims with fact. Reno occasionally succumbed to sarcasm. In an article headlined, "Anti-fluoridation Experts are Pretty Hard to Find," Reno charged that some of the doctors the anti-fluoride group cited could not be located. He added derisively, noting that "the ones we do locate are individuals who say they 'live on prune juice and seaweed.'"[35] Fraser became so exasperated by such politically charged statements made on radio talk shows by the opposition that in October 1966 he wrote to the Federal Communications Commission to inquire about the limits of free speech on the radio and asked for an investigation of talk shows. He informed the FCC that "certain individuals are calling each station, each day, repeatedly, and in their calls they charge that the dentists, doctors, the Mayor, and others pushing this program are at the very least Communist dupes." Fraser described one such incident involving a caller to a local radio station:

A man called into the program and said, "The big rush to get fluoride in is being financed by the Socialist Party. It is part of a big conspiracy, and I think the Mayor is being paid by the Socialist Party to promote fluoridation." A few days ago, a woman on this same station said, "Moscow has given orders to the Communists to have Billings fluoridated by 1967, and here are the names of the traitors who are carrying out Moscow's orders.[36]

Among the names mentioned were Mayor Fraser, city attorneys James Thompson and James Reno, and Russ Hart of Hart-Albin.

Both sides of the fluoridation proposal ran an extensive ad campaign promoting their positions. On March 29, the anti-fluoride Committee for Free Choice[37] placed an ad that consisted of eight questions and answers, such as "Q: Does the Committee oppose the treating of city water with chlorine?" ("A: Chlorination treats water to make it safe—fluoridation is designed to treat people.") and "Q: Isn't it true that the opponents of city water fluoridation are 'crackpots,' 'witch doctors' or 'extremists'?" ("A: Let those who hurl such charges name a single one.") Then, on April 1—just two days before the election—the opponents ran a more alarming ad. One segment carried the headline, "Mistakes of U.S. Public Health Service." The FDA approval of thalidomide and the resulting birth defects was mentioned, while other medications—lithium, some antibiotics, polio vaccines, imitation vanilla, sodium iodide—were listed without providing evidence of their alleged negative effects. Elsewhere, the ad linked "mongolism" with the accumulation of fluoride in a mother's body based on a 1956 French article, and it generally warned of huge hidden costs to taxpayers and property owners.[38]

The day before the election, the Citizens for Fluoridation upped the ante, running a full-page ad with the headline, "If You Can't Trust Your Doctors—Who Can You Trust?" It bore photos of thirty-six Billings doctors and dentists and a list of eighty-five doctors and dentists who "urge you to vote yes for fluoridation." It also included direct quotes in favor of fluoridation from twelve of the doctors, such as Dr. Kenneth Steffensen's statement: "The effectiveness and safety of fluoridation as a decay preventative measure has been well established."[39]

Fraser had to worry not only about the outcome of the fluoridation vote but about winning a third term as mayor. His opponents in the race were Republican Ted Lacklen and Francis Deisz of the Citizens Committee for Free Choice and Pure Water, who ran as an independent despite having run as a Republican in the 1966 primary for the Montana House. Alderman Wharton accused Fraser of running as an independent to avoid being responsible to anyone but himself, adding that neither party would have him anyway. Nevertheless, Fraser continued to eschew partisan politics in city government and declared that the 148 Republican signatures on his filing application were evidence of his bipartisan appeal.[40] Willard's declaration proved to be true. In the April election, Fraser earned his best plurality—47.8 percent or 8,503 votes—of his three elections and a 1,414 margin over second-place Republican Ted Lacklin, a notable accomplishment in a predominantly Republican city. Francis Deisz received just 2,113 votes—5,800 fewer than Fraser. An editorial in the *Gazette* noted, "Despite the hue and cry about discord in mayor-council relations, the voters returned Mayor Fraser and all but one councilman to office."[41]

The record turnout of 16,292 total voters in the 1967 city election may have resulted from widespread interest in the library bond and the fluoridation issue. The library bond passed, but fluoridation was rejected by 4,070 votes. City attorney James Reno, who had chaired Citizens for Fluoridation, said the outcome "was a triumph for ignorance and stupidity," a statement for which he was chided in a *Gazette* editorial. Seeking to calm the tension, the editors wrote, "This page has long advocated fluoridation, but we respect the intelligence of those who differ with us, and hope that in time their fear of fluoridation will be overcome and we can have fluoridated water for the children of this community."[42] After a nearly four-year battle, the city aldermen agreed that the fluoride issue was dead. "The people have spoken," declared council president Harold Hultgren.[43]

Reminiscing about the fluoride fight decades later, Dr. Donald Harr commented about one of the most vocal opponents of fluoridation, Leona Deisz: "She put out a lot of poisonous, false information that frightened people.... Fear can cause much damage."[44] There were no immediate quotes in the paper from Fraser regarding the stunning defeat of fluoridation, but when he spoke to a classroom of eighth graders several weeks later, he said simply, "Fear and hate defeated fluoridation."[45] However, his disgust at the unfounded claims and fearmongering of the anti-fluoride contingent was palpable in a letter to one of the opponents, in which Fraser lambasted the victory of fearful ignorance over medical evidence in one breathless sentence:

> I am always amazed in this age of technical knowledge [that] we have people who would disregard the advice of our knowledgeable medical men, but then I recall that thousands

and thousands of mothers had to die in childbirth because these same sort of ignorant people refused to accept the fact that doctors could save lives, and, of course, this has been repeated over and over again as thousands and thousands and thousands of people had to die of smallpox just because the silly ignorant minority would not accept the suggestions of the wise men of medicine, and these same people are today forcing thousands and thousands and thousands of children to suffer from toothache and thousands and thousands and thousands of elderly people to die of broken hips and other bones, heart attacks, and other unnecessary ailments because of the silly people who listen to the nuts among us say things about fluoride that are neither true, honest, Christian, nor just plain American decent.[46]

Early in the fluoride controversy, Sam Blythe had reported in the *Gazette* that the "normally scrupulously polite mayor was seen to lose his temper" over the stance of the fluoride foes.[47] While Fraser may have maintained his composure in public, this letter suggests his still sizzling anger over the fallacious arguments of the anti-fluoride crowd: he ended the letter with a single, short sentence: "The stuff you sent me is *pure* crap."

More than a half century later, fluoridation continues to be controversial, with heated argument on both sides of the issue. The American Dental Association and the American Medical Association are unwavering in support of fluoridation, and the Centers for Disease Control (CDC) cites it as one of the ten most important public health accomplishments of the twentieth century.[48] The CDC website states there is no credible evidence supporting the claims that it causes cancer, Down syndrome, heart disease, osteoporosis, low intelligence, Alzheimer's disease, allergic reactions, or autism as some opponents have claimed.[49] A 2008 article titled "Fears Over Fluoride" in the *U.S. News and World Report* concluded that while too much fluoride is harmful, too little causes tooth decay.[50] Most tap water in the United States is fluoridated at the CDC-recommended amount of 0.7 ppm (parts per million), and in 2014, it was estimated that 74 percent of Americans have access to fluoridated public water.[51] Nonetheless, some cities continue to vote fluoridation down. In 2013, the residents of Portland, Oregon, rejected a fluoridation measure for the fourth time after opponents—echoing the unproven claims made by Montana's opponents in the 1960s—cited concern about negative health effects and the argument that the state cannot make an individual ingest a chemical without that person's consent.[52] Since the Fraser-era fluoridation war in Billings, the controversy over adding fluoride to the city's water has reemerged from time to time, but as of 2020, Billings still does not have fluoridated water. It seems "America's Longest War" is not over.

Although the unsuccessful fluoridation referendum was a significant loss for Fraser, the ebullient mayor remained undaunted and optimistic about making Billings the best city in America. His inaugural dinner in 1967 featured a Scottish piper and a main address by Dr. Lawrence Small, president of Rocky Mountain College. The thrice-elected mayor spoke of what he referred to as the "accomplishments of the whole community working together," rather than the failed fluoridation proposal.[53] Not sidelined by obstruction, Fraser continued to broaden his network of supporters, peers, and friends by keeping up an impressive volume of communication. The multitude of letters and memos that he wrote as mayor served as an important instrument for dispensing his ideas and advice, building support for important issues, staying abreast of current events, and—of course—promoting Billings and Montana. Willard used his talents for communication to initiate new friendships and to instill in others his unflagging enthusiasm for the world.

CHAPTER FOURTEEN

"All it took was a five-cent stamp"

IT IS SAFE to say that Mayor Fraser gave more speeches, covered more miles, participated in more parades, and met with more Billings citizens than any previous mayor had. Without a doubt, he also wrote more letters. Enamored of words and possessed of an irrepressible urge to share stories and information, Willard penned letters to the famous and the ordinary, to those he knew and those he never met. He wrote about important and mundane topics, often dispensing advice, offering support, or requesting more information. Some of his letters now archived at the MSU–Billings Library simply share a humorous anecdote or express Willard's views on an issue. Many of them reveal his humanitarian values, and many more promote the virtues of Billings and Montana.

Willard Fraser loved language, and he used it with confidence and panache. At home, he stayed up late typing letters, and Robin often fell asleep to the sound of Willard's typing.[1] As soon as he became mayor, Willard bought a Dictaphone, a purchase that helped make it possible for him to churn out fifty or more letters a day. His secretary during his last term, Abby Ferguson, confessed, "It was hard to keep up. He was in the office before me and stayed after I left."[2] The blizzard of communications issuing from the mayor's office included not only the dozens of letters and proclamations his secretaries typed, but also the informal memos that Willard himself often typed. In August 1965 alone, he issued nearly one hundred such memos.

The range of topics covered in Willard's memos is head-spinning. He addressed the "salteric language of the landfill guy," flu shots for city employees, mud holes in front of the convent, weeds in various locations,

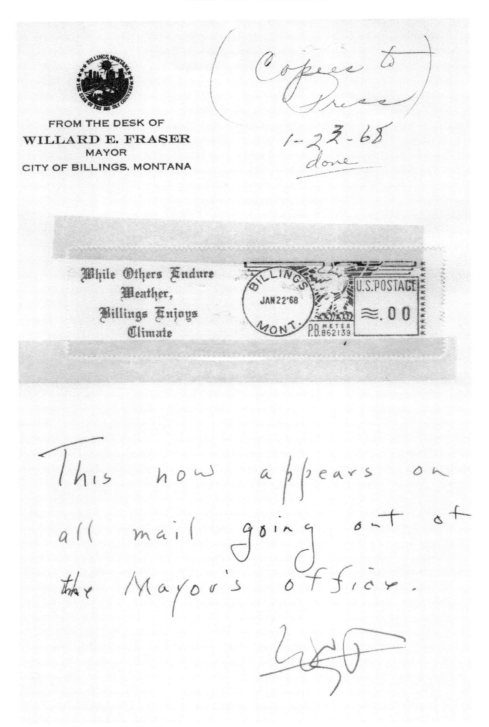

Willard Fraser churned out dozens of letters daily, and one of Fraser's favorite sayings became part of the postal mark during his tenure. Mayor Willard E. Fraser Collection, MSU–Billings Library

cockroaches in restaurants, speeding on city streets, and waitresses who defied sanitation by carrying glasses by the rim rather than by the sides. Most memos to department heads ended with "Let's get with it" or a similar call to action. Fraser even got involved in matters of dress. He wrote a memo to police chief Beven to say, "Why not have cotton-khaki-type pants as part of the summer uniform for police? It seems to me wool is pretty darned hot."[3] This suggestion was followed, and the police department adopted cotton trousers for summer wear.

Willard's letters were not the standard businesslike dispatches of a businessman or politician. They frequently ran several pages in length and veered from the business at hand to a gem of a story he'd heard recently and could not resist retelling. Occasionally, Willard's letters were short and to the point, as when he wrote to a Billings man, "You know, some night I wish you would invite me over for dinner. I have several matters I would like to discuss with you. Give me a ring so we can set a time. Mayor's rights you know."[4]

The mass of Fraser's letters preserved in the MSU–Billings Library go beyond giving supplemental information about his political activities.[5]

One of the many people Willard Fraser corresponded with regularly was U.S. News and World Report *editor Grant Salisbury (left), despite the two men's opposing political views. They are pictured together here floating the Flathead River.* Courtesy Stu Conner

They provide rich material to assemble a collage of Willard's personality, his philosophy of life, and the many relationships he forged. Grant Salisbury of *U.S. News and World Report* probably gets the prize for receiving the most letters from Willard, but Willard's correspondence reflects an array of other contacts—from college students to celebrities to mayors of other cities.

Like many of his other undertakings, Mayor Fraser's passion for letter writing got him into some trouble with the city council for exceeding his printing, stationery, and postage budgets. The previous mayor, Harold Gerke, had spent $174.83 on stationery and printing and $77.25 for postage in the 1962–1963 fiscal year. Consequently, the council budgeted $240.00 for printing and stationery and $100.00 for postage for Mayor Fraser. With four months to go in the 1963–1964 fiscal year, Willard had already overspent both budgets, and by May, with one month to go, he had spent $373.95 on printing and stationery and $250.00 on five-cent stamps. A *Gazette* article explained, "Aldermen get copies of the mayor's pronouncements. Department heads get them. Senators get them. The press gets them. Friends get them."[6] The article did not mention the scores of letters Mayor Fraser also wrote to city residents and sundry others to friends and acquaintances outside Billings and Montana.

As mayor, Fraser set himself the task of marketing Montana and protecting its image. He was ever on alert for anything published about Montana in the media that he felt misrepresented his favorite state. When he spotted such a transgression, he fired off a letter to set the perpetrator straight, often lacing his jabs with humor. The *Chicago Tribune, Saturday Evening Post, Los Angeles Times, Christian Science Monitor, Redbook*, and *Harper's* were among the publications admonished by the Billings mayor. Frequently, these objections involved weather. When the *Monitor's* radio show, broadcasting from Rockefeller Center, reported on Easter morning 1966 that a "howling blizzard is sweeping Montana," Fraser quickly responded, "Well at Indian Caves . . . meadowlarks, [the] most melodious of songbirds, were pouring out their hearts. . . . It was beautiful—both birdsong and morning. And yet Monitor is putting out that sort of nonsense. You should do something about it." Then he added a favorite statement: "Others have weather. We have climate."[7]

When the travel editor of the *Los Angeles Times* commented unfavorably about Montana's "climate," Fraser wrote that it was "salubrious," saying, "Our Montana cold is an honest cold, not hampered or untempered by humidity, for ours is a sunny bright cold. We enjoy a phenomenon known as 'sunshine,' something the be-smogged areas of America rarely see. Our winter has an exhilarating freshness about it that those of the humid East would never never understand."[8] He could, however, sound a less swaggering tone when writing to friends. More than once he described a frigid Montana day with the mysterious simile, "It's as cold as a dead priest."[9]

Willard gave full rein to hyperbole and professed indignation when *Redbook* referred to the western swath of states including Arizona, California, Nevada, New Mexico, and Utah as "Big Sky Country," a term novelist A. B. Guthrie coined for Montana when he published the book *The Big Sky* in 1947. Fraser admonished *Redbook*'s editor:

> The natives of this "real" Big Sky Country are mighty restless these days and girding their loins to go on the warpath.... You might steal our cattle, and our horses, and get away with it, but when you steal our colorful name, and give it so blithely away to others, then you are going to have to take the consequences.... You can give other appellations to Arizona, such as the "Land of the Great Stillness," or California, the "Land of the Great Confusion," or Nevada, the "Land of He who Takes a Chance," or New Mexico, the "Land of the Dancing Gods," or Utah, the "Land of the Dedicated," but "Big Sky Country" belongs to the people of the "Land of the Shining Mountains," and we want you to know it.[10]

A self-described chauvinistic Montanan, Fraser built and protected Montana's positive image in myriad ways. "As soon as a child is born in Billings," he wrote to the League of Women Voters in 1969, "he receives a letter from the Mayor of Billings congratulating him on his wisdom in choosing Billings as a place of birth rather than foolishly selecting ... some other, less desirable far-off community."[11] Expanding on Montanans' love of place, Fraser told the editor of *TIME*, "I can attest that I have yet to hear of a single Montanan expressing any desire of leaving Montana for Heaven—or any place else in His World for that matter."[12]

Willard's appearance in the national press sometimes initiated unexpected long-distance relationships. When the *Chicago Tribune* printed some unkind comments about Montana winters, Willard responded with a letter of protest, which appeared in a subsequent issue. A Chicago couple, Mr. and Mrs. Phillip Scott, were so impressed by his letter that they decided to come to Billings to explore it as a home for their retirement. In expressing his pleasure at their visit, Mayor Fraser said, "All it took was a five-cent stamp."[13] The affection and admiration the Scotts developed for Willard resulted in a regular correspondence and subsequent positive pieces in the *Chicago Tribune*.

The letter-writing mayor came up with various creative methods to bring people to Montana. Dozens of letters among his papers invite various organizations to hold conventions in Billings. He wrote to the League of Women Voters, the State Hairdressers and Cosmetologists Association, the Daughters of the American Revolution, and the Consulting Engineers Council, among others. He even asked the Holtzhacker Buam Milwaukee, a society established to uphold Bavarian culture, to come to Billings. Some of these invitations succeeded. A group of Irish priests convened in Billings in 1966, and the American Public Health Association met in the city that same year. Jim Thompson maintains that the fact that Willard attracted business to Billings earned him the support of the conservative business-men who voted for Willard in successive elections.[14]

Fraser with Hollywood filmmaker Austin Green in 1965 at the premiere of Gates of Hell. *The mayor enjoyed hobnobbing with celebrities and politicians, many of whom he later corresponded with and invited to visit Billings.* Dennis Calkin, photographer. PAc 2003-07.79, MHS Photograph Archives, Helena

Willard's love for Montana did not preclude or take second place to his love for America. He warned that because Montana is thousands of miles from the nation's capital, it risks "a costly provincialism which we cannot afford. We must be part of the world and century in which we live."[15] Thoroughly American, his patriotism was reinforced by his family history with the Civil War, his own experience in World War II, and an intellectual life steeped in history. He expressed his belief in America's melting pot in a letter to a diplomat in the Norwegian Embassy: "I have always maintained that in becoming an American citizen, one should never give up the knowledge of history, love, taste for foods, poetry and song of the land native to his ancestors. It is by bringing all those attributes to our land and implanting them into our culture that has made this Western country of ours the fun that it is."[16] He was proud to be the son-in-law of an *American* poet, and he stressed Frost's identity as such. He often gave a framed copy of Marjorie Frost Fraser's poem "America" as a gift.

This literary mayor was still a consummate politician, and his many letters espoused his political opinions and philosophy. Fraser was especially fond of expressing his definitions of the terms "conservative" and "liberal." Addressing these concepts in a letter to the League of Women Voters, he wrote, "Liberal has come to mean 'let me get my hands into your pockets and spend your money.' Whereas, the term liberal ought to mean 'opposition to tyranny'—and tyranny can come from the left as well as from the right. By the same token, many people confuse the term 'conservative' with being 'against' and doing nothing. A true conservative should be one who believes in the wise use of resources, human, natural, physical and spiritual."[17] In another letter, this one to Lillian Frost, he spoke of false conservatives who "know nothing, do nothing, spend nothing, and anyway be against it."[18] He often railed against those who, out of ignorance, objected to change.

Fraser frequently shared his political thoughts with friends and wrote to state and national politicians—among them Herbert Hoover, Lyndon Johnson, Hubert Humphrey, Stewart Udall, Carl Albert, Edmund Muskie, Lee Metcalf, Mike Mansfield, and Burton K. Wheeler—to voice an opinion or comment on a vote. As friend Jim Thompson commented, "He thought people needed to hear from him."[19] In the summer of 1971, Fraser sent a Wheeler letter to Sam Guilly of the Montana Historical Society for inclusion in the Wheeler papers there, commenting in his transmittal letter, "Senator Wheeler is one of the truly Greats of Montana. . . . When I walk with Senator Wheeler, I feel I am walking with history."[20] A few months later, when he wrote to Wheeler to regret that he could not attend Wheeler's ninetieth birthday celebration, he said, "To be ninety, still storming around the country and keeping an active interest in that country is great."[21]

Willard's letters demonstrate that he was often bipartisan in his opinions and loyalties. That he was a close friend of Grant Salisbury, for instance, illustrates his ability to listen to opposing views and yet build positive personal relations with those of a different intellectual perspective. Writing to Salisbury after the 1968 election, he spoke out in favor of a Montana Republican candidate: "One of our very best legislators, a Republican . . . very qualified, competent, and very conversant with water problems . . . was defeated." He went on to make a scathing comment that he would not have uttered for public consumption: "[A]nd three absolute numbskulls were elected."[22] Fraser was much more apt to be critical of misguided politicians than he was of marginalized or mistreated citizens.

Letter writing enabled Fraser to expound at length on his strongly held feelings about race and injustice in politics. When it was reported that Nixon wanted a strict constructionist on the Supreme Court, Fraser expressed his opinion in a letter to his nephew, John B. Fraser:

> [He] is really saying he wants a mediocrity, with no imagination, a rule follower, with neither a sense of justice or compassion in his makeup—and one that all too often money can buy, or is overly impressed by men of position and wealth and therefore has an obsequiousness about him that can be deadly. . . . Chief Justice Taney was such a man, and his sense of justice made the Civil War inevitable. His Dred Scott verdict said, and I think I quote verbatim: "The Negro has no rights that the white man is bound to respect."[23]

Willard's quote was almost verbatim. Judge Taney's sentence was introduced by the statement that the black race was "an inferior class of beings" and thus "they have no rights that the white man was bound to respect."[24] As he did in this instance, Willard commonly buttressed his opinions with historical facts and events.

History, as well as personal experience, informed many of Willard's views on humanity and increased his compassion for all. During the 1930s, he had an experience that reinforced his empathy for the poor and indigent. Writing to a woman in McCook, Nebraska, in 1970, he recalled when, as a young man, he jumped a freight train while traveling across Nebraska and shared a boxcar with four or five hobos. He was scared to death, afraid of being clubbed or knifed in the ribs. One of the men asked him if he had any money, and he said he did not, although he did have just under a hundred dollars. In McCook, Willard got off "but fast." When he was fifty feet away, one of the "bums" called, "Here, kid, go get yourself something to eat," and threw him seventy-five cents. "I've been pro-bum ever since," Willard wrote.[25]

Like coming of age during the Great Depression, living in Billings' South Side neighborhood fostered Willard's compassion for the under-privileged. The economic disparity between this industrial, working-class neighborhood and the more upscale, residential neighborhood north of the tracks created two separate cultures. Both the South Side's ethnic and racial diversity and the generally lower socioeconomic standing of its residents made them a target of prejudice in the mid-twentieth century. Jim Ronquillo, who grew up among the South Side's Mexican community during the 1950s and '60s, recently described some of the attitudes that persisted into Fraser's terms as mayor and that Fraser worked to dispel. Ronquillo's father, Senaido, one of eleven children, moved to Billings in 1929 and met his Bohemian wife at the Colonia, a housing settlement established by the Great Western sugar company. Jim's parents, like most early immigrants in Billings, initially worked in the sugar beet fields, later in the packing houses; and finally, Jim's father worked for the city's street department. After school, Jim and his friends went to Minnesota Avenue to shine the shoes of people leaving the bars on "Skid Row." That "was where things happened," he remembered. "It was the center of activity for the neighborhood. It was the real melting pot because both South Side people and those from the North would frequent the area. The judges and lawyers all came to the bars. There were the Oasis, Casey's Pheasant, Maple Leaf, the Standard, the Silver Dollar."[26]

As Jim approached adulthood, the discrimination against Mexican Americans and other South Siders affected him directly. The Silver Dollar Bar did not admit Native American or Mexican Americans. African Americans were allowed to swim in the public pool only on Sunday, before the weekly draining of the pool. As a young man, Jim thought he might want to be a cop, and he took the application test. A few days later, a detective drove by the house where Jim, in work clothes, was painting.

"So you think you want to be a cop?" the detective asked.

"Yeah, I think so," Jim replied.

"Well, you can't wear those clothes, you know," the detective said. He went on to warn Jim that cops had to pay their bills. Jim decided being a cop was not worth putting up with such distrust and humiliation. He went on to become the first Mexican American given a permanent position at Montana Dakota Utilities, and he served as a ward councilman from

2006 to 2014. In a similar vein, Ronquillo once recommended to a construction company that they hire two Native Americans. When the two reported for work, they were given pickaxes to break up concrete blocks. Given the difficulty of the task, the two did not last the day. "See, they don't work," said the man in charge of hiring. The next day, two white men applied, and they were given jackhammers to break up the concrete.[27] Ronquillo would have been a young man during Fraser's terms as mayor, and his experiences are indicative of the types of discrimination Mexican Americans and American Indians faced in Montana during that era.

Loyal to his fellow South Side residents, Fraser did not just speak against prejudice; he also took steps to counteract it and to support those who suffered from it. He recounted one such incident in a letter to Rev. Robert Hudnut, likely less because of his indignation and more because the story itself merited the retelling. Willard described a phone call from South Side resident Delsie Kenoly, a 102-year-old "Negro lady," who said, "I just wish the Mayor would call on me." Willard's response was, "Anyone who is 102 should say, 'Mayor, Dammit, you get out here and see me right away!' I shall be right out in twenty minutes." The mayor immediately paid a visit to the elderly woman, who had done sewing, laundry, and housework for Billings families. In their ensuing conversation, Delsie said, "You know, Mayor, some folks—they just ain't civilized. They don't like [blacks] around here." His response was, "Oh, don't pay any attention to them. You tell them that you're a friend of the Mayor and to treat you right."[28]

When Delsie died in early 1967, Mayor Fraser was asked to serve as a pallbearer at her funeral. "I'd be proud to," he said. Afterward, he wrote to Reverend Hudnut that Delsie's obituary mentioned that she had been born to slave parents on the plantation owned by Confederate general Jubal Early, who was involved in several major Civil War battles including Fredericksburg, Chancellorsville, and Gettysburg. Willard recalled that Delsie had said to him, "My father was a white gentleman," and he speculated that Delsie could have been an offspring of General Early. This thought activated Willard's impish streak, and he wrote in the letter to Hudnut, "I think I should write a letter to the Daughters of the Confederacy and say, 'Hey, you know what? The Mayor of Billings was pallbearer to Jubal Early's daughter last week.' Bet that would shake them."[29]

This speculation would be difficult to corroborate. It is true that Early grew up on a plantation with many slaves, and he was actively involved in fighting during most of the Civil War. However, there is scant evidence on Early's whereabouts in the fall of 1863 when Delsie would have been conceived.[30] Nonetheless, the notion, however unfounded, provided

Willard with a moment of characteristic levity while underscoring his desire to confront racist attitudes.

A Congregationalist in a heavily Protestant city, Willard counted poet and Catholic priest Fr. James Kittleson among his close friends at a time when a Catholic could not be hired to teach in the Billings public schools.[31] He wrote letters to Fr. John Dimke of St. Patrick's Church and to Rabbi Samuel Horowitz of the local synagogue to bring them into city affairs. Willard often sounded a plea for tolerance and acceptance in his letters. Adopting a jocular tone, he once wrote to a Montana woman, after hearing about a marriage in her family, to say, "So you're getting a Christian Scientist in the outfit? As I say, every family ought to have a Catholic, a Methodist, a Lutheran, and what not in their midst, including a Christian Scientist."[32] Upon receiving a letter from a young African American soldier, he responded with a long commentary on prejudice and reflected on the bias against Germans when he was growing up, saying, "Today, the grandsons and granddaughters of the same undesirable 'Germans' own vast areas in the Yellowstone Valley and are amongst our finest citizens. . . . We are citizens of this world, and we must act and perform as God gives us the intelligence and right to perform, and none of us—Negro, Jew, German, Irish, or Indian, can point with disrespect at the past of any of our ancestors."[33]

In Montana, American Indians were a common object of racism, but Willard did not sympathize with those whites who viewed American Indians as inferior. Nor was his view of Montana Indians a romanticized one. When Fraser ran for governor in 1968, he wrote to Clarence Adams of the Montana Inter-Tribal Policy Board in Helena to say that, if he were elected governor, he "would bring our Indian citizens into full and active participation in State Government."[34] In a carefully worded response to an apparent offer of charity to the Cheyennes, he wrote, "The Cheyenne, like many other fine peoples have only within a matter of a few short years been thrust from the age of hunting to jet exploration, which of course brings its problems . . . [and] while there is always room for charity, there must also be wisdom in its application. . . . [The] Cheyenne are emerging into this interesting world of ours, and I predict that in the future they will contribute greatly as they have in the past."[35] The statement shows a balance of respect for the dignity and potential of the Cheyenne people along with Willard's acknowledgment of the struggles the tribe was facing in the mid-twentieth century.

In addition to illustrating his political and social views, Willard's letters reveal his personal philosophy and attitudes toward life. His persistence

Northern Cheyenne elders meet with the Billings mayor, 1971. Left to right: James Blackwolf, Willis Medicine Bull, Charles Sitting Man, Dan Seminole, Willard Fraser, Daniel Pine, Albert Tallbull, Leroy Pine, Oran Charles Wolfback. Fraser made a point of establishing good relationships with Crow and Cheyenne people and did not hesitate to write letters to the editor when they were maligned in the press.
Courtesy Abby Ferguson

in running for office after recurrent failures verifies that he was an incurable optimist. Indeed, he detested a dour outlook, writing puckishly at one point, "I told the people of Billings that it's always an ancient practice to give up something they hold dear during Lent, and too many people thoroughly enjoy being pessimistic; so I was asking those people to quit being pessimistic for the forty days of Lent, and be optimistic." He added a favorite line: "How do you like that?"[36] Fraser applied this positive frame of mind to dealing with people in general. In thanking someone for a letter of appreciation, he said, "A pat on the back is worth [more than] a kick in the butt any day."[37]

Fraser's letters often counseled patience and consideration, sometimes buttressed with Twain-like humor. To one correspondent he wrote, "A long time ago, I thought if you treat a man like a man, he will usually act and respond like a man, but if you treat him like a dog, he's liable to bite you."[38] In another letter, Willard encouraged a young journalist to consider the law in the context of humanity:

> Laws are made to be enforced by executives with a human understanding of human weaknesses and strengths. A few years ago, a friend of mine was principal of one of our Billings high schools. I once heard him admonishing his teachers before a football game, 'Now when you find small boys trying to sneak into the game without a ticket, you chase them. Run like hell. But do not ever run quite as fast as those small boys.' It still seems to me that was good advice then, and remains as sage advice today.[39]

Frequently, Fraser's letters and memos are in response to complaints from Billings citizens. While some problems could be referred to the appropriate agency, others required the mayor's attention. When a resident grumbled about delayed garbage pickup, Fraser's written reply encouraged forbearance: "I think the fact of the matter is that they merely emulate the Mayor, who is constantly on a dead run trying to catch up to an impossible schedule. We try, the garbage men and I."[40]

Willard himself often bemoaned how much of the mayor's time was taken up by dealing with citizen complaints about dogs. Nevertheless, he gamely dealt with one such complaint in a memo to police chief Beven, sending a memo to say, "Neighbors are complaining about a dog in heat in the area of 22nd Street West between Colton and Lyman. The lady says that every 'he dog' in town is concentrated wishfully and hopefully in that area—wishfully because it seems the lady dog in question is fenced in. What can you do to alleviate the stress and strain of not only the 'he dogs' but of the neighbors? In any event, do something. Thanks."[41]

Another letter from Willard to the Billings sheriff seems to have been motivated by a complaint about how a young deputy handled a situation of finding a young couple canoodling in a car parked on the Rimrocks. Apparently, the deputy had grabbed the young man by the hair, slapped him across the face, and used rough language when confronting the couple. Fraser admonished, "It seems to me we must accept . . . looking the other way when the young man is receiving cooperation from a young lady . . . not that I approve of or condone promiscuity, but I am inclined to accept the world as I find it, and lust has its place."[42] Fraser was not rigid in his views on youth, but he did draw the line at some behavior. In a separate memo he asked the police chief to check out the "extremely enthusiastic lovemaking" neighbors were complaining about in a certain area.[43]

Addressing an instance of premarital sex, he responded with tact and concern. He wrote a long, earnest letter to a couple to persuade them to attend the wedding of their son and his pregnant girlfriend. He told this conservative couple that not attending would be an un-Christian act that they would regret, and he asked them to take the wider view of the situation:

> Sex has always been a strong, and overpowering drive, and because of this fact, you and I are here. . . . The fact that sex sometimes occurs in premarital moments does in no way lessen its results, and babies so conceived are no less loved. Babies conceived in or out of wedlock are still deserving of love of both their parents and most especially of the love of their grandparents, who being older must be the more understanding. I would doubt if there be a family in America that has not at one time or another had babies conceived before the marriage of their parents. . . . Such things happened in our generation, too. . . . My own feeling is . . . you are going to have one of the most creative, exciting, and interesting of grandchildren. And you would not want him to start life with family ill feelings now would you?[44]

Fraser concluded the letter by saying that if it would help them to attend, he would host them for breakfast at the Northern Hotel and then go with them to the church for the wedding.

Willard could be less patient when responding to a complaint from out-of-state. One such situation was dealt with jaw-dropping audaciousness. He wrote to the mayor of Billings, Missouri, and enclosed a letter he had received from Germany "that states a certain soldier boy from Billings left an illegitimate child in Germany that he is not supporting. I want to assure you that not one of our Billings, Montana boys would have done such a thing, I'm sure."[45] The letter ends there. There is no record of how the mayor of Billings, Missouri, responded to this cheeky passing of the buck.

The impudent attitude displayed in the letter to the mayor of Billings, Missouri, does not signify disregard for the competence of his fellow mayors. In fact, Fraser sent a plethora of letters of inquiry to other mayors, citizens, civic groups, and public agencies seeking information on topics affecting Billings. He once wrote to the U.S. Department of Health, Education, and Welfare to ask, "Will you send me any and all information you might have available regarding cockroaches carrying diseases."[46] He asked the Midwest Rubber Reclaiming Company in East St. Louis, Illinois, for suggestions on what to do with old tires. Identical letters went to mayors of Denver, Phoenix, Los Angeles, San Diego, Greenwich, and Grand Rapids. He wrote to the Bureau of Standards in Washington, D.C., and to the mayors of Cleveland, Duluth, Denver, and Detroit for recommendations on the use of salt on the streets. Among scores of letters to other mayors, Willard asked the mayor of Wichita, Kansas, for that city's ordinance regulating female café entertainers; the mayor of Orlando, Florida, about their "fabulously fine new library"; and the mayor of Dallas for its ordinance prohibiting the keeping of poisonous reptiles. In soliciting expert advice though letters and correspondence, Willard was constantly seeking to add to his already considerable store of knowledge and information.

No topic was too mundane, no problem too small for the attention of this mayor. Nor did he hold back on his opinions about how things ought to be done. When Willard wrote to the manager of Skyview Terrace at Billings' Logan Field to arrange the menu for the annual George Washington birthday lunch for international students, he specified the American menu of fried chicken, corn, and cherry pie and then added, "If you could have real, fresh shoestring potatoes, that would be nice too. I would be sort of embarrassed if you served them any of those 'embalmed' potatoes that seem to be the way of life in too many restaurants in this day and age."[47] Fraser seemed picky about his potatoes. After spending a weekend in Yellowstone National Park, he wrote to thank the kitchen staff: "Most especially I want to commend you on that baked potato that you served at Old Faithful on Saturday night. That is the first decent and edible baked potato that I have eaten in a restaurant in the past year. All I seem to get are those steamed, tinfoil wrapped objects, that are neither edible nor digestible."[48]

Willard confessed to friends or acquaintances that he stole stories from them, although he once told a nun that you could not really steal from someone who had taken a vow of poverty. When he heard Edward P. Morgan comment on ABC News in 1971 that there might be one or two Spanish-American War veterans left in America, Fraser wrote to Morgan to fill him in on Col. Joe Montgomery, a Lewistown resident who had fought with Teddy Roosevelt.[49] Ninety-six-year-old Montgomery was a living Montana legend with a reputation as a political prognosticator. Like Fraser, he was also a storyteller with a fondness for history. Fraser wrote to the old-timer in 1972 to say he had passed some of his yarns on to visiting Californians. "I specifically pointed out, however, that you have always admonished me with the warning that your tales were half-truths, half lies and half bourbon."[50] In particular, Fraser delighted in Montgomery's version of the trajectory of the life of Irishman Thomas Meagher, acting Montana territorial governor in 1867. According to Montgomery, when Queen Victoria saw a photo of Meagher when he was jailed in Ireland on a charge of sedition, she declared he was "too pretty a boy" to be executed. Thus, he was instead banished to Tasmania. Montgomery also claimed that it was Scotland Yard that plotted Meagher's death in the swirling waters of the Missouri River at Fort Benton on July 1, 1867.

Willard could not resist a good story, and an especially shocking or unusual story bore repeating. In the spring of 1972, he went to Broadus High School to speak at a banquet. While there, he commented to a woman about a pretty girl sitting at a nearby table. The woman said, "Yes, but did you know she chews tobacco?" Willard reported this incident in at least three letters with the comment, "It turned out tobacco chewing is the 'in thing' for the girls in Broadus High School. I had nightmares in which I dreamed of kissing a girl with a mug full of tobacco juice."[51]

Although Fraser might not meet the gender awareness test of the twenty-first century, he was certainly progressive in his views of women

Great Falls mayor Marian Erdmann, Spanish-American War veteran Joe Montgomery, and Willard Fraser in the Moccasin Mountains, August 1968. Montgomery delighted in telling his own versions of historical events, and Fraser took pleasure in the retelling. 943-988, MHS Photograph Archives, Helena

for his time, perhaps because he had a mother who did not fit a traditional mold. When he wrote to a history professor to congratulate him on his marriage, he added the comment, "As a historian, have you ever stopped to consider the part women play in history?"[52] It was a rare man who expressed such thoughts in 1965. His references to women are neither patronizing nor dismissive. Some have a teasing quality—as when he wrote to a female member of the Billings Business and Professional Clubs: "It takes a brave man to nominate a woman who has excelled over and above others in a city that has so many women who excel. But to show you I am a man of courage, I am going to nominate two women."[53] During one of his many hospital stays, he wrote to Grant Salisbury, "A few days in the hospital will convince you that this idea of the female of the species being the weaker sex is all baloney, perpetuated by us males to maintain our male ego. The way those nurses will throw you about."[54] When Frances Elge, a pioneering woman lawyer, was chosen as Montana's Woman of the Year in 1971, Willard wrote to congratulate her, saying, "Did you ever read the proceedings of our Constitutional Convention, and the great wonderfully masculine arguments of how 'Our women just shouldn't be subjected to the horrors of the ballot box, jury duty and the other onerous tasks of citizenship'—too onerous for frail women to shoulder. We men can be so ponderously masculine—and stupid in some of our thinking."[55]

Of the barrage of letters Willard sent to people—young and old, celebrities and ordinary citizens—only occasional responses are filed among his papers. They include letters from Jacqueline Kennedy, Adlai Stevenson, Herbert Hoover, Norman Cousins, Dustin Hoffman, and Hubert Humphrey. The editor-in-chief of Houghton Mifflin answered a letter of Willard's that drew attention to an omission of Montana on a map. The editor wrote, "Your letter concerning the undoubted civic and geographic virtues of Billings, Montana, was a positive delight to editors who are all too accustomed to either carping letters of criticism or legitimate errors of fact. We confess to a sin of omission!"[56] Willard promptly fired off a return letter with a story about a carping letter he had received from a lady "who was most unhappy because a hungry bobcat had chewed up her dog for a bobcat breakfast."[57]

Another of the rare letters from a correspondent is one from Richard Glendinning, a Florida writer who had once participated in the Yellowstone River Boat Float and became a Fraser friend. Glendinning wrote, "I read aloud to cast assembled your splendid letter dealing with the Bobby Burns birthday celebration and your cavalier approach to Scottish history. On the strength of your letter I am now being lionized. The word has gone

Fraser (left) celebrated Bobby Burns Day and his Scottish heritage, sometimes donning his kilt and tam o'shanter for the festivities. Billings Gazette, Dec. 3, 1964

out all around Town. . . . Everyone wants me as a guest—provided I bring along the latest letter from Willard Fraser to read aloud. . . . Listen, Willard, you've got to come to Sarasota. Those people think I've made you up."[58]

During Fraser's nearly eight years as mayor of Billings, his letters and the press chronicled how he sought to implement his vision for Billings, the problems he grappled with, and the vast network of human relationships he established along the way. They also encapsulate Fraser's attitude toward life, best expressed by Willard himself in one of his letters: "It is a great world, and a world that I have always found terrifically, and sometimes terrifyingly interesting—but never dull, and so you will find it."[59]

"I am not city limited"

ONE OF Mayor Fraser's friends once cautioned, "Don't go out of town with Willard or you'll end up in a parade." Stuart Conner learned this lesson while serving as city attorney during Fraser's first year in office. Along with two aldermen and the person in charge of city garbage, Conner and Fraser traveled to Arizona in 1963 to see if Billings should replicate Phoenix's garbage collection system. Along the way, they stopped in a small town where Willard knew the mayor and discovered the town was about to have a parade. Years later Conner recalled:

> It wasn't the Fourth of July or anything. I don't have any idea why they were having the parade, and I said, 'I'm not going in any parade.' The people had no idea who we were. Willard finally browbeat me into it. He wouldn't take no for an answer. So, we went down through this line of people. I think the mayor was in the car in front of us, and I could just tell by the look on the faces of these poor observers that they wondered who in the hell these people were and why are they in the parade.[1]

Willard's pleasure in parades is evident in photos of him beaming from a parade car. After a parade in Laurel in 1967, he told a local radio station, "That was fun . . . riding a horse through Laurel on Sunday."[2] Billings's Western Day Parade was a favorite outlet for Willard's love of pageantry, an affection he justified by saying, "I advocate pomp and circumstance in city government, for in no small measure was it pomp and circumstance that kept the Holy Roman Church rolling along in dignity and color for lo these 2,000 years, and the British Empire for the past 300 and a bit."[3]

Whether joining a parade or speaking to a crowd, Willard loved to take part in public events, and his mayoral duties and personal interests frequently allowed him to participate.

Mayor Fraser did not let city limits or the state's borders hem him in; rather, he saw his role as the city's number-one advocate as a platform for wider engagement with the world. He visited other Montana cities regularly, corresponded frequently with other elected officials, and attended national conferences in a commitment to staying informed on issues of importance to American communities. He accepted out-of-state speaking engagements and testified in Helena and in Washington, D.C., on some of his favorite causes. In part, Willard was driven by his enthusiasm for sharing ideas, but his ability to envision Billings within a wider historical, geographical, and political context motivated this mayor to get involved in issues at a regional, state, and national level.

Willards's love of history—and the value he placed on it—inspired his participation in many projects both within and outside the city limits. Within Billings, for instance, he encouraged an upgrade of the Boothill Cemetery, where residents of the nineteenth-century settlement of Coulson are buried, and he promoted enhancement of the grave of soldier, scout, and hunter Yellowstone Kelly on the Rimrocks. Beyond the city, Fraser was instrumental in protecting Pictograph Cave and Pompeys Pillar as national historic landmarks. Both sites are culturally important to the region's Indigenous peoples. Friend and colleague Stuart Conner remarked that Fraser "was probably the first mayor who ever paid any attention to the Indians. We have two reservations close by, the Crows and the Northern Cheyenne. He made much ado about the Indians."[4] Undoubtedly, the time spent unearthing the life patterns of ancient civilizations and the contact with Navajos during his college years fed Willard's drive to preserve sites of historical and cultural significance to Montana tribes and reinforced his respect and admiration for American Indians in general.

One of Mayor Fraser's first significant clashes with the Billings city council concerned his efforts to preserve the three-cave complex originally called Inscription Cave, then popularly known as the Indian Caves, and finally officially named Pictograph Cave. Crow elders regard Pictograph Cave, or "Where There is Rock Writing," as "a place with great power, where war parties and hunters left offerings and sought blessing for their ventures."[5] The caves, located six miles south of Billings, united Fraser's interests in history, Indigenous peoples, and archaeology, and he was inspired to preserve the site. During the Great Depression, geologist H. Melville Sayre and amateur archaeologist Oscar Lewis began to excavate

*Stu Conner (left) and Fraser prepare invitations to the 1966 Yellowstone River Boat
Float. Both Conner and Fraser were members of the Billings Archaeological Society.*
Bill Tutokey, photographer. *Billings Gazette,* Jun. 3, 1966

the caves as part of a Works Progress Administration (WPA) project.
Archaeological work revealed artifacts from the Middle Prehistoric Period
(3000 BC to AD 500) and Late Prehistoric occupation (AD 500 to 1800).
Indications suggest that by the 1700s, the caves were no longer used as resi-
dences.[6] In 1940, archaeologist William Mulloy took over the excavation
until it was halted by World War II. After the war, Fraser and Stu Conner,
as members of the Billings Archaeological Society, worked with others to

outfit the increasingly popular site with tables, a water pump, and outdoor toilets to accommodate the growing number of visitors. Within a year, however, vandals and thieves had destroyed their good work.[7] Throughout the years, many of the artifacts in the caves were lost to souvenir-seeking tourists or defaced by vandals.[8]

In November 1963, when Fraser signed a permit from the state park commission for Billings to administer the twenty-two acres around the caves, the city council erupted with objections. "He's got no authority to do this," Alderman Joe Leone said, basing his criticism on the caves' location outside the city limits. To defend his signing of the permit, Fraser noted the trouble that Thomas Jefferson, Andrew Jackson, and Theodore Roosevelt encountered when they expanded the nation's territory. "This is a project of the future; I don't want to see that land lost forever," he said.[9] A month later, the council voted 7–2 to nullify his action, and Fraser called the decision "the antithesis of conservatism."[10] The controversy over the caves was noted statewide. Helena's *Independent Record* commented, "Billings Mayor Willard Fraser is trying to save what is left."[11]

After the council shot down Fraser's efforts to have the city manage the caves, the mayor replied with a memo asking the councilmen to reconsider. He reminded them that "the Indian Caves are not of importance just today, but for all time to come," emphasizing that the caves "are one of the finest historical areas in the northwest" and as such offered ample research potential for future archaeologists and scholars. The mayor also cautioned the council that the state could easily enough sell the land to a private party, thereby jeopardizing Indian Caves' future and making the site off-limits to the public. Hoping to convince reluctant council members to see the caves' potential economic benefits to the city, Fraser pointed to a recent survey that recommended Indian Caves be protected and developed as a tourist attraction.[12]

Committed to his goal, Fraser garnered enough support from the public and from organizations such as the Billings Art Association and the Billings Archaeological Society to create a Cave Commission in early 1964, with the intention of preventing any further desecration of the caves and the pictographs inside them. The members of the Cave Commission were Dr. Wilson Clark (Eastern Montana College), Chester Brooks (National Park Service), Ted Wirth (landscape architect), Harold Hagen (Billings Archeological Society), Conna May (Montana Dude Ranchers' Association), and Rockwood Brown Jr. (Billings Parks Board). The commission was in charge of overseeing volunteer help, and they arranged to have graffiti and other non-prehistoric "art" removed from the site.

In July 1964, the U.S. Department of Interior designated Indian Caves a national historic landmark to join nine others in the state. Willard commented proudly, "Stu Conner and I have been pointing out the value of this site for a long time. Now we're vindicated."[13] On the same date, the Hagan archaeological site near Glendive, which contains the remains of a permanent Native American village dating to the fifteenth century and which was also excavated by Lewis, was granted national historic landmark status. Landmark status provides these sites with a measure of protection against development and recognizes their significance to American history. When J. O Brew, Willard's friend from his summers in the Southwest and now the director of Harvard's Peabody Museum, visited the caves in 1965, he commented that the preservation "should set an example for other municipalities and states."[14]

In 1991, the Indian Caves site became Pictograph Caves State Park, one of fifty in Montana at the time.[15] The twenty-three-acre park offers magnificent views of the surrounding hills and sandstone formations, as well as a visitor center, hiking trails, a picnic area, and interpretive

Members of the Cave Commission established by Fraser in 1964 to manage the Indian Caves, now Pictograph Caves State Park. Willard E. Fraser Collection, MSU–Billings Library

signs detailing the many centuries of use and habitation by Indigenous peoples. A plaque in the visitor center commemorates Fraser's contribution to preserving the caves and lists members of his Cave Commission. While several of the pictographs are intact and can be viewed by today's visitors, few of the roughly thirty thousand artifacts excavated from the cave complex remain in Yellowstone County. Many were plundered long before the site was preserved, while others have been relocated. Some are in collections at the University of Montana, Montana State University, and Montana Technological University, formerly the School of Mines, in Butte.[16] Nonetheless, because of the forward-thinking efforts of Fraser, Conner, the Billings Archaeological Society, and the Cave Commission, the Pictograph Cave complex is now protected as a cultural site that draws thousands of visitors annually.

Building on his success at preserving Pictograph Cave, Willard promoted the preservation of another historic site in the area: Pompeys Pillar. Located twenty-eight miles northeast of Billings, Pompeys Pillar is a stunning 150-foot-high rock promontory illustrated with thousands of pictographs, petroglyphs, and etchings. In addition to bearing significance to the region's Indigenous peoples, Pompeys Pillar holds the only remaining physical evidence of the Lewis and Clark Expedition in the region.[17] On the expedition's return journey in 1806, Captain William Clark carved his name and the date—July 25, 1806—on the sandstone pillar. The site is named after Jean Baptist Charbonneau, whom Clark nicknamed "Pomp." The son of Clark's guide Sacagawea, a young Shoshone woman, and French Canadian explorer and expedition member Toussaint Charbonneau, "Pomp" was eighteen months old when Clark carved on the pillar. Once part of the Crow Indian Reservation, the land surrounding the pillar was ceded to the federal government in 1904. The government sold it to a private owner in 1916.

When Don and Stella Foote, ranchers and collectors of historic artifacts, bought the land in 1954, they replaced an iron screen protecting Clark's signature with glass and opened the site to visitors. Willard knew the Footes and understood the importance of the signature, and he wanted to make sure the public could see this unique Montana landmark. During the construction of I-94 in the early 1960s, Fraser wrote to the highway department in Helena to urge that they add an exit so that travelers could stop to see Pompeys Pillar. A highway representative informed the mayor that the traffic didn't warrant an exit. Undaunted, Fraser wrote to Senator Mike Mansfield to plead for a change in the highway plans.[18] His action must have worked; today, Exit 23 offers a convenient route to the site.

Ranchers and landowners Stella and Don Foote, photographed in 1955 next to Clark's signature on Pompeys Pillar, worked with Fraser to protect this culturally and historically important site as a national historic landmark. 950-261, MHS Photograph Archives, Helena

In March 1965, Fraser wrote to the National Park Service to "again" talk of the possibility of having Pompeys Pillar designated a national historic landmark. This was not his first time making this suggestion, and his persistence paid off. In April, Interior Secretary Stewart Udall indicated the designation would occur.[19] Always ready to promote historic Montana places, Mayor Fraser invited William Clark Adreon, great-great-grandson of Captain Clark, to come to Billings to see his forebear's initials. On July 19, Adreon, "led by a hearty band of area historians and the intrepid Mayor Willard E. Fraser," climbed to the top.[20] A year later, Adreon, his son, and an estimated crowd of three thousand people attended the dedication of Pompeys Pillar.[21] As part of the visit, the two Adreons joined the annual mayors' float down the Yellowstone River, which his great-great grandfather had navigated 160 years earlier. In 1991 the Bureau of Land Management purchased the site, and Fraser would have been delighted to learn that in 2001, President Clinton declared Pompeys Pillar a national monument, protecting it from development, mining, oil exploration, and motorized travel.

Willard Fraser (right) shows Clark Adreon Sr., the great-great grandson of Captain William Clark, the views from Pompeys Pillar, 1965. Pat Connolly, photographer. *Billings Gazette,* Jul. 20, 1965

Fraser's combined passion for archaeology and his zeal for publicity inspired him to participate in commemorating another historic Montana site—Little Bighorn Battlefield, then called Custer Battlefield, located sixty-two miles east of Billings. In the 1960s, Custer was still generally regarded as a hero and a martyr. Fraser judged Custer's character vainglorious and his actions ill-conceived, a view many historians later supported.[22] He pointed to the false, idealized image that Custer's widow, Libbie, had promulgated through her books and speeches. When *TIME* published a glowing article on Custer, Fraser felt the need to admonish them for buying Libbie Custer's version of her husband. The magazine, he said in a letter to its editor, "still lives in a heroic, dream-world illusion that Custer was a 'nice guy.'"[23] Fraser's own view of Custer was illustrated in a macabre comment he was fond of repeating: "Custer liked this country so much that he stayed here."[24] Recognizing the importance of acknowledging the Lakota and Cheyenne victors in the 1876 battle, Fraser wrote to the Board of Geographic Names in 1968 to ask, "Have you ever thought of changing the name of Custer Battlefield to Custer–Sitting Bull Battlefield? Wouldn't that be more in keeping with the victor's side of the case?"[25] Although the board failed to act on Fraser's suggestion at the time, Congress changed the site's name to Little Bighorn Battlefield National Monument in 1991, although a few years later there was opposition to the installation of artwork commemorating the Cheyenne and Lakota victory.[26]

Mayor Fraser enthusiastically promoted the battle's annual reenactment. In 1966, the ninetieth anniversary of the Indigenous victory, national publications, including the *Saturday Evening Post, U.S. News and World Report,* and *National Observer,* covered the event.[27] As a self-appointed Montana host, Fraser sent invitations to a broad swath of local and national figures. When he invited President Johnson to the 1966 reenactment, he pitched it by saying the president's presence would be good for race relations.[28] Unfazed by Johnson's absence, Fraser extended another invitation to the president for the 1967 event, saying, "In white circles it is known as the Custer massacre and in red circles as a great victory."[29] Again the president declined the appearance, but when Johnson delivered his 1968 "Forgotten American" speech focusing on problems facing American Indians, Willard wrote to commend him.

In 1966, Fraser became involved in local efforts to "rescue" Major Marcus Reno of Custer's command from his ignoble grave in Washington, D.C., and reinter him in Little Bighorn's military cemetery. Willard's view on Reno's reputation was entwined with his assessment of Libbie Custer. Always eager to correct what he saw to be a false interpretation of history, Fraser later wrote to Grant Salisbury that he felt Reno's negative reputation was a victim of Libbie's "vicious" pen. "The fact is," Fraser wrote, "he is now one of our national figures in history, and we have treated him

Crow tribal member Henry Old Coyote (foreground) played the role of Sitting Bull during the 1966 re-enactment of the Little Bighorn Battle, an event Fraser enjoyed promoting and attending. 946-646, MHS Photograph Archives, Helena

very shabbily."[30] Reno, who led his men in a retreat across the river when outflanked by warriors, was criticized for being a coward and abandoning Custer. In June, the *Gazette* ran an article with the headline, "Fraser Would Bring Reno Back." Fraser noted that Chet Shore of the American Legion in Helena had suggested the move of Reno's remains.[31] Despite the credit Fraser gave Shore, Shore took umbrage at the implied importance given to Fraser, and he spoke out to say that he had started the drive five years previously and wanted "to keep it his project."[32] Fraser, who had been accused of stealing the show from key players in previous projects, replied that he was only supplying the assistance that Shore had requested of his office. "I will continue to help bring Reno back," he said.[33]

In January 1967, Fraser wrote first to the Department of Interior and then, at their suggestion, to the Review and Correction Board of the Department of the Army, suggesting a reburial be scheduled for Memorial Day that year.[34] The ceremony was eventually held on September 6. Shore and Fraser evidently made peace with each other, because as preparations were made for the ceremony, Fraser wrote to Shore to accept an offer: "I will be happy to work as Chairman of the Distinguished Guest Committee for the reburial of Reno."[35]

Reno's reburial began with a procession in Billings followed by rites at Custer National Cemetery. Distinguished guests included Governor Babcock, John Woodenlegs of the Northern Cheyenne tribal council, and Edison Real Bird of the Crow tribal council—both of whom took part in the ceremony. In typical fashion, Willard had sent out a blizzard of invitations to the event—to Hubert Humphrey, Burton K. Wheeler, associate justice of the Montana Supreme Court John Harrison, Senators Mansfield and Metcalf, the mayor of Great Falls, and Edward Thompson, editor of *LIFE*. He later described the reburial as "the flashiest funeral in years" and noted, "There was no necessity of tears, weeping or wailing at the grave."[36]

When Fraser was elected to the board of trustees of the St. Louis-based Jefferson National Expansion Memorial Association in June 1965, his influence extended from Montana to Missouri. The association's mission was to establish a memorial to those who made possible the western expansion of the United States, particularly President Jefferson and Lewis and Clark. Fraser's interest in and knowledge of the link between St. Louis, Lewis and Clark, and Montana made him an avid participant in this endeavor.[37] As a member of the board, Fraser became acquainted with G. Edward Budde, public information officer for the Jefferson Memorial.[38] After a tour of St. Louis's Jefferson Memorial led by Budde in early June 1965, Fraser's thank-you note included his observation that a map in Budde's office included only the Missouri River as part of the Lewis and Clark Expedition, ignoring the fact that on their return trip, the two explorers separated near Lolo Pass. Lewis took a northern route to the Marias and Missouri Rivers, while Clark traveled down the Jefferson River to its confluence with the Gallatin and Madison Rivers (now Missouri Headwaters State Park), then overland through today's Gallatin Valley to the Yellowstone River near present-day Livingston, and from there down the Yellowstone to meet Lewis near the convergence of the Yellowstone and Missouri Rivers in what is now North Dakota. Fraser urged Budde to include Clark's 1806 journey down the Yellowstone on the map, as it "encompassed some of the most beautiful scenery of the region."[39]

The grand plan for the Jefferson National Expansion Memorial, conceived during the 1930s, consisted of a park with a memorial as the central feature. Construction of the memorial arch, designed by Eero Saarinen, began in February 1963 and was finished in October 1965, several months after Fraser's trip to St. Louis. The completed 630-foot arch is the tallest memorial in the United States and the tallest stainless-steel monument in the world.

To complement the work of the Jefferson Memorial Association, the Lewis and Clark Trail Commission was established by Congress in 1964 to preserve and mark the explorers' route. Eleven states participated in the Trail Commission. Orvin Fjare, state advertising director, represented Montana and served as chair of the Montana Committee. Fraser friend and Harlowtown newspaperman Hal Stearns was the vice chair. In February 1966, a train carrying members of the Trail Commission stopped in Billings en route from St. Louis to Portland. At Union Station in Billings, Stuart Conner organized a welcome party consisting of Crow Indians, Miss Indian America Sharron Ahtone (Kiowa), Stan Lynde, Don Foote, and Mayor Fraser. Foote and Fraser joined the trip from Billings to Portland. Clark Adreon Sr., whom Willard had hosted the previous summer for a tour of Pompeys Pillar, was also aboard the train. Lloyd Old Coyote presented Adreon a letter of welcome, and Roger Stops gave Adreon a hand-carved horse as "repayment" for the thirty-six horses the Crows stole from Lewis and Clark. Conner also arranged to have smoke signals set off from Pompeys Pillar, so they would be visible to those in the train. Commission members returned to Billings that summer for their quarterly meeting and the dedication of Pompeys Pillar and to join the annual Yellowstone River Boat Float, which featured a Lewis and Clark costume ball one evening. The Lewis and Clark interpretive markers along Montana's highways resulted from the 1966 Trail Commission meetings.[40]

Left to right: Clark Adreon Sr.; Don Henke dressed as Captain Clark; Mayor Fraser; G. Edward "Gus" Budde of the Missouri's Lewis & Clark Trail Commission; actor Robert Taylor; and Clark Adreon Jr., during the Yellowstone River Boat Float, 1966. Bill Whithorn, photographer. 2006.044.7233, Yellowstone Gateway Museum, Livingston

As the only upriver member of the Jefferson National Expansion Memorial Association, Fraser shared the speaker's platform at the dedication of the Gateway Arch in St. Louis on May 25, 1968, with Vice President Hubert Humphrey and Interior Secretary Stewart Udall, who officiated. Artist J. K. Ralston and his wife, Willow, and Hal Stearns accompanied Fraser to St. Louis, where Ralston's painting *Into the Unknown* was unveiled as part of the dedication. The painting depicts members of the Lewis and Clark Expedition leaving a Shoshone village at the Beaverhead River before going over the Continental Divide. It hung in the Museum of Westward Expansion in St. Louis once it was completed. Fraser brought a Montana sagebrush plant to be planted in the museum grounds at the dedication, saying, "St. Louis is going to smell a whole lot nicer."[41] In 2018, the memorial was designated a national park and renamed Gateway Arch National Park.

In high demand as a public speaker, Willard Fraser traveled hundreds of miles within the state and thousands of miles beyond its borders to speak at sundry events and on a wide variety of topics. He did not have a booming orator's voice; instead, he established a personal connection with his audience, a connection further cemented by his enthusiasm, humor, and knack for storytelling. As mayor, he spoke at numerous high school graduations. As a political official, he chaired the Montana Water Congress, an organization dedicated to protecting the state's water resources for Montana's benefit, and was the featured speaker at the Dawson County Jefferson-Jackson dinner, an annual Democratic Party fundraiser, in Glendive. As a supporter of the arts, he participated in the Governor's Council on the Arts in Helena. As a public relations man, he addressed the Advertising Association of the West in Santa Ana, California, and the Tri-State Travel Editors in Yellowstone National Park, while as a proponent of fluoridation, he moderated a dental panel in Washington, D.C. When he spoke at a 1964 geological meeting in Regina, Saskatchewan, Fraser commented, "We're not only city unlimited now; we're country unlimited."[42]

The more Willard spoke at public ceremonies, the more invitations he received. He did not accept every invitation. When the King of Norway visited Minneapolis, Fraser was invited to represent Billings, and he declined, saying, "When it comes to royalty, autocrat that I am, I am a democrat at heart."[43] Fraser did not turn down an invitation to present at Crow Fair, the largest Native American event in Montana and one of the biggest powwows in the country. The fair, held in Crow Agency, features a parade, horse racing, evening powwows, and a daily rodeo, drawing as many as fifty thousand spectators to the Crow Reservation each August. Until the 1980s, most tribal members spoke Apsáalooke as their first language.[44] When he spoke at Crow Fair in 1964, Fraser worked with a translator to have his speech translated into the Apsáalooke language so that he could deliver it in that difficult tongue.[45]

Because of Willard's ready repertoire of facts and stories, he could adapt his speechmaking to a variety of occasions. His experience as a speaker was a decided advantage when he was invited in 1968 to give a presentation to what he thought was the Yellowstone Geological Society. He prepared something about Yellowtail Dam and Bighorn Canyon, thinking it would appeal to his audience. When he got to the location, he thought, "My golly, that's a funny looking group of geologists. Perhaps they decided to bring their wives." When the chair introduced Willard, it became apparent that the group was, in fact, the Yellowstone *Genealogical* Society. Fraser walked to the rostrum, reevaluating his planned presentation. He talked instead about his Scotch ancestors, Catholics and the early padres, and the Mormons. "I made out," he recalled.[46]

Many of Willard's speaking engagements outside of Billings involved testifying for proposals that would benefit Billings and Montana. Fraser's earlier work on Yellowtail Dam had made him a veteran participant in congressional hearings, and he continued to testify in both Helena and Washington, D.C., about state and national issues. He advocated for a reservoir proposal for Billings and, at the request of Governor Anderson, testified before the Environmental Protection Agency in Helena about proposed sulfur emission standards. In D.C., he testified against the closing of Glasgow Air Force Base and the Miles City Veterans Hospital in addition to speaking on the dangers of air pollution. He also spoke to a congressional aviation subcommittee on a proposal for the federal government to finance national airport systems as it had financed the interstate highway system.

Willard was never at a loss for ideas. "I like ideas. Do you have any?" he once wrote to a councilman.[47] This open, inquisitive attitude fueled much of Mayor Fraser's involvement in conferences and inspired him to make connections with other elected officials. He attended the annual U.S. Conference of Mayors, whether it was in New York City, New Orleans, Philadelphia, Honolulu, St. Louis, or Chicago. He "did Bourbon Street" with Mayor John Lindsay of New York City and struck up friendships with Detroit mayor Jerome Cavanagh and Baltimore mayor Thomas D'Alesandro III.[48] Both mayors were leaders who were early advocates of hiring or appointing African Americans to their city boards and commissions, but they were also tested by destructive, violent riots in their cities—in Detroit in 1967 and in Baltimore in 1968. Fraser's exposure to such charismatic and forward-thinking leaders affirmed his own resolve to pursue his progressive goals in Billings.

In 1971, D'Alesandro accepted Fraser's invitation to visit Billings. A military history buff and someone who had "read almost everything written" about the Little Bighorn Battle, D'Alesandro toured the battlefield and met Crow veteran Barney Old Coyote and president of the Billings American Indian Council, Sam Rides the Horse. Fraser also introduced him to Beth McNally, mother of Orioles pitcher Dave McNally, who was on the 1966 and 1970 Orioles World Series championship teams. The Baltimore mayor sat in on a city council meeting and later wrote to Fraser, "You were the perfect host. I marvel at the enthusiasm that you have for your city and your part of America and respect your dedication to public service as I witnessed your conduct in the City Council and the warmth with which you greet your fellow man."[49]

Fraser's connection with Chicago mayor Richard J. Daley strengthened as a result of the 1968 mayors' conference in Chicago. Shortly after Fraser returned to Billings that summer, Mayor Daley, too, had to deal with riots—this time with protesters at the Democratic National Convention. Fraser's reaction to the Chicago riots was certainly influenced by his personal positive feelings toward Daley, about whom he said, "He knows what he's doing, and he's a very able man." He sent a supportive telegram to Daley for his "maintenance of law and order."[50] Given Fraser's humanistic qualities, it seems unlikely that he would have continued to support the actions of the Chicago police given the perspective of time and with more information on what transpired outside Convention Hall.

Willard's acquaintance with big city mayors didn't cause him to neglect mayors or concerns of other Montana cities. By 1967, Marian Erdmann of Great Falls had been replaced by Democrat John McLaughlin, and Howard Dix of Missoula had been replaced by Richard Shoup. That year, Fraser joined with Shoup, McLaughlin, and Montana's congressmen in a Great Falls meeting to attempt to prevent Glasgow Air Force Base from closing, and he joined McLaughlin in advocating for an I-90 interchange at Glendive.[51] In July, Fraser and McLaughlin journeyed together to Salt Lake City to testify at a Civil Aeronautics Board meeting considering plane service between Billings and Los Angeles.[52]

Unsurprisingly, Willard kept a packed suitcase at home so he could take off at a moment's notice.[53] That seemed a sensible approach, given this energetic mayor's travel schedule. However, travel costs money, and therein lay more clashes with Fraser's city council. Budget skirmishes over his travel expenses made local headlines in 1966, when the council cut his car allowance from $1,200 to $900. In addition, he had a $2,000 travel allowance, but he maintained he paid more than $1,000 out of his own pocket to travel for "legitimate city business."

Controversy about his travel expenditures and objections from city council members continued into Fraser's last term. In December 1971, a *Gazette* column with the headline "Jet-set Fraser Flies on Red Ink" described the mayor, back from the national conference of the League of Cities in Hawai'i and with his travel budget in the red, smiling and telling newsmen that he planned to go to Wolf Point to speak to the chamber of commerce and then perhaps to Washington, D.C., to check on progress on funding for Billings' bus and water systems. Columnist Roger Clawson had admitted in an earlier column that Willard had brought federal funds to Billings as a result of a connection he made in Philadelphia and a subsequent visit to D.C.[54] Despite his success at such fundraising, the mayor continued to meet resistance from his city council, led by Aldermen Donald Baker and Roy Rye, but he never capitulated to the council's attempts to rein in his travel. After Baker accused him of "abuse of power," Fraser "chuckled" in his office and told newsmen he was off to Red Lodge

Fraser (left) in Washington, D.C., in March 1965 with Representative James Battin (center) to testify against the closing of Miles City's Veterans Administration hospital.
2027.15.222, Western Heritage Center, Billings

to address a high school class. Fraser was rightly convinced his traveling was good for Billings and Montana.

Willard was just as audacious about his preferred method of getting to his various commitments. Rather than driving his own ancient 1956 Packard or, later, his white Mercury, he used city policemen as his personal chauffeurs with no compunction. Some felt this wasn't right, but others said it was a lot safer for Willard to be driven by the police. Friend and journalist Addison Bragg said, "It scared the hell out of you if you drove with him in a car. I once drove to Red Lodge with Willard and then started looking around for someone to drive back to Billings with."[55] Willard evidently knew his talents did not extend to automobile driving. Mac Fraser recalls being summoned to drive his uncle to the Crow Fair one year, and Paul Jakab, the son of friends, remembers driving Willard to a sun dance ceremony.[56] Willard's letters recount numerous times when he invited Jim Thompson or Stuart Conner to come along to an event—and, by the way, do the driving. When Willard finally agreed to stop using police cars as his own taxi, Bragg quipped, "The good news is that Willard is going to stop riding around in police cars. The bad news is that Willard is going to start driving himself."[57] Willard shared his feelings about the issue when writing to a staff member of the *Great Falls Tribune* to say that "the editor of the Billings *Gazette* . . . does not understand that a mayor can learn a great deal from riding with the police."[58]

As Willard's schedule became busier, he hired local pilots to fly him to and from engagements. Police chief Beven, airport manager Robert Michael, rancher Gerhardt Blaine, and local businessman and engineer Fred Liquin all played a part in flying the mayor around the state and beyond its borders. Some of these flights must have been terrifying, as Fraser hints at in the description of a trip to Billings from Rapid City: "It was terrifically stormy weather and we were almost forced down. I told him [Michael] not to worry about landing as the Cheyenne are friendly now. He, being a pilot, and knowing more about it [the possible danger] than I, was really in a sweat; however, we did arrive in Billings."[59] After flying over Livingston, a town located at the intersection of powerful crosswinds, Fraser exclaimed, "[T]he turbulence was unbelievable. We dropped once over 700 feet. I still have a sore spot on my head where we hit the roof."[60]

Willard sometimes suffered severe asthma attacks as a result of his determination to engage in the world outside of Billings. "Your air pollution did my breathing no good," he admonished a friend upon returning from a meeting in Missoula.[61] After a mayors' conference in Philadelphia he reported, "Your Philadelphia weather coupled with air conditioning at the Bellevue-Stratford did me in."[62] Outdoor air pollution, humidity, and air conditioning all threatened Willard's health, but cigarette smoke was particularly dangerous. This eternal foe earned his ire after a trip to Hawai'i: "Honolulu was great but those *damnable* smokers on the plane."[63] He had to stay in a hotel for two days to gain strength to come back to Billings. This experience inspired a letter to Frontier Airlines in which he outlined why they should ban smoking on flights.[64] Willard's request to the airlines would not be honored for another thirty years.

Mayor Fraser's ability to see Billings as part of the larger Montana and American landscape inspired him to pursue interests, correspondence, and travels that took him far beyond Billings. His journeys were motivated by his belief that it is important to "reach beyond the city limits, for we are all a single community, and must work and act as such."[65] John Bohlinger, who ran Fraser's 1971 mayoral campaign, referred to Willard as "The Mayor of the State" for his reach and influence, while James Thompson said, "He was the Mayor of all Outdoors."[66] After man landed on the moon in 1969, Willard made an observation that rings true today: "One of the positives to come from the Moon Landing it seems to me is that it will inevitably bring home to all people that we are 'in this world together' . . . pollution-wise, governmental-wise, and . . . we must tackle problems as ONE World, for it is truly that."[67]

CHAPTER SIXTEEN

"What is a city without lively youngsters in it?"

"DON'T TRUST anyone over thirty" was a popular slogan of disaffected youth in the 1960s, an era when the media devoted much coverage to juvenile delinquency and to public handwringing over the alleged moral decay of the young. Despite his own occasional fretting over young people's unkempt appearance, Willard valued young people and paid attention to their needs. "What is a city without lively youngsters in it?" he responded to grumblings from "the little old ladies from both sexes."[1] As mayor, Fraser took young people's concerns as seriously as he did other issues, and he valued and respected them as responsible, thoughtful citizens. Willard's genuine interest in youth represents a hallmark of his mayoral tenure and, in many ways, was unique to his brand of governance.

Fraser demonstrated his advocacy for children in his daily activities and his positions on public policy. A December 1964 *Gazette* headline, "Fraser Clinches Toboggan Vote," was a wry take on the mayor's support for blocking off streets near Pioneer Park so that children could go sledding on the hill. The mayor asked those who were inconvenienced to "bear with transient childhood . . . let us accept the inexorable rules of childhood and cooperate with them for these brief periods."[2] A few years later, when some of the city aldermen pushed to charge a fee for the public swimming pool, he responded, "I have always thought some things in life should be free and among these should be the right of small boys and girls to go swimming."[3] Early in his tenure, Fraser began working on establishing a Boys Club in Billings, a goal he accomplished in 1970.

In 1968, hoping to foster a deeper appreciation for history among local youth, while also promoting fun—Willard was always in favor of having

Mayor Fraser and Stan Lynde lead dozens of boys on the "No Mom's Bike Hike," an overnight excursion to Pompeys Pillar instituted by the mayor in 1968. Courtesy Western Heritage Center, Billings

fun—the mayor established an overnight bike ride for boys aged eleven to sixteen. The ride, which came to be called "No Moms Bike Hike," took them from Billings to Pompeys Pillar to get a close look at this evidence of the Lewis and Clark Expedition. In July 1970, four hundred boys embarked on the forty-plus-mile venture. Before the boys turned in for the night, Apsáalooke World War II veteran Joe Medicine Crow explained Indian smoke signals, artist Ken Ralston and cartoonist Stan Lynde discussed their portrayals of the West, and Fraser himself recounted William Clark's escape from grizzly bears.[4] A year later, when six girls proposed a "No Dads Bike Ride" to Laurel, Mayor Fraser was all for it.

One of Willard's favorite speaking gigs was to talk to elementary or middle school students. Teachers frequently invited Willard to speak or read to their classes, even during the two years between his third and fourth terms when he was an ordinary citizen. He often read Frost's poetry or spoke on civics or the environment, and he relished the letters students sent him after such presentations. After Fraser spoke to one elementary school class about the history of the American Indian people in Montana, a young boy wrote to tell him, "You made me proud to be an Indian."[5]

Fraser answered letters from school-aged children with pages, not paragraphs, of encouragement and advice. He seldom missed an opportunity to plug his favorite causes, such as air pollution and civic responsibility. "I hope you are a nonsmoking bicycle rider," he wrote to a student who inquired about air pollution. To another student, he sent a three-page response in which he said, "Increasingly today with our growth of the cities, and with people living immediately next door to the other, we are needing more and more order so that we can stand each other. And this is what government is mostly all about." He concluded the letter by inviting the young man to take a tour of the police department.[6] When a student from Glasgow wrote seeking information about Fraser's father-in-law, Robert Frost, Fraser's full-page response ended with the line, "Trusting this will help you get an 'A' in your class" followed by the Fraser signature with a flourish.[7] Many of his letters to young people share a common positive tone. "You sound like a responsible young citizen," a typical letter begins; in another he says, "It is precisely because of the active, interested, and intelligent boys and girls like you that I am able to be a good Mayor."[8]

At least once, Willard's enthusiastic efforts to instill local pride in Billings' young people earned him some indignant criticism. While adults could take Willard's sometimes-liberal interpretations of history with a chuckle and a grain of salt, the mother of a third grader wrote to the *Gazette* with concern because her son had come home to report that Mayor Fraser said that Billings is the oldest city in the United States.[9] This was a common "Fraserism," a statement by Willard that could not be swallowed whole. This particular declaration was based on his knowledge of the area near the Yellowstone River as an early gathering place for Indigenous peoples. Objections such as this one from the third grader's mother did not stymie Fraser's glorification of the history of the region.

Mothers were not the only people who sometimes questioned the mayor. In a 1970 *Gazette* column, Addison Bragg reported that ex-mayor Fraser "was up to his old tricks again" by using the sheriff to take him to a local school to read poetry in an English class.[10] Fraser responded with a letter of explanation to the editor. He said that at a meeting in the Northern Hotel, a gentleman had told him an English teacher from Will James Middle

School wanted to meet him and ask a favor. Still healing from a broken hip and knee, Willard replied, "Bring her over, her legs are better than mine." When the teacher asked him to read to a 9:00 a.m. class, Willard declined, saying he was undergoing an asthma attack and getting his tubes cleared out, so driving a cold car at that time would leave him too short of wind. The sheriff overheard this conversation and offered to drive him.[11]

A true politician, he pushed young people to speak up about issues that mattered to them, and he enjoyed an opportunity to share their concerns with the city council. When a girl wrote to him about a plan for a softball field, he let her know that "about four years ago we drew up plans to make a softball complex out of Stewart Park. Just lately one of our Council men has been objecting to it, and I am sending your letter to him. It is letters like this from interested active citizens such as yourself that help. If you have other friends who would like to write too I would pass their letters on likewise."[12] Of course, Fraser would have been delighted to have his "obdurate" councilman confronted by such letters. Construction on the softball complex began in the fall of 1972, and it was dedicated on June 1, 1974.

In an era when gender roles often dictated separate spheres of activity, Fraser supported many opportunities for boys.[13] He was not, however, oblivious to the inequalities girls faced. "As a father of a daughter," he addressed a Campfire Girls gathering, "I think we ought to be doing more for girls than we are in this community."[14] Occasionally, the mayor was asked to judge beauty contests, a popular aspect of American culture at the time. As he did when encouraging confidence in young men, he also strove to instill self-assurance in the contestants. After judging the Miss Wyoming contest, a woman judge and Fraser received letters from the chosen young woman. Their replies could not have been more opposite. "The woman [judge] said, 'I wrote her a letter and said not to let it go to her head. Be humble.'" Fraser recalled, "I then admitted that I had written the girl and said, 'Stick out your chest, lift up your head, and live it up! You're queen for such a short time.'"[15] His advice to the pageant winner reflects his own ability to believe in himself regardless of the critical views of others.

Willard retained an appreciation for a child's sense of fun, and he generously indulged it. Friend and clothing store owner John Bohlinger commented on Willard's attentiveness to his children, recalling, "He once asked if I'd like to have a fire truck pick them up and take them home. Sure enough, that day there was a fire truck in front of the store to take them home."[16] Fraser's secretary, Abby Ferguson, related that when Fraser traveled out of town, he sent postcards to her daughter. She said, "He loved children, and my daughter who was six or seven at the time adored him."[17] Willard enjoyed getting young people outside to be active. In his sixties, he reported that he took his nephew's children on "every ride" at the local fair.[18]

After breaking his hip in 1968, Mayor Fraser began riding a bicycle—with balloon tires and no gears—regularly, and he soon found that doing so helped him get a child's-eye view of local happenings. Recommending bike riding to a patient at St. Vincent's, Willard said, "The kids of the neighborhood ride along beside me to tell me of all the latest in school and the neighborhood gossip."[19] In 2019, Billings resident Lance Grider remembered, "My friend Bill Kreiner and I were riding our bikes downtown one summer day in the '60s and Mayor Willard cycled by on his bike. We recognized him immediately and said, 'Hi, Mr. Mayor' and he gave us a cheery, 'Hello, Boys,' as he biked to work. How can you not like a guy like that?"[20] Willard, too, saw his bike riding as a positive relationship builder.

Mayor Fraser was open to young people's opinions on issues, and he gave merit to their views. He wrote to a Dawson County High School senior, "What is the position your classmates take regarding the proposition of eighteen-year-olds voting? In the past, I tended to oppose this, but lately have changed my position." He then added a favorite question, "What do you think about that?"[21] He believed that citizens in a democracy should engage in government, and that belief extended to young people. When an opportunity arose, he sought to introduce students to important national figures. When Hubert Humphrey spoke to the state legislature in Helena in 1959, Willard made arrangements for his nephew Mac to take the train from Missoula to Helena so he could see and hear Humphrey in person. As part of the experience, and characteristic of his combination of instruction and generosity, Willard took Mac out for lunch at the historic Montana Club off Last Chance Gulch in Helena.

Mayor Fraser and the Boy Scouts promoting bike safety, 1963. In addition to supporting the scouts, Fraser founded Billings's first Boys' Club and established a Youth Committee to advise the city administration on young people's issues.
Billings Gazette, Oct. 2, 1963

Both Willard and his sister, Jeanne, were involved in the lives of Marvin's five children. Willard applied his nearly missionary fervor to encourage a positive future for young people to his niece and nephews. As they reached college age, Willard's message to them was, "You have to go to college." Marvin thought that Mac's job at a gas station was just fine, but Mac's mother, Mary Louise, agreed with Willard in his push for a college education for the young Frasers. Mac said she "wanted her kids to get a different flavor of life."

Despite Willard's own financial struggles, he supplemented his educational advice with contributions to college expenses, giving Mac and his brother John $1,000 (roughly $9,000 in today's dollars) per year toward tuition, nearly three-quarters of the tuition in the late 1950s. In return, the brothers performed such tasks as scrubbing and polishing floors and painting in the Fraser buildings during their college summers. In the 1960s, Willard also shepherded his brother Bob's son, Robert Fraser, and Lesley Frost Ballantine's grandson, Doug Wilber, into Montana colleges.

Beyond providing financial assistance, Willard monitored the academic progress of his young relatives. While they were attending the university, he would drive the 350 miles from Billings to Missoula and take them out to lunch at the locally renowned Florence Hotel, where he would sit and twirl his pen between his fingers while he quizzed them about their grades. Sally Fraser, daughter of Willard's cousin Harold, was part of this group and commented that the lunches were fun but also an obligation.[22] What Willard couldn't communicate in real time, he committed to letter. When Michael Fraser, who attended college in California, was not performing as well as his mentor expected, Willard sent him several admonishing letters telling him, "Get with it—you have the ability, and now you ought to use it."[23] Mac said he, too, received letters from his uncle that "lectured me and told me what to do and how to do it." Mac expressed this without rancor. Rather, he commented in a tone of respect, "Willard made you think and held your feet to the fire. He wanted people to be the best you can be."[24]

With support and encouragement from Willard and their parents, all of Marvin Fraser's children did well. Four of the five attended the university in Missoula. Pepper (John) graduated in 1961, and the youngest, Wendelanne, in 1973. Pepper and Mac went on to successful business careers. Willard was proud of them and in a letter spoke positively of Mac's "vim and vigor." Michael became a professional musician, playing for the San Francisco Symphony. Jerry managed hotels and motels, and Wendy became a therapist.

Willard had several godsons, among them Ted Cross, the son of his longtime friend Frank Cross. Ted remembered Willard as "always trying to do things for people." Willard took Ted to parades, bought him yearly subscriptions to the *Junior National History Magazine*, and never forgot his birthday. Recognizing Ted's intellectual talents and interests, Willard told his godson he should go into sanitation engineering because garbage was such a big problem "it will overrun us all." Instead, Ted became an electrical engineer and worked for the Defense Department analyzing Russian missiles.[25]

Willard frequently referred to daughter Robin's five children—David, Marjorie, Joshua, John, and Benjamin—as "the world's greatest grandchildren," and the letters he wrote to his grandchildren are especially long and often filled with advice. When grandson David wrote to him and confided that he got in trouble with his teacher for talking too much, Willard's reply pointed to the merits of being a capable speaker:

> Perhaps the next time you have a teacher who thinks you talk too much, tell her it is because you have so much to say; and that your grandfather, who is an expert on conversationalists, says she should listen more to what you have to say. Also tell her that "talking" was bred into you. . . . For instance, tell her that Edward Everett Beecher, one of the greatest and most consistent talkers of the last century is in your blood lines, then that one of your grandfathers is the best Presbyterian preacher and talker of this land and the other is Mayor of Billings and he got to be Mayor because he was a constant talker—that your dad is a lawyer—and lawyers are famous for talking, and your mother is a woman—a sex famous of having the last word—so to expect you to be quiet is just to expect too much. . . . Tell her to listen to what you have to say, and then talk sense to her.[26]

When eight-year-old Marjorie asked her grandfather who the most lovable American president was, Willard sent her a seven-page letter in which he appraised the lovability of seventeen presidents. Aware that the criterion was "lovable" not "great," Fraser discounted Lincoln because he dealt with too many problems and didn't have time to be lovable. About Teddy Roosevelt, Fraser said, "Cuddly he was not." His evaluation of Taft, meanwhile, included a mental picture of the three-hundred-pound president dripping beside his custom-made bathtub. Willard opined that FDR had too much "high Church fancy deviousness," and although he admired Kennedy, he determined that JFK was "too much of a jock." In the end, Fraser declared Truman to have been the most lovable president.

Willard with Marjorie Hudnut, Robin's daughter, ca. 1965. Fraser relished the role of uncle and grandfather and helped put some of his young relatives through college.
Courtesy Marjorie Hudnut Renner

He singled out Truman's fatherly/grandfatherly image and wrote at length about Truman's ability to "cuss out the rascals," adding that "with these outbursts of earthiness . . . did Truman wind and wrap his way into our heartstrings and [give] Americans all that certain feeling of security and warmth, for with Harry Truman in the White House, with his fists up, and chin thrust out, we knew that he and we could lick any S.O.B. who dared to criticize or challenge his family, friends, state of Missouri, and Nation."[27] As a grandfather and as a politician, Willard was forthright in his opinions and, like Truman, loyal to those he loved. His positive view of Truman was likely influenced, at least in part, by the fact that Burton K. Wheeler was a close friend of Truman, who wrote after becoming president, "Burt Wheeler was one of the few Senators who was in any way decent to the Junior Senator from Missouri and I can't forget that. That doesn't necessarily mean that he has any influence with me as to policy, but I shall continue to like him as long as I live."[28]

Willard enjoyed hosting his grandchildren for extended summer visits to Billings. "Montana is for boys and sad is the boy who doesn't experience Montana," was a favorite Fraser saying. During one of his grandson David's summer visits, Willard wrote to Robin to say he had taken him to three movies—*Fiddler on the Roof, Nicholas and Alexandra*, and *Damn Yankees*. He added, "David is having a great time. He is riding in police cars [and] fire wagons, [and] has attended banquets, conventions, Council meetings, and last night he saw the Council at its worst. He has been swimming and many other things. Tomorrow he goes on the Bike Hike."[29]

David's version of one visit to see his grandfather was more elaborate and demonstrates Willard's urge to educate and get young people involved in community affairs. Thirteen-year-old David accompanied Willard to his office, where the mayor asked his secretary to call the police chief in. David remembered,

> He introduced me to the chief and said, "You know, Davy doesn't know much about police work. Is there an officer he could drive round with today?" So Willard walked me down, and I drove around in a squad car for four hours. Then we got a call in the squad car to come to prison, the city jail. Willard was there. "Come on, Davy, we're going to prison," he said. An officer walked us around, and we went from cell to cell. Willard knew many of the people. He would ask that the doors be opened, we walked in, sat down, and Willard introduced me. If the resident was an Indian, he used their Indian names. He was always respectful of Indian names. A typical conversation would include a comment like, "Gosh, we've been working so hard to get you a job and you've been promising me you were going to break through. Why are we seeing you here again?" We visited at least eight people. We were there three hours.[30]

As he did for his grandchildren, Mayor Fraser paid attention to local teenagers and their needs. He established a Youth Advisory Council in his first years as mayor in order to involve teens in city affairs and to instill a sense of civic engagement. More than fifty years later, Billings resident Russ Davidson remembered hearing an announcement on KOOK radio that anyone interested in being on the mayor's youth council should call the mayor's office. Davidson did so, and after meeting with the mayor, Russ served with about twelve other students on the 1968–69 council. Council students represented all three high schools (West, Central, and Senior) and both middle schools (Will James and Lewis and Clark). Each meeting began with the mayor asking what the students thought the city could do for the youth. Russ said, "For me and those in that council it was a big deal that political leaders really cared about our ideas and actually listened. He never talked down to us but was very sincerely interested in what we had to say." He went on, "I absolutely believe we made a difference." As a result of the meetings, students hosted rock concerts at Pioneer Park once a month, and a building at 2032 Grand Avenue was opened as a teen dance and music venue. The youth council also created a crisis hotline for kids on bad drug trips. "Mayor Fraser was absolutely the best," Russ said. "It was because of him that I first got excited about political science, a subject I eventually taught for 40 years."[31]

Willard served as a role model even for those with whom he didn't have a personal relationship. In 2009, Fred Van Valkenburg, county attorney of Missoula County, was asked by former legislator Bob Brown what in his life motivated him to become involved in the public sector. Before mentioning Mike Mansfield, Bobby Kennedy, and George McGovern, Van Valkenburg said, "There was a mayor of Billings, Willard Fraser. . . . He was a colorful figure, . . . somebody who you could kind of look at and say, 'Well, it wouldn't be too bad to follow in those footsteps.'"[32] Van Valkenburg had grown up in Billings and served in the state senate for many years before being elected Missoula county attorney. Decades later, another man who had been a teenager in the 1960s remembered Fraser in a different situation. As the young man and friends were enjoying a kegger at Pictograph Cave, the mayor suddenly appeared. They were sure they were busted. Instead, Fraser gave them a lecture about littering and not polluting the environment and then took his leave.[33]

In 2020, Paul Jakab, a California lawyer, recalled Willard's influence on him during his formative years. The Jakabs had fled the Hungarian Revolution in 1956 and arrived in Billings in 1957, where they established Jakab's Art Gallery and where Paul's parents, Elmer and Ruth, became friends with Willard Fraser and Stuart Conner. Paul had heard his parents talk about Willard for years, but he and Willard did not become acquainted until Paul was in high school. As the 1968 Billings High School student body president, Paul was elected student "mayor of the day" and went to work with Willard, his adult counterpart. When it came time for Paul to choose a college, Willard urged him toward Harvard. His persuasion prevailed. During Paul's college years, Willard sent him long, encouraging and instructive letters. When Paul was on the staff of a Harvard publication, Willard brokered an interview for him with Chet Huntley, NBC newsman and founder of Big Sky Resort. Later, when Paul was in law school at Columbia, Willard arranged for Paul to meet Jeanne and her husband Ben Blackford, whom he described as a "sensible Republican." The Blackfords' hospitality expanded to an invitation to their condo in Florida and time on Long Island Sound on their boat, *Flicka*.

Willard also introduced Paul to poetry, politics, and the world at large. "I would not have appreciated Robert Frost nor the plight of the Indians without him," Paul recalled. He remembered driving Willard to Laurel one day over back roads while Willard discussed *Fiddler on the Roof*—the story of a Jewish family's flight during the pogroms in turn-of-the-twentieth-century imperial Russia. This was the first time Paul had heard of the musical. Paul echoed Russ Davidson's statement that he majored in political science because of Willard, but because Paul had witnessed the adversity Willard faced, he made the choice not to become an elected official. "Billings didn't appreciate what they had," Paul observed. He knew how poorly Willard was paid, and he decided he would not go into politics if it meant being beholden to or dependent on others for his financial existence, as Willard was.[34]

Humor and wit were natural Fraser characteristics, but they also protected him from the emotional cost of defeat and adversity—as did his constant quest for knowledge. Paul Jakab's perceptive observation of Fraser's sacrifice suggests that Willard's enduring optimism was, in part, a deliberate choice stemming from a childhood plagued with asthma and financial insecurity and maintained through successive illnesses and frequent public rejection of his talents and ideas. During Willard's childhood and his adult years, asthma played a role in developing his reading habits, which in turn helped broaden his mind and buoy his spirits. Having benefited from extensive reading, he encouraged a young Olympic athlete also afflicted with the debilitating illness: "Having asthma does give one time to read, as in my own case I all too often wake up coughing and wheezing at three or four in the morning and not being able to lie down or go back to sleep, I do get in a lot of reading."[35]

Fraser used his position as mayor to encourage young people to use higher education as a steppingstone toward full participation in the wider society. For instance, when a Crow youth ran afoul of the law and had to spend a night sobering up in jail, Willard wrote to him. "There is no one, no color, no sex, or age—be he red, white, black, blue, purple or pink polka dot who can handle alcohol safely," Willard admonished. "So, get with it, get to your books and get on to college . . . and get an education because the Mayor of Billings needs educated Crows as well as educated whites."[36]

Another young Crow man who benefited from Willard's intervention was Bill Yellowtail, who attended Dartmouth College in New Hampshire in the 1960s.[37] Willard did not know Yellowtail but knew some of his family members, so he wrote to him in his freshman year to encourage him in typical Willard fashion by telling him, among other things, that he was there to civilize the "New England savages."[38] In the second spring of this youth's time at Dartmouth, pro-segregation politician George Wallace visited Dartmouth, and apparently the protests against Wallace created an atmosphere of chaos during which the boy "did several things, including stealing some beer." He was expelled.[39]

Willard immediately began a correspondence with Dartmouth president John Dickey to advocate for the student's reinstatement. He emphasized the great strain "put upon the boy taken from a small Montana reservation town and entered into your Ivy League student body." Fraser emphasized the importance of the boy's education, saying that "the Crows so need the type of leadership he is potentially capable of giving."[40] He continued to advocate on the boy's behalf throughout the summer, telling Dickey, "I can understand your position, and yet I cannot too strongly emphasize the fact that this boy. . . comes from a completely different environment and culture, and his people so need educated men. . . . I once made such an exception with a boy of Mexican birth, and this June that boy's son graduated number one from the Law School."[41] Willard's considerable

Always an advocate for education and literacy, Fraser (right of center) attended the groundbreaking of Eastern Montana College's new library. Taking the first turn at the shovel is EMC librarian Jean Davis. MSU–Billings Library

effort did not have an immediate effect; however, Yellowtail returned to Dartmouth two years later and graduated in 1972.

Fraser witnessed prejudice against different races and religions during his boyhood, while serving in the military, and in his South Side neighborhood. He spoke decisively against such intolerance and exhorted young people to be open-minded. In a two-page letter to a student at Rocky Mountain College, he catalogued groups of humanity that had been maligned and mistreated at various points in history—the Scots by the English after the Battle at Culloden, the Irish ("as filthy a name as one could be called in the 1840s"), the Germans ("the terms 'Kraut' or 'square-head' were exceedingly dirty words when I was a boy"), and the Jews ("a few years ago the term was one of great disrespect"). He followed this list with a call to respect all people.[42]

Sometimes Fraser used drama, underscored with humor, to make a case against prejudice. North Dakota jokes were popular in Montana at the time and often made North Dakotans out to be simpletons. For example, one joke asked, "How many North Dakotans does it take to screw in a light bulb?" Answer: "Three. One to hold the bulb and two to rotate the ladder." Writing to the editor of the *Bismarck Tribune*, Fraser spoke of these "horrid North Dakota jokes" and said, "Personally, I have never liked jokes that had to rely on the degrading of someone else whether it be jokes on the Catholic, Irish, Jew or Negro."[43] But rather than issuing a passionate tirade, Willard planned a mass funeral for North Dakota jokes during the 1967 North Dakota Days in Billings.[44] As part of the event, referred to by its chairman as "the mayor's private baby," jokes were put into a gray coffin shrouded with a black cloth, and six pallbearers bore the "coffin" in a procession in downtown Billings. Four of the pallbearers were young men from Billings attending college in North Dakota.[45]

As the 1960s progressed, tensions between America's youth—who often espoused open-minded and countercultural ideals—and the more conservative, older generations in power became pronounced. When Fraser saw a production of the popular and controversial antiwar musical *HAIR*, he connected the decibel level of the music to a plight of the nation's young people. He opined that because Washington refused to hear or answer the legitimate questions American youth were asking, the music of the young generations got louder and louder, as some American soldiers did when speaking to Germans or French—thinking if they just talked louder, they would be understood.[46]

Unlike some of his generation, Fraser was not conflicted about the values that became popular among young Americans in the 1960s. He voiced his more open views in a letter to Salisbury, saying, "I just can't get carried away with those who are crying that the colleges have all gone "hippie," "Pinko," "Commie" or whatever adjectives you want to use. . . . One of the obligations of our generation, it seems to me is to . . . keep college kids in true perspective."[47] However, Willard drew the line at the poor personal hygiene and unkempt appearance that some young adults had adopted. When some young men alleged to Senator Mansfield that Fraser had his police department eject them from a park because they had long hair, Mansfield passed the complaint on to Fraser. The mayor responded, "If the youth today want to wear long hair, so be it. I will accept it in grace and so will and so does the Police Department and the City of Billings." Fraser then said the young men had come into his office to complain about the police harassing them, which Fraser contended was not true. He described the young men as having "the most incredibly foul, offensive odor that you can imagine" and concluded the letter by asserting, "As a Mayor, I have waged a continual battle against slum housing, dirty air, dirty land, and dirty water, and if we have to include dirty people . . . so be it."[48]

He was more tactful but just as adamant in a letter to a young man who had applied for a teaching position at Eastern Montana College. He wrote, "I am very happy to endorse you but I must advise you [that] you leave a lot to be desired in your personal grooming right now. Your hair is too long; your mustache is too silly." After a bit of lecturing about the importance of teachers being role models, Fraser ended the letter with "Hoping that as soon as you receive this letter you head for the nearest barbershop and buy a razor blade, and with that hoping to see you teaching at Eastern Montana College next year."[49]

Similarly, Fraser did not overlook instances when young people misused language. He wrote to one young man, "To learn to speak, and to know your language, is of utmost importance." He went on to say, "First of all, I should correct your English, for it is going to be a big handicap to you through your years in college, if you use incorrect grammar. You should have said 'My brother and I' instead of 'Me and my brother.' A word of the wise from a Mayor who knows and understands."[50] While most of Fraser's comments were delivered gently, occasionally he could be caustic in his criticism. For instance, when a young man from Missoula wrote to disparage some of Fraser's statements regarding "citizenship stupidity" and "oddballs," the young man could not have expected to hear this: "That really is an awful letter that you wrote me. I wonder if you know how many words were misspelled. Awful in context, form, grammar, and text." Fraser's

Fraser (second from left) at EMC's commencement ceremonies, 1967. Fraser encouraged young people to obtain a college education so that they could participate in the civic and political life of their communities. MSU–Billings Library

response was a four-page diatribe that ended with, "Snap to, get with it, and let's build Montana together."[51] In Fraser's view, the ability to write and speak fluently was part and parcel with responsible citizenship.

Lecturing was not Fraser's usual approach with people. Mr. and Mrs. Phil Scott, Fraser's acquaintances from Chicago, were so inspired by a report of Fraser's handling of a potential disruption of civic life that Phil Scott wrote a letter to the editor of the *Chicago Daily News*. He described a contingent of Black Muslims coming into Fraser's office and announcing they were going "to take over the city" by taking up stations at all prominent corners to extoll the virtues and merits of their philosophy.

> The mayor, a man of wit and astuteness . . . looked up from his desk, smiled, and leaned back in his chair and proclaimed: "Fine, we are glad to have you in our midst but before you start your day, why don't you all be my guests for breakfast so that you can start the day right." (He's that kind of man). It

happened. No incidents—no name calling—no fighting—no flaring tempers—no additional local police patrols and no calling of the National Guard. It was an orderly day, as most always they are in Billings.[52]

While Scott may have overstated the potential for civic disruption from these young men, the letter captures Fraser's essentially benevolent attitude toward friends and strangers alike, as well as his ability to avert conflict.

A consummate politician, Willard Fraser was also a natural humanist. His efforts to involve students in government and to encourage them toward a positive future went beyond benevolence. Knowing that the fate of the world depended on the young, mentoring them was part of Willard's effort to foster an educated and engaged American populace who would be informed voters in a progressive democracy. Throughout the cultural revolution and the political and global chaos of the 1960s, Fraser maintained his advocacy for young people and his belief in their essential goodness. He expressed his faith in Montana's youth in an article for the *American Observer and Weekly News Review*, which the editor introduced with the statement, "From one of the big Rocky Mountain states comes a vigorous expression of confidence in American youth." Mayor Fraser's article began, "In Billings, Montana, we do not have a juvenile problem, even though once in a while we do have a few young people who act as irresponsibly as some adults." He commended them, saying, "In spite of all the temptations we place in the hands of our youth, they resist us and—I repeat—are a better generation than we were."[53]

"The confusions of the hour are immense"

WILLARD FRASER served as mayor of Billings during an era characterized by cultural and political upheaval, a time dubbed by *LIFE* as the "Decade When Everything Changed."[1] Fraser had been in office less than a year when President John Kennedy was assassinated; by the end of the decade, Robert Kennedy, Martin Luther King Jr., Medgar Evers, and Malcolm X had also been killed.[2] Mourning publicly, Fraser also expressed concern for what the assassinations of these political and civic leaders meant to, and said about, the nation. When he issued the proclamation to fly flags at half-mast after Senator Kennedy's assassination, he entreated his fellow citizens to reflect on "the conditions existing in our country that make such events tragically possible. . . . I am also asking that the clergy of Billings emphasize the meaning of this tragedy, and pray for a better understanding of the meaning of Hope and Goodwill for all mankind in these tragic times."[3]

The years encompassing Willard's mayoral tenure were among the most tumultuous in a century. Unlike the immediate postwar era, the 1960s and 1970s were marked by violent riots and demonstrations, assassinations, and armed conflict. Simultaneously, dissatisfaction with the status quo sparked a cultural revolution in music, clothing, sexual attitudes, and hair styles as popular culture reflected the undercurrents of political change. Even as America became entrenched abroad in the Vietnam War, a progressive shift in politics on the national level birthed the Civil Rights Act of 1964, the Voting Rights Act of 1965, the War on Poverty legislation, and the rise of Indigenous self-determination. The progressive changes in the nation's laws caused many southern Democrats to become Republicans, creating a historical change in the demographics of the two major parties. Given his open mind and humanistic approach, Fraser was uniquely suited to—but at the same time challenged by—his leadership position during this era. "The confusions of the hour are immense," he observed, and they required his ability to reflect, assess, and sometimes change his mind.[4]

Willard's views on the national political scene of the 1960s appear only occasionally in the Billings press, but his letters illustrate more clearly how his attitude toward the Vietnam War changed over the course of a decade. Initially, he agreed with President Johnson on the war in Vietnam—a view that Fraser would abandon as the war escalated during Johnson's presidency. It is interesting to compare Willard's views with those of his contemporary and fellow politician, Mike Mansfield, whose views also evolved as the war progressed. Montana's senior senator had succeeded Lyndon Johnson as Senate majority leader in 1961, and he was a powerful Democratic voice throughout the Vietnam era.

Mansfield had been instrumental in America's support of Vietnamese nationalist Ngo Dinh Diem in the 1950s. Despite Diem's personal weaknesses and the subsequent brutality and autocracy of his government, Mansfield

Senator Mike Mansfield meets with Montana college students about their concerns regarding the crisis in Southeast Asia, 1970. Left to right: Bill Philip, John Kelly Addy, Dean Hart, Mansfield, Robert Quinn, Bob Brown. 99.0493, Archives and Special Collections, Mansfield Library, University of Montana-Missoula

continued to support Diem until 1962 because of Diem's anti-Communist views.[5] Mansfield voiced public support of the Johnson administration's actions in Vietnam in the early years of the war. "I would recommend that if you oppose the Viet Nam policy that you do so constructively. If you don't like what's being done, come up with an alternative," he said before a gathering of Lee newspaper editors in 1964.[6]

At that time, Fraser's stance was similar to Mansfield's, perhaps because both men were veterans who had dedicated their careers to public service. Mansfield had served in the U.S. Navy, the U.S. Army, and the Marines during World War I. Fraser's innate sense of patriotism predisposed him to support this war as a matter of backing the nation. "In the beginning," he wrote later, "I accepted the statements of the State Department and Defense Department brass that Viet Nam was necessary."[7] As an American soldier in Europe during World War II, Fraser had seen the devastation wrought by World War II, and he had passionately condemned that destruction. Ironically, Fraser had followed Wheeler in initially being against American involvement in World War II, but then served in the army for more than four years. His attitudes reversed in the Vietnam War. Fraser initially supported the war then turned against it as the loss of young lives increased and justification for the war became untenable.

In the first years of the war, Fraser wrote to soldiers overseas to offer encouragement, and his correspondence often included lighthearted humor. "The Army usually puts one Montanan in every outfit—just to jell its backbone," he wrote to one young Marine.[8] As a symbol of support from home, the mayor sent state flags to soldiers in Vietnam, making frequent requests to Orvin Fjare of the State Advertising Department to send him yet another flag, which he would then forward to a Montana soldier. The *Gazette* headline, "State Flag Flies Over Khe Sanh," capped an article about the Montana state flag flying at a U.S. Marine Corps billet in Khe Sanh, South Vietnam. Willard had sent the flag in response to a request from Marine W. S. Persoma. By August 1968, he had sent at least twenty flags to Vietnam.[9] Meanwhile, at home, Fraser ordered flags to fly at half-mast for each death of a Billings soldier. After one of the first casualties, he wrote, "I caught hell from three or four of the 'John Birch types' because I put the flags at half-mast. They say, only a President can do that. But I do. It seems so little that we can give to one who has given so much—so to hell with them!"[10] Fraser attended every funeral of a Billings soldier when he could. When he could not attend, he sent his city attorney or another representative. He also carried out the grim task of writing sympathy letters to bereaved parents. These were not perfunctory missives but heartfelt condolences from a man who knew what it was to grieve the untimely loss of a loved one.

The escalation of the war in 1965 marked a change in Mansfield's attitude toward it. In February 1965, the first bombing raids on North Vietnam were conducted, and in July, Johnson committed ground troops to Vietnam. In private meetings with President Johnson and his military advisors, Mansfield's opposition became apparent. From then on, Mansfield's primary goal regarding Vietnam was to persuade Johnson to negotiate a peace conference, though his public statements about the war were less forceful than those of antiwar legislators such as Senators Wayne Morse of Oregon and J. William Fulbright of Arkansas.[11] In May 1965, Fulbright called for a bombing halt, and in June, he opposed escalation in a Senate speech.[12] In contrast, when asked about his relationship with Johnson in a 1966 interview with Kenneth Sheibel of the *Gazette*'s Washington Bureau, Mansfield's only comment was a terse, "We differ on Viet Nam."[13]

Despite the deep distress he felt over the loss of young life in the war, Fraser was not yet ready to abandon his support for American military intervention in Vietnam. In 1967, he received newspaper coverage when he refused to allow an antiwar protest march up Airport Hill and past Eastern Montana College. His refusal seems surprising coming from a mayor who would later tell a high school student council, "[T]o hear the President of the City Council of Billings advise the Student Council that they should never attempt to stand up for issues or ideals unless they have more than a 50–50 chance of winning same must not go without contradiction." He went on to say it is important to "dare to face up to new ideas and issues."[14]

Fraser's concern for peace and law and order was behind his stance against the march. In a memo to department heads, he expressed his reasoning for objecting to the march: "I am the Mayor, and I represent government, and as Mayor, I must support my government." Ever the historian, he cited Emperor Diocletian, who stabilized the Roman Empire, and Charles V, the Holy Roman Emperor, both of whom "manned the barricades against the barbarians. . . . I told him [the boy] to think it over and come back in a week or ten days and if he still wants to do it, I will grant permission. . . . The boy never came back."[15] One wonders if this 1967 decision would have been made differently two years later, after Fraser's view of the war had changed.

By the end of 1967, the number of troops in Vietnam had reached half a million, and casualties were increasing. Early in 1968, Fraser landed in the papers with an outrageous proposal that belied his private disquiet over the war. Perhaps picking up on Mansfield's focus on arranging a peace conference, Fraser issued an invitation for President Johnson and Ho Chi Minh to come to Billings for peace talks. The *Gazette* quoted Fraser as saying that Billings was "a notably neutral community that can be reached in but a few short hours from any corner of the globe." He added, "Our people are a most cosmopolitan lot," noting that the committee making arrangements would include names such as Fujwara, Giovetti, Jovanovich, Kansala, Kamalski, Leone, MacKenzie, Ohmdahl, Perkins, and Vandegenachte—all names of Billings residents.[16] Fraser must not have received a response to his invitation. If he had, it surely would have been publicized.

As the deaths mounted and the war continued, Fraser began to question the actions of the U.S. government, but in 1968—one of the most violent, tumultuous years of that decade, and perhaps of the century—Fraser's reaction to some of the major events seems contradictory. During this time, he wrote frankly and frequently to Grant Salisbury of the conservative *U.S. News and World Report*. Perhaps their very different political allegiances stimulated the steady political commentary in Willard's many letters to Salisbury during this period. Commenting on the national scene before the 1968 primaries, Willard observed, "LBJ is having his troubles with Bobby [Kennedy], [Eugene] McCarthy, and others—but then Democrats always tend to act like college kids in the springtime and kick up their heels in many directions."[17] Despite their shared support for civil rights, Willard had no use for 1968 Minnesota presidential hopeful Eugene McCarthy, whose candidacy focused on his antiwar stance. When asked by McCarthy's campaign to support his candidacy, Fraser declined. "Can I possibly say to their parents or wives that [the soldiers] have died for naught?" he wrote, adding, "I don't have the heart, and isn't that essentially what McCarthy is saying?" He declared he was against McCarthy's position "even though I deplore the way it [the war] must seemingly be fought—it is so reminiscent of the attrition-stupidities of the military (both sides) of World War I."[18] In a postelection letter, Fraser called McCarthy an S.O.B., accused him of having a "deep-seated malevolence," and remarked, "There are many people in this area who will not read the obituary of Senator McCarthy with great wailing and weeping."[19]

Fraser's condemnation of McCarthy seems uncharacteristically vehement, but his view of McCarthy can be explained by his impression that McCarthy was dividing the nation. Sowing the seeds of division contradicted Fraser's adherence to his belief that elected officials should "support the National Administration on affairs, foreign."[20] Mansfield, too, had declined to support McCarthy in the 1968 primary election, and when asked to comment on McCarthy entering the race, his succinct comment was, "It's a free country."[21] McCarthy, both at the time and later in retrospect, criticized Mansfield's reticence to publicize his private criticism of Johnson's Vietnam policy.[22] However, by 1968, the *Gazette* had carried several articles that described Mansfield as a "frequent critic of Johnson's war policies," a very different portrayal from that in the same paper four years earlier.[23]

Shortly after the Conference of Mayors in Chicago in June 1968, protestors and police clashed at the Democratic National Convention, a violent event sparked by the delegates' failure to adopt McCarthy's antiwar plank. Although no one was killed in the ensuing chaos, Chicago police charged violently into the assembled protestors, creating what was later called a "police riot." Fifty years later, Bob Nolte, a reporter for the *Chicago Tribune* at the time, agreed with the term "police riot," but he also called the protestors a "dangerous mob," and said, "[T]he protestors, the cops and everybody is [*sic*] just going wild."[24] The Chicago clash polarized the Democratic Party and much of the nation, with one faction supporting the aggressive action of Mayor Daley and the police and the other faction vehemently objecting to the attack on protestors.

Having just returned from Chicago, where Mayor Daley had treated him well, Fraser spoke out to commend the efforts of that city's mayor and police force to maintain law and order. In a letter to a Billings youth attending Yale, he explained that "any Mayor must attempt, for he is duty bound by his oath, to preserve law and order, for without order—all is lost. . . . It wasn't just the immediate protesters that the police had to contend with. The spark that once started could have erupted in a holocaust for which we all would have paid dearly." He made the point that not all the youth in Chicago were idealists and expressed sympathy for those caught in the crossfire, concluding, "We need activists in the political world, and you must be a leader . . . but violence I cannot, (at least civic violence) condone."[25] It is difficult to know whether Fraser knew at the time he made these statements of the extent of the atrocities committed by the police. If he did, his support for Daley seems to contradict his expressed beliefs.

By 1969, Fraser's attitude toward the war was changing, both because of the high number of American casualties and because of his belief that the war itself was a mistake. "The feeling that Viet Nam has now bogged down into another war of attrition is shoving me mightily toward the side of the doves," he wrote, adding, "After all, it is the young who are being asked to die."[26] He considered the assertion that the war was prolonged by those who stood to profit from it, conceding that "one cannot but feel there is some truth in that statement."[27] By the summer of 1970, he was

Coinciding with Vietnam War Moratorium Day events around the nation, students from Eastern Montana College held a quiet vigil for Montanans killed in the Vietnam War, October 15, 1969. Billings Gazette, Oct. 16, 1969

more definite in his stance against the war: "I know enough of history to know that few people mind another's sons going off to war, and the cries of the war advocates usually outshout the pacifist. No pacifist I, but I am a complete Dove now."[28] It was more than the deaths of young men that got to Fraser; he felt the war—and the dismissive attitude toward the violence it engendered—was brutalizing America. He told Salisbury about a radio interview of a twenty-year-old soldier who was home on leave: "Then the announcer asked if he had ever killed a child. 'Yes. I shot a nine-year-old boy just before I left last week.' He said it in a tone [like], 'Yes, I killed a rabbit last week.' . . .These boys are that mild, yet now they accept killing and death, and the brutalizing that wars always bring in their wake—but the brutalizing of the Viet Nam struggle is pervading our whole nation in a disastrous way."[29] Fraser was concerned about the potential effect on the entire nation if the younger generation became desensitized to violence.

By 1970, Mansfield, too, had become more forthright in public about his statements on the war. The *Gazette* ran an AP article quoting Mansfield saying, "In Viet Nam I think we're in over our heads."[30] Willard would have arrived at his loss of faith in governmental wisdom and his conversion to being an outspoken dove as the war progressed through his own analysis, but he was in sync with Montana's senior senator. The *Gazette* featured a column in which "roses" were awarded to favorable events; on June 29, 1971, it read, "A rose to Mike Mansfield who has tagged the renewal of the Draft Act with a clause demanding the complete withdrawal of U.S. troops in Vietnam within nine months."[31]

The public tide was also turning. The *Gazette* and newspapers around the nation increasingly carried headlines such as "Disgusted with War," "Veterans Protesting at Arlington," and "Endless War, Endless Grief." Protests to the war began to coalesce in Montana, mostly through the actions of the state's young people. In April 1969, Dr. Benjamin Spock, bestselling author of infant care books and outspoken foe of the Vietnam War, visited the University of Montana in Missoula to speak with students. After his address, about two dozen young men publicly turned in their draft cards.[32] On October 15, students and faculty at five Montana colleges— MSU in Bozeman, the University of Montana in Missoula, Carroll College in Helena, Eastern Montana College in Billings, and the College of Great Falls—joined millions of Americans in a nationwide Vietnam War moratorium. The antiwar activities included a march from Carroll College to the Selective Service Office and canceled classes at Eastern, while the event in Missoula drew two thousand participants.[33] In July 1970, Miss Montana, Kathy Huppe, who had participated in protests against the war, submitted her resignation from the Miss America pageant because her contract stipulated that her political views should be "middle of the road." "I would put my belief above the pageant," she said.[34] Her stance resulted in a photo in the September 18 issue of *LIFE* magazine. When a peace demonstration was organized in Lewistown in September, however, it became clear that antiwar protesters did not represent all Montanans. Some residents distributed posters reading, "Wanted: 50 Cowboys with Shears and Clippers

. . . to patrol Main Street," a declaration of their strong opposition to the long-haired liberal protesters.[35]

So profound was Fraser's eventual revulsion toward the Vietnam War that this World War II veteran could not condemn the young men who became conscientious objectors or who left the country to avoid service. This topic was certainly another "confusion of the hour." In a five-page letter, "To a Young Friend," Fraser counseled a young man wrestling with a decision about seeking conscientious objector status or fleeing to Canada. He described an encounter he had had in a Montreal airport after hearing an announcement on the TV that there were 70,000 young men—U.S. citizens who had escaped the draft—in Canada. The Canadian boy sitting next to him said, "If I were an American, it would be 70,001," and another piped up to say, "I would be 70,002." Fraser's military service and his upbringing amid traditionally patriotic Americans argued against draft evasion and conscientious objector status, and he worried about the legacy such acts would leave for the descendants of the young men who chose such paths. However, after warning the "Young Friend" to think about the long-term consequences of his decision, Fraser counseled,

> Whatever you do, I will understand, and as one who has worn his country's uniform in war, I will point out that there is a pride in knowing and proving that one was once a man among men, men who were not afraid to go. . . . I know that with the bulk of these young men that are going to Canada or seeking conscientious objector status today, fear is not the motivating force. It is deeper than that. . . . But do what you must, and I will be your partisan either way, but I must truthfully say, "I hope you don't but . . . I know I could be wrong."[36]

Fraser couldn't wholeheartedly support draft evasion or conscientious objector status, but knowing what Montana's young men faced, neither could he condemn their choice to avoid service in a war that he and many Americans now opposed.

Fraser turned to history to put his quandary over draft evaders into perspective. In early 1972, he watched Senator Edmond Muskie of Maine, who had been outspoken against American involvement in the war, discuss Vietnam on *60 Minutes*.[37] Fraser, who was acquainted with Muskie, wrote to say,

> Your television interview of Sunday brought to mind my boy-hood in our Yellowstone Valley in Billings after World War I. . . . We had many, many immigrants homestead in our valley

from Germany, whose descendants now number some of our finest citizens. It was a very common thing for one of them to be pointed out as having been "smart" enough to have skipped out of Germany to evade the prewar draft of the Kaiser. In my boyhood they were considered to be very honorable men for having done as they did. Nowadays the shoe is on the other foot, and it is some of our own men who have been skipping to Canada to evade the draft. Which is right and which is wrong, and when are they right and when are they wrong? That is the question that had no real answer then, nor has it now.[38]

Undoubtedly, the Vietnam War played into Fraser's views on other national politicians. Fraser expressed his disillusionment with President Johnson's mishandling of the war and his assessment of Nixon in a letter to Salisbury in 1970: "I had to carry a cross named LBJ on my Democrat back, and now you've got to bear with one called Nixon. I suspect that down in our partisan hearts we viewed . . . and view them in about the same light."[39] In Fraser's view, neither president dealt honorably with the war.[40] When the 1970 election approached, Fraser predicted that McGovern would carry Montana. "Personally, I think the country is so fed up with Vietnam and having found that Nixon did not really do much more than play with us in

Billings Young Men Who Died in the Vietnam War

George David Anderson, *Marines*, 3/06/68

Alan F. Ashall, *Navy*, 8/29/68

Charles Goodhue Boyer, *Marines*, 3/28/68

Larry James Burkhardt, *Army*, 5/07/68

James Lynn Burns, *Army*, 12/21/67

Kenneth Lee Derheim, *Army*, 12/19/65

Frank Garcia Jr., *Marines*, 8/4/67

Gregory Allen Gifford, *Navy*, 2/8/68

Gerald Thomas Greene Jr., *Army*, 10/29/69

Gary O'Neal Griffin, *Army*, 5/23/69

Douglas Duane Kern, *Army*, 11/16/66

Daniel W. Margrave, II, *Marines*, 2/25/69

Steven Bernard Melnick, *Air Force*, 8/17/70

Michael David Padilla, *Marines*, 4/20/68

Charles Calvin Snider Jr., *Army*, 9/9/71

William Eugene Taylor, *Marines*, 3/23/70

Bernard Jeffrey Uhren, *Army*, 10/1/68

Dennis Elmer Ulstad, *Marines*, 1/26/69

Barclay Leonard Volk, *Army*, 4/17/70

Dennis William Wear, *Army*, 9/10/68

John Robin Wiest, *Army*, 10/12/68

Ralph Leroy Williams, *Army*, 2/15/68

Although he initially backed the government's stance on the war, Mayor Fraser lowered the flag to half-mast for Billings-area soldiers killed in the Vietnam War, sent letters to their families, and attended their funerals. Source: Vietnam Conflict Extract Data File, Defense Casualty Analysis System Files, Record Group 330, Office of Secretary of Defense

that issue, that will be McGovern's strongest point."[41] The strong point did not prevail. Nixon was reelected in a landslide four months later.

Six months before the war ended, Fraser wrote to Salisbury that he had lowered the flag to half-mast thirty-nine times for Billings boys killed in Vietnam, "and that is a whale of a lot for a community of our size."[42] Fraser's count is more than the number of Billings young men listed on the official military site or on the Vietnam National Memorial (22), because he likely included casualties from Yellowstone County or those who had been natives of Billings but were no longer Billings residents when they entered the service. By the end of the war, 267 Montanans and 58,307 Americans had lost their lives. Mayor Fraser's letters to grieving families conveyed his shared anguish over what increasingly seemed to be a senseless loss. To one set of parents, he acknowledged, "The tragedy you two have lately had to undergo is one no one should ever have to face. I just don't think I would have the physical strength to bear such a loss myself, and I can only hope you are stronger than I fear I would myself be under similar circumstances." As Fraser often did in letters of sympathy, he included Frost's "Never Again Would Birds' Song Be the Same," the poem he said his father-in-law had written after Marjorie's death. "It will help just a little in helplessly trying to explain the unexplainable," Willard offered, concluding, "Sometimes there is nothing left but poetry and God."[43]

Fraser suggested to the American Legion Veterans Council that they establish a memorial for the Billings boys killed in the war. "Vietnam has been such a hopeless, discouraging war," he said, "and it seems to me that the parents of the boys who died—as well as all the boys who have served in Vietnam must feel a great frustration as well as a great lack of appreciation from the citizens of the country for what they have done, and given."[44] Sadly, no separate Vietnam memorial was erected in Billings following the war, but in November 1997 a multi-war memorial was dedicated in honor of all those who died in World War I, World War II, the Korean War, and Vietnam.

"This has not been one of my better years"

Six months into Willard's third term, the Fraser family suffered a tragedy. On November 12, 1967, Bobby Fraser, the son of Willard's brother Robert, was killed in a car accident on Highway 212 near Red Lodge. The driver had been speeding, the car overturned, and both Bobby and the driver were ejected. The driver survived, but twenty-year-old Bobby died.[1] Willard's grief over Bobby's death was shared by Bobby's grandmother. As Sadie left for Connecticut to visit Jeanne in December, Willard wrote to his sister, "She [Sadie] really took Bobby's death pretty hard."[2] To his old friend Charlie Borberg, Willard confided, "I have felt like hell ever since. Damn, damn, damn."[3]

The tragedy of Bobby Fraser's untimely death was the beginning of more than a year of difficulty for Willard. He had begun his third term with his usual optimism and a burst of activity to further his myriad plans to better Billings and Montana. In the first few months, he traveled to Helena to testify at the Water Pollution Control Board, wrote to the State Highway Commission to advocate for an interchange on the interstate at Glendive, traveled to Salt Lake City and Washington, D.C., to testify at airline hearings, and attended the U.S. Conference of Mayors meeting in Hawai'i, where he was on the Resolutions Committee. The storm drain system was progressing, and he hoped to make significant progress on combating air pollution in Billings. However, over the next two years, Willard encountered significant personal and political setbacks that battered his morale and sapped his energy.

The frequent standoffs between the mayor and his council escalated as the council strove to rein in Mayor Fraser's authority. Soon after he was reelected, the city council passed an ordinance that gave the council, rather than the mayor, the power to name the city's standing committees. Fraser vetoed this and another ordinance that permitted a person from the council to be added to the Park Committee. In both cases, he was overruled, which undermined his power as mayor. Fraser created an Air Pollution Advisory Committee, but when the committee's recommendations came to the council, he was frustrated by their lack of support in effecting action against the refineries and other industries in the city. The *Great Falls Tribune* pointed out the inevitability of the council's continued obstruction of the mayor's plans: "Fraser can expect a 7–3 vote against his desires. Great Falls mayor John J. McLaughlin can expect 7–3 support."[4]

Outside of Billings, however, Fraser received public praise. A letter to the *Gazette* editor from a Missoula resident praised Fraser's testimony at the Water Control Board. The writer said others—representatives of the chamber of commerce, Montana Power, Montana-Dakota Utilities, and Pacific Power and Light—only gave lip service to the Yellowstone River's potential while Fraser's testimony was "more constructive and more far-sighted."[5] The *Great Falls Tribune* noted that "Billings started slowly in its building rehabilitation program, but the tempo picked up greatly under the vigilance of Mayor Willard E. Fraser."[6] The *Tribune* also wrote an editorial thank-you to Fraser for his actions on behalf of the Glendive interchange: "Great Falls owes a debt of gratitude for his support. The Billings mayor, one of the most alert and farsighted officials in Montana, has demonstrated once again he doesn't think narrowly or selfishly."[7] A year later, an editorial in the *Tribune*, titled "A Question of Leadership," took issue with Mayor McLaughlin's lack of forcefulness, commenting, "An effective leader must not shy away from strong stands that might create disharmony."[8]

Fraser could not be accused of shying away from strong stands, even when it meant not falling in line with the expected Democratic Party stance. As the primaries for the 1968 presidential election approached, he did not support Bobby Kennedy's candidacy even though he had been an admirer of President Kennedy. His opinion of the younger Kennedy had been formed during Bobby Kennedy's visit to Billings in 1966, after which the *Gazette* commented on the abrasive and apparently condescending behavior of Bobby's entourage and Fraser's disapproval of that behavior. Fraser's resulting negative view of Bobby seemed to derive more from those surrounding him than from Bobby himself.[9] Additionally, Fraser's belief in the importance of a mayor's role influenced his support for New York City's John Lindsay and Minneapolis's Hubert Humphrey as candidates. He wrote before the national conventions, "I have, as a Mayor, more

Left to right: Representative John Melcher, Representative Lee Metcalf, Senator Robert Kennedy, Mayor Willard Fraser, and Stan Lynde at a political convention in Billings, October 25, 1966.
AP Photo. MHS Photograph Archives, PAc 99-49.1

interest in either Lindsay as a Republican candidate or Humphrey as a Democratic candidate . . . for they alone of all the candidates understand the problems of our cities."[10]

Encouraged perhaps by his favorable press in Montana cities such as Great Falls and Missoula, Fraser began thinking about running for governor in 1968. Stuart Conner tried to dissuade him. "I pleaded with Willard not to run for governor," he said. Despite his own affection and respect for Willard, Conner felt he did not have sufficient financial backing. He also feared that, statewide, Willard was still viewed more as an eccentric than as a serious politician.[11] Missoula mayor Richard Shoup had a different opinion. He visited Billings in February 1968 and supported Willard's candidacy. "More people are living in urban areas than in rural areas. And we do not have proper representation at the state level," Shoup commented.[12] Willard's optimism and desire prevailed, and he filed as a candidate for governor on April 24. Newspapers around the state gave the news mixed coverage. Butte's *Montana Standard* observed, "Most [Democrat] party leaders have little love for Fraser who was elected as an independent in Billings' city campaigns."[13] Given that the Democratic Party's choice for governor was attorney general Forrest Anderson, and that four other Democrats were running in the June primary, Fraser was a definite underdog.

Several newspapers around the state ran an Associated Press story reporting on the widespread concern by key Democrats that Fraser would take votes away from Forrest Anderson, but the charge seemed not to bother Fraser, who "went on his merry way telling jokes, saying Montana needs some levity and salesmanship in its top office, and declaring that he is in it to win."[14] In an editorial about Willard's candidacy, Helena's *Independent Record* opined, "We're glad Willard Fraser is running for governor. He won't win, of course. . . . It's not that he shouldn't. It's just that he won't." Still, the *Independent Record* pointed out the benefits of Willard's participation: "He'll challenge the voters to think, which is probably why he'll lose this time. . . . The political pros will tell you the voters don't like candidates who make them think. . . . Fraser's campaign should be an educational experience, and for this reason we welcome his candidacy."[15] The *Great Falls Tribune*, a regular Fraser cheerleader, commented just before the primary election, "It seems to us that Willard Fraser has advanced more ideas than the other candidates although he doubtless is an underdog as a late starter."[16] Newsmen continued to concentrate on Willard's colorful reputation in their coverage, with one reporter saying, "It is difficult to tell whether he is running for poet laureate or governor."[17]

Fraser campaigned on issues that would have gained more traction in later years but fell flat in the late 1960s. When he filed, he charged that the other candidates were "running on motherhood and old clichés," and in a press conference in Helena, he spoke of becoming a visionary governor who would develop Montana's "crops" of winter sports, tourism, youth opportunity, and state history. He advocated consolidation of city and county governments and proposed a limited tax-oriented constitutional convention to revise Montana's tax system. He declared, "I preach positivism" and asserted, "You don't build empires, states or cities with people being against things." Later, he opposed incumbent governor Tim

Babcock's proposed sales tax and declared that "to add a sales tax without a constitutional revision would be shortsightedly immoral." Visiting Libby Dam shortly before the primary, he sounded a favorite theme—the conservation of Montana's water—saying, "Water should be treated as one of Montana's most important crops." He decried the "greedy and needy downstream states" who had plans to steal Montana's water.[18]

The results of the gubernatorial primary on June 5 confirmed Conner's prophecy: "I knew he was going to lose. He was so insistent that he wasn't

Former governor Tim Babcock and Missoula mayor Richard Shoup on the steps of the U.S. Capitol, ca. 1970. Shoup supported Fraser for governor in the 1968 Demoratic primaries. 94.4657, Archives and Special Collections, Mansfield Library, University of Montana-Missoula

going to lose. I didn't want him to be hurt. And he was hurt."[19] Attorney general Forrest Anderson won the Democratic nomination with 39,057 votes over second-place Eugene Mahoney's 35,562 votes, and he would go on to win the governor's seat in November. LeRoy Anderson came in third, and Willard fourth with 8,525 votes. Hanford Gallup and Merrill Riddick came in a distant fifth and sixth, with just over 1,000 votes apiece.[20] In the post-primary analysis, the *Independent Record* acknowledged that Fraser "got in too late and with too little money. . . . His ideas were good but often too vague and over the heads of most voters."[21] The "too little money" statement was certainly true. A later article listed Fraser's personal and club expenditures for the race at $1,707, making it even less than the amount spent by sixth-place Riddick. In contrast, winner Forrest Anderson spent $47,427.[22]

Fraser's residence in eastern Montana was not a factor in losing this race, but it may have been a factor in his placing fourth among the six candidates. A unique feature of Montana political history is the Butte background common to some of the state's most prominent politicians in the first half of the twentieth century. Senators Walsh, Wheeler, and Mansfield and FDR assistant James H. Rowe Jr. all had Butte roots. In *A Century of Politics on the Yellowstone*, author Lawrence F. Small writes about the secondary role of eastern Montana in the state's politics: "It is revealing of Yellowstone's [county] place in Montana politics that so few of its citizens have made it to high elective office." Writing in the early 1980s, Small postulated that because most of the state's wealth and population were centered in its western counties, leaders from Yellowstone County had less financial and popular support when running for state office. By the 1960s, however, this pattern of western Montana political dominance had begun to shift, and Billings Republican Tim Babcock served as governor from 1962 to 1969. In 1968, however, Willard seems to have overestimated the effect that his increased exposure as the three-term mayor of Billings would have in his run for governor.

Barely a week after his defeat in the primary election, Willard flew to Chicago to attend the Conference of Mayors. There, he intended to introduce two resolutions: to eliminate custom charges to aircraft owners and operators flying between the United States and Canada and to commend President Johnson for establishing the new National Council on Indian Opportunity and major new policies of significant benefit to the Indian population.[23] However, an accident would prevent him from attending the conference. After checking in at Palmer House, an elegant and historical Chicago hotel, he decided to take a bath.[24] The bathtub had no mat, and

Mayor Fraser working from his bed at St. Vincent's Hospital in Billings, 1968, where he was convalescing from a broken hip. Visiting him is a Billings police officer.
Courtesy Western Heritage Center, Billings

Fraser slipped and fell on his right side, fracturing his upper right femur in two places. Despite fighting a blackout because of excruciating pain, he managed to pull himself out of the tub and get to the phone. An ambulance took him to Passavant Hospital, where Willard reported, "I had my hip pinned with a nine-inch pin and a plate about four inches going off at an angle, and countless screws so I believe I would be able to supply enough metal to reconstruct the Battleship Maine."[25] He remained in Passavant for a month.

When news of his injury reached Billings, the *Gazette* announced, "Fraser's Plans Tumble with Him."[26] Robin came to Chicago from Detroit, and Willard's Chicago friends Mr. and Mrs. Phillip Scott visited. His accident and hospitalization received front-page coverage in the *Chicago Daily News*, where he was referred to as a "Montana fireball."[27] Chicago's Mayor Daley telephoned and sent flowers. The *Gazette* quoted Sadie Fraser on her son's condition: "He needed a rest so badly that God took a hand. Now he will get the rest he has needed for a long, long time."[28] So many letters and flowers arrived for Fraser that his secretary asked that no more flowers be sent to the Chicago hospital room; the *Gazette* aired her request under the headline, "Cease! Desist!"[29]

Despite the good wishes and his own usual cheerfulness, Willard was not enjoying the therapeutic "rest" his mother wished for him. While he was in recovery, council president Howard Hultgren became acting mayor at city council meetings, but Fraser still did his best to carry out mayoral duties from his hospital bed. Newspapers in Chicago and Billings bore a photo of a smiling Fraser in hospital garb to show him as an active, albeit physically compromised, public figure. While still in Chicago's Passavant Hospital, Fraser backed allotting $33,260 in the 1968–69 budget for an air pollution department. Furthermore, responding to a request by Philip Beaumont, a Crow member of the Billings human relations committee, Fraser proposed busing Crow students the thirty-eight miles from Pryor to Billings rather than to a smaller school in Edgar. Beaumont argued that, in Billings, the children "would be with white students and thereby be better equipped for the life they should and must lead as adults if they are to be proper citizens."[30] Willard recalled that Senator Robert Taft in the late 1940s had criticized the South "for failing to educate the Negro."[31] Accordingly, he sent a letter in July 1968, to state superintendent Harriet Miller requesting this option.

In Fraser's absence, the 1968–69 city budget had to be submitted. Hultgren put a five-mill tax request to city voters in an effort to balance the city budget, but it was voted down. Consequently, Billings cut five firemen, five police officers, and seven other city employees. Fraser's salary was also cut. A $10,000 yearly salary for the mayors of Montana's large cities had been set by the state legislature in 1968, but Fraser's salary was reduced by $1,800 in the 1968–69 budget, leaving him a monthly check of $602.39. In addition, his car allowance was cut from $75 a month to $50 a month and his travel allowance was trimmed by 25 percent. The councilmen also received a cut in their salaries.[32] A curtailed income was another dispiriting event in a year of disappointments and medical problems.

When Fraser returned to Billings on July 11, he had lost 18 pounds and was down to 140 on his five-foot, ten-inch frame. Taken immediately by ambulance to St. Vincent's Hospital, Fraser reported to the Scotts in Chicago, "I was awfully glad to hit the bed at St. Vincent's. My foot was getting quite swollen and painful."[33] Days later, he missed participating in the Yellowstone Float for the first time. Jim Thompson and Stan Lynde represented Fraser in his black rubber boat.[34] He left the hospital briefly to officiate at a council meeting on July 15 and a week later was discharged from St. Vincent's on crutches. On August 14, he reported that he made it to the office for a couple hours a day, but his foot continued to swell painfully if he was up too long. He wrote of the "sheer agony" of this experience, but his public comments about pain or discomfort are more moderate.[35] In Butte's *Montana Standard*, Fraser did admit he had been through a "rough ordeal."[36] Only much later was he able to joke about his injury, writing to Salisbury in December 1968 that, in a recent talk to students at Eastern Montana College, he had mentioned that he was reconsidering his views of hippie philosophy, "especially the part that has to do with non-bathing. I can see a lot of sense in keeping out of bathtubs."[37]

When Willard resumed his public role in the summer of 1968, he was soon confronted with a familiar antagonist—Leona Deisz. During the July 15 meeting, the city council approved new electrical, plumbing, and building codes to meet state and Housing and Urban Development (HUD) requirements. This was one issue on which the mayor and the council were in agreement, but Deisz organized a misinformation campaign to stymie the new building safety measures. She opposed the new codes and started a petition to put the codes to a city referendum. Moreover, Deisz was quoted in the paper as saying that when she was finished with the petition, she would start work to recall the entire Billings city council and the mayor and would call for the firing of two city officials.[38] It was not clear how she planned to do this, and any efforts she made toward these goals did not succeed.

After securing enough signatures, Deisz instigated a public campaign on radio talk shows to garner support for defeating the codes. Her arguments, like her tactics, echoed those the Deiszes had used during the fluoride fight. The charges made on the radio included callers saying that the council president was a Communist and that the city council would tear down all the houses from Grand Avenue south to Lewis. She claimed that programs for air pollution, water pollution, slum clearance, urban renewal, fluoridation, and building codes were directed from Moscow. Fraser refuted the charges, point by point, in a *Gazette* article, stating in response to the last one, "Moscow has its own problems and in all likelihood has never heard of Billings."[39]

Decades later, Fraser's niece, Wendy, remembered the building code war for its heated rhetoric and for Deisz's role:

> There was a local woman who would call in to the radio every day to criticize, demean, and say really mean things about my uncle, the mayor. Uncle Will would listen attentively to her tirades and on more than one occasion comfort me as those

tirades would sometimes bring me to tears. Willard would calmly remind me that people's words often reveal more about them than about him, so [it is best] to turn a deaf ear, develop a thicker skin and have tolerance and kindness for their shortcomings.[40]

Fraser was not as calm when discussing the radio call-ins with others. In a letter to the editor of the *Gazette*, apparently in response to a printed statement that he had shut down Leona Deisz in a council meeting, Willard replied that it was his "duty to keep the Council functioning with decorum and dignity, protect them, and not let aldermen be subject to irresponsible abuse by every 'Moscow Molly' that comes along."[41]

As a public figure, Leona Deisz was the subject of an extensive profile in the *Gazette* in September 1968. The article began with her favorite quote from Billy Graham: "If the Lord does not judge America soon, He'll have to apologize to Sodom and Gomorrah." She credited J. Edgar Hoover as starting her on a "thirst to understand government better" by sending her information on Communists and recommending *Masters of Deceit*, Hoover's book warning about the dangers of communism.[42] Months later, Fraser continued to ruminate about the effect of such scare tactics on undermining public confidence in elected leadership: "It is mediocrity and negativism that scares me far more than any threats of communism, but with the cries of communism one can raise such hideous bugaboos and scare the 'holy socks' off the uninformed."[43] Undoubtedly, Deisz's approach of spreading misinformation and ratcheting up fear epitomized the power of negativity to sway public opinion.[44]

As the *Gazette* noted later, Leona Deisz was an expert at "planting seeds of doubt," and in the April 1969 city elections voters rejected uniform housing, plumbing, and electrical codes. The *Gazette* quoted city clerk Fry citing that Deisz's referendum cost the city $1,239.50, but the cost was much higher.[45] Without the adoption of new building codes, Billings was not eligible to receive Housing and Urban Development grants for the next two years, a loss amounting to nearly eight million dollars in support of such city programs as parks, additions to public schools, and storm sewer projects. Only programs approved by the city and its people were eligible for the direct cash grants.[46]

While the building codes conflict was playing out, Fraser attended the 1968 Montana League of Cities and Towns convention in Butte on crutches, and soon he began to accept speaking engagements. When he was invited to speak in West Yellowstone at an economic-political conference put on by the University of Montana, he invited Fr. Eugene Hruska, a former teacher at Billings Central Catholic High School and then a pastor in Forsyth, to accompany him. He cautioned Father Hruska that his acceptance might involve serving as a part-time valet: "I am still unable to put on my left sock, shorts, and pants," he wrote.[47] Despite his physical challenges, Willard seemed to be making a gradual comeback to his active public life.

On September 25, Fraser's recovery was delayed by another accident. That morning, he arrived on crutches at city hall, where he was to receive a meritorious service award for public display of patriotism from the Yellowstone branch of the American Legion in recognition of his support for Vietnam soldiers and their families. As he navigated the stone stairs of City Hall, he fell down eight steps. The *Gazette* reported he bruised his hand and his forehead but that he went through with the ceremony.[48] In fact, Fraser had broken his right kneecap. "I was so shaken after that fall the other morning that I hardly knew what to say or do for it was all I could do to keep my composure," he wrote later to Clarence Nybo, a veteran who had been present at the American Legion ceremony. "It was really much more of a fall than you probably knew. Since then I've hardly been able to move a muscle, but fortunately, I didn't do any real harm to my hip."[49] Fraser was back in St. Vincent's Hospital for another four weeks, writing to Lesley Frost Ballantine in October that taking six steps "seemed like six miles." During this time, he left the hospital only occasionally to attend events, transported in a van that accommodated his wheelchair. With much satisfaction, Willard told Lesley, "Udall is coming out to dedicate Yellowtail. We are not going to leave it to the Republicans to dedicate as the Republicans fought the dam all along the way."[50] He attended the joint dedication of Yellowtail Dam and the Bighorn Canyon National Recreation Area on October 31 in a wheelchair.

While recovering in St. Vincent's, Willard retained his sense of humor and interest in world and national events. When Jackie Kennedy married Aristotle Onassis, he chuckled, "This is the year of the Greek! The nurses and nuns are all abuzz over the idea of Jackie marrying that Greek. It does seem a letdown, doesn't it? One of my prerogatives as a mayor is to marry folk, but I will never marry a young chick to an old goat or vice versa."[51] In a letter thanking Governor Babcock for accompanying him to the Montana Chamber of Commerce meeting in Sidney, he teased, "Red Welsh says you should have gotten a picture of yourself pushing me around in the wheelchair, just to show how you have come up in the world, and how Governors rate with their ability to push Mayors around."[52]

In letters to friends and relatives, he issued opinions on the upcoming presidential election. Fraser expressed his opinion of Richard Nixon, the Republican candidate, in a letter to Salisbury. "One of the crusty old nuns here at the hospital was in to tell me that there were two women down the hall who were going to vote for Nixon. 'What shall we do?' she asked me. 'Give them a cold-water enema,' I suggested. 'That will fix them.'"[53] Despite his opposing political alliance, Salisbury replied, "If Nixon does win, I hope he displays more backbone than he has in the campaign—and more finesse. He is going to need plenty of both."[54] After Nixon won the election, Fraser grumbled to Salisbury, "His television program election eve was pretty nauseating. . . . It's that Madison Avenue, Hollywood phoniness that galls the intellectual crowd, and I'm sure he galled them all that night."[55]

Keeping abreast of political events elsewhere, Fraser paid particular attention to the statewide election in California, where one of his several godchildren lived. He expressed alarm at Ronald Reagan's election as governor. As an actor, Reagan did not fit Fraser's concept of a statesman: he was not well versed in history, nor was he up to speed on important issues of the time—such as the Vietnam War and environment concerns. "It would appear . . . that California has gone to hell," he wrote to a friend. In a parody of Frost's line, "Something there is that doesn't love a wall," he continued, "How come? Something there is that really doesn't respond to a Hollywood actor in the Governor's chair." He questioned whether "the glamour boys" were equipped to solve the problems of the age, adding, "Perhaps I'm wrong, but I wonder . . . and tremble."[56] He distrusted popularity achieved purely through emotional appeal. Months before the election, Fraser had written to Charlie Borberg to say, "Intelligent people are too busy attending to their own affairs in business to participate [in politics]; so we give the leeway to all the crackpots. At the moment they are all gathering around Ronald Reagan. What a lot he would turn loose if he were elected President—and it could happen although I would hope the American people have more sense—but California didn't."[57] Fraser was again prescient. Reagan became the fortieth president of the United States in 1981, nearly a decade after Fraser died.

In Montana, Democrat Forrest Anderson won the governor's chair over incumbent Republican Tim Babcock. Montana political reporter Chuck Johnson later explained Anderson's victory over a popular Babcock in a year when a Republican won the presidency. First, Babcock had failed in his attempt to win Democrat Lee Metcalf's Senate seat in 1966; second, and more importantly, Anderson had campaigned against Babcock's proposed sales tax proposal with the effective slogan "Pay More? What For?"[58] Following a long-established pattern, Montana's eastern congressional seat went to Republican James Battin, while Democrat Arnold Olsen was elected from the western district.

On the local political level, Fraser continued his campaign against one of his chief concerns: air pollution. Smog was no stranger to Montana's largest cities—Missoula, Butte, Great Falls, Billings. Although Billings' problem was not as severe as Missoula's, the mayor said he received after-midnight calls about the "stench" in Billings, although some residents forgave the industrial smell, saying it was "the smell of money."[59] After four years of wrangling, the Montana legislature had passed an Air Pollution Control bill in 1967, but while the bill set standards for emission control, it depended on local air control programs.[60] In December 1968, Fraser met with county commissioners and the chamber of commerce to gain support for creating a local air pollution control board. One commissioner urged a "go-slow approach," and the chamber expressed doubt that residents wanted to spend for it.[61] The next day, Fraser vented his frustration in a letter to Salisbury: "There was a mayor once who died and went to Hell and was there three weeks before he discovered that he wasn't on vacation. This week I feel like I was that mayor."[62] He continued to apply his persuasive powers to gain cooperation from state regulators and scientists to address the poor air quality in Billings. He wrote to Humble Oil, Continental Oil, and the Farmers Union Central Exchange to say he had received calls from local residents complaining that the smog was so bad that "one couldn't see the city from the airport. . . . Your help to clean up this intense smog is appreciated."[63]

As 1968 came to an end, Willard lamented, "This has not been one of my best years."[64] He had been hospitalized for a total of ten weeks, lost in the gubernatorial primary, endured vitriolic and unfounded charges from a small segment of the city population in the quest to establish building codes, and had not yet succeeded in curbing the valley's nagging air pollution problem. To cap it off, he came down with the flu in December.[65] While 1969 would present some exciting new opportunities, the year would not be measurably better—although Fraser would finally manage to establish an Air Pollution Commission in April 1969, just weeks before his third term ended.

During the winter of 1969, Fraser experienced some uplifting moments. In a singularly successful coup, Fraser's salesmanship brought a major Hollywood film company, Stockbridge Productions, to the Billings area. The company had originally thought of filming near Durango, Colorado, but Fraser "had spent nearly four months badgering the company to shoot around Billings."[66] Fraser was ecstatic. "Just killed a bear in that I have secured the movie 'Little Big Man' to be filmed in Billings," Fraser wrote to Hal Stearns in March, adding, "It is the type of industry we need . . . [and] no smoke, no grime will be left after."[67] Stuart Millar of Stockbridge Productions came to Billings in early February to locate housing for the production crew and cast of *Little Big Man*, directed by Arthur Penn and starring Dustin Hoffman and Faye Dunaway. When the production manager, Dick Gallegly, and livestock manager, Kenneth Lee, arrived in March to survey shooting sites, Gallegly commented in an interview with the *Gazette*, "I might say it is due to your mayor's efforts we are here."[68] Filming would begin in July, and the company would spend at least two million dollars in Billings.

That winter, Willard had traded his crutches for a cane and was able to participate in the annual Jaycee Livingston Snowmobile Race. He earned a first-place trophy in the Mayors' Race. That same month, the *Great Falls Tribune* featured a photo of Willard on the dance floor at the Governor's Ball honoring new governor Forrest Anderson at the Civic Center in Helena. Fraser's mother Sadie accompanied him. Sadie seemed a political asset for her son. She had delivered the replacement city keys to Lady Bird Johnson and Muriel Humphrey and had spoken on the radio during at least one of Willard's campaigns. When Sadie turned eighty-two that month, the *Gazette* ran a feature story about her with an accompanying photo. The article used such adjectives as "dignified, active, and effervescent" to describe the mayor's mother and made the point that she acted as a part-time secretary to Fraser.[69]

In the early spring of 1969, Willard Fraser filed to run again for mayor in the April 1969 election. Running against him were Howard Hultgren and Leona Deisz. In his ads for mayor, Fraser highlighted pollution control as an important ongoing project and published positive quotes about himself from newspapers in Billings, Helena, and Harlowton. Hultgren, meanwhile, focused on promising "improved administration" in his campaign and stressed his experience as a seven-year member of the city council, four as president. Deisz stated her purpose for running for public office was "to cut expenses, eliminate waste, stop unnecessary services being forced on taxpayers and clean up, not cover up."[70] She proclaimed she would stop violations of citizen rights as set forth in the Ninth and Fourth Amendments to the Constitution. She claimed the inspections mentioned in the proposed city codes—up for a referendum vote in the same citywide election—violated the people's rights against unreasonable searches as set forth in the Fourth Amendment, and she cited the Ninth Amendment guarantee against unlisted rights.

As the election drew near, Willard's precarious health again sapped his energy. "When I get a cold, I am laid low," he complained to Richard Shoup, the mayor of Missoula, "as it does complicate my asthma."[71] Paul Jakab remembers Willard convulsing at times from a terrible cough.[72] With a limp, multiple hospitalizations during the year, and his obvious struggle with asthma, Willard projected a picture of a physically weak, elderly man. James Thompson reported that a Billings voter commented to him before the election, "The best thing I can do for Willard is vote against him. He needs a rest."[73]

Three days before the election, the *Gazette*'s editorial page endorsed council president Hultgren for mayor, citing the improved administration he would provide. The editorial admitted that Fraser had done a great job of public relations, had made excellent appointments to boards and commissions, and had presented challenging ideas. It also pointed out that at times he overstepped his legal authority, was not a compromiser, and lacked a business-type leadership quality.[74] When Willard was criticized for not participating more actively in the budget process, his stock response was, "I was elected to be a mayor, not a bookkeeper."[75] The *Gazette* was not the first entity, nor would it be the last, to voice the opinion that businessmen were best qualified to run government. In contrast, Willard believed the business of government should be conducted with levity and imagination and in a way that sought input from those in the arts and in business.

On election day, April 7, 1969, Howard Hultgren became mayor of Billings with a 44.5 percent plurality, the lowest plurality in mayoral elections since 1963. Fraser trailed Hultgren by just 799 votes—5,497 to Hultgren's 6,296. Leona Deisz earned 2,338 votes, likely taking votes from Hultgren than from Willard. In Butte, incumbent Thomas Powers was also defeated, but Missoula mayor Richard Shoup and Great Falls mayor John McLaughlin were reelected. In Fraser's concession speech, he quoted Martin Luther, saying, "I have made tracks." He added that he hoped there would be "a continuation of the slum clearance program, the fight against air pollution, the upgrading of the caliber of city employees, and that recreation programs aren't abated." He concluded, "I wish my successor well, and I thank the public."[76] The *Gazette* editorial following Fraser's defeat expressed the hope that Hultgren would show the same commitment that Fraser had to good planning, pollution controls, sensible zoning, and slum clearance, but the paper also expressed its belief that there would be greater cooperation, harmony, and a more businesslike approach in city hall.[77]

When Salisbury—who sometimes addressed Willard in his letters as "Yerhonner"—heard the news of Willard's defeat, he wrote, "Though a few knuckleheaded voters of Billings have failed to bestow again upon you the title of Mayor, you will always be 'Yerhonner' to me if that is any comfort."[78] In his own letters to friends and supporters, Fraser communicated his defeat with a Gaelic reference to the Sassenach (outsiders): "The Sassenach had their way and now I am an ex-Mayor. Wouldn't you know."[79] He struck the same vein in a letter saying, "In this town, as you so well know, Republicanism is a brand of religion. I understand it and accept it."[80] In another, more thoughtful letter, Fraser reflected on the important issues of the time: air, land, people, and water pollution, urban renewal, and development of historic sites and natural resources. He said, "In all of these I have attempted very much, and, of course, will in the future . . . I was too limited in finances and [by] a reactionary Council to do so adequately, but nevertheless I tried."[81]

Willard had to grapple with both his defeat and his conviction that the issues he had devoted so much of his mayoral energy to would receive no attention from the newly elected city leadership. "I can assure you," he griped to an acquaintance, "that the 'present' Council and the 'next' Mayor could care less. In not one single instance while I have been Mayor has [Hultgren] manifested interest in pollution in any form, but in truth has always opposed every single step we have taken toward control of the same."[82] An embittered Fraser took a sly swipe at incoming mayor Hultgren in a memo to the city council:

> By no means would I want to embarrass Mayor-elect Hultgren by leaving my Dictaphone in his office—for as you will recall he many times and oft did repeat for the benefit of all at Council Meetings, Budget Hearings, and to the press that the Mayor should not have a Dictaphone in his office. Therefore, I am this date transferring my Dictaphone to the Recreation Department to avoid his embarrassment on having such a modern office to contend with during his administration.[83]

Cane at hand, Fraser conducted his last city council meeting on April 28 as a defeated mayor. As he urged the council to do something about some unfinished houses on Avenues E and F in Billings, councilman Allen Wharton, a longtime Fraser adversary, passed a note to newsmen attending the meeting. The note said, "The SBA [Small Business Administration] gave Willard $135,000 to fix his building; it hasn't been done yet."[84] Such a surreptitious jab at Fraser during his last council meeting must have seemed unnecessarily cruel to Fraser, who was not able to ignore it. The next day, Wharton was lunching at the airport when Fraser walked by and confronted him over the allegation. According to Wharton, Fraser then "picks up his cane, runs it at me like a sword, and shouts at me." Wharton said the point of the cane poked him in the ribs. The press called the incident a "caning," a word that brings to mind a brutal beating.[85] This uncharacteristic outburst of anger was an ugly blot on the last days of Fraser's third term.

Before leaving office, Fraser took time to advocate for saving the old Parmly Billings Library building, which now stood empty. He released to the press a letter he received from a group of students who hoped the structure could be saved, and he proposed it be used as a law library by the city's lawyers.[86] He found new homes for the international flags in his office, giving the Mexican flag to the Guadalupe Church, the Norwegian to Eastern Montana College's language department, the Irish to Fr. John Moore, the Canadian to Police Chief Dunbar, and the Israeli to Rabbi Samuel Horowitz. Knowing it would be best appreciated there, he donated the Plenty Coups bust by Billings sculptor Dolly Felt to the museum at Chief Plenty Coups State Park in Pryor. He wrote dozens of thank-you notes to supporters and boxed up six years of correspondence, which he donated to the Eastern Montana College library for their newly established archives. Having completed what tasks he could, Willard declared to the press he had no immediate plans except to "sleep for a month."[87] It would become apparent over the next two years that Willard would do much more than sleep.

"Tell 'em Willie Boy is here"

WILLARD disappeared from newspapers for nearly a month before he was back in the public eye. A month after he left office, some city officials and the chamber of commerce considered hiring Fraser as a publicist for Billings to attract new industry to the city and to promote tourism. The city and the chamber would split expenses. The final decision was announced with the *Gazette* headline, "Chamber Axed Job for Fraser." Apparently, the chamber feared Willard's "unpredictableness" and worried that he would run through the allotted budget before the year was out and then ask for more money. This decision sparked a scolding letter to the editor from a Billings resident. "Who ever heard of a predictable publicist?" the writer asked after admonishing the chamber on not taking advantage of Fraser's ability as "one hell of a publicist."[1]

Press coverage and Willard's personal letters demonstrate that the former mayor was only nominally a private citizen during his two years out of office. As he did every year, he invited scores of people to the increasingly popular Yellowstone River Boat Float, and he accompanied his mother and some Kansas aunts to Yellowstone Park. Much of the time, however, Willard remained involved in many of the public events and causes he had participated in as mayor. He judged the Miss Billings Scholarship Pageant and once again led more than two hundred boys on the No Moms Bike Hike to Pompeys Pillar.[2] He accepted invitations to speak at a variety of venues and on sundry topics. "I am speaking today to the college and at the Catholic Church. Then I am drinking beer with the boys on Skid Row. They are part of the city's population too," he wrote.[3] Willard did not abandon his zeal to oppose pollution while he was out of office. He addressed classrooms to dissuade students from littering and received *Gazette* coverage for writing to the Montana Air Pollution Council to advocate for stricter air standards and enforcements.[4] When the legislature was considering the Montana Environmental Policy Act (MEPA), he traveled to Helena and delivered a statement of support for the act.[5]

During the summer of 1969, Willard devoted much of his time and attention to the filming of *Little Big Man*, the first major film shot in Montana in a decade. After enticing Stockbridge Productions of North Hollywood to Billings, Fraser served as an informal resource for the company. He helped locate housing for stars Dustin Hoffman and Faye Dunaway, producer Stuart Millar, director Arthur Penn, and all actors and crew. Two homes on Virginia Lane housed the extended Hoffman family, and houses on Azalea Lane and O'Malley Drive were made available for key movie people. A block of nearly seventy-five rooms was set aside in the Northern Hotel for additional cast and crews. In an early July *Gazette* article titled "Lose Your Razor," Willard advised local men who were interested in parts as extras to grow "beards, mutton-chop whiskers and western-style mustaches." Casting director Gene Lasko had told Willard that "bewhiskered applicants" would stand the best chance of being cast.[6] Willard also recommended Stuart Conner, local collectors Don and Stella Foote, artist J. K. Ralston, and local Western historian John Popovich as consultants on costumes and artifacts used in the film.[7] For a battle scene, he collaborated with Crow tribal chairman Edison Real Bird and *Hardin Tribune* editor Helen Peterson to recruit Crow and Cheyenne tribal members as horsemen. In a letter to Peterson, Fraser reported that 397 showed up on Monday, and 50 the next morning. "So great was the Indian bareback riding ability," Fraser noted with pride, that the filming of the enactment took just three days instead of the ten days the filmmakers had expected.[8]

Filming of *Little Big Man* began in late July and lasted through early October. Portions of the film were shot on a ranch southeast of Billings that was owned by Earl and Antoinette Rosell. Earlier, Willard had asked Earl Rosell to guide producer Stuart Millar during a weekend visit. Rosell remained involved with the film, including playing a minor role.[9] Director Arthur Penn made good use of Montana's wide-open landscapes, shooting battle scenes near Crow Agency, at the Little Bighorn Battlefield on the Crow Reservation, and at the historic ghost town of Nevada City. In early October, the crew moved to Ennis, Montana, for a few days and then on to Calgary, Alberta, where a winter scene was filmed.

Wendy Fraser recalled a memorable day during the early fall of 1969 when she was a college freshman and her uncle invited her to lunch.

Actor Dustin Hoffman and his wife visit with Crow tribal members during the filming of Little Big Man *in 1969. Willard Fraser persuaded the producers to shoot the movie in Montana and helped recruit over four hundred Crow and Cheyenne horsemen for the film.* Billings Gazette, Sept. 19, 1969

Expecting "a fancy lunch at the Northern Hotel," she was surprised when he directed her to drive to the Crow Reservation. Wendy described their day:

> As we drove toward the reservation, Willard explained that he had been writing to Hollywood directors and producers raving about the beauty and history of Montana that was abundant and untapped at that time. His goal was that Billings would become a destination for moviemakers. The game changer came when we were greeted at the movie set of *Little Big Man*, and I spent the next two hours with Dustin Hoffman. Oh, my goodness—so exciting! Willard was full of experiences like that and was always generous about sharing them with family and friends.[10]

A year later, in early October 1970, Fraser, who was on his way to Europe, stopped in New York City to discuss a premiere date for *Little Big Man* with the publicity division of the film's producers.[11] The result was that on December 16, 1970, Billings hosted the movie's premiere in the 1,400-seat Fox Theater (now the Alberta Bair Theatre). The event was unusual enough that Governor Anderson declared the day to be *Little Big Man* Day in Montana. Sam Rides Horse and Jake Athone planned a full day of Indian activities, including dancing, athletic contests, fry bread, and a game of shinny (Indian hockey played without skates). At the theater, the first seats were reserved for Indians who had been in the movie, then those Indians who participated in the celebratory powwow on Broadway that day, then the Billings American Indian Council. The rest of the seats were first-come, first-served. Afterward, a publicity agent for the film wrote Willard a thank-you letter, saying, "A big thank you for making *Little Big Man* Day possible in Billings. December 16th will go down as one of the most successful movie preview dates in memory."[12] Willard seemed to bask in the day's success, writing to Grant Salisbury, "You should have seen the Indians in town for 'Little Big Man.' It was the first time in Hollywood's Un-Indian history that real Indians got a "First-Showing" free, or otherwise."[13]

Since its debut in 1970, *Little Big Man* has been recognized as a film of historic merit because of its sympathetic portrayal of nineteenth-century Cheyennes and its critical presentation of George Armstrong Custer and the U.S. cavalry as ruthless marauders intent on annihilating the Cheyenne. "What really set the movie apart from so many previous westerns was its depiction of Native people. The Cheyenne are not merely noble savages or bloodthirsty braves," says film critic Kimberly Lindbergs, who wrote a synopsis of the film's significance when *Little Big Man* was chosen for preservation in the National Film Registry in 2014. "*Little Big Man* humanized Indians in a way that few Hollywood films had dared to, and they suddenly seemed as complex and divided as their white brothers and sisters. They were our neighbors, our friends and family members."[14] That the film's makers employed hundreds of Cheyenne and Crow tribal members to play Cheyenne people on their own turf is significant in film history as well, as many films of the era either cast non-Indians as Natives or recruited Indians to shoot "Westerns" filmed in Hollywood rather than on tribal lands.[15]

Without a doubt, the choice of Montana as the primary location for filming a major motion picture benefited the state. Estimates for the money spent in the Billings area during the filming vary from two million to sixteen million dollars, certainly a financial boon for a midsized city.

On February 18, 1971, the Montana chapter of the National Association of Theater Owners honored Fraser for his work in securing the film. They presented him with a plaque at a special showing in Helena for legislators, public officials, and news media representatives.[16] The filming of *Little Big Man* in the state was significant because it took place before the Montana Film Office was established in 1974 to promote film production in the state.[17] Since then, many films have been shot in Montana as a result of the work by the Montana Film Office, but *Little Big Man* came to the state primarily through the efforts of one individual who recognized Montana's environmental and cultural potential—Willard Fraser. Commenting on the location search, production manager Dick Gallegly told the *Gazette* in 1969 that "Willard Fraser. . . wrote such convincing letters about Billings that we came up here to look around. And we're staying to shoot."[18]

Seeking additional outlets for his energy and skills, Willard—a lover of words and spinner of tales—wondered if he might use his verbal talents to reach a broader audience. Following the recommendation of friend and novelist A. B. Guthrie, he wrote a letter to the literary agency Brandt and Brandt, now Brandt and Hochman, proposing various writing projects. He enclosed articles he had written on Custer, frontier scout James Beckwourth, and a World War II relationship between an Irish girl and a Navajo soldier.[19] When nothing came of Willard's attempt to venture into the literary world, he shifted his wide-ranging intellectual interests and his talent for public relations to other interests.

In 1970, Willard was drawn into *Gazette* employee Kim Larsen's efforts to preserve the Rimrocks, the dramatic sandstone cliffs abutting Billings. Larsen had conducted an intensive letter-writing campaign to the press, hoping to prevent commercial development on the sandstone promontory. As a result, Senator Mansfield wrote to the National Park Service to request that a task force come to Billings to assess and determine the feasibility of the Rimrocks becoming a national monument.[20] When the task force arrived on September 28, 1970, Concerned Citizens for a Better Billings organized a reception where the three task force members were presented with Larsen's proposal along with histories of different aspects of the Rimrocks written by Billings geologist George Darrow, Stella Foote of the Yellowstone Historical Society, and Willard Fraser. On a subsequent tour of the Rimrocks, Fraser and J. K. Ralston served as guides.

Willard's interest in preserving the Rims was not new. In a March 1970 letter, he cited Ray Hart's attempt as the state's WPA director thirty years previously to keep the property on the Rims out of private hands. Willard testified that the city council and county commissioners at the time had scoffed at Hart's plan as being that of an egghead dreamer. Willard denounced those who had opposed the preservation of the Rims in the 1940s as "men of no imagination and no vision" and grieved in 1970, "Now the City has slept on its rights too long, and property on the Rims belongs to private individuals who now proceed to develop their property."[21] In the end, the government decided the Rimrocks could not be designated a national monument because too much of the area had already been developed.[22] The men that Willard had accused of having "no imagination and no vision" decades earlier had indeed squandered an opportunity to preserve a unique and impressive natural feature.[23]

Willard also embarked on a project that combined his interest in archaeology and history with a primary focus on Crow culture and people. Stuart Conner had already taped two interviews on vision quests with Crow tribal member John Cummins for the American Indian Research Project at the University of South Dakota. Conner's connection there opened the door for Willard to conduct oral history interviews with additional tribal members. Willard taped fourteen interviews, all of which are archived at the University of South Dakota. His interviewees included

During his two years off from mayoral duties, Willard interviewed Joy Yellowtail Toineeta (left) and Joe Medicine Crow (right) for an oral history project now archived at the University of South Dakota in Vermillion. Courtesy Stu Conner

Alice Bull Tail, Barney Old Coyote, Phil Beaumont, Tom Yellowtail, Joy Toineeta, Joe Medicine Crow, Mickey Old Coyote, and Eloise Pease. The topics ranged from cultural practices—such as the sun dance, the Crow clan system, Crow wedding ceremonies, and practices of Crow medicine men—to current tribal issues, such as the problems caused by alcohol on the reservation, the preservation of tribal documents, unemployment, and tribal government. One interview included a discussion of the portrayal of Native Americans in films such as *Little Big Man*, a topic that would certainly have been of interest to Fraser.[24]

Throughout his life, Willard fostered friendships with Crow and Cheyenne tribal members, among them Susie and Tom Yellowtail, Barney Old Coyote, Edison Real Bird, and Johnny Woodenlegs. He attended many tribal events, such as Crow Fair and sun dance ceremonies. Among Willard's writings is a detailed description of a Crow funeral that could only have been written by an eyewitness.[25] He also cheered for tribal athletic teams, telling one friend in the fall of 1970, "Going down to Lodge Grass on the morrow to watch and cheer for the Lodge Grass Red Skins as they take after the scalps of the Harlowtown Engineers."[26] Later that month, he reported that he "attended an Indian meet today. . . and tomorrow to a meeting of Tribal chiefs from over the state."[27] In turn, the Crows saw Fraser as a friend and an advocate, inviting him to weddings and graduations and calling on Willard when he could be of assistance. When the *Gazette* published a letter from a white woman accusing Indians of receiving government hand-outs, Minnie Ellen Fritzler of Lodge Grass wrote a long, detailed letter of rebuttal.[28] The *Gazette* refused to print Fritzler's letter unless she edited it down to three hundred words. Incensed, Fritzler wrote back to the paper, including Mayor Fraser and Helen Peterson in her response, and told the *Gazette* that the mayor had invited her to bring the letter to his morning press conference.[29] Fritzler's letter was published eight days later, but it had been edited down to the requisite three hundred words.

Willard was fond of emphasizing that the Indians had been victorious against Custer at the Little Bighorn, and he also delighted in stories that highlighted Indian wisdom versus white man's logic. For instance, he enjoyed repeating Barney Old Coyote's well-timed response to the question of whether he was a full blood. Old Coyote, who had just given blood, responded, "All but one pint." Willard also shared the following story more than once. In 1970, Crow tribal member Braids on Top (Phillip Beaumont) was finishing his education at Eastern Montana College when he was called into the dean's office and told he could not graduate that year because he lacked a foreign language credit. Braids on Top replied, "What do you

Willard with Susie Walking Bear Yellowtail, Montana's first Native registered nurse, at a Crow wedding, ca. 1970. Courtesy Stu Conner

mean, I've not been taking a foreign language? Haven't I been taking English for four years? Until I was ten or twelve I spoke only Crow, and to us Crows English is a foreign language." Willard happily reported in a letter to Salisbury that EMC president Stanley Heywood agreed with Braids on Top, who would graduate in 1971.[30]

As always, Willard's interests and opinions extended beyond Montana, and even as a private citizen he was compelled to express his opinions on political events. The actions of President Nixon gave Willard an opportunity to expound on the relationship between religion and government. When Nixon became president, he instituted fairly regular Sunday services in the White House, the first president to do so. Theologian Reinhold Niebuhr criticized these services in the journal *Christianity and Crisis*. Calling attention to the fact that the nation's founding fathers had "expressly prohibited establishment of a national religion," Niebuhr observed, "It is wonderful what a simple White House invitation will do to dull the critical faculties, thereby confirming the worst fears of the Founding Fathers." He contended that by hosting a religious service in the White House, Nixon had circumvented the Bill of Rights' first article.[31]

Niebuhr's article struck a chord with Willard, and he penned a congratulatory letter to the seventy-seven-year-old theologian. Willard quoted Robert Frost as saying that Franklin Roosevelt, an Episcopalian, had no press present at private religious services at Hyde Park, and he noted that Truman, a Baptist, also had private services. Fraser continued, "When Eisenhower was elected, the whole blankety blank world went to church in the papers, over the radio, and on television. And now, with Richard Milhous Nixon in the White House, the whole world goes to frenzied Camp Meetings every week, with the usual fornication and seductions going on in the wings, and woods. . . . So it is good to hear of you and many another clergyman starting to speak up." Willard received a note of thanks from Niebuhr and a handwritten note from Niebuhr's wife.[32]

As mayor, Fraser, a member of Billings' First Congregational Church, had begun council meetings with a prayer, but he distrusted ostentatious displays of both religion and patriotism. "Excessive flag waving by politicians is all too often an attempt to cover up shady purposes just as is too much Bible shouting," he wrote to one correspondent. "I've found that when politicians quote the Bible and Jesus and wave the flag at the same time, one had better reach for his wallet, and keep a firm hand on it."[33] He wrote to the editor of *TIME*, "From infancy I have been taught to respect the man of the cloth in the proper church pulpit, but to always beware of the man shouting 'Jesus' from the street corner or circus tent, the ones Henry L. Mencken always referred to as 'Theological Prostitutes.'"[34]

Although Willard sustained a spirited interaction with public figures, friends, and institutions, his own medical and financial difficulties resurfaced during 1969 and 1970. After construction of the federal building led to the loss of his tenants at 804 North 29th Street, Willard searched fruitlessly for a new tenant or for a new purpose for the office building. He could not pay a loan previously negotiated for a remodel, and foreclosure began in November 1969. The headlines this created were not the kind of publicity Willard generally received or relished. In January 1970, the federal government sold the Fraser Company office and apartment buildings at a sheriff's sale, a loss against which the Fraser family had little financial cushion.[35] The income from the two buildings had provided major support for Willard and his parents. His prior income as mayor would have funded only a very basic lifestyle, and he had minimal savings; thus the loss of his buildings was a major financial blow.[36]

In addition to his financial woes, the ordeal of Willard's broken hip persisted. Willard had decided to file a suit of negligence against Palmer House in Chicago because there was no mat in the tub when he fell. James Thompson commented in 2019 that Willard was "very critical of the judge" who presided at the juried case. A letter from Willard to his lawyer corroborates this view and includes a litany of evidence to support his belief that he was the victim of a "great injustice in Chicago." At the trial, the judge reminded the jury that he himself had often visited Palmer House (without falling) and, according to Willard, the foreman of the jury admitted to owning hotel stock. The defending attorney downplayed Willard's injury by claiming it would have been impossible for someone in great pain to get out of the tub and phone for help as Willard did. Willard explained, "It was simply something I had to do. There was no alternative unless I wanted to stay in the tub until the maid came in the next morning, go into shock, and probably die." He then described a soldier from his outfit in World War II who, when "German shrapnel slashed off both feet at the ankles, . . . ran several feet in shock on stumps."[37] Willard said that the "nodding heads and faces" of the jurors prepared him for the eventual loss of his suit against the Palmer House.

In the spring of 1970, Willard faced another medical procedure related to his injury. Pins and other pieces of metal used to repair his hip had to be removed. He often joked about this hardware, "The first year of medical school—and I swear it—is spent at a blacksmith's forge." The surgery was originally planned for February 1970, but it was postponed when his asthma kicked up, and the metal was finally removed in May. In preparation for the metal removal and to regain his strength afterward, Willard began riding a bike up to ten miles each day. He was no stranger to bike riding, having participated in the annual No Moms Bike Hike for years, but now he began riding regularly with a specific intent. After the metal had been removed from his hip in May, he wrote to his sister and brother-in-law, "I am doing a lot of biking, trying to get strength back into my hip muscles."[38] The exercise seemed to help curb his asthma as well, and Willard reported that the summer of 1970 was "the best breathing summer I've had in years."[39] His bicycle became a part of his lifestyle and would soon become an important political symbol as well.

With his health improving, Willard took advantage of his time out of the mayor's office to devote attention to matters concerning his late father-in-law. He made a trip to San Francisco to view *Once by the Pacific,* a movie about Robert Frost's early life in that city. He corresponded regularly with Will Gahagen, the director of the Frost Center in San Francisco, and several Frost biographers communicated with Willard over the years as part of their research on the Frost family. After the sudden death in 1939 of scholar Robert Newdick, who had begun a biography of Frost, Lawrance Thompson undertook an official, three-volume biography of the American poet.

Thompson had visited Billings in 1961 to speak at several Montana colleges. Afterward, Willard and Thompson corresponded, and Willard contributed ten letters to the volume of Frost letters that Thompson published in 1964. When the first of three volumes of Thompson's biography, *Robert Frost: The Early Years, 1874–1915,* appeared in 1966, Willard wrote Thompson a two-page letter, "having long since finished your book." Willard's letter is interestingly absent of praise except for saying he appreciated the "brains and sweat" that went into the book. Willard then took issue with Thompson's portrayal of Elinor Frost as a glum person. Robin, after reading the book, asked, "Did Grandmother never smile?" Willard told Thompson, "She did smile and often. Treat her kindly. Without her, RF would have been nothing." The remainder of the long letter ignores the book and discusses JFK and a visit from Cheyenne children from the school at St. Labre.[40]

Willard's true feelings about Thompson's book emerged in a later letter to the editor of *Mainliner,* a United Airlines magazine, in response to its article titled, "Robert Frost's New England." In defense of Frost, Willard exclaimed, "I often wonder . . . at the surprise biographers of R. F. seem to feel at finding him to have been a man of great toughness of body, mind, and spirit. What is surprising about that? He got to the top, didn't he? And what tougher top to get to than the top of the poetry world? Sure, he was a hotheaded, supersensitive, egoist hard as Vermont or Montana granite—all in the finest sense—who loved attention because he knew he had earned it." Of Elinor Frost, he wrote, "She had such a strong understanding softness—softness not to be confused with weakness."[41] Despite his apparent ambivalent feeling about Thompson's first volume, Willard continued to correspond with him, writing several letters to him in the first months of 1967.

Robert Frost, 1941. Willard Fraser defended his father-in-law's reputation and countered the image of Elinor Frost portrayed in Lawrance Thompson's biography of the American poet. Fred Palumbo, photographer. 3c20742, Library of Congress, Washington, D.C.

When Thompsons's second volume, *Robert Frost: The Years of Triumph, 1915–1938*, came out in 1970, the Frost family was taken aback by Thompson's negative profile of Frost's character. Willard's emotional commitment to the Frost family inspired a loyal defense of his father-in-law's reputation. He wrote to Lesley Frost Ballantine, who was then living in Spain, to say, "Like you, I too am receiving numerous copies of reviews sent me by friends and acquaintances. . . . Few people here have read Thompson's book, but many have read the reviews."[42] Lesley expressed her opinion of the book in a letter to the *New York Times Book Review*, stating she was "speechless with the shock of surprise at what appears to be a book written by one who hated my father instead of loving him."[43] There is no record of a letter from Fraser to Thompson about this volume, but Willard expressed his views to friends and reviewers in several letters. Both Judson Jerome of the *Writer's Digest* and literary critic and Frost friend Louis Untermeyer published rebuttals of Thompson's portrayal of Frost as a "moral monster," and Willard wrote to commend them for their support of Frost.[44] Willard sent a letter to Jerome suggesting that Thompson's unfavorable treatment of Frost stemmed from Frost's inability to defend himself: "I suspect that he is taking vengeance for slights, and brusqueness of Frost. . . . You know the phrase 'kick the dead lion'? Never more apt."[45] In another letter, Willard said, "It does seem to me that much of Thompson's stuff is both unnecessarily cruel, and far from the real, or whole truth."[46]

Many critics, at the time and since, agreed with Fraser that Thompson created a subjective and unfairly negative picture of Frost the man. A 1999 biography by poet and academic Jay Parini devoted pages to Thompson's treatment of Frost and asked, "Was Frost as Thompson suggests, really such a selfish, egomaniacal, dour, cruel, and angry man? Certainly, the evidence of many who knew the poet well runs counter to this claim. And there is in the poems themselves a deep core of natural sympathy for human beings that would seem to oppose this assessment."[47] More recently, *New York Times* reviewer Jonathan Miles called Thompson's book "a big fat voodoo doll of a biography with Thompson puncturing Frost from every angle."[48] Critic Peter Stanlis called the Thompson biography "badly flawed" and said, "Thompson not only failed to understand Frost's character and critical reflections, but [Thompson's] own wooden, literal-minded, humorless and rigid temperament made him incapable of appreciating Frost's audacious literary imagination."[49] Unfortunately, Thompson, as Frost's official biographer, exercised undue negative influence on Frost's personal reputation, and many English majors, teachers, and students since 1970 have accepted as truth what Stanlis called a "deliberate character assassination of the poet."[50]

Despite Willard's evident feeling that Thompson betrayed his trust, he aided other critics in their research on Frost and the Frost family. During the winter of 1970, Willard served as a source for a book by Don McCarthy, *Afternoons in Montana*, a collection of essays published in 1971 about significant or interesting people with connections to Montana. Specifically, the essay "A Bird in Her Arms" about Marjorie Frost Fraser is based on letters and information from Willard.[51] When Arnold Grade was working on *Family Letters of Robert and Elinor Frost*, which appeared in 1972, Willard sent him a 1933 letter from Frost to Willard and Marjorie and the photo of Willard and Robin before Willard left for World War II. Both appeared in Grade's book. Willard also corresponded with William Sutton, who had undertaken the task of publishing Robert Newdick's unfinished biography and the corresponding notes.[52]

In the fall of 1970, Willard embarked alone on a trip to Europe. Typically, his network of connections provided experiences unlike those of the ordinary tourist. The previous winter, Willard had hosted the burgermeister of Billings, Germany. This, in turn, paved the way for Willard's visit to Billings, Germany, where he gave a speech at the dedication of their new Rathaus (town hall) and was feted by the townspeople. In Cologne, he encountered an American who told Willard he was a Catholic and was going to mass at the city's famous Gothic cathedral. Willard responded, "I am not a Catholic, but I am going to mass too. I want to hear the organ thunder Bach."[53] In France, he visited Don Nunley, who had been the property manager for the *Little Big Man* filming near Billings. Nunley was working onsite for the filming of *Le Mans*, a film about the famous auto race, starring Steve McQueen. After meeting McQueen, Fraser reported to protégé Paul Jakab, "I rode in a racing Porsche with him [McQueen], and when we hit 110 miles on the Le Mans raceway—a regularly used road—I said, 'Don't you think that is fast enough?' 'We are still in low' was his [McQueen's] comment. . ... We left the ground—I swear—every time we went over a fallen leaf." In Iceland, Willard ate whale blubber for lunch but "did not ask for seconds." He rode a bike "all over Amsterdam," although nephew John Fraser, who was living in Holland at the time, told him that riding a bike in that city "took more guts than brains."[54]

Writing to Hal Stearns, Willard described his method of touring Rome. Upon arrival, he called the North American College at the Vatican and said, "I am an American from Montana. Are there any Americans from Montana roaming around the Vatican?" By this means, he got a Missoula boy on the phone and told him to get his buddy, who was also from Montana. "I will take you both to dinner," Willard insisted. "I can say that he and Norm showed me some of the high spots and low spots of Rome," Willard later reported to Stearns.[55] Of course, he invited both boys to the Yellowstone Float the following summer.

Willard relished "fun," but even when having fun, he ruminated on how to improve the world and Billings and Montana in particular. He returned to Montana from his European trip with his mind brimming with ideas. He wrote to the Billings school board recommending exchange programs with Billings, Germany, and he wrote to the Agricultural Experiment Division at MSU to ask why the Flathead couldn't become a "massive wine-producing region.[56] In Austria, he had shared a cable car with skiers from New York and asked them why they didn't come to Montana to ski. The chance meeting made Willard aware that Montana needed to do a better job advertising its ski areas and natural wonders so as not to lose potential winter recreation tourists. He also visited four or five mayors while in Europe and compared how they handled municipal garbage and health programs. In what could be interpreted as a subtle prelude to the 1971 mayoral campaign, Willard said of his European travels, "Any mayor should be worldly knowledgeable."[57] This may have been a sly dig at Mayor Hultgren who, in contrast to Willard, was more city limited.

Gazette reporter Roger Hawthorne introduced his appraisal of Mayor Hultgren's first year with the statement that the mayor had "revealed himself as a very capable administrator, a forceful fighter for city projects, and an official who seems to distrust the public." He cited another Hultgren shortcoming: the new mayor made appointments that suggested conflicts of interest. Overall, Hawthorne's assessment was that Hultgren made improvements in city facilities but without engaging the press or the public in his endeavors.[58] Implicit in the statement was an unfavorable comparison to Fraser's regular communication with the press and his continual contact with Billings citizens.

Without Willard in the mayor's seat, *Gazette* headlines focused less often on the city's mayor. Nevertheless, Mayor Hultgren and the council created some buzz in the press, reminiscent of conflicts between Willard and the council. A year into Hultgren's tenure, the July 6, 1970, meeting featured a shouting match between Republican councilman Roy Rye and attorney Arnold Berger, who was representing the Tampico Café on a license issue. The district court was in abatement proceedings against the café, and the council was considering revoking Tampico's license. Rye's conduct, including inviting Berger to a physical fight, was so outrageous that on August 10, the council voted 7–3 to remove Rye from its ranks. After some legal maneuvering, Rye was reinstated on September 14.[59]

Willard Fraser, John Bohlinger, and Jean LeBar prepare to distribute campaign signs in 1971. Phil Bell, photographer. *Billings Gazette*, Mar. 28, 1971

The dramatic ordeal did no favors for the city council's reputation. The *Gazette* quoted city residents as saying the "council is acting like a bunch of children," and references to the "fighting in city hall" suggested Billings' city government was not running smoothly. While one individual commented that Hultgren was "at least trying to do something," such incidents demonstrated that a fractious council was not unique to a Fraser mayoralty.[60]

In early 1971, Willard announced he would run for mayor in the spring election. He declared that the 1,700 signatures on his nominating petition made the pressure to seek the office again "pleasantly irresistible." He decried the "cronyism, dullness, and inability to make decisions" that characterized the current city hall.[61] Upon hearing of Willard's candidacy, Stuart Millar of *Little Big Man* wrote to say, "Good luck with the campaign. I just hope Billings' citizens share the respect and admiration that you won from Dustin [Hoffman], Arthur [Penn], and the rest of us. I have traveled many places and met many persons, but seldom have I met a man who loved and *served* his home town so wisely and well."[62]

Locally, councilmen Cornelius Riedl and Joe Leone stated their support for Fraser in their own campaign advertisements. Harvard University student Paul Jakab paid for an ad declaring "There is No Generation Gap." The Crow Nation also purchased an ad in support of Fraser, prompting him to quote a line from *Little Big Man* when he told the Crow tribal council that his "heart soared like a hawk" at seeing the ad.[63] Some two hundred supporters, including several Republicans, attended a fundraising dinner at the Northern Hotel, where Hal Stearns said of Fraser, "We need men to match our mountains."[64] Buoyed by such support, the 1971 Fraser campaign for mayor echoed the excitement and optimism of his 1963 campaign.

Willard stumped with enthusiasm and an upbeat message. He appeared on college campuses, where he was greeted with "Tell 'Em Willie Boy is Here" signs, inspired by the movie of that title. Campaign manager, friend, and clothing store owner John Bohlinger, a Republican, came up with novel and successful campaign ideas.[65] He decided that Willard's bicycle would best symbolize youth, vigor, and support for a clean environment.[66] Fraser's campaign posters simply bore a bicycle and the word "Yes!" Newspaper ads included the slogan, "Fraser Makes Things Happen." Bohlinger also organized a Women for Willard Tea event. From the fifty women who attended the first tea, "ladies held teas that drew more ladies who held more teas to draw more ladies."[67] This use of the power of women as organizers and voters was a new—and effective—tactic for an election in Billings.

Once again, Willard would face incumbent mayor Howard Hultgren and write-in candidate Leona Deisz in the April 4 election. Deisz's campaign never took fire and, days before the election, she dropped out and endorsed Howard Hultgren, whom she called a "gentleman," while simultaneously saying, "Sixty minutes of Fraser, a fluoride-pushing dictator, would be a disaster."[68] This time, Fraser's war chest was much closer to that of Hultgren's than it had been in the previous election. In all, his campaign costs came to $4,145.97 while Hultgren spent $4,402.00.[69] Two of the larger donations to Fraser's campaign came from Billings businesses, an indication that Willard's perennial promotion of Billings reaped practical rewards. The harshest criticism Fraser leveled against the incumbent mayor was that as a practicing chiropractor, Hultgren was only a part-time mayor. Hultgren, in

I'm Afraid It's Still Just Me, John

This newspaper cartoon from February 7, 1971, shows a dapper John Bohlinger, Fraser's campaign manager, working to improve Fraser's appearance and his appeal to young voters. Curtiss, artist. *Billings Gazette,* Feb 7, 1971

turn, charged Fraser with "fiscal irresponsibility" and said he himself was an administrator while Fraser was a "public relations man." Hultgren stated that his job as mayor was to run the city, not to attract attention.[70] Willard's response to such criticism was always that any attention he attracted was good for Billings and would help him put it on the map.

Gazette columnist Roger Clawson predicted that Fraser would win by a small margin. "The attacks on the old warrior have failed to draw blood," he noted, "and Fraser has declined to retaliate. The council fights are forgotten, foreclosure has slipped from memory." Clawson commented that incumbent Hultgren, unlike Fraser, was more at home behind a desk than in the center of a powwow, and he observed that Hultgren was not a raconteur. Clawson lauded Hultgren's acquiring more park lands and bringing the traffic system out of the horse and buggy era, but he conceded that Hultgren had also had some issues working with the council.[71]

On election day, Clawson's prediction of a Fraser victory by a "slim margin" proved wrong. Fraser won a decisive victory, winning a solid majority: 9,234 votes compared to Hultgren's 5,821. The *Great Falls Tribune* declared that Willard "trounced" Hultgren, and a few days later the paper applauded Fraser's victory, saying, "Willard Fraser is a colorful man with imagination and spark. We congratulate him on his election."[72] Under the headline "Hail, Willard!" the *Independent Record* declared, "There are pros and cons about his administrative ability but no question about his ability to bring a lot of attention to Billings—and himself."[73] Willard was exuberant. As befitted his new image, the victorious mayor-elect rode his bicycle into the Northern Hotel where a celebration was held on election night. One member of the cheering crowd, Alderman Joe Leone—who at times had publicly denounced Fraser's actions—gushed to the press, "I'm so happy I'm crying. I wouldn't face another two years with Hultgren and you can quote me on that."[74]

Willard described his joy both at being reinstated in the mayor's office and at the festivities of the inauguration: "The Royal Pipe Band piped and marched this Mayor from the Inaugural Banquet at the hotel four blocks to the City Hall in Billings, where I was installed in office at the first council meeting. It was great. It was fun. It was colorful. It was enjoyed by all."[76] A week after the victory, Willard wrote to Harry Hornblower in Boston, "April was a great month in Montana, for again I became Mayor of Billings."[77]

Watched by members of a local bagpipe band and Willard Fraser, a young man fastens a campaign flag to Fraser's bicycle. Fraser rode the bike into his election night party at the Northern Hotel. Billings Gazette, *Apr. 4, 1971*

"I am looking for men who will think 50 years ahead, instead of 50 years backward"

ON MAY 3, 1971, sixty-four-year-old Willard Fraser began his fourth term as mayor. Robin traveled to Billings to participate in the inaugural ceremonies. The *Gazette* snapped a photo of Willard and Robin—both beaming—as they walked to the inaugural dinner. In the background, the World Theatre announced *Little Big Man* on the marquee. The newspaper caption mentioned that Fraser and the movie had boosted each other. Certainly, Willard's role in bringing the filming of the movie to Billings, the resulting publicity for the city, and the millions it brought to the economy burnished his image, but positive memories of his previous six years as mayor was probably a more significant factor in his victory. Fraser moved into his final term as Billings's mayor displaying characteristic optimism and brimming with ideas.

By 1971, the city's population was approaching one hundred thousand, making it Montana's largest city since surpassing Great Falls. Billings's steady growth presented the mayor and city council with the question of how to manage that growth. The postelection council of 1971 seemed to promise less obstruction than the heavily Republican councils of Fraser's first three terms, but the mayor's pet issues faced opposition from at least some councilmen as well as the community's conservative contingent. Nevertheless, Willard charged ahead with his progressive hopes for Billings, declaring, "As citizens of Montana's number one city we must provide the area with leadership."[1]

Delighted to be back in the top spot of Billings' government, Fraser immediately began to make sure the public had access to him and that he was a visible mayor. To showcase his availability, he met with the press in his office every morning, and he suggested to KULR TV that they institute a "Tell it to the Mayor" program. His open attitude toward the press guaranteed frequent coverage. Billings citizens always knew what their mayor was up to and what he thought. He also issued plans for a revived Western Day Parade in the summer of 1971. Beginning in 1939, the city's Go Western Parade had attracted as many as fifty thousand spectators. By the 1950s, it had evolved into the Western Day Parade. In 1968, the procession of horses, antique autos, stagecoaches, and marching bands stretched for a mile. The event then lapsed until Fraser reinstituted it. He announced that the Edelweiss Marching Band and, "of course, my Scots" would participate that year. He requested that Crow leader Sam Rides Horse participate, saying it was important "to bring him and others of his race in to meet and join with the rest of us in building Billings."[2] Naturally, the mayor would also be part of the parade. The Western Heritage Museum in the former

Robin Fraser Hudnut and Willard Fraser celebrate the start of Fraser's fourth term as mayor, May 3, 1971. Billings Gazette, *May 4, 1971*

Parmly Library building would be dedicated before the parade. It was an auspicious beginning to Mayor Fraser's fourth term.

Willard's personal largesse, as always, extended to family and friends in the hot, dry summer of 1971. He took his nephew's children to the Midland Empire Fair in Billings, where they rode "every sort of impossible mechanical contraption."[3] Lesley Ballantine's grandson, twenty-one-year-old Doug Wilber, spent part of that summer with Willard and Sadie, and at one point three young men from France, a connection made through Willard's World War II friend Guillaume Auger, spent some time with the Frasers. During their visit, it became apparent that Sadie's memory was beginning to falter. After the visit from the young Frenchmen, Willard wrote to Auger to apologize after learning that one morning Sadie, who was then eighty-four years old, had uncharacteristically forgotten to feed the young men breakfast. Her difficulties continued, and she entered a nursing home in October 1971. The next month Willard wrote to Robin, "She [Sadie] is quite bright and alert most of the time, but still very forgetful. It just seems to me that it is just too much of a hazard to bring her home for any length of time at all. Marvin, myself, and Jerry drop in every day."[4] Willard was now living alone for the first time in the house at South 38th Street.

Almost immediately, Mayor Fraser resumed his traveling ways, much to the angst of his city council. Two weeks after his inauguration, he went to Hollywood to try to draw more moviemakers to Montana. In June, he went to the Conference of Mayors in Philadelphia. In October, Fraser accepted an invitation to participate in the annual Baconian Dialogues, named for Sir Francis Bacon, in Minnesota. Initiated by Montana native Hugh D. Galusha Jr., president of the Federal Reserve Bank of Minneapolis, the Baconian Dialogues brought approximately forty leaders from different professions together to discuss societal issues.[5]

When Fraser went to Hawai'i in December for the national conference of the League of Cities, his budget wrangles with the council came to a head. This Hawai'i trip depleted his travel budget, and two aldermen said they would refuse to honor future travel claims. Undaunted, Fraser cheerfully told newsmen that he had no intention of staying home. "You should compare the dollars I have brought into Billings with those I have spent travelling," he countered.[6] Fraser simply charged future travel expenses to a "film and industrial development" fund, dubbed a "champagne fund" by Alderman William Fox. Later that term, Mayor Fraser invited international students in Billings to a lunch on George Washington's birthday, as was his tradition.[7] When he submitted a claim for $50 to the city for hosting the twenty students, three aldermen rejected the claim, saying the mayor should pick up the tab himself.[8] Fraser did so but grumbled, "In many ways it [the lunches] has paid off, yet today the Council turned down my bill for same. What about that for international good will?"[9]

The mayor-council relationship supplied plenty of fodder for the press. Republican Donald Baker led the opposition of the fractious council, and Republicans Ed Leuthold, Charles Lidderdale, and William Fox, and occasionally Democrat Cornelius Riedl, tended to side with Baker. Five councilmen—Democrats Joe Leone and Russell Fillner, Republicans Roy Rye and William Chapel, and independent Norman Schoenthal— supported Fraser early on, but as his fourth term progressed, even they sometimes challenged or opposed him.

Perhaps as a result of his frustration with Fraser's return to power, Baker proposed in June 1971 that Billings adopt a city manager form of government, in which a trained professional appointed by the council would conduct the city's day-to-day business. The head of the Yellowstone Republican Party also supported such a change, stating, "Now is the time for a public study of an alternate form of city government."[10] Naturally, Willard, who loved having a position from which to realize his many ideas, was opposed to any plan to rein in the mayor's power. In his first televised news conference, he assailed the city manager proposal as a half-baked and purely theoretical notion, calling it a "long-haired idea."[11]

Several months later, as the Montana Constitutional Convention was deliberating in Helena, Fraser sent a persuasive letter on the issue of city leadership to Dr. George Rollins, an Eastern Montana College professor and delegate to the convention. "In this age of urbanization, the mayor needs increasingly to have the power to exercise immediate responsibility that the people have placed upon him," Fraser wrote, adding, "Just as Governor Anderson has been attempting a reorganization of state government, so we are in need of reorganization of city government." He went on to say that no city should have more than four to six council members, and that a mayor should have more power in appointments.[12]

Despite his ongoing power struggles with the council, Fraser was able to achieve some important accomplishments early in his fourth term by working within the traditional mayor-council form of government. He proposed a one-mill levy to support a city-run bus system to replace the current privately run service. He proposed that citizens over sixty-five would ride the buses free. The proposal passed on a 6–4 vote, and Fraser complimented the council, saying, "The council in its wisdom and courage has taken the right road."[13] In September the Billings Transit Authority was organized, and it applied for federal grants. The grants were secured, and city-owned buses were scheduled to be delivered in the fall of 1972.

Billings Gazette staff writer Roger Clawson's column provided regular and prolific commentary on all things related to Fraser and his city council. Clawson was often skeptical of Fraser's actions and ideas, but he also had fun with the role-defying actions of the mayor. In August 1971, Clawson used his column to imagine a three-act play about "Willard Fraser—Super Mayor" and the Monday night city council meeting, which he referred to the meeting as "the best comedy by an elected body." Clawson opened the first act with an atmosphere of harmony, with five Boston cyclists appearing as Fraser's guests. "The mayor said they [the cyclists] were all wonderful and they said the mayor was wonderful and presented him with a plaque," Clawson wrote, but the play's tone devolved from there. The first act ended with the aldermen "assassinating a Fraser proposal to make the northern six feet of Parkhill Drive a bike expressway." In the second act, aldermen discussed the council's annual garage sale, and the "curtain closed with the clatter of marketplace drowning the chatter of the council." The third act, hitting close to home, began with "the Knights of the Semi-Circular Table [the ten aldermen] plotting to cut the king's purse strings."[14]

In September, when Willard renewed his campaign for a gravity-flow water system for Billings, Clawson continued to play devil's advocate to Fraser's progressive ideas and to highlight any turmoil that occurred in council meetings. Regarding the gravity water system, Clawson questioned whether Fraser was a dreamer or a hallucinator, commenting, "Only a fool would pretend he totally understood Willard Fraser."[15] Two months later, Clawson felt compelled to protest charges from readers that he was knifing the mayor in the back in his columns. "When my articles have portrayed Fraser as a clown, it was because he was clowning," Clawson declared. "When my stories reported the mayor engaged in pressure politics, the mayor was engaged in pressure politics." He then provided a "portrait of my friend, the mayor," who is "also a compassionate human being." For instance, he described Fraser spending Thanksgiving visiting people on Skid Row and families down on their luck. His article concluded, "What's more, he is the same man in all situations. I like the mayor because he doesn't cry. Politicians who wail that they are maltreated by the press and misunderstood by the public bore me. If Fraser were that sort of man, I wouldn't be writing this."[16] Clawson's assessment brings to mind John Bohlinger's later comment that Fraser had once said he "had no enemies, only friends who didn't know [him] well."[17]

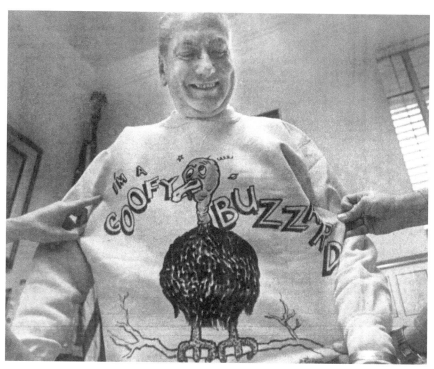

Capitalizing on media attention, Fraser donned a "Goofy Buzzard" shirt after an alderman tried to insult him with the term. William Tutokey, photographer. *Billings Gazette,* Dec. 20, 1971

Gazette columnist Addison Bragg also drew attention to Willard when he turned the topic of the mayor-council sparring into a lighthearted *Gazette* photo. After councilman Donald Baker called Willard a "goofy buzzard" in a December 1971 council meeting, Bragg was instrumental in commissioning a sweatshirt featuring a sketch of a buzzard and the caption, "I'm a Goofy Buzzard." A grinning Fraser donned the sweatshirt for a *Gazette* photograph, a result that Baker probably neither anticipated nor appreciated.[18]

Of course, Willard was quite capable of garnering publicity on his own. In late 1971, he joined a Montana Chamber of Commerce tour in Malta, and in response to a question about how to bring industry into the state, he said that Montana was handicapped by misinformation about its climate. He contended this false image of Montana being as frigid as the North Pole was due in part to Charlie Russell's "damn cow." The drawing he referred to was Russell's famous sketch, *The Last of 5,000,* of a gaunt cow suffering in a severe blizzard during the harsh winter of 1886–1887. The *Gazette* quoted Fraser on the Russell drawing, national media picked it up, and it became nearly as big a story as that of Lady Bird Johnson stealing the city key in 1963. It was featured on Paul Harvey's daily radio program and received coverage in newspapers on both coasts.[19]

Passionate about marketing Montana's "salubrious" climate, Willard came up with a new marketing ploy—to stamp the day's temperature on the mail from all city departments—and he issued a memo containing that directive. The idea could not have been more untimely, because the winter of 1971–1972 was unusually cold and snowy. Fraser proposed that the city buy a snow blower to clear city streets, but the council refused to pay for one. Fraser blamed the many spring potholes on the failure to keep snow and ice off the streets. In a twist on one of his fondest sayings, "Others endure weather while Montana enjoys climate," city residents joked, "Billings endures potholes while others enjoy streets."[20]

That winter, the mayor and the council began work on a comprehensive zoning plan for a growing Billings. The city had first adopted some zoning measures in 1955, but the mayor and the council agreed that the ordinances needed to be redone and modernized. Working with city planners, they drew up a new zoning plan. They did not anticipate that they were ushering in a fight evocative of the fluoride war. As soon as activist Leona Deisz heard of the new zoning proposal, she began to marshal her forces to block it.[21]

The Deiszes' confrontational rhetoric resulted in an ugly incident. On December 4, 1971, a car pulled up outside the Deisz residence and the occupants burned a cross on the Deiszes' lawn. They assumed, undoubtedly correctly, that the action was taken to protest their stand on the zoning plan. That the cross was burned on the lawn of a perennial Fraser foe made no difference in Fraser's reaction. He fired off a memo to Police Chief Dunbar directing him to make it a priority to locate and take action against those who committed the cross burning. "This is the type of hooliganism we must not permit to go unpunished . . . for it is the type of activity that can lead to much evil."[22] This was not the end of the public furor over zoning for Billings.

Aware of some public opposition to the comprehensive zoning plan, the council at the January 17, 1972, meeting postponed voting on the ordinances for thirty days until a committee had vetted the plan. The council asked the mayor to form such a committee composed of two people in favor of zoning and two people opposed. The committee would choose a fifth member. Fraser appointed Leona Deisz to serve as one of the opponents, but Deisz refused to serve on the committee, saying she was not interested in compromise. Fraser declared that he would not accept her resignation because she was a "dissident of dissidents" and the council wanted two dissidents on the committee.[23] If Deisz did not attend, Fraser said, she would simply be marked absent, and the committee would resume their work. After meeting, the committee reported to the council with a "do pass" recommendation, but the council again delayed voting on the zoning plan at their February 28 meeting so that proposed changes could be incorporated. On March 13, the council finally approved the new codes, which were set to go into effect in sixty days.

Declaring that zoning itself was unconstitutional, Leona Deisz immediately began collecting signatures to force a referendum on the codes, just as she did during the fluoride fight. On May 3, Deisz submitted a petition with enough signatures to ensure a referendum, which prevented the codes from going into effect later that month. The next day, the *Gazette* ran Fraser's letter to the editor describing to the public how lack of zoning would adversely affect the city. The mayor explained, for instance, that some mortgage companies would not approve a home mortgage unless a property was zoned for residential use.[24] Deisz argued that zoning codes would erode an individual's right to own property. Furthermore, she demanded that the city council and the mayor be recalled, using fear tactics to distort the public's perception of their elected officials "We have ten men and a dictator setting out to oust people from their homes," Deisz told the *Gazette*. While Deisz stirred up a zoning feud, the city council enacted the housing codes killed by Deisz's campaign in 1969, indicating they were prepared to defeat her opposition to such regulations.[25] In July 1972, the council approved putting the zoning to a public vote during the November 7 general election rather than at the April 1973 municipal election favored by Deisz.

When the *Great Falls Tribune* interviewed Fraser in September, the mayor alluded to Deisz and her misinformation tactics when he commented, "We have a local woman who's very active in stopping the wheels of government. . . . She's one of the most costly people in the city."[26] Deisz's petitions and forced referendums certainly did cost the city some money, as well as time, and Fraser pointed out that her earlier successes in blocking fluoridation and building codes resulted in long-term expenses as well as the loss of federal funds. Over the ensuing months, Deisz's Citizens for Free Choice and the proponents of zoning, Citizens for Orderly Growth, waged separate campaigns to influence the votes of Billings citizens. The *Gazette* ran several strong editorials in favor of zoning, declaring Deisz's arguments were "nonsense" and stating that "an orderly community demands orderly growth." The Citizens for Free Choice ran an ad featuring a bulldog attacking "High Taxes, Excessive Controls, and Power Grabbing."[27] As it had during the fluoride campaign, the Deisz strategy relied heavily on calls to radio talk shows. This time, however, Deisz's hype against practical city planning failed to gain wide support, and the city's new zoning codes were voted in on November 9, 1972.[28]

As Billings grew, so too did the air pollution that was a byproduct of the city's burgeoning industry. Although many city residents continued to excuse the foul air produced by toxic emissions from the refineries and other plants because it was "the smell of money," the Billings mayor didn't see it that way, and he renewed his attacks against air pollution knowing that he faced an uphill battle against his council. Past councilmen had refused to fund air pollution studies in the early 1960s, but Fraser persisted. Even before the Montana legislature enacted its first air pollution control bill in 1967, he had created a city Clean Air Committee, which evolved into the Air Pollution Commission in 1969. During Fraser's fourth term, he invited state Department of Health officials to Billings to analyze and report on its smog and odor. The resulting report named four major industries—Montana Power Company's Corette plant, Great Western Sugar Company, Continental Oil Company, and Montana Sulfur—as major contributors to the "foul" air. Addressing the city's air pollution problem was not a simple matter. Air pollution control officer James Glenn directed both the air monitoring and enforcement programs, but he had neither the cash nor the manpower to operate both.[29] Still, some progress had been made since 1967. By early 1972, Great Western had spent more than $600,000 on control devices, but fighting air pollution continued to be one of Mayor Fraser's ongoing battles.

While fighting for city zoning regulations and trying to curb toxic smog, Fraser became embroiled in a conflict with his council and the fire department. According to a *Gazette* article, the U.S. Department of Labor had criticized city departments in Billings as being too white, a situation that Fraser was very much ready to rectify. The police department had previously admitted two Mexican Americans to the force. Fraser's two recommendations for new admissions to the fire department included David Albin, grandson of B. R. Albin, and Larry Garcia, a Vietnam veteran and Crow/Mexican American. Both men took the department's entrance test and failed it. Albin retook the test and passed. The subsequent standoff between Fraser and the council and the fire department involved the application of Larry Garcia, who in addition to failing the test, did not have a high school diploma. Fraser charged that the department's opposition to Garcia was because of his race. When it was revealed that six years earlier the teenaged Garcia had been caught stealing beer, Fraser responded with disbelief, telling the newspaper, "Not many reach adulthood without getting into some trouble. . . . I belonged to an arch group of criminals that stole apples."[30] Privately, he wrote to another critic, "Should a youthful transgression be held against a man forever?"[31] Fraser went on to charge that the department's entrance exam was culturally biased, and Billings psychologist Dr. Eugene Wiesner corroborated that charge. In response, the department dropped that exam and went to work formulating a new one. Nevertheless, the fire department and the city council refused to approve Fraser's selection of Garcia.

Fraser did not suffer this defeat quietly. He wrote to a Yellowstone County court official to say, "I can no longer in good conscience sign any statement on any grant stating that the City of Billings does not have racial discrimination."[32] Shortly thereafter, he issued a memorandum to the clergymen of Billings citing the Garcia family's history of military service: Larry's father died while serving in World War II, his twin brother died in Vietnam, and Larry served in the Marine Corps. Larry was, in Fraser's words, a "boy who is now denied an opportunity to fight fires for the city of Billings, but not our country's enemies."[33] A *Gazette* editorial called the issue "complex" but admitted good might come out of the incident by revamping employment procedures. However, the paper also claimed that the incident "set back race relations in Billings." It appears Willard pulled a veil off some racist attitudes that until then had not been acknowledged.

Fraser maintained his reformist urge through the spring and summer of 1972. In August, he wrote to friend Cal Taggert, mayor of Lovell, Wyoming, "Things are lively in Billings, as you know, but that is what happens when they have an activist as a Mayor, as again you so well know—it is easy to sit and do nothing, but one does not build empires that way."[34]

Despite having depleted his travel budget earlier in his term, Fraser continued to go places, sometimes charging travel-related expenses to the industrial development fund, his so-called champagne fund. Fraser incorporated participation in Bobby Burns Day in Miles City with mayoral duties, but when he accepted an invitation to speak in Broadus that April, he did so with a caveat. "If you wish to pay for the gas and lodging it will be fine," he told the teacher who had invited him, "for while I think this is a neighborliness due an important neighbor (and Broadus is important to Billings), there are members of the Billings city council who do not feel this way."[35] Willard combined a visit with Jeanne and Ben Blackford in Connecticut with a "treasury raiding" trip to Washington, D.C., to seek funding for the Calamity Jane Reservoir.[36] Shortly after, he attended the

As a gimmick, Fraser hitchhiked part way to Helena in the summer of 1972. While his poor health sometimes necessitated being chauffeured, city councilmen objected to him asking police officers to drive him to events.
Phil Bell, photographer. *Billings Gazette,* Aug. 30, 1972

U.S. Conference of Mayors in New Orleans, where New York's Mayor Lindsay seconded his resolution to require auto manufacturers to remove one junked car for each new car delivered.[37] When Rapid City, South Dakota, suffered from catastrophic flooding in June of 1972, Fraser flew to that city to offer help and support. He compared the ravaged city to the bomb-leveled cities he saw in southern France during World War II.[38] He continued to believe his errands of goodwill, his public appearances, and his participation in state and national events brought business and a favorable reputation to Billings.

Quibbles over Fraser's travel budget created a characteristic publicity splash when Governor Forrest Anderson invited the Billings mayor to Helena in late August to testify at the Environmental Protection Agency's public hearing on proposed sulfur emission standards for smelters such as the Anaconda Company. Willard accepted but wrote a note saying that because the council had cut his travel budget, he might have to hitchhike. The quip blossomed into a photo in the *Gazette* of hitchhiker Fraser standing on the interstate overpass, suitcase in hand, holding a sign, "Mayor of Billings. Destination Helena." When it was discovered that Fraser had orchestrated a ride to Laurel, where he picked up his own car to drive to Helena, Fraser shrugged it off, saying, "Sometimes it's easy to get carried away with being mayor."[39] Clearly, he had a point he wanted to make to his council.

Given the fairly consistent accusations from his council about Willard's financial irresponsibility, it is interesting that shortly after the publicity over Fraser's hitchhiking stunt, the *Great Falls Tribune* ran an article dubbing Willard the "Oracle of Billings." Journalist Frank Adams introduced the article by saying he was motivated to interview Fraser in part because Fraser had "been able to maintain a balanced budget in all of his nearly eight years as mayor of Billings, while red ink has run like water through the streets of Great Falls." The article ended with Willard saying that good government depended on people taking time to serve on the council, the board, and committees. "Government is only as good as the people in it," the Billings mayor declared.[40]

Fraser's secretary, Abby Ferguson, also came to his defense. Ferguson composed a twelve-page memorandum to "Members of the Press" that consisted of a résumé of the major accomplishments in different city departments and commissions during Fraser's tenure. Her comprehensive catalog, intended to generate positive press coverage, included finally achieving new building codes; progress in slum clearance; additional tracts annexed to the city; chip sealing on arterial and residential streets; many improvements by the engineering and traffic departments; adoption of a city bus system; drafting a city zoning ordinance; hiring another sanitarian in the Health Department; creation of the Air Pollution Board; improvements in the fire, police, park, and water departments; and the creation of the Mayor's Youth Committee and the Committee on Aging. Additionally, Ferguson mentioned that the flu shots Fraser had made available to city employees cut down on absenteeism, and, of course, that he had succeeded in putting Billings on the map. Ferguson concluded her exhaustive summary by listing several projects Fraser was still working on, including bike and saddle routes throughout the city, the acquisition of new park lands along the riverfront, a solution to the city's air pollution, and a paved road to Pictograph Caves.[41]

Like the positive coverage Willard received in the *Tribune*, the picture of Fraser's mayoralty projected by Abby Ferguson and the picture projected by *Gazette* coverage could produce quite different impressions. Ferguson did not mention Fraser's grandstanding, while the *Gazette* often ignored Willard's serious side. In truth, Willard Fraser was a complex combination of a determined politician working against the odds to accomplish idealistic goals and a fun-loving humanitarian who loved ideas and being the center of attention.

Looking ahead to the second year of his fourth term, Fraser expressed a sense of urgency about the goals he had not accomplished. He had for some time envisioned a Calamity Jane Reservoir and a Five Finger Lake project for the Billings area. In March 1972, he wrote to the State Conservation Office saying that "a Mayor's time is always limited by his short term in office and as a Mayor definitely interested in developing the Five Finger Lake project in Billings, time is running out."[42] The Soil Conservation

Service of the U.S. Department of Agriculture informed Fraser that, due to lack of funding, the feasibility report had not been completed.[43] They predicted the report's completion in five months, but it did not happen. Time did indeed run out for this project.

Never one to despair, Fraser wrote to Robert Hudnut in early September 1972 to say, "Why shouldn't I be happy?" He cited his daughter and her family and that he lived in the "last paradise in this world" as reasons for his happiness.[44] Willard visited Robin and her family in California fairly often, and he enjoyed such visits as the one from his grandson, David Hudnut, that summer. As mayor, he was in the satisfying position to make things happen in Billings that would enrich the lives of his diverse constituency. Encouraging the celebration of special occasions in Billings, he wrote to the city librarian and asked, "Would you please have a display of things Mexican . . . and all books that you have on Mexico. . . . The 16th of September is Mexican Independence Day, and our Mexican community is having quite a celebration that weekend so please do what you can to add to it. Thanks."[45] Mayor Fraser never missed an opportunity to add some sparkle to the Magic City.

In mid-September, Fraser prepared to welcome a national figure to Billings to commemorate Yellowstone National Park's centennial birthday. More than a century earlier, the Washburn-Langford-Doane expedition spent several weeks surveying the Yellowstone region. While the group camped at Madison Junction on September 19, 1870, expedition member Cornelius Hedges purportedly revived the suggestion that the area be set aside for the public's enjoyment. Hedges, a Helena journalist, continued to promote the idea in articles in the *Helena Herald*. Two years later, on March 1, 1872, President Grant signed the bill establishing Yellowstone as the nation's first national park.

On September 19, 1972, First Lady Pat Nixon and Interior Secretary Rogers C. B. Morton stopped in Billings on their way to a rededication of Yellowstone Park. This was the kind of public event Willard Fraser relished, and he planned to greet them with his usual love of pomp. The mayor reminded the Billings Police Department security officers, "Mrs. James Thompson is bringing her small daughter Elizabeth to the airport Tuesday morning armed with a bouquet of marigolds to present to Mrs. Nixon. Be assured there will be no bomb in the marigolds."[46]

A smiling Fraser presided at the lectern during the welcoming ceremony for Mrs. Nixon on what began as a pleasant fall day. The Billings bagpipe band played as the mayor escorted the First Lady from the plane to receive the flowers from Elizabeth Thompson and then down the receiving

Mayor Fraser and young Elizabeth Thompson greet Pat Nixon upon her arrival in Billings, September 19, 1972. Willard E. Fraser Collection, MSU–Billings Library

line and to the speaker's platform. Former governor Tim Babcock and his wife, Betty, were among the Republicans in the receiving line. Willard presented Mrs. Nixon with a leather-bound copy of J. K. Ralston's *Rhymes of a Cowboy*, but—recalling Lady Bird Johnson's visit in 1963—not a key to the city.[47] Estimates of the crowd assembled at the Billings airport to greet Mrs. Nixon ranged from one thousand to four thousand people, including a

contingent of about six hundred Crow Indians in tribal regalia led by Crow tribal council chairman David Stewart. After a short welcoming ceremony, Fraser, ever an ambassador and host for Montana, prepared to depart with the First Lady and her entourage by plane to the park. Just before boarding, Willard beckoned to Addison Bragg, saying, "Come here. You going to be around Monday? Come by the office. I want to talk to you."[48]

The weather had turned windy and cold as the afternoon progressed, and the temperature had dropped into the forties. When the entourage arrived at the West Yellowstone airport, a driving rain and near sleet conditions prevailed. A long line of people greeted Pat Nixon there, but she said only a few words before hurrying inside to warm up. From West Yellowstone, the entourage traveled an hour and a half first to see Old Faithful and then to Madison Junction, where the outdoor rededication was held in the amphitheater. The National Park Service described the event at Madison Junction: "Preceding the evening ceremony, the participants and several hundred guests were served typical American fare, a barbecue dinner. . . . As the diners huddled around picnic tables in the campgrounds adjoining Madison Junction in near-freezing weather, darkening clouds and chilling winds suggested the ceremony might be memorable for more than one reason." Interior Secretary Rogers "gave the Centennial address amid rain, hail, sleet, and snow."[49] The First Lady was sheltered by an umbrella which protected her from the rain but not the cold. This was not salubrious weather for Billings's asthmatic mayor.

After the Madison Junction event, Willard traveled with his city attorney, Cal Calton, and Cal's wife, Fran, north to Mammoth, where they had reserved rooms at the Mammoth Hot Springs Hotel. The three visited in the lobby for a while and then Cal, who was tired from the day's events, said to Fran, "You and Willard can sit in front of the fire. I need to go up and rest." As the mayor and Fran warmed by the fire, Willard talked, among other things, about memories of his visits to Mexico. Finally, Willard said, "It's about bedtime. Tell Cal to relax and sleep in. I'll meet you in the morning for breakfast." When Fraser did not show the next morning, Cal went to Fraser's room and found him on the bathroom floor, lifeless.[50] A consulting doctor concluded that sixty-five-year-old Willard Fraser had died of a heart attack.

Mayor Willard Fraser, Sept. 19, 1972. The sixty-five-year-old mayor of Billings died of a heart attack later that night at Mammoth Hot Springs Hotel in Yellowstone National Park. Willard E. Fraser Collection, MSU-Billings Library

Back in Billings the *Gazette* devoted the entire front page of its September 20 evening edition to Willard Fraser's death, and papers in Missoula, Great Falls, Butte, Kalispell, Helena, and elsewhere around the state announced his death. An obituary appeared in the *New York Times* the next day. In Fraser's honor, flags at the Montana Capitol were flown at half-mast on September 21.[51] That afternoon, in the city hall, the stunned aldermen bowed their heads in prayer at a special council meeting. Addison Bragg took charge of answering the phone at 118 South 38th Street. He would not be meeting with the mayor on Monday.

The Native American community had felt at home for the first time in city hall when Willard was elected, and after he died, the Crow and Cheyenne people's unique tributes demonstrated their affection and regard for him. There were no public viewings at the funeral home, but a representative from the Crow Tribe arranged permission for tribal members to come to the funeral home to see Willard in his casket. The day before Fraser's funeral, about a dozen Crow women visited Sadie at the Fraser

Billings residents, including children on bikes, paused to listen to the funeral service for their popular mayor though a loudspeaker. The panel announcing Fraser's death was erected by city employees.
Billings Gazette, Sept. 24, 1972

home, dancing and circling throughout the house. Without a drummer, they kept beat with their feet and quietly filled the living area of the Fraser home as they paid their respects to the Fraser family.[52]

On the morning of Saturday, September 23, 1972, Fraser's flag-draped casket resided in the city hall foyer, attended by firemen and policemen. One of the floral tributes flanking the casket was an arrangement of juniper, sunflowers, pinecones, sagebrush, and shrubs picked from the Rimrocks by Eastern Montana College professor and city councilman Norm Schoenthal and his students. The funeral was held that afternoon at First Congregational Church. Bach and bagpipes played accompaniment to tears and eulogies. During the ceremony, tribal representatives dressed in full regalia lined both sides of the sanctuary. A Crow Nation flag hung in the front of the church.[53] Former governor Tim Babcock attended as a personal representative of President and Mrs. Nixon. "And the people came," Bragg noted for the paper. "They were grade schoolers who remembered a man who was never too busy to visit a classroom. They were young mothers carrying babies. They were college students in jeans and others—men who grew up with him; much older who remembered him as a youngster from the South Side."[54] Outside the packed church, more people listened to the services on loudspeakers next to a memorial panel erected by city employees.

Robin's words on the front of the memorial program attested to Willard's positivity: "He would not want his going away from us to make us sad. He would hope for us to leave this beautiful place inspired and ready to carry on the good fight." Likewise, the music before and during the service reflected Willard's optimistic personality, his patriotism, and his spirituality. The preservice organ selection consisted of three Bach pieces: "Fugue in C Major," "When in the Hour of Utmost Need," and "Sheep May Safely Graze," as well as Mendelssohn's "Sonata II." As the service began, the organist played "This Land Is Your Land," "America the Beautiful," "Montana," and "What Child is This?" The songs during the service were Simon and Garfunkel's "Bridge Over Troubled Water" and the hymns "Joyful, Joyful We Adore Thee," and "A Mighty Fortress Is Our God." *Harlowton Times* editor Hal Stearns delivered the eulogy, and Wendy Fraser and Paul Jakab read the poem, "America," by Marjorie Frost Fraser. Four of Robin's five children placed bouquets on the casket, one for each season—tulips, wildflowers, autumn leaves, and paper snowflakes.

The pallbearers were close friends and former city attorneys James Thompson and Stuart Conner, nephew Jerry Fraser, Crow veteran Joseph Medicine Crow, EMC president Dr. Stanley Heywood, Leslie Frost

Ballantine's grandson Douglas Wilber, journalist Addison Bragg, longtime friend Frank Cross, artist J. K. Ralston, Dr. Aaron Small of Rocky Mountain College, and J. Lawson Lee, a Fort Peck Sioux Tribe member who represented the Montana Bureau of Indian Affairs. Police Chief Gerald Dunbar in a police car led the procession to Mountview Cemetery followed by fire chief Curtis Magruder in a pumper truck. At the cemetery, the West Mosby Volunteer pipe band played "Loch Rannock," a traditional funeral march. There, under a windy, wet sky, Mayor Willard Edward Fraser was buried next to his wife, Marjorie Frost Fraser.

Willard's death elicited a flood of comments and memorials. The *Gazette* columnists—Gary Svee, Roger Clawson, and Addison Bragg—who had had such fun covering Willard in life each wrote an affectionate column of tribute. Stuart Conner expressed the thought of many locals when he said, "The sparkle has gone out in Billings' star."[55] Missoula mayor George Turman stated that Fraser's "zest in politics enlivened and enriched the process of government."[56] J. O. Brew of Harvard's Peabody Museum wrote, "I have always considered Billings to be one of the great cities in the country because they had sense enough to elect him mayor."[57]

Montana's Democratic statesmen paid tribute to Fraser and his life. Senator Lee Metcalf's public statement included the fact that while Willard had opposed entering World War II, when war was declared, Fraser was one of the first from Billings to enlist. Senator Mike Mansfield wrote separate condolence letters to Robin, Sadie, and Marvin Fraser. In his letter to Sadie, Mansfield said, "His accomplishments as a civic leader, a student of history and a great humanitarian will remain as a tribute to his memory for generations to come."[58] Mansfield read a statement about Fraser into the Congressional Record and included a copy of Hal Stearns's eulogy.[59]

Joseph Leone, president of the city council, was sworn in as acting mayor on October 16. On October 24, a somber council met in closed session to approve the last of Mayor Fraser's expense accounts: a trip to Helena, one to Hardin, and one to Cody for a total of just under $460. There was no evidence of the former budget wars between Fraser and the council in the October 24 session. All Fraser's expenses were approved with no discussion. Even those councilmen who had fiercely opposed Willard's travel expenditures offered no objection. Willard had finally united the council.

On November 11, 1972, during halftime at the Billings Senior–West High football game, students performed a tribute to the mayor who had paid special attention to young people.[60] The program for the event bore

Flanked by firemen and policemen, pallbearers carry Fraser's flag-draped coffin from First Congregational Church, September 23, 1972. Addison Bragg, Stu Conner, Frank Cross, Joe Medicine Crow, Jerry Fraser, Stanley Heywood, J. Lawson Lee, J. K. Ralston, Aaron Small, James Thompson, and Douglas Wilber Jr. served as pallbearers. Billings Gazette, *Sept. 24, 1972*

images of the sombrero, the Christian cross, and the Indian tipi, with the comment that Fraser had brought them all together in Billings. The students made a presentation to Sadie Fraser, who outlived her son by three years.[61] Both high schools' marching bands formed the word "Will" on the playing field. They then formed a bicycle followed by the initials VIP, which changed to RIP. Songs played during the tribute were "Yakety March" (a city hall favorite), "Montana," and "Taps." The tribute ended with a quote from Robert Frost's poem, "Stopping by Woods on a Snowy Evening":

> The woods are lovely, dark and deep
> But I have promises to keep
> And miles to go before I sleep
> And miles to go before I sleep.

Reflecting on the life and career of Billings's most colorful mayor, Billings architect and state legislator Harrison Fagg summed up the sentiments of those who had known him: "There will never be another Willard Fraser. He was unique."[62]

A RECKONING

"This is your mayor!"

To ANYONE who called him, no matter where they were calling from or what they were calling about, Willard Fraser's standard telephone greeting was always, "This is your mayor!" Fellow Democrat and South Side alderman Joseph Leone once called Fraser "the worst damn mayor we've ever had," but by the end of Fraser's fourth term, Leone was a stalwart supporter. The citizens of Billings performed the same about-face, voting against Fraser in five mayoral elections and then placing him in the mayor's chair four times. "He exasperated me sometimes," recalled Addison Bragg, "but I voted for him every time."[1]

That Willard was elected to serve multiple terms as Billings' mayor is remarkable, because he was a progressive in a deeply conservative city where Republicans far outnumbered Democrats. Although a Democrat by affiliation, he often railed against partisan politics and did not hesitate to disagree with the party line. More than a party loyalist, he was a proud American with a deep understanding of history.

Willard's perseverance in achieving public office was rooted in his firm belief in the importance of good government that was open and accessible to the public. In a 1964 Constitution Week Proclamation, he stated, "The pitfalls of Free Government are all too often created out of fear, ignorance, and prejudice. . . . Free Government, Learned Government, and Sound Government can only exist through education and knowledge being provided for all our people."[2] His investment in young people stemmed from affection as well as his belief that an informed, well-educated youth built a strong nation. Similarly, he believed in and promoted a government without prejudice and inclusive of and responsive to all people.

As a candidate, Willard envisioned improvements and modernization that would put Billings on the map. As mayor, he worked to make those ideas become reality. After Willard's death, Burton K. Wheeler spoke to that vision when he wrote to Stuart Conner, "He had a brilliant mind but was quite a good many years ahead of his contemporaries."[3] Twenty-seven years later, former councilman Norman Schoenthal, who had chaired Fraser's Air Pollution Control Board, echoed Wheeler's statement: "He was the most wonderful, crazy visionary in the world, . . . but he was fifty years ahead of his time."[4] Friend, historian, and journalist Hal Stearns praised Willard for his ability to see what was possible, saying, "Little mortals cannot deny him his place as a Big Man with Big Visions, Big Dreams—no little ones."[5]

Some Fraser ideas thought to be "zany" in the 1960s later proved viable and demonstrated his forward-looking vision. Recognizing the recreational potential of Montana's beautiful scenery and waterways, he collaborated with other mayors to start the Yellowstone River Boat Float, still an annual event. He abolished smoking in City Hall in 1965; Montana abolished smoking in bars and restaurants in 2009—forty-four years later. He fought industrial air pollution while the federal government was still working to identify toxic pollutants and create emissions standards, and he challenged the leaching of agricultural waste into waterways before the passage of the 1972 Clean Water Act.[6] Looking back, attorney Fred Van Valkenburg remembered that Fraser's leadership on environmental issues was unique at the time because he "made much of the environment" before environmentalism became a movement. Indeed, Fraser often railed against "those who insult God by not seeing the wonders of His world."[7]

Likewise, Willard weighed in on issues still current in the twenty-first century, writing to friend Charles Borberg in 1968 that small guns should be controlled and advocating for laws requiring helmets for motorcyclists. Although some of his signature visions—a tunnel under the Rims, a gravity-flow water system for the city, Calamity Jane Reservoir, and Five Finger Lake—did not materialize, the concepts still have proponents today. Willard's dream of an Indian Study Center at Eastern Montana College—a dream he shared with many tribal members and college educators—became a reality when the Office of American Indian Outreach and the Native American Achievement Center were established to attract and retain American Indian college students.

In 2017, *Gazette* editor Darrell Ehrlick called Willard "Billings' greatest mayor."[8] Any reckoning of his greatness must go beyond assessing the improvements he made to his beloved city and include the equally important example he set as both a politician and a humanitarian. He was a politician who supped with inhabitants of Skid Row as readily as he dined with the city's upper swells. A member of the Democratic Party, he won the support of many Republicans as he sought to build a better Billings and a better Montana. Interested in integrating marginalized populations into the city mainstream, Willard appointed women to key positions in city government. At a time when many Montanans looked askance at the Women's Liberation Movement, Willard wrote to the head librarian at the Billings Public Library to say, "In this age of Women's Lib . . . it seems to me that we are remiss in our duty, and thereby failing all womankind, if we do not subscribe immediately to that new female magazine . . . entitled *Ms*."[9] Fraser also worked for the inclusion and participation of racial minorities, paying particular attention to the area's Mexican American and Native American residents and making his office accessible to their needs and concerns.

Mayor Fraser also strove to promote the arts and to beautify Billings. The city today enjoys more trees and parks because of his efforts. And because of his appreciation for history and the natural world, some of these parks have more interesting names—Two Moon Park, Meadowlark Park, Sacagawea Park.[10]

Willard was adept at attracting attention to himself—no one ever had more fun being mayor—but the publicity he garnered was conjoined with his efforts to promote Billings and Montana.[11] His ability to entertain sometimes obscured the light he shone on such important issues as environmental safety, racial justice, and urban growth. The enthusiasm and vigor he infused into the daily lives of his city and state—and sometimes the nation—were accompanied by a sense of compassion that gave his governance a humanitarian quality.

Willard's impact did not die with him in September 1972. He donated his entire collection of mayoral papers to Eastern Montana College as the founding collection for the college's regional archives, which continue to grow in size and importance as a regional repository. At the time, EMC history professor Robert Smith recognized the papers' significance to the city and state's history:

> Perhaps even more important, the papers will become an inspiration to many young people who will grow up in Billings in the future. They will see that the written word is important; they will realize the importance of the mayor's office; and perhaps if they look into the boxes which house the papers, they will find that there was a man who lived in Billings who cared

about children and young people and tried to make Billings a place where it was fun to grow up. They would learn that had there been no Willard Fraser there would have been no Indian Caves, no float trip on the Yellowstone, no bike ride to Pompey's Pillar and no Smokey Lane.[12]

Tributes to Willard Fraser have been plentiful in the subsequent months and years. In 1972, a Fraser bust by sculptor Rink Davis was placed in the *Gazette* atrium. The Billings Boys Club, now the Boys and Girls Club, established a memorial fund in Willard's name. When Willard died, his family asked that memorials be in the form of contributions to the Willard Fraser Memorial Scholarship at Eastern Montana College (now MSU–Billings), which provides "financial assistance to history majors at MSU Billings who share the broad interests which motivated Mr. Willard Fraser's life, such as public service, love of country, style, and 'pizzazz.'" Willard's daughter, Robin Hudnut, continues to receive thank-you notes from students who received the scholarships. Two years after Fraser's death, Chris Michels, violinist with the band Applejack, organized a six-hour concert in Pioneer Park to celebrate the mayor's memory. Michels recalled, "It was Fraser who always encouraged young people to use the parks for pleasure, for enjoyment and to appreciate the beauty there . . . He authorized the first 'summer fest' events."[13]

A decade after Willard's death, a group of friends organized a "Remembering Willard" night when they told stories and shared letters from his papers. Two hundred people showed up for the memorial dinner in June 1982. Those sharing reminiscences included J. K. Ralston, Joe Medicine Crow, Basil Andrikopoulas, John Bohlinger, James Thompson, Stan Heywood, Denes Istvanffy, Hal Stearns, Addison Bragg, and Stan Lynde.[14] Earlier that year, Stearns had written a letter to the editor titled "What a Salesman," which began, "How we miss Willard Fraser." Stearns's letter, published in the *Gazette* on May 16, 1982, cited how Fraser was a treasure for his beloved Montana and ended with, "Please, Lord, make us a clone of Willard."[15] Columnist Roger Clawson couldn't forget Willard either. In 1975, Clawson wrote, "While he dreamed, the city slept." Reminiscing about Willard some years later, Clawson again described him as a visionary, a dreamer, and a lover of film and foreigners. "Somewhere there should be room for a dreamer," he concluded.[16]

On February 26, 1993, the Boys and Girls Club of Billings hosted a dinner and night of entertainment in memory of Willard Fraser. The

Gazette reported, "In celebration of Willard's appreciation of diversity the night will feature Crow and Cheyenne pow wow singers, bagpipers, a mariachi band, an Indian gospel singer, a Crow flute player, and more." Proceeds of the evening benefited the club.[17]

In 1999, twenty-seven years after Willard's death, a ninety-two-foot bike and foot bridge across Alkali Creek, linking the Kiwanis Trail with Coulsen Park, was dedicated as the Willard Fraser Memorial Bridge. The Caledonian Pipe Band played at the dedication, and Robin Fraser Hudnut rode her father's bicycle over the bridge. In an interview about the bridge, Donald Baker, the alderman who had called Willard a "goofy buzzard" years earlier, said, "He was one of those guys who had an idea a minute and some of them were pretty darn good and, of course, some were not."[18] In 2017, *Gazette* editor Darrell Ehrlick published a four-part series on Fraser in *Magic*, the *Gazette*'s quarterly magazine. Willard Fraser is not forgotten.

Willard's successor, Joseph Leone, was the last Billings mayor to enjoy the executive power Willard exerted. Just a week after Willard's death, Councilman Baker revived his argument that "Billings doesn't need a mayor—we need a change in our form of government." That change would be for a "capable, experienced and objective city manager." The state of Montana was apparently ready for a change. The 1972 Montana State Constitution, ratified six months before Fraser's death, required cities and counties to elect commissions to study city and county government structures, recommend necessary changes, and put the recommended changes to a vote. In 1976, the City Study Commission in Billings wrote a new city charter that would place a professional administrator—a city manager—as head of city government instead of the elected mayor.

This new charter came up for a vote before the Billings city council on September 14, 1976. In what the *Gazette* called a light turnout, the new form of government was approved by a 7,245 to 6,271 vote. According to the *Gazette*, the more affluent and Republican-leaning precincts voted in favor of the new government headed by a city manager, while Democrats tended to vote for the old form of government.[19] The result of the vote ushered in a new era of mayors. Although decades later mayors Chuck Tooley (1996–2005) and Tom Hanel (2009–2017) surpassed Willard's nearly eight years in office, they could not exert the same executive authority Mayor Fraser had exercised. Truly, there will never be another Willard Fraser.

Hal Stearns described Willard's far-ranging influence and emphasized the talents with which Willard infused every aspect of his life: "As a student, he never ceased to learn. As a soldier, he did his duty. As a man

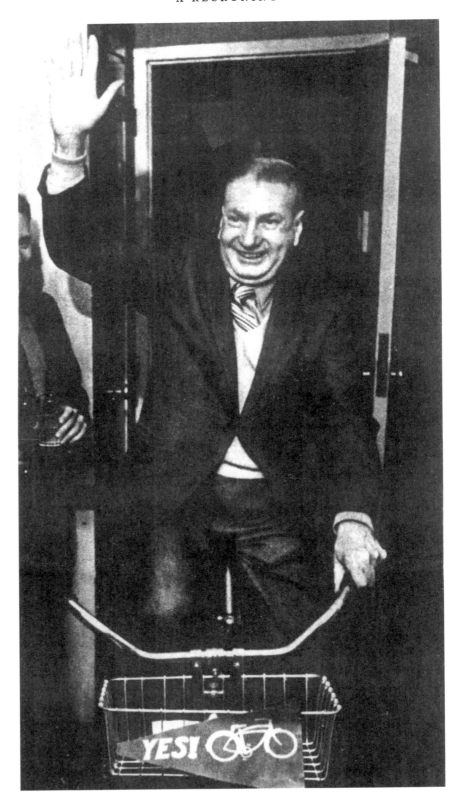

of intellect and curiosity and concern, and as a public servant—he knew no prejudice."[20] Nephew Mac Fraser likewise summed up Willard's character: "Willard never lost his gumption. He just wanted to make the world a better place."[21] Willard's zeal to improve his city, his state, and his nation was conjoined with a sense of humor and an innate belief in the goodness of people. The life of Willard Edward Fraser, the thirty-third mayor of Billings, offers us a view of a transformative time in Montana history and stands as an example of a politician dedicated to serving all the people and the community he loved. With panache.

Willard E. Fraser, Montana's visionary mayor, riding his iconic bicycle into Northern Hotel to celebrate his victory in 1971. His daughter, Robin Fraser Hudnut, rode the same bike over the Willard E. Fraser Memorial Bridge when it was dedicated in 1996. Billings Gazette, Apr. 7, 1971, reprinted Sept. 24, 1972

Bibliography

Books and Web Resources

Anderson, Margaret Bartlett. *Robert Frost and John Bartlett: The Record of a Friendship.* New York: Holt, Rinehart and Winston, 1963.

Bain, David Haward, and Mary S. Duffy. *Whose Woods These Are: A History of the Bread Loaf Writers' Conference, 1926–1992.* Hopewell, NJ: Ecco Press, 1993.

Benson, Jackson J. *Under the Big Sky: A Biography of A. B. Guthrie Jr.* Lincoln: University of Nebraska Press, 2012.

Berg, A. Scott. *Lindbergh.* New York: G. P. Putnam's Sons, 1998.

Boden, Anneke-Jan. *Billings, the First 100 Years.* Norfolk, VA: Donning Co., 1981.

Bragg, Addison. *The Best of Bragg: A Collection of Columns from the Pages of the* Billings Gazette. Billings, MT: Unicorn Communications, 1985.

Brown, Bob. Fred Van Valkenburg Interview, June 23, 2009. https://scholarworks.umt.edu/brown/69. The original interviews are held as Oral History Collection 396, Archives and Special Collections, Mansfield Library, University of Montana–Missoula.

Calamur, Krishnadev. "A Short History of 'America First': The Phrase Used by President Trump Has Been Linked to Anti-Semitism during World War II." *The Atlantic* online, Jan. 21, 2017. https://www.theatlantic.com/politics/archive/2017/01/trump-america-first/514037/.

"Civil War on the Western Border: The Missouri-Kansas Conflict, 1854–1865." http://www.civilwaronthewesternborder.org/encyclopedia/quantrill. Accessed Aug. 26, 2020.

Clawson, Roger, and Katherine A. Shandera, *Billings: The City and the People.* Billings: *Billings Gazette* and *Montana Magazine,* 1993.

Connell, Evan S. *Son of the Morning Star: Custer and the Krishna Little Bighorn.* San Francisco: North Point Press, 1984.

D'Ambrosio, Brian. *Shot in Montana: A History of Big Sky Cinema.* Helena, MT: Riverbend Publishing, 2016.

Devitt, Steve. "Billings Hispanic Community: A Contemporary Look," *Montana Magazine,* Sept. 1, 1987, 6–13, 10.

Ehrlick, Darrell. "Then Comes the Fall: The Rise, Fall, Resurrection and Legacy of Billings Mayor Willard Fraser." *Magic City Magazine* 15:1 (Mar. 2017).

Frost, Robert Lee, Elinor Frost, Lesley Frost, and Arnold E. Grade. *Family Letters of Robert and Elinor Frost.* Albany: State Univ. of New York Press, 1972.

Frost, Robert, and Lawrance Thompson. *Selected Letters of Robert Frost.* New York: Holt, Rinehart and Winston, 1964.

Frost, Robert, and Louis Untermeyer. *The Letters of Robert Frost to Louis Untermeyer*. London: J. Cape, 1964.

Frost, Robert. *The Complete Poems*. New York: Holt, Rinehart and Winston, 1949.

Haaland, Tami. "The Frost Family in Montana: A Story of Poetic Generations." Essay. In *These Living Songs: Reading Montana Poetry*, edited by Lisa D. Simon and Brady Harrison, 16–29. Missoula: The University of Montana Press, 2014.

Hart, Sue. *Billings: Montana's Trailhead*. Virginia Beach, VA: Donning Co. Publishers, 2009.

Hart, Sue, and Katherine A. Shandera. *The Call to Care, 1898–1998: Saint Vincent Hospital and Health Center, the First 100 Years of Service*. Billings, MT: Saint Vincent Hospital and Health Center, 1998.

"Helena As She Was—An Open History Resource for Montana's Capital City," 2006. http://helenahistory.org. Accessed Jan. 11, 2021.

History.com Editors. "Jubal Early." History.com. A&E Television Networks, November 9, 2009. https://www.history.com/topics/american-civil-war/jubal-a-early. Accessed Aug.12, 2020.

Jensen, Margaret. "Float the Yellowstone." Essay. In *Writers Under the Rims: A Yellowstone County Anthology*, edited by Sue Hart, Donna Davis, Ken Egan, and Joyce Jensen. Billings, MT: Parmly Billings Library Foundation, 2001.

"John Brown." Kansas Historical Society. https://www.kshs.org/kansapedia/john-brown/11731. Accessed Aug.26, 2020.

Johnson, Chuck. "Modern Revolution and Counter-Revolution in Montana." Lecture, Oct. 9, 2018. Montana Club, Helena, Montana.

Johnson, Marc C. *Political Hell-Raiser: The Life and Times of Senator Burton K. Wheeler of Montana*. Norman: University of Oklahoma Press, 2019.

Katz, Sandra. *Elinor Frost: A Poet's Wife*. Westfield, MA: Institute for Masachusetts Studies, 1988.

Korn, Jerry. *War on the Mississippi: Grant's Vicksburg Campaign*. Alexandria, VA: Time-Life Books, 1993.

Lang, William L. "In the Yellowstone." Essay. In *Stories from an Open Country: Essays on the Yellowstone River Valley*, edited by William L. Lang, 13–28. Billings, MT: Western Heritage Press, 1995.

LIFE, The Editors of. *The 1960s: The Decade When Everything Changed*. New York: Time Inc. Books, 2016.

Linker, Damon. "'A Man and His Presidents: The Political Odyssey of William F. Buckley Jr.' by Alvin S. Felzenberg." *New York Times Book Review*, May 14, 2017.

Lister, Florence C., and Robert H. Lister. *Earl Morris & Southwestern Archaeology*. Albuquerque: Univ. of New Mexico Press, 1981.

Logevall, Fredrik. *Embers of War: The Fall of an Empire and the Making of America's Vietnam*. New York: Random House Trade Paperbacks, 2014.

Malone, Michael P., Richard B. Roeder, and William L. Lang. *Montana: A History of Two Centuries*. Seattle: University of Washington Press, 2001.

McCarthy, Donald. *Afternoons in Montana*. Aberdeen, SD: North Plains Press, 1971.

Miles, Jonathan. "All the Difference." *New York Times Book Review*, May 11, 2008: 14 ff.

Morris, Ann Axtell. *Digging in the Southwest*. Santa Barbara, CA: P. Smith, 1978.

Morrison, John, and Catherine Wright Morrison. *Mavericks: The Lives and Battles of Montana's Political Legends*. Helena: Montana Historical Society Press, 2003.

Oberdorfer, Don. *Senator Mansfield: The Extraordinary Life of a Great American Statesman and Diplomat*. Washington, DC: Smithsonian Books, 2003.

"Obituary of William Fraser." *Gardner Gazette*. Apr. 28, 1921.

Olberding, Janelle M. *Butte and the 1918 Influenza Pandemic*. Charleston, SC: The History Press, 2019.

Olson, Gregory A. *Mansfield and Vietnam: A Study in Rhetorical Adaptation*. East Lansing: Michigan State University Press, 2012.

Paladin, Vivian A., and Jean Baucus. *Helena: An Illustrated History*. Helena: Montana Historical Society Press, 1996.

Parini, Jay. *Robert Frost: A Life*. London: Pimlico, 2001.

Pictorial History of the Second World War. New York: Wm. H. Wise & Co., 1944.

Pritchard, William H. *Frost: A Literary Life Reconsidered.* New York: Oxford University Press, 1984.

Proto, Neil Thomas. *Fearless: A. Bartlett Giamatti and the Battle for Fairness in America*, 1st ed. Albany: State University of New York Press, 2020.

"Remembering Willard." *Billings Gazette.* Feb. 25, 1993.

"Remembering Mayor Willard Fraser." Episode in *Piece of Mind with Mark Tokarski.* Community 7 Television, Billings, MT, 1982.

Small, Lawrence F. *A Century of Politics on the Yellowstone.* Billings, MT: Rocky Mountain College, 1983.

Stanlis, Peter J. "Rehabilitating Robert Frost: The Unity of His Literary, Cultural, Political Thought." *Imaginative Conservative,* Jul. 26, 2016. https://theimaginativeconservative.org/2012/04/rehabilitating-robert-frost-unity-of.html. Accessed November 19, 2019.

Stanlis, Peter. *Frost: The Poet as Philosopher.* Wilmington, DE: ISI Books, 2007.

Stegner, Wallace Earle. *The Uneasy Chair.* First Vintage Ebooks Kindle edition. New York: Random House, 2015.

Sturdevant, Anne, and Dave Walter. "White Hoods under the Big Sky: Montanans Embrace the Ku Klux Klan." Essay. In *Speaking Ill of the Dead: Jerks in Montana History.* Helena, MT: Two Dot Press, 2000.

Sturdevant, Anne. "The Ku Klux Klan in Montana During the 1920s" (undergraduate thesis, Carroll College, Helena, MT, 1991). https://scholars.carroll.edu/history_theses.

Swibold, Dennis L. *Copper Chorus: Mining, Politics, and the Montana Press, 1889–1959.* Helena: Montana Historical Society Press, 2006.

Tester, Jon. *Grounded: A Senator's Lessons on Winning Back Rural America.* New York: HarperCollins, 2021.

Thompson, Lawrance. *Robert Frost the Years of Triumph.* New York: Holt, 1970.

Waldron, Ellis L. *Montana Politics since 1864: An Atlas of Elections.* Missoula: Montana State University Press, 1958.

Walter, Dave (ed). *Speaking Ill of the Dead.* Guilford, Ct: Globe Pequot Press, 2000.

Woodhead, Henry, and Thomas H. Flaherty, series directors. *Time-Life Books.* Alexandria, VA, 1986.

Work, Clemens P. *Darkest before Dawn: Sedition and Free Speech in the American West.* Albuquerque: University of New Mexico Press, 2005.

"You Know You're from Billings, Montana If . . ." Public Group. https://www.facebook.com/groups/157498974325938/. Accessed Aug. 27, 2020.

Newspapers

Unless otherwise noted, newspapers were published in Montana.

American Observer and Weekly News Review (Washington, DC)

Billings Gazette

Billings Herald

Choteau Acantha

Conrad Independent-Observer

Daily Inter Lake (Kalispell)

Daily Missoulian

Eastern Montana Clarion (Rygate)

Gardner (KS) *Gazette*

Great Falls Tribune

Havre Daily News.

Helena Independent Record

Harlowton Times

Montana Standard (Butte)

Reporter Dispatch (White Plains, NY)

Ryegate Clarion

Times Clarion (Harlowton)

Western Progressive (Helena)

Interviews

Augunas, Wendelanne Fraser. Interview by Lou Mandler, Camden, ME, Jul. 29, 2018.

Albin, Jo. Interview by Lou Mandler, Billings, MT, Aug. 2, 2018.

Bohlinger, John. Interview by Lou Mandler, Billings, MT, Jul. 17, 2017.

Calton, Frances. Interview by Lou Mandler, Billings, MT, Oct. 21, 2017.

Conner, Stuart. Interviews by Lou Mandler, Billings, MT, Dec. 14, 2016; May 2018; Oct. 23, 2018; and Jul. 2, 2019.

Cross, Ted. Telephone interview by Lou Mandler, Jul. 10, 2019.

Ehrlick, Darrell. Interview by Lou Mandler, Billings, MT, Apr. 30, 2018.

Fagg, Harrison. Interview by Lou Mandler, Billings, MT, Oct. 17, 2018.

Ferguson, Abby. Interview by Lou Mandler, Billings, MT, Apr. 10, 2017.

Fraser, Robert Macmillan (Mac). Telephone interviews by Lou Mandler, Dec. 4, 2017; Jan. 15, 2018; Jan. 31, 2018; Jul. 11, 2018; Sept.22, 2018; and Feb. 26, 2019.

Harr, Dr. Donald. Interview by Lou Mandler, Billings, MT, on Oct. 19, 2018.

Hudnut, David. Telephone interview by Lou Mandler, Sept. 6, 2018.

Hudnut, Robin Fraser. Telephone interview by Lou Mandler, Apr. 7, 2022; email correspondence with Lou Mandler, Apr. 19–26, 2022.

Jakab, Paul. Telephone interview by Lou Mandler, Jul. 15, 2020.

Johnson, Chuck. Interviews by Lou Mandler, Helena, MT, Jul. 13, 2017; Apr. 2018; and Jul. 20, 2019.

Koonce, Judy. Telephone interview by Lou Mandler, Feb. 16, 2018.

Moskol, Sally Fraser. Interview by Lou Mandler, Bozeman, MT, Oct. 22, 2017, and Apr. 2018.

Ronquillo, James. Interview by Lou Mandler, Billings, MT, Apr. 30, 2018.

Thompson, James. Interviews by Lou Mandler, Billings, MT, Oct. 3, 2016; Apr. 6, 2017; Jun. 28, 2017; Jul. 17, 2017; and Jun. 27, 2019.

Van Valkenbury, Fred. Telephone interview by Lou Mandler, Mar. 22, 2020.

Wiltgen, Cathy Albin. Interview by Lou Mandler, Billings, MT, Oct. 23, 2018.

Archives

Stuart Conner, Private Collection. Billings, MT.

Edmund B. Craney Papers, 1916–1979. Craney, Edmund B., 1905–1991. MC 122 (6:3–4). Montana Historical Society, Helena, MT.

Abby Ferguson, Private Collection. Billings, MT.

Mayor Willard E. Fraser Collection. Montana State University–Billings Library, Billings, MT. This archive is shortened to Fraser Papers.

Fraser Clipping File. Billings Public Library, Billings, MT.

Robert Frost Collection, 1887–2008 (mainly 1920–1963). Amherst College Archives and Special Collections, Amherst College Library, Amherst, MA. This archive is shortened to Frost-Amherst.

Robert Frost Collection. Frost MS-1178. Rauner Special Collections, Dartmouth College, Hanover, NH. This archive is shortened to Frost-Rauner.

Robert Frost Family Collection 1923–1988. University of Michigan Library, Special Collections Research Center, University of Michigan, Ann Arbor, MI.

Robert Frost Collection. Jones Library Special Collections, Jones Library Inc., Amherst, MA.

Lesley Frost Ballantine Papers 1890–1980. Collection MC 185. Milne Special Collections and Archives, University of New Hampshire Library, Durham, NH. This archive is shortened to Ballantine-Milne.

Gardner Historical Society. Gardner, KS.

Dr. Sean Haling, Private Collection. Jackson, WY.

Robin Fraser Hudnut, Private Collection, Tiburon, CA.

Judy Koonce, Private Collection. Gardner, KS.

Mike Mansfield Papers 1903–1990. MSS 065. Mansfield Library Archives and Special Collections, Maureen and Mike Mansfield Library, University of Montana-Missoula. This archive is shortened to Mansfield Papers.

Lee Metcalf Papers, 1934–1995, bulk 1934–1978. Metcalf, Lee, 1911–1978. MC 172 (9:2–6). Montana Historical Society, Helena, MT. This archive is shortened to Metcalf Papers.

Sally Moskol, Private Collection, Big Sky, MT.

James E. Murray Papers 1918–1969. Archives and Special Collections, Maureen and Mike Mansfield Library, University of Montana-Missoula. This archive is shortened to Murray Papers.

Burton Kendall Wheeler Papers. MC 34 (1:3–7). Montana Historical Society, Helena. This archive is shortened to Wheeler Papers-MHS.

Cathy Wiltgen, Private Collection, Absarokee, MT.

Notes

Introduction

1. Stuart Conner, interview with author, Dec. 14, 2016.

2. Robert Lee Frost et al., *Family Letters of Robert and Elinor Frost* (Albany: State Univ. of New York Press, 1972), 255. When Frost wrote this letter in 1949, Lesley had been divorced from James Dwight Francis since 1931; she would marry diplomat Joseph Ballantine in 1953. Erma married John Cone in 1926, but they separated in 1944 and divorced in 1946. Cone subsequently became a successful architect. Erma's mental illness and eventual commitment to an institution probably did not lead to a close Cone/Frost relationship.

3. Robert Smith, "The Fraser Papers" (introduction to the Mayor Willard E. Fraser Collection), Montana State University–Billings, n.d.

4. Robin Fraser Hudnut, interview with author, Apr. 7, 2022.

5. *Billings Gazette*, Dec. 20, 1971.

6. James Ronquillo, interview with author, Apr. 30, 2018.

7. Hal Stearns, eulogy to Willard E. Fraser, Sept. 23, 1972.

Chapter One

1. The Miles City Caledonian Society, established in 1908, honors Scottish poet Robert Burns (1759–1796) near his January 25 birthday with an annual dinner. In 1971, 630 Scots or would-be Scots attended the event.

2. Willard E. Fraser (hereafter WEF) to Grant Salisbury, Feb. 22, 1970, Mayor Willard E. Fraser Papers, MSU–Billings Library, Billings, MT (hereafter Fraser Papers).

3. "Remember Willard," *Billings Gazette*, Feb. 25, 1993.

4. WEF to Addison Bragg, undated but would be 1968, Fraser Papers.

5. The Fraser family history is based on research done by Judy Koonce.

6. WEF to Ann Hardy Bosworth, Jun. 29, 1965, Fraser Papers.

7. WEF to unstated recipient, Jan. 15, 1968, Fraser Papers.

8. Jerry Korn, *War on the Mississippi: Grant's Vicksburg Campaign* (Alexandria, VA: Time-Life Books, 1993), 93.

9. Ed Blair, *History of Johnson County Kansas* (Lawrence, KS: Standard Publishing Company, 1915), http://kancoll.org/books/blair/index.html, accessed Sept. 2017.

10. Copy of William Fraser's discharge papers and memorandum from prisoner of war records from Judy Koonce.

11. Information on prisoners from "Prisoners of War (Civil War)" in *Encyclopedia of Arkansas History and Culture*, https://encyclopediaofarkansas.net/entries/prisoners-of-war-8634/, accessed Aug. 25, 2020.

12. Information on Third Iowa Cavalry, http://www.iagenweb.org/clinton/history/military/cw/book/cwbk_3c.html, accessed Sept. 11, 2017.

13. Ibid.

14. *Gardner (KS) Gazette*, Apr. 28, 1921.

15. "John Brown," Kansas Historical Society, Aug. 26, 2020, https://www.kshs.org/kansapedia/john-brown/11731.

16. "Civil War on the Western Border: The Missouri-Kansas Conflict, 1854–1865," Sept. 11, 2017, http://www.civilwaronthewesternborder.org/encyclopedia/quantrill., accessed Aug. 26, 2020.

17. WEF to Ann Bosworth, Jun. 29, 1972, Fraser Papers.

18. Family legend from Judy Koonce.

19. WEF to Mike Zeetner, April 1972, Fraser Papers.

20. Max Evans, "Raid on Gardner," *Olathe (KS) News*, May 21, 2005.

21. WEF to Olive Fraser, May 30, 1972, Fraser Papers.

22. WEF to Ann Bosworth, Jun. 29, 1972, Fraser Papers.

23. WEF to Mrs. Mary Eaton, Nov. 7, 1968, Fraser Papers.

24. John Brown Fraser was commonly known as J. B. or Jack. In Gardner he had been known as Don.

25. *Gardiner Gazette*, Nov. 7, 1913.

26. In 1898, Willard's uncle James moved to Billings, where he began a promising career. He became an associate and friend of A. L. Babcock, a prominent and influential Billings leader.

27. Sadie Fraser obituary, *Gardner Gazette*, Oct. 1, 1975,

Chapter Two

1. WEF to KD Van Wagenen of Wyoming Charter Coach Tours, Nov. 4, 1965, Fraser Papers.

2. WEF to Dan McCarthy, Sept. 30, 1970, Fraser Papers. After Fraser introduced his young bride, Marjorie Frost, to Billings, she shared his enthusiasm for his hometown. Years later, Fraser said of Marjorie, "She thought, and I always have, that people of Billings and Montana should out-Chauvin both Texans and Vermonters." In typical fashion, he went on to explain the derivation of "chauvinistic"—that it came from the name of one of Napoleon's very loyal soldiers.

3. Hoxie, Frederick E., "An Undeniable Presence: Indians and Whites in the Yellowstone Valley, 1880–1940," in *Stories from an Open Country: Essays on the Yellowstone River Valley*,

William L Lang, ed. (Billings: Western Heritage Press, 1995), 44–47.

4. According to legend, Sacrifice Cliff's name is derived from a result of a smallpox epidemic. The story is that two Crow warriors returned from a hunting trip to find the people in their camp dead, including the warriors' lovers. In their grief, they chose to join their dead relatives. They blindfolded their horses and jumped from the cliff.

5. For the source of the Apsáalooke name, see Apsáalooke Place Names Database, http://lib.lbhc.edu/index.php?q=node/200&a=I .

6. The Parmly Billings Library, built in 1901, was donated in memory of Frederick Billings's eldest son. Carroll Van West, "Good Times, Bad Times," in *Stories from an Open Country: Essays on the Yellowstone River Valley*, ed. William L. Lang (Billings, MT: Western Heritage Press, 1995), 119.

7. Roger Clawson and Katherine A. Shandera, *Billings: The City and the People* (Billings: *Billings Gazette* and *Montana Magazine*, 1993), 53. In September 1882, General James Sanks Brisbin wrote to a Chicago newspaper and described Billings' incredible growth as "magic." Brisbin had served in the Civil War and in 1876 commanded the 2nd Cavalry in Montana Territory. He had been a lawyer before the Civil War and contributed several articles to eastern magazines. https://en.wikipedia.org/wiki/James_Sanks_Brisbin.

8. Van West, "Good Times, Bad Times," 121–23.

9. Sources on the history of Billings include—in addition to Carroll Van West—Lawrence F. Small, *A Century of Politics on the Yellowstone* (Billings, MT: Rocky Mountain College, 1983); Karen D. Stevens and Dee Ann Redman, *Billings from A to Z*, (Billings, MT: Parmly Billings Library, 2000); Anneke-Jan Boden, *Billings, the First 100 Years* (Norfolk, VA: Donning Co., 1981).

10. A. L. Babcock is not related to the future governor Tim Babcock.

11. In the late 1960s, Mayor Fraser was unsuccessful in his plan to build a new library, and this utilitarian structure, the old hardware store, became the Billings Public Library—much to his dismay.

12. Small, *A Century of Politics*, 9.

13. Willard Fraser, in one of his letters, claims that automatic dialing came to Billings in 1912, twenty years before it came to New York City.

14. *Gardner Gazette*, Jan. 1, 1915.

15. James and Mary Ella Fraser's children, Frances and Harold, remained lifelong residents of Billings, and Willard, his sister Jeanne, his brother Marvin, and Marvin's children maintained a close relationship with their cousin Harold and, later, his children. Another Fraser, Mr. R. B. Fraser, who was not related, moved to Billings with his family in the early 1930s and became a prominent rancher. His daughter Antoinette Fraser Rosell became the first female state legislator from Yellowstone County. The Rosells were also involved in various movies filmed in Montana, some of which were shot on their ranch.

16. WEF to Shirley Day, Aug. 19, 1965, Fraser Papers.

17. WEF to League of Women Voters, Oct. 19, 1969, Fraser Papers.

18. WEF to Grant Salisbury, Mar. 20, 1970, Fraser Papers.

19. Robin Fraser Hudnut, interview with author, Apr. 7, 2022.

20. Family history from author's telephone interview with David Hudnut, Sept. 6, 2018.

21. James Thompson, interview with author, Oct. 3, 2016, and Jun. 28, 2017; Stuart Conner, interview with author, Dec. 14, 2016.

22. Mac Fraser, interview with author, Dec. 4, 2017.

23. *Billings Gazette*, Sept. 13, 1936.

24. *Billings Gazette*, Nov. 20, 1927.

25. *Billings Gazette*, Aug. 19, 1928.

26. Ibid.

27. Mac Fraser, interview with author, Jan. 15, 2018.

28. Robin Fraser Hudnut, interview with author, Apr. 7, 2022.

29. *Billings Gazette*, Dec. 14, 1919.

30. *Billings Gazette*, Aug. 14, 1959.

31. Marvin Fraser's daughter, Wendy, feels she, too, owes her own love of literature to her grandmother's reading to her.

32. WEF to Matt Garrett, Apr. 5, 1965, Fraser Papers. Stratemeyer used the pseudonyms Victor Appleton and Arthur Winfield for the Tom Swift and Rover Boys books. millions of copies sold and credited as inspiring future science fiction writers and scientists.

33. Regarding raising rabbits, see WEF to Isabelle Stewart, Apr. 16, 1965, Fraser Papers; WEF to Dave Rogers, KGHL Radio, Jan. 10, 1969, Fraser Papers.

34. WEF to Jim Gisi, Jul. 15, 1971, Fraser Papers.

35. WEF to John Beslanevitch, Jan. 27, 1966, Fraser Papers.

36. WEF to Grant Salisbury, Oct. 18, 1967, Fraser Papers.

37. Todd S. Harwell, Stacy L. Anderson, Greg S. Holzman, MD, and Steven D. Helgerson, MD, "The Biggest Public Health Experiment Ever," *Montana The Magazine of Western History* 69:3 (Autumn 2019): 47–69; *NY Times*, Dec. 31, 2020.

38. Janelle M. Olberding, *Butte and the 1918 Influenza Pandemic* (Charleston, SC: The History Press, 2019), 47.

39. *Billings Gazette*, Oct. 11, 1918.

40. *Billings Gazette*, Oct. 16, Oct. 21, and Nov. 25, 1918.

41. *Billings Gazette*, Dec. 4, 2018.

42. Olberding, *Butte and the 1918 Influenza Pandemic*, Location 1732; and an Apr. 2020 article in the *Missoulian*, which was based on Pierce Mullen and Michael Nelson, "Montanans and 'the Most Peculiar Disease': The Influenza Epidemic and Public Health, 1918–1919," *Montana The Magazine of Western History* 37:2 (Spring 1987): 50–61.

43. Sue Hart and Katherine A. Shandera, *The Call to Care, 1898–1998: Saint Vincent Hospital and Health Center, the First 100 Years of Service* (Billings, MT: Saint Vincent Hospital and Health Center, 1998), 24–29, gives an accounting of Dr. Allard's role during the two epidemics.

44. Robert Lee Frost et al., letter dated Oct. 5, 1918, in *Family Letters of Robert and Elinor Frost* (Albany: State Univ. of New York Press, 1972), 31; Robert Frost and Louis Untermeyer, letter dated Jan. 4, 1919, in *The Letters of Robert Frost to Louis Untermeyer* (New York: Holt, 1963), 79.

45. WEF to Robert Soloman, Public Health Department, Dec. 14, 1965, Fraser Papers.

46. Clemens P. Work, *Darkest before Dawn: Sedition and Free Speech in the American West* (Albuquerque: Univ. of New Mexico Press, 2005), 81–82.

47. Michael P. Malone, Richard B. Roeder, and William L. Lang, *Montana: A History of Two Centuries* (Seattle: University of Washington Press, 2001), 276–78.

48. Work, *Darkest before Dawn*, 151–53.

49. WEF to Robert Gest, Sept. 12, 1965, Fraser Papers.

50. *Billings Gazette*, Feb. 12, 2018.

51. Anne Sturdevant, "The Ku Klux Klan in Montana During the 1920s" (undergraduate thesis, Carroll College, Helena, MT, 1991), gives a good overview of the topic. Her essay, "White Hoods Under the Big Sky," in *Speaking Ill of the Dead*, Dave Walter, et. al, (Guilford, CT: Globe Pequot Press, 2011) is derived from her thesis.

52. *Missoulian*, Sept. 22, 1923.

53. *Billings Gazette*, Nov. 15, 1924.

54. *Missoulian*, Sept. 22, 1923.

55. *Butte Miner*, Oct. 7, 1921.

56. *Billings Gazette*, Sept. 24, 1926.

57. *Missoulian*, Apr. 9, 1922.

58. *Missoulian*, Apr. 14, 1922.

59. Sturdevant, "The Ku Klux Klan in Montana During the 1920s."

60. *Billings Gazette*, Jun. 23, 1926.

61. *Billings Gazette*, Apr. 30 and May 28, 1924; May 31, 1925; June 23, 1926.

Chapter Three

1. Michael P. Malone, Richard B. Roeder, and William L. Lang, *Montana: A History of Two Centuries* (Seattle: University of Washington Press, 2001), 295.

2. WEF to Dwight Morrow, May 25, 1932, Fraser Papers.

3. Charlie Borberg's written memories, n.d., Fraser Papers.

4. Dr. Reynolds is commemorated at the university today in its George F. Reynolds Fellowships and in Boulder in the George F. Reynolds Branch of the Boulder Public Library.

5. WEF to Dwight Morrow, May 25, 1932, Fraser Papers.

6. Florence C. Lister and Robert H. Lister, *Earl Morris & Southwestern Archaeology* (Albuquerque: Univ. of New Mexico Press, 1981), 176.

7. WEF to J. O. Brew, Jul. 30, 1965, Fraser Papers.

8. The notion that Willard "talked his way into" the expedition comes from a note from Dr. Robert Lister on a letter that Stuart Conner wrote soliciting information about Willard. Conner's letter is dated October 27, 1972, and Lister returned the letter with notes. A contradictory letter from Dwight Morrow to Stu Conner, dated May 3, 1973, says Morris hired Willard "because he was so much impressed by Willard's efficient management of the cafeteria."

9. Ann Axtell Morris, *Digging in the Southwest* (Santa Barbara, CA: P. Smith, 1978), 241. Ann Morris was Earl Morris's first wife.

10. General information from Morris, *Digging in the Southwest*.

11. WEF to J. O. Brew, Jan. 2, 1969, Fraser Papers.

12. When Willard met the Morrows, Dwight's sister, Anne, had recently married Charles Lindbergh, who had become an international celebrity after a successful solo, non-stopflight across the Atlantic. During a political campaign years later, Willard was asked to use his Morrow connections to entice Lindbergh to speak in Montana. Willard declined.

13. Dwight Morrow to Newton F. McKeon, Director of Amherst College Library, Jul. 8, 1963, Robert Frost Collection, bx 8, fldr 73, Amherst College Archives and Special Collections, Amherst College Library, Amherst, MA, (hereafter Frost-Amherst).

14. Robert Frost and Louis Untermeyer, *The Letters of Robert Frost to Louis Untermeyer* (London: J. Cape, 1964), 169.

15. The Morrow Family Letters at Smith College's Nielson Library contains letters from Dwight to his mother and sister describing some of the archaeological finds and camp experiences during his summers in the Southwest. Dwight mentions Willard several times.

16. Robin Fraser Hudnut, interview with author, Apr. 7, 2022.

17. Deric O'Bryan was the stepson of Jesse Nusbaum, who was noted for his archaeological work both in the Yucatan and Mesa Verde, and who served as superintendent of Mesa Verde National Park and senior archaeologist for the National Park Service.

18. Deric O'Bryan to Stuart Conner, Nov. 16, 1972, Fraser Papers.

19. Elinor Frost to Ethel Manthey-Zorn, Sept. 6, 1934, bx 9, fldr 93, Frost-Amherst.

20. Lucille Morris was Earl Morris's second wife. His first wife, whom Willard met while working in the Southwest, was Ann Morris.

21. WEF to Peter Tufts, Glacier National Park, Jun. 25, 1965, Fraser Papers.

22. WEF to Mrs. Herbert Gehskepf, Mar. 16, 1970, Fraser Papers.

23. WEF to J. O. Brew, Jul. 20, 1965, Fraser Papers.

24. Stuart Conner, interview with author, Dec. 14, 2016.

25. Stuart Conner to Deric O'Bryan, Nov. 26, 1972, Fraser Papers.

26. Beside the relationship with Lindbergh and his ties with Smith and Dartmouth, Dwight Morrow Sr., was a prominent banker, an ambassador to Mexico, and a U.S. senator. Dwight Jr.'s life had been one of privilege—summering on Maine's Penobscot Bay, spending winter vacations in Nassau, and socializing with the Rockefellers and the Vanderbilts. A. Scott Berg, *Lindbergh* (New York: G. P. Putnam's Sons, 1998), 182.

27. Margaret Bartlett Anderson, *Robert Frost and John Bartlett: The Record of a Friendship* (New York: Holt, Rinehart and Winston, 1963), 157.

28. WEF to Dwight Morrow, Jun. 1, 1931, Fraser Papers.

29. Anderson *Robert Frost and John Bartlett*, 161.

30. Robert Frost and Lawrance Thompson, *Selected Letters of Robert Frost* (New York: Holt, Rinehard and Winston, 1964), 382–83.

31. Frost and Thompson, *Selected Letters*, 284.

32. WEF to Dwight Morrow, Jun. 23, 1932, Fraser Papers.

33. Elinor Frost to Edith Forbes, Jun. 24, 1932, in *Selected Letters*, 388.

34. WEF to Mrs. Frances Perkins, Apr. 17, 1972, Fraser Papers.

35. Lawrance Thompson, *Robert Frost: The Years of Triumph* (New York: Holt, 1970), 657. When Florence and Robert Lister published *Earl Morris & Southwestern Archaeology* in 1968, Willard was especially pleased that Frost's poem, "A Missive Missile" was included as a frontispiece. Willard wrote that the poem was the result of "my sending him one of the arrowheads" from a dig, but the Listers gave Morris credit for the gift to Frost. WEF to J. O. Brew, Jan. 3, 1969, Fraser Papers.

36. This report is in box 34 in the Fraser Papers.

37. Deric O'Bryan to Stuart Conner, Nov. 16, 1972, Fraser Papers.

38. Ibid.

39. WEF to Dwight Morrow, May 25, 1932, Fraser Papers.

40. WEF to Dwight Morrow, Jun. 23, 1932, Fraser Papers.

41. Charlie Borberg's written memories, Fraser Papers.

42. Elinor Frost to Ethel Manthey-Zorn, Jul. 27, 1932, bx 9, fldr 87, Frost-Amherst.

43. Marjorie Frost to Helen Browning Lawrie, Nov. 6, 1932, Frost-Rauner.

44. WEF to Dwight Morrow, Nov. 11, 1932, Fraser Papers.

45. Marjorie Frost to WEF, Dec. 1932, quoted in Donald McCarthy, *Afternoons in Montana* (Aberdeen, SD: North Plains Press, 1971), 48.

46. Marjorie to Helen Browning Lawrie, Mar. 3, 1933, Frost-Rauner.

47. McCarthy, *Afternoons in Montana*, 49

48. Marjorie to Helen Browning Lawrie, Mar. 3, 1933, Frost-Rauner.

49. WEF to Dwight Morrow, Nov. 11, 1932, Fraser Papers.

50. Sandra Katz, *Elinor Frost: A Poet's Wife* (Westfield: Westfield State Univ., Institute for Massachusetts Studies, 1988), 139.

51. McCarthy, *Afternoons in Montana*, 54.

52. Ibid., 56.

53. *Billings Gazette*, Apr. 4, 1933, gives election results, and the Dec. 7, 1933, issue announces Tilton's death at age forty-nine.

54. *Western Progressive*, Montana Historical Society Research Center Archives, MHS, Helena.

55. Dennis L. Swibold, *Copper Chorus: Mining, Politics, and the Montana Press, 1889–1959* (Helena: Montana Historical Society Press, 2006), 271, 317.

56. Marjorie Frost to Sadie Fraser, undated, in McCarthy, *Afternoons in Montana*, 49.

Chapter Four

1. Robert Lee Frost et al., *Family Letters of Robert and Elinor Frost*, Arnold Grade, ed. (Albany: State Univ. of New York Press, 1972), 156.

2. WEF to Don McCarthy, Apr. 27, 1970, Fraser Papers. This very long letter serves as the basis of the chapter "A Bird in Her Arms" in Donald McCarthy, *Afternoons in Montana* (Aberdeen, SD: North Plains Press, 1971).

3. Elinor Frost to Lesley Frost Francis, postmarked Jun. 3, 1933. Lesley Frost Ballantine Papers (1890–1980) Collection, MC 185, bx 3, fldr 3, Milne Special Collections and Archives, University of New Hampshire Library, Durham, NH (hereafter Ballantine-Milne).

4. *Billings Gazette*, Jun. 4, 1933.

5. WEF to "Folks," Jun. 6, 1933, Robert Frost Collection, Frost MS-1178, bx 12, fldr 38, Rauner Special Collections, Dartmouth College, Hanover, NH (hereafter Frost-Rauner).

6. Marjorie to Helen Lawrie, Jul. 11, 1933, Frost-Rauner.

7. Legend has it that Helena's main street was named Last Chance Gulch because prospectors in the 1860s had decided to give the stream in the gulch one last chance before they struck gold.

8. Marjorie to Helen Lawrie, Jul. 11, 1933, Frost-Rauner.

9. "Cathedral of Saint Helena," Helena as She Was, http://www.helenahistory.org/cathedral_of_saint_helena.htm, accessed Aug. 18, 2021.

10. A devastating earthquake in 1935, several major fires, and an aggressive urban renewal project in the 1970s destroyed many historic buildings; others remain. Willard would return again and again to Helena in his various roles as newspaperman, lobbyist, and mayor.

11. Marjorie to Helen Lawrie, Jul. 11, 1933, Frost-Rauner.

12. William H. Pritchard, *Frost: A Literary Life Reconsidered* (Oxford: Oxford Univ. Press, 1984), 176. Lawrance Thompson's *The Years of Triumph* quotes Frost as saying Marjorie had pneumonia (289) in addition to the appendicitis, pericarditis, and nervous listlessness cited by Pritchard.

13. Robert Frost and Louis Untermeyer, letter dated October 11, 1928, in *The Letters of Robert Frost to Louis Untermeyer* (New York: Holt, 1963), 191.

14. Lawrance Thompson, *Robert Frost: The Years of Triumph* (New York: Holt, 1970), 306, 307, 328.

15. Marjorie to "Mama and Papa," Jun. 10, 1933, bx 12, fldr 37, Frost-Rauner.

16. Marjorie to "Mama and Papa," undated but would be Jun. 6, 1933, bx 12, fldr 37, Frost-Rauner.

17. Ibid.

18. WEF to Don McCarthy, Apr. 27, 1970, Fraser Papers.

19. Marjorie to Helen Lawrie, Nov. 9, 1933, Frost-Rauner.

20. Willard describes this time in the letter to McCarthy on Apr. 27, 1970, and in an Oct. 20, 1933, letter to "Bob" (Robert Frost). He wrote in this letter about his quandary regarding what to call his new father-in-law. He considers Mr. Frost, Dad, Robert, Papa. In future letters, he addresses

them "Dear Folks." Gumbo is a fine, clay-like soil that becomes viscous when wet.

21. This would have been the Fort Peck Indian Reservation in northeastern Montana, home to Assiniboine and Sioux Tribes.

22. This is an early expression of Willard's future support of Montana dams including the Yellowtail and Libby Dams, and an indication of his focus on projects that would benefit both rural and urban people. WEF to Frost, Oct. 20, 1933, bx 12, fldr 38, Frost-Rauner.

23. Lung function tests were developed in the 1940s, but medical treatment was unavailable until the 1950s, when inhaled glucocorticoids were proven effective. This remains the standard treatment for asthma. *New England Journal of Medicine*, https://www.nejm.org/doi/full/10.1056/nejmra1102783, accessed Aug. 1, 2021.

24. Marjorie Frost Fraser to "Mama and Papa," undated but would be winter 1934, bx 5, fldr 20, Ballantine-Milne.

25. Marjorie to Helen Lawrie, Nov. 9, 1933, Frost-Rauner.

26. WEF to Don McCarthy, Apr. 27, 1970, Fraser Papers.

27. Marjorie letter to her parents, undated but would be winter 1934, bx 5, fldr 20, Ballantine-Milne.

28. Frost to WEF, Feb. 1934, in Robert Frost and Lawrance Thompson, *Selected Letters of Robert Frost* (New York: Holt, Rinehard and Winston, 1964), 406. In the summer of 1931, when the Frosts visited Marjorie in Colorado, she and Elinor helped Frost make the final choice of poems to be added to the anthology *The Book of Living Verse: English and American Poetry from the Thirteenth Century to the Present Day*. Frost and Untermeyer, *The Letters of Robert Frost*, 211.

29. Robin Fraser Hudnut, email to author, Apr. 26, 2022.

30. Pritchard, *Frost*, 180.

31. WEF to Don McCarthy, Sept. 30, 1970, Fraser Papers.

32. Robert Frost to Carol Frost, Sept. 9, 1933, in Frost and Thompson, *Selected Letters*, 400. Carol Frost later preferred his name to be spelled Caroll, but Frost continued to use the original spelling.

33. Frost to WEF, in Frost and Thompson, *Selected Letters*, 404.

34. Elinor Frost to Ethel Manthey-Zorn, Mar. 2, 1937, bx 10, fldr 9, Frost-Amherst.

35. WEF to Robert Frost, Oct. 30, 1933, bx 12, fldr 38, Frost-Rauner.

36. The *Western Progressive* ceased publication in 1936.

37. Marjorie to "Mama," undated but would be Feb. 1934, bx 5, fldr 20, Ballantine-Milne.

38. Marjorie to Helen Lawrie, Nov. 9, 1933, Frost-Rauner.

39. At the time of Marjorie's marriage, the eldest Frost child, Lesley (1899–1983), had two daughters and had recently divorced Dwight Francis. She later married diplomat Dr. Joseph Ballantine in 1952. Lesley, the longest-living Frost child, became the family spokesperson. Son Carol (1902–1940) married Lillian LaBatt, a high school friend of Marjorie's, and they had a son, Prescott. Carol's prime occupation was farming on the Vermont family property and later in California, but he struggled with mental illness and finally took his own life. Daughter Irma (1903–1967) married John Cone, and they had a son, John. Irma, too, suffered from mental illness, and after her divorce and some difficult years, she spent the last twenty years of her life in a mental institution. Two other Frost children died in infancy or early childhood, four-year-old Elliott of cholera in 1900 and day-old Elinor in 1907.

40. Marjorie to "Mama," undated but would be Feb. 1934, bx 5, fldr 20, Ballantine-Milne.

41. WEF to Don McCarthy, Sept. 30, 1970, Fraser Papers.

42. Marjorie to WEF, undated but would be Apr. 1934, in Donald McCarthy, *Afternoons in Montana* (Aberdeen, SD: North Plains Press, 1971), 57.

43. Marjorie gave birth at a hospital that was the precursor of Billings Clinic. The clinic was called Movius, Bridenbaugh, Culbertson, and Rathman. It became Billings Clinic in 1939. Two of the physicians who attended her were Dr. Ratham and Dr. Movius.

44. Lillian Frost to Helen Lawrie, Aug. 1, 1934, Frost-Rauner.

45. WEF to Don McCarthy, Jun. 26, 1970, Fraser Papers.

46. Margaret Bartlett Anderson, *Robert Frost and John Bartlett: The Record of a Friendship* (New York: Holt, Rinehart and Winston, 1963), 174–78.

47. Mary Wollstonecraft, the mother of *Frankenstein* author Mary Shelley, died about a week after Mary's birth in 1797.

48. Safiya Shaikh, "'The Contagiousness of Puerperal Fever' (1843) by Oliver Wendell Holmes," The Embryo Project, Jul. 26, 2017, https://embryo.asu.edu/pages/contagiousness-puerperal-fever-1843-oliver-wendell-holmes. General information from: https://en.wikipedia.org/wiki/Historical_mortality_rates_of_puerperal_fever, accessed Jun. 27, 2018; https://jezebel.com/the-silent-and-painful-killer-childbed-fever-5130504, accessed Jun. 27, 2018; and https://en.wikipedia.org/wiki/Oliver_Wendell_Holmes_Sr., accessed May 11, 2020; Review of *The Tragedy of Childbed Fever*, by Irvine Loudon in the *New England Journal of Medicine*, Aug. 24, 2000, https://www.nejm.org/doi/full/10.1056/NEJM200008243430819, accessed June 27, 2018.

49. *The Tragedy of Childbed Fever* by Irvine Loudon (Oxford Univ. Press, 2000) is a book-length discussion of this postpartum infection.

50. British physician Leonard Colebrook demonstrated the effectiveness of sulfonamides against puerperal fever in 1936–37. Peter M. Dunn, "Dr Leonard Colebrook, FRS (1883–1967) and the chemotherapeutic conquest of puerperal infection," June 2008, researchgate.net/publication/5425817_Dr_Leonard_Colebrook_FRS_1883_1967_and_the_chemotherapeutic_conquest_of_puerperal_infection.

51. WEF to Don McCarthy, Apr. 27, 1970, Fraser Papers.

52. Robert Frost to Carol Frost, Apr. 18, 1934, from 244 Burlington Ave., Billings, MT, in Frost et al., *Family Letters*, 164.

53. Elinor to Lesley Frost Francis, Apr. 27, 1934, in Frost et al., *Family Letters*, 167.

54. WEF to Don McCarthy, Sept. 30, 1970, Fraser Papers. The Polytechnic Institute in Billings merged with Intermountain Union College in 1947 and was renamed Rocky Mountain College.

55. Elinor Frost to Lesley Frost Francis, undated but would be in Apr. 1934, bx 3, fldr 3, Ballantine-Milne.

56. Lillian Frost to Helen Lawrie, Aug. 1, 1934, Frost-Rauner.

57. WEF to Don McCarthy, Sept. 30, 1970, Fraser Papers. Dillinger was shot to death in a movie theater in Chicago three months later.

58. Frost and Untermeyer, Apr. 29, 1934, in Frost and Untermeyer, *The Letters of Robert Frost*, 240.

59. Elinor Frost to Lesley Frost Francis,

undated but would be Apr. 1934, bx 3, fldr 3, Ballantine-Milne.

60. Marjorie is also listed on the Frost tombstone in the Bennington, Vermont, cemetery.

61. Lillian Frost to Helen Lawrie, Aug. 1, 1934, Frost-Rauner.

62. WEF to Robert and Elinor Frost, Aug. 1934, Frost-Rauner.

63. Elinor to Edith Forbes, Jul. 15, 1934, in Frost et al., *Family Letters*, 412.

64. Pritchard, *Frost*, 196. In her remaining years, Elinor took care to make arrangements to see Robin as much as possible. In fact, four-year-old Robin was part of the family group, along with Carol and his family and Lesley, who were staying near Elinor and Robert in Gainesville, Florida, when Elinor died.

65. Frost to Untermeyer, May 15, 1934, in Frost and Untermeyer, *The Letters of Robert Frost*, 241.

66. Untermeyer, 241.

67. Frost to Untermeyer, Oct. 8, 1935, in Frost and Untermeyer, *The Letters of Robert Frost*, 184.

68. *Franconia* is now out of print.

69. Elinor Frost to Joseph Blumenthal of Spiral Press, undated, but would be 1935, The Robert Frost Collection, Jones Library Special Collections, Jones Library, Inc., Amherst, MA.

70. Tami Haaland, "The Frost Family in Montana: A Story of Poetic Generations," in *These Living Songs: Reading Montana Poetry*, eds. Lisa D. Simon and Brady Harrison (Missoula: Univ. of Montana Press, 2014), 16–29, 27. Poem used by permission of Robin Fraser Hudnut.

71. WEF to Don McCarthy, Apr. 27, 1970, Fraser Papers. Frost critics and biographers, including Jay Parini and Lawrance Thompson, state that the poem was written for Kay Morrison, and, in fact, Frost himself once said it was for Kay. However, Jay Parini's discussion of the origin of "The Silken Tent" could also apply to "Never Again Would Birds' Song Sound the Same." Because Lesley Frost claimed "The Silken Tent" was written while Elinor was alive, Parini states that it is possible the poem was originally written to Elinor, but Frost's later dependence on Kay may have caused him to credit it to her. Perhaps the same is true of "Never Again. . ."

72. Marjorie Hudnut Renner, email to author, Aug. 31, 2021.

73. WEF to Don McCarthy, Sept. 30, 1970, Fraser Papers.

74. Written memories of Borberg and Cross, Nov. 11, 1972, Fraser Papers.

75. WEF to Lesley Frost Ballantine, Feb. 22, 1972, bx 3, fldr 1, Ballantine-Milne.

Chapter Five

1. WEF to "Folks," Aug. 21, 1934, bx 12, fldr 38, Frost-Rauner. As part of his "mean attempt to keep things going" that summer, Willard accepted a request to speak in favor of Josephine Roche's run for governor in Colorado in 1934. (Roche, Denver's first female police officer, became chair of Colorado's Progressive Party and later Franklin Roosevelt's Assistant Secretary of the Treasury.) As he spoke, an old man in the front listened carefully, nodding his head, and Fraser thought he had won him over. However, afterward the man said to him, "That was a mighty fine speech young man, but we don't want a woman for governor now, do we?" WEF to Josephine Roche, Jun. 7, 1965, Fraser Papers.

2. WEF to Richard Mulligan of NYC, Aug. 31, 1971, Fraser Papers.

3. *Billings Gazette*, Feb. 24, 1906, clipping from Cathy Wiltgen, granddaughter of B. R. Albin.

4. Although many assumed that the Albins were Jewish, according to an account by B. R.'s mother, Ferdinandina Bethke Albin, B. R. and his brother Leo were baptized Lutherans. Family history from Cathy Wiltgen.

5. The Hart-Albin Store endured to become the oldest family-owned department store in Montana before closing in 1990.

6. Russ Hart and Jeanne Fraser divorced in 1941.

7. "As It Was," *Billings Gazette*, Feb. 9, 1952, citing events in 1917.

8. Brochure courtesy of Dr. Sean Haling. At the time, Billings was not yet Montana's largest city.

9. WEF to Robert and Elinor Frost, Jun. 6, 1933, bx 12, fldr 38, Frost-Rauner.

10. WEF to Don McCarthy, Apr. 27, 1970, Fraser Papers.

11. Frost to Marjorie Robin Fraser, Dec. 17, 1940, in Robert Lee Frost et al., *Family Letters of Robert and Elinor Frost* (Albany: State Univ. of New York Press, 1972), 223.

12. Jo Albin, interview with author, Aug. 2, 2018; Mac Fraser, interview with author, Sept. 22, 2018; Wendelanne Fraser Augunas, interview with author, Jul. 29, 2018; and Cathy Wiltgen, interview with author, Oct. 22, 2018.

13. WEF to Charles Searl of Billings Chamber of Commerce, Aug. 11, 1971, Fraser Papers.

14. B. K. Wheeler to B. R. Albin, Dec. 11, 1934, and Jan. 5, 17, 21, 1935, Burton Kendall Wheeler Papers, MC 34 (1:3–7), MHS (hereafter Wheeler Papers-MHS). The bulk of Wheeler's papers are at the Montana State University–Bozeman, but some of his papers are at the Montana Historical Society in Helena.

15. Marc C. Johnson, *Political Hell-Raiser: The Life and Times of Senator Burton K. Wheeler of Montana* (Norman: Univ. of Oklahoma Press, 2019), 267.

16. "As It Was," *Billings Gazette*, Sept. 28, 1959, referring to a *Gazette* article of Sept. 28, 1924.

17. *Billings Gazette*, Oct. 15 and Dec. 22, 1935.

18. Vada Albin kept a diary during this trip, which recounts the cocktail parties, shuffleboard, and shopping trips on the journey. The telegram and diary are part of Dr. Sean Haling's personal collection, which includes the dinner menu of the SS *President Grant* bearing signatures of those in the congressional party. I was able to see the diary through the courtesy of Dr. Sean Haling.

19. *Montana Standard*, Sept. 6, 1939.

20. Elinor Frost to Ethel Manthey-Zorn, Sept. 6, 1934, bx 9, fldr 93, Frost-Amherst.

21. During the Frasers' visit to Rockford, Illinois, Willard was included in a meeting of Robert Frost and Chicago poet Carl Sandburg.

22. Elinor Frost to WEF, Oct. 14, 1934, in Lawrance Thompson, *Robert Frost: The Years of Triumph* (New York: Holt, 1970), 663n.

23. *Billings Gazette*, Mar. 7, 2015.

24. Western Heritage Center, Billings, "The Southsiders" exhibit, Jan. 2018.

25. Sadie Fraser once supervised the hobos in the creation of a rock garden at the Fraser house. Marjorie Hudnut Renner, email to author, Jun. 21, 2020.

26. J. B. died in 1959, and Sadie lived with Willard at their South Side Billings house until she went into a nursing home in 1971.

27. Robert (Mac) Fraser, interview with author, Feb. 2020 (hereafter Mac Fraser).

28. WEF to Robert Frost, Oct. 20, 1933, bx 12, fldr 38, Frost-Rauner.

29. Dennis L. Swibold, *Copper Chorus: Mining, Politics, and the Montana Press, 1889–1959* (Helena: Montana Historical Society Press, 2006), 163–67.

30. Swibold, *Copper Chorus*, 270. The Corrupt Practices Act survived for nearly a century. However, in 2010, in a case before the U.S. Supreme Court, Citizens United, a conservative nonprofit, argued that secret spending by corporations, labor unions, and nonprofit organizations to influence American elections is free speech protected by the First Amendment. The Supreme Court ruled in favor of Citizens United in that case and in a similar case two years later. Montana senator Jon Tester has sponsored a constitutional amendment to undo the Citizens United decision, and an effort to overturn Citizens United persists. Jon Tester with Aaron Murphy, *Grounded: A Senator's Lessons on Winning Back Rural America* (New York: HarperCollins, 2020), 230–31.

31. *Billings Gazette*, Oct. 21 and Dec. 23, 1936; *Great Falls Tribune*, Nov. 1, 1936.

32. *Montana Standard*, Oct. 23, 1936.

33. *Missoulian*, Oct. 23, 1936; *Great Falls Tribune*, Nov. 1, 1936.

34. *Great Falls Tribune*, Nov. 3, 1936.

35. *Great Falls Tribune*, May 22, 1936; *Independent Observer*, Oct. 8, 1936

36. In March 1947, Montana adopted a quota system, limiting the number of liquor licenses in each area based on its population, a system that pushed the price of a commercial liquor license to as much as $100,000 by 1992, and in 2015, the resale value of a license was as high as $500,000. All Montana liquor stores continue to be state owned, although liquor can also be bought at bars with package licenses. Wine and beer can be sold in grocery and convenience stores. https://www.stateliquorlaws.com/state/MT.

37. WEF to Frosts, undated but probably 1935, bx 12, fldr 38, Frost-Rauner.

38. Elinor Frost to Ethel Manthey-Zorn, Mar. 1935, in Robert Frost and Lawrance Thompson, *Selected Letters of Robert Frost* (New York: Holt, Rinehard and Winston, 1964), 419. Ethel's husband, Otto, was a German

professor at Amherst. Robert Frost stayed in the Manthey-Zorn home when he traveled to Amherst for Elinor's funeral in 1938.

39. Frost and Thompson, Jul. 8, 1935, *Selected Letters*, 420. See also, Robert Frost and Louis Untermeyer, *The Letters of Robert Frost to Louis Untermeyer* (London: J. Cape, 1964), 260.

40. Elinor Frost to Ethel Manthey-Zorn, Aug. 23, 1935, box 9, fldr 99, Frost-Amherst.

41. Elinor Frost to Ethel Manthey-Zorn, Jan. 15, 1936, bx 10, fldr 1, Frost-Amherst.

42. WEF to Frosts, Feb. 12, 1936, and Mar. 4, 1936.

43. *Billings Gazette*, Mar. 7, 1936. At the time, Montana paid a bounty for killing predators, particularly coyotes, whose population had grown dramatically after wolves were exterminated throughout the state.

44. WEF to Frosts, undated, but probably 1935, bx 12, fldr 38, Frost-Rauner.

45. Lesley Frost Francis to "Papa," Feb. 1, 1939, bx 12, fldr 12, Frost-Rauner.

46. *Montana Standard*, Jun. 1, 1936.

47. *Great Falls Tribune*, Jul. 20, 1936.

48. Ibid.

49. *Billings Gazette*, Nov. 3, 1936.

50. Roosevelt's Social Security Act of 1935 was in part a response to the popular support of the more generous Townsend Plan. https://socialwelfare.library.vcv.edu/eras/great-depression/townsend-dr, accessed Sept. 23, 2017.

51. WEF to Frost, Jan. 26, no year, probably 1937.

52. Johnson, *Political Hell-Raiser*, 404n.

53. Historian Kevin Starr was California's state librarian (1994–2004) and wrote a multi-volume history of California.

54. WEF to Frost, Feb. 12, 1936, bx 12, fldr 38, Frost-Rauner.

55. WEF to Dr. Larry Thompson, Jan. 30, 1967, Fraser Papers.

56. RF to Bernard DeVoto, Mar. 26, 1937, in Frost and Thompson, *Selected Letters*, 442.

57. Elinor to Lesley Frost Francis, Oct. 21, 1937, bx 3, fldr 4, Ballantine-Milne.

58. Frost wire to Willard re Elinor's death, Mar. 21, 1938, in Frost and Thompson, *Selected Letters*, 468.

59. WEF telegram to Frost, Mar. 21, 1938, bx 12, fldr 38, Frost-Rauner.

60. WEF to Frost, "Tuesday," bx 12, fldr 38, Frost-Rauner.

61. Frost to WEF, Jul. 28, 1938, in Frost and Thompson, *Selected Letters*, 472.

62. Yellowstone County began sending eight representatives to the Montana State House in 1952, and for many years a "straight eight" Republican team went to Helena. Lawrence F. Small, *A Century of Politics on the Yellowstone* (Billings, MT: Rocky Mountain College, 1983), 86; and Michael P. Malone, Richard B. Roeder, and William L. Lang, *Montana: A History of Two Centuries* (Seattle: Univ. of Washington Press, 2001), 382–87.

Chapter Six

1. WEF to Frost, undated but just before war was declared (but not after Pearl Harbor), bx 12, fldr 38, Frost-Rauner.

2. John Morrison and Catherine Wright Morrison, *Mavericks: The Lives and Battles of Montana's Political Legends* (Helena: Montana Historical Society Press, 2003), 111–15.

3. Morrison and Morrison, *Mavericks*, 120. Both Marc C. Johnson, *Political Hell-Raiser: The Life and Times of Senator Burton K. Wheeler of Montana* (Norman: Univ. of Oklahoma Press, 2019) and Michael P. Malone, Richard B. Roeder, and William L. Lang, *Montana: A History of Two Centuries* (Seattle: University of Washington Press, 2001) state that Walsh's cause of death was never determined.

4. Johnson, *Political Hell-Raiser*, 133, 134

5. Also discussed in Malone, Roeder, and Lang, *Montana*, 305.

6. Ibid.; and Burton K. Wheeler with Paul F. Healy, *Yankee from the West* (Garden City, NY: Doubleday, 1962), 294.

7. Malone, Roeder, and Lang, *Montana*, 302, 307; Marc Johnson, *Montana Free Press* interview, Apr. 2019, and Johnson, *Political Hell-Raiser*, 369.

8. Johnson, *Political Hell-Raiser*, 273.

9. *Billings Gazette*, Jan. 19, 1938.

10. WEF to Frosts, Apr. 19, 1939, bx 12, fldr 38, Frost-Rauner.

11. *Havre Daily News*, Jan. 18, Jan. 19, Mar. 14, and Mar. 20, 1940.

12. *Billings Gazette*, Apr. 3, 1940.

13. Malone, Roeder, and Lang, *Montana*, 307; and Johnson, *Political Hell-Raiser*, 202.

14. WEF to B. R. Albin, Oct. 5, 1939, Wheeler Papers-MHS.

15. Johnson, *Political Hell-Raiser*, 255. Jeannette Rankin was the first woman elected to Congress, in 1916, and became famous for voting against the United States entering both World War I and World War II. Jeannette Rankin's brother, wealthy rancher and lawyer Wellington Rankin, was a Wheeler friend.

16. WEF to Joan Kinne, Jun. 10, 1965, Fraser Papers.

17. WEF to Wheeler, Jan. 16, 1940, Wheeler Papers-MHS.

18. WEF to R. Bailey Stortz, Oct. 17, 1940, Wheeler Papers-MHS.

19. WEF to Wheeler, May 7, 1940, Wheeler Papers-MHS.

20. Wheeler to WEF, May 10, 1940, Wheeler Papers-MHS.

21. WEF to R. Bailey Stortz, Oct. 26, 1940, Wheeler Papers-MHS.

22. WEF to Frost, Dec. 31, 1940, bx 12, fldr 38, Frost-Rauner.

23. Outside the realm of politics, Willard was a sponsor for the DeMolays, a branch of the Masons for youths ages twelve to eighteen. A chapter met at the Fraser home in November 1941.

24. War broke out between Japan and China in 1937, preceding the start of World War II in Europe.

25. Johnson, *Political Hell-Raiser*, 258; Damon Linker, review, "'A Man and His Presidents: The Political Odyssey of William F. Buckley Jr.' by Alvin S. Felzenberg," *The New York Times Book Review*, May 14, 2017, 1–33 (nonconsecutive), 33.

26. A 2020 biography of Yale president A. Bartlett Giamatti covers the America First movement in New Haven quite thoroughly. Neil Thomas Proto, *Fearless: A. Bartlett Giamatti and the Battle for Fairness in America*, 1st ed. (Albany, NY: State Univ. of New York Press, 2020).

27. *Billings Gazette*, Aug. 3, 1941. Bundists belonged to the German-American Bund, a pro-Nazi group in the United States in the 1930s and 1940s.

28. Later, right-wing political activist and public speaker Gerald L. K. Smith, formerly aligned with the Townsend movement and the Union Party, continued to use the name for his America First Party, formed in 1943, which espoused anti-Semitic and pro-Nazi views. After the war, Fraser truthfully denied any connection with Smith's America First Party. Smith eventually changed his party's name to the Christian Nationalist Crusade and continued his anti-Semitic and pro-segregation rhetoric. The America First name was again resurrected during the 2016 U.S. presidential campaign despite the negative associations evoked by its history. See, for example, Krishnadev Calamur, "A Short History of 'America First': The Phrase Used by President Trump Has Been Linked to Anti-Semitism during World War II," *The Atlantic*, Jan. 21, 2017, https://www.theatlantic.com/politics/archive/2017/01/trump-america-first/514037/, accessed Sept. 1, 2020.

29. WEF to B. R. Albin, Jul. 7, 1941, Wheeler Papers-MHS.

30. A. Scott Berg, *Lindbergh* (New York: G. P. Putnam's Sons, 1998), 407.

31. WEF to B. R. Albin, Jul. 7, 1941, Wheeler Papers-MHS.

32. Proto, *Fearless*, 91, 105

33. *Billings Gazette*, Jun. 27, 1941.

34. A. Scott Berg, *Lindbergh* (New York: G.P. Putnam's Sons, 1998), 425–30, and *Great Falls Tribune*, Sept. 15, 1941. Lindbergh's words and actions before and during the war, including his apparent sympathy for Fascism and the much later revelation that he maintained a second, secret family in Europe, have clouded his once heroic image. In 2004, Philip Roth's novel *Plot Against America* presented a chilling picture of Lindbergh as a president who began a gradual program of persecuting American Jews. Roth's title was part of the title of a sensational book in 1943—*The Plot Against America: Senator Wheeler and the Forces behind Him*—which made the false accusation of Wheeler consorting with Hitler. In Roth's novel, Lindbergh's vice president is a fictionalized Wheeler. In a 2020 HBO adaptation of Roth's novel, no parallel between the vice president and Wheeler is mentioned. See Johnson, *Political Hell-Raiser*, 352, 353, and "How It Could Have Happened Here," *New York Times*, Mar. 16, 2020.

35. *Independent Record*, Sept. 18, 1941.

36. WEF to "Robert," Nov. 30, 1941, bx 12, fldr 38, Frost-Rauner.

37. Lewis Penwell to B. K. Wheeler, Nov. 6, 1939, Wheeler Papers-MHS.

38. Johnson, *Political Hell-Raiser*, 238–42.

39. Metcalf also had the distinction of being the first Montana senator born in the state.

40. Johnson, *Political Hell-Raiser*, 244.

41. Chuck Johnson, email to author, Oct. 26, 2020

42. That Metcalf and Mansfield were not Wheeler partisans may have prevented the relationships between Fraser and Mansfield, and especially between Fraser and Metcalf, from being close in later years, even though both Fraser and Metcalf often expressed similar views on environmental issues. Fraser maintained a cordial and respectful but not close relationship with Mansfield and Metcalf, and as mayor, he worked with both on securing federal funds for municipal issues such as storm drains, dams, and other federal projects.

43. Ruth Jeanne Fraser, who preferred to be called Jeanne, was emerging from some difficult years. She and Russ Hart had married in 1935, and Jeanne gave birth to a son in December 1936. The baby died six weeks later, and in the coming years their marriage soured. In November 1941, the couple's divorce was finalized

44. Jeanne Fraser remained in D.C. during the war and worked as a secretary at the Pentagon, where she met Benjamin Blackford, whom she married. Blackford eventually became president of the State National Bank of Connecticut, and the Blackford home in Greenwich, Connecticut, became another East Coast destination for Willard, Robin, and the family of Marvin and Mary Louise Fraser.

45. Robin Fraser Hudnut, interview with author, Apr. 7, 2022.

46. *Billings Gazette*, Dec. 9, 1941.

47. Johnson, *Political Hell-Raiser*, 316.

48. WEF to Frost, Sept. 12, 1939, bx 12, fldr 38, Frost-Rauner. Refers to "Tuesday before War was declared." This would be the war in Europe, not when America entered the war. Fraser's view was undoubtedly influenced by Robert Frost, who was in turn influenced by his friend Edward Thomas, who had declared that when one's country goes to war, one should be a part of it. Thomas lost his life in World War I.

49. A copy of this application is in Box 34 of the Fraser Papers.

50. WEF to Ed Craney at KGIR in Butte, "Tuesday," 1941, Edmund Craney Papers 1916–1979, MC 122 (6:3–4), Montana Historical Society, Helena. Craney, a pioneer in Montana broadcasting, was a lifelong friend of Wheeler. He played a key role

in founding the Burton K. Wheeler Center at Montana State University in Bozeman.

51. RF to Marjorie Robin Fraser, Dec. 17, 1940, in Robert Lee Frost et al., *Family Letters of Robert and Elinor Frost* (Albany: State Univ. of New York Press, 1972), 223.

Chapter Seven

1. Sue Hart, *Billings, Montana's Trailhead* (Marceline, MO: Walsworth Publishing, 2009): 75.

2. WEF to Frost, May 5, 1942, Frost-Rauner

3. WEF to Frost, May 30, year not written but likely 1942.

4. WEF to Frost, Jan. 29, 1943, Frost-Rauner.

5. WEF to Frost, Feb. 22, 1946, Frost-Rauner.

6. Borberg reminiscences, n.d., Fraser Papers.

7. Lillian Frost to Robert Frost, undated but fall 1943, Frost-Rauner

8. Ibid.

9. WEF to Frost, Nov. 29, 1943, bx 12, fldr 38, Frost-Rauner.

10. Marjorie Hudnut Renner, email to author, Nov. 12, 2021. The devastating effect of the war on European families stayed with Willard. When he came home for Christmas for a very short furlough in 1944, he would not let the family use lights on the Christmas tree because he said parents in Europe were putting their children to bed at 4 p.m. reasoning the children would not be so hungry once they were asleep. (Robin Fraser Hudnut interview with author, Apr. 7, 2022.)

11. https://gitrail.com/eisenhower-trail-fermanagh-tyrone, accessed Aug. 26, 2018. When Eisenhower died in 1969, Mayor Fraser issued a memorial that said in part, "Three times I passed in review before General Eisenhower, once while on desert maneuvers with the Eighth Infantry Division in the Arizona Desert, the second time on Tennessee maneuvers, and the third when the Division was bivouacked in Northern Ireland while awaiting his signal for the invasion of Europe." He also referred to Eisenhower's "touch of idealism, touch of gentleness." *Billings Gazette*, Apr. 3, 1969.

12. Qub.ac.uk/irishhistoryResources/Northern IrelandandWorldWarII. Accessed Mar. 21, 2022.

13. WEF to Sister Marie Cordell, Aug. 9, 1968, Fraser Papers. Fraser wrote to thank Sister Marie

Cordell for the homemade bread that she had given him during his hospital stay after he had broken a hip, and in that letter, he recalled his appreciation for the homemade bread that had sustained the Eighth Infantry Division in Northern Ireland.

14. WEF to William Ed Burns Jr. of the U.S. Navy, Mar. 29, 1967, Fraser Papers.

15. These poems are part of the Fraser Papers at MSU Billings.

16. Lillian Frost to Robert Frost, May 22, 1944, Frost-Rauner.

17. WEF to B. R. Albin, Apr. 30, 1944, Wheeler Papers-MHS.

18. https://history.army.mil/books/wwii/utah11.htm, accessed Aug. 25, 2018; "Liberating Cherbourg, Normandy's Great Port," https://warfarehistorynetwork.com/2016/11/29/liberating-cherbourg, accessed Sept. 20, 2021.

19. WEF to Corporal Neal Barhight, Aug. 14, 1968, Fraser Papers.

20. Mason General Hospital operated as a military hospital for the years 1944 to 1946.

21. WEF to Frost, n.d., "Saturday," bx 12, fldr 38, Frost-Rauner.

22. WEF to Frost, May 1, 1945, Frost-Rauner

23. WEF to Helen Lawrie, August 3, 1945, Frost-Rauner

24. Le Havre, World Heritage Site, http://unesco.lehavre.fr/en/understand/world-war-ii, accessed Mar. 9, 2022.

25. WEF to Frost, Aug. 20, 1945. bx 12, fldr 38, Frost-Rauner.

26. WEF to Robert Frost, May 23, undated but 1946, Frost-Rauner.

27. WEF to Gene Michael Thomas, Feb. 1, 1972, Fraser Papers.

28. Lillian Frost writes to Robert Frost on November 11, 1945 that she had received three cards from Willard from France, England, and Scotland. This is likely while he was on his Benedictine adventure.

29. WEF to Paul Grandcamp in Poulouse, France, Nov. 10, 1965; and WEF to Grant Salisbury, Jan. 11, 1966.

30. WEF to Mrs. J. C. Thompson, Nov. 20, 1967, Fraser Papers.

31. Sally Moskol, interview with author, Oct. 22, 2017; and WEF to Ann Bosworth, Jun. 29, 1965, Fraser Papers.

32. Robin Fraser Hudnut interview with author, Apr. 7, 2022.

33. David Hudnut interview with author, Sept. 6, 2018.

34. WEF to Frost, Apr. 21, 1946, bx 12, fldr 38, Frost-Rauner.

35. WEF to Frost, Feb. 22, 1946, bx 12, fldr 38, Frost-Rauner.

36. Willard and Dwight were still in touch in 1971, when Dwight married for the second time.

37. WEF to Frost, Apr. 21, 1946, bx 12, fldr 38, Frost-Rauner.

38. A copy of Willard's discharge papers are in Box 34 of the Fraser Papers.

39. Marjorie Hudnut Renner, email to author, Nov. 12, 2021.

40. Michael P. Malone, Richard B. Roeder, and William L. Lang, *Montana: A History of Two Centuries* (Seattle: University of Washington Press, 2001), 309–10.

41. WEF to Frost, Feb. 22, 1946, bx 12, fldr 38, Frost-Rauner.

Chapter Eight

1. WEF to Frost, May 23, 1946, Frost-Rauner.

2. The secretary of Veterans for Wheeler was Jack Mahan. *Billings Gazette*, May 19, 1946. Mahan later was president of the Veterans for Kennedy and Veterans for Johnson organizations.

3. WEF to Frost, Jul. 22, 1946, bx 12, fldr 38, Frost-Rauner.

4. Robin recalls one of Willard's invented games in which the first one to see a white horse had to buy the other a milkshake. Willard noticed and commented on everything they passed. "Why," he once asked, "are the silos the color of concrete? Why not paint them different colors?" On some trips, he took Robin to formal dinners, even to the Senate dining room in Washington, D.C. Robin Fraser Hudnut, interview with author, Apr. 7, 2022.

5. *Great Falls Tribune*, Jul. 10, 1946.

6. Marc C. Johnson, *Political Hell-Raiser: The Life and Times of Senator Burton K. Wheeler of Montana* (Norman: Univ. of Oklahoma Press, 2019), 350.

7. WEF to Frost, Jul. 22, 1946, bx 12, fldr 38, Frost-Rauner.

8. Michael P. Malone, Richard B. Roeder, and William L. Lang, *Montana: A History of Two*

Centuries (Seattle: University of Washington Press, 2001), 313.

9. *Billings Gazette*, Nov. 19, 1946.

10. *Choteau Acantha*, Jan. 9, 1947.

11. BKW wire to WEF, 1940, bx 12, fldr 38, Frost-Rauner.

12. *Choteau Acantha*, Jul. 3, 1947.

13. *Billings Herald*, Dec. 9, 1948. The *Herald* ceased publication in 1951.

14. *Billings Gazette*, Jan. 16, 1958.

15. Built in 1880, the hotel was severely damaged by fire in 1927 and 1953 but survived to be finally demolished after another fire in 1967.

16. Robin Fraser Hudnut, interview with author, Apr. 7, 2022.

17. *Billings Gazette*, Nov. 18, 1947.

18. RF to WEF, Sept. 1948, from Ripton, in Robert Frost and Lawrance Thompson, *Selected Letters of Robert Frost* (New York: Holt, Rinehard and Winston, 1964), 533.

19. *Billings Gazette*, Oct. 8, 1948.

20. *Billings Gazette*, Sept. 9, 1948. The Taft-Hartley Act, also known as the Labor Management Relations Act, restricted the power of unions. It became law on June 23, 1947.

21. *Billings Gazette*, Oct. 24, 1948.

22. WEF to Mike Mansfield, Nov. 14, 1948, bx 11, fldr 13, MSS 065, Mike Mansfield Papers, Mansfield Library Archives and Special Collections, University of Montana, Missoula, MT (hereafter Mansfield Papers).

23. Leon Choquette to Mike Mansfield, Dec. 23, 1949, bx 11, fldr 2, Mansfield Papers.

24. *Billings Gazette*, Apr. 3, 1949.

25. *Billings Gazette*, Jul. 19, 1950, states President Truman asked Mansfield to stay in Washington, and D'Ewart said he wouldn't leave Washington during the crisis. The Korean War has been referred to as "the forgotten war" because it has received less coverage than the World Wars or the Vietnam War. Nevertheless, when it ended on July 27, 1953, almost forty thousand Americans had died in addition to about 10 percent of Korea's prewar civilian population. https://www.history.com/topics/korea/koean-war, accessed Sept. 12, 2021.

26. D'Ewart's view of Senator Joseph McCarthy's Communist hunt was revealed in a 1950 interview of D'Ewart by Kelly and Dugan of Billings. D'Ewart stated, "I think Senator McCarthy did a splendid job, against great odds, to let the American people know about an evil thing that has grown up in our government." Wesley D'Ewart Papers, MSU–Bozeman.

27. *Billings Herald*, Nov. 30, 1950.

28. *Great Falls Tribune*, Nov. 11, Nov. 13, and Nov. 28, 1952; Apr. 6, 1954.

29. *Billings Gazette*, May 27, 1956.

30. *Billings Gazette*, Jan. 26, 1960. The AMVETS was organized in 1944 by World War II veterans and chartered by Congress in 1947. The organization provides veterans and their families with services and promotes programs and public policy to support veterans and their families.

31. *Billings Gazette*, May 11, 1950.

32. Characteristically, Willard's letters to the Murrays contained more than discussion on the proposed Yellowtail Dam. Shortly after Senator Joseph McCarthy first made national news by accusing Cedric Parker of the *Madison Capital Times* of being a Communist, Fraser added a prescient judgment in a postscript to a 1949 letter to Senator Murray: "I think McCarthy should be sent back to Wisconsin." He made this comment three years before Senator McCarthy launched his national anti-Communist hunt with a speech in Wheeling, West Virginia, and five years before the Senate hearings that resulted in McCarthy's censure in December 1954.

33. *Billings Gazette*, Jun. 4, 1949.

34. *Billings Gazette*, Jun. 30, 1949.

35. *Billings Herald*, Feb. 15, 1951.

36. This incident was related both by David Hudnut, Willard's grandson, in a September 6, 2018, phone conversation, and by Robin Hudnut in an April 19, 2022, email.

37. WEF to Robert Frost, Apr. 6, 1960, bx 12, fldr 40, Frost-Rauner.

38. Reinemer, a native of Circle, Montana, served as executive assistant to both Senator Murray and his successor, Lee Metcalf. Murray died in 1961, a few months after retiring.

39. *Great Falls Tribune*, Apr. 5, 1949.

40. *Billings Herald*, May 17, 1951.

41. *Billings Herald*, May 10, 1951.

42. *Billings Herald*, Feb. 15, 1951. Firm energy is energy guaranteed to be available.

43. *Montana Standard*, Dec. 23, 1955. See also Megan Benson, "The Fight for Crow Water,

Part II: Damming the Bighorn," *Montana The Magazine of Western History* 58:1 (Spring 2008): 4–5.

44. Whiteman to Anderson, Mar. 12, 1958, bx 128, MC 172 (9:2–6), Lee Metcalf Papers 1934–1995, Montana Historical Society, Helena, MT (hereafter Metcalf Papers).

45. Lederer was the author of *The Ugly American*.

46. *Across the Wide Missouri* won a Pulitzer Prize in 1948 and *The Course of the Empire* won a National Book Award in 1952.

47. Wallace Earle Stegner, *The Uneasy Chair*, First Vintage Ebooks, Kindle edition (New York: Random House, 2015), location 6387.

48. Stegner, "Chapter VII: Full Career" in *The Uneasy Chair*, locations 5935 and 6387 of 9170. Metcalf originally supported the Knowles Dam on the Flathead River until persuaded otherwise by Montana's Freda Beazley, a Fort Peck Assiniboine who served as the vice president of the National Congress of American Indians, the president of the Affiliated Tribes of Northwest Indians, and the secretary of the Montana Inter-Tribal Policy Board. Freda Augusta Beazley Ppaers, 1960–1975. MC 187, MHS Research Center, Helena.

49. *Billings Gazette*, Oct. 30, 1952.

50. *Great Falls Tribune*, Oct. 1, 1952.

51. *Billings Gazette*, Oct. 21, 1952.

52. Willard would join future float trips down the Bighorn Canyon in 1957, 1964, and in 1965—the last trip before dam construction began.

53. Senator Murray to WEF, July 8, 1955, bx 831, fldr 6, Murray Papers.

54. Senator Murray Press Release, Jul. 14, 1957, bx 404, fldr 3, Metcalf Papers.

55. Edison Real Bird to Senator Lee Metcalf, Jul. 20, 1967, bx 128, fldr 1, Metcalf Papers.

56. Statistics taken from a 1967 Department of Interior memo, bx 128, Metcalf Papers.

57. Benson, "Crow Water," 22.

58. Bighorn Canyon National Recreation Area, www.nps.gov/bica/planyourvisit/bighorn-river-in-montana.htm.

59. *Billings Gazette*, Jun. 23, 1968.

60. "Environmentalists and Dam Operators Start Making Peace," *New York Times*, Oct. 14, 2020.

61. Robin Fraser Hudnut email to author, Apr. 25, 2022.

62. Robin Fraser Hudnut, interview with author, Apr. 7, 2022.

63. *Billings Gazette*, May 16, 1948; Apr. 12, 1959.

64. WEF to Grant Salisbury, Feb. 22, 1971, Fraser Papers.

65. WEF to RF, Nov. 12, 1949, bx 12, fldr 38, Frost-Rauner.

66. Montana writer A. B. Guthrie was also a Bread Loaf Fellow and faculty member.

67. Robin's speech is included in a letter from WEF to Mrs. Joseph Jenkins, Sept. 20, 1970, Fraser Papers. The letter is a five-page response to a request for information about Robert Frost.

68. The meeting between Sandburg and Frost occurred in the fall of 1934 when Willard and his mother met the Frosts in Rockford, Illinois, to exchange infant Robin from the care of Robert and Elinor to Willard and his mother.

69. In the Tigers-Cardinals World Series, the Detroit Tigers first baseman, Hank Greenberg, was also later voted into the Baseball Hall of Fame.

70. WEF to William Sutton of Ball State, Mar. 14, 1972, Fraser Papers. Frost's love for baseball was also a feature of his friendship with Edward Lewis, a fellow Amherst resident and president of the University of New Hampshire, who had been a pitcher for the baseball team that later became the Boston Braves. Frost and Lewis's conversations were also more about baseball than about education and literature.

71. WEF to Mrs. Joseph Jenkins, Sept. 26, 1970, Fraser Papers.

72. This poem has the title "Take Something Like a Star" in *The Poetry of Robert Frost*, ed. Edward Connery Lathem (New York: Holt, Rinehart and Winston, 1969), 403.

73. *Billings Gazette*, May 20, 1952. The poem is "The Need of Being Versed in Country Things," in Lathem, ed., *The Poetry of Robert Frost*, 241. Before leaving Billings, Frost stopped by the Marvin Fraser home where Mary Louise Fraser, in work clothes, was on a ladder painting the outside of the house. Mary Louise's initial embarrassment at being caught in her painting clothes dissolved when she and the noted poet had a natural, easy conversation. Author phone interview with Mac Fraser, Jan. 15, 2018.

74. Willard's admiration for Smith graduate Anne Lindbergh Morrow added to his conviction that Robin should attend Smith.

Chapter Nine

1. *Billings Gazette*, Mar. 22, 1953.

2. Author phone interview with Mac Fraser, Sept. 22, 2018; Mac Fraser's 1953 diary.

3. *Billings Gazette*, May 25, 1953. Bernard DeVoto (1897–1955), writer and champion of public lands, began to argue for continued federal control of public lands in his "The Easy Chair" column in the late 1940s and continued to write columns on public land problems until shortly before his death in 1955. DeVoto wrote letters to Senators Metcalf, Dodd, and Aiken and railed against "the cowboy clique" that advocated more grazing rights for stockmen. Wallace Stegner's biography of DeVoto, *The Uneasy Chair*, thoroughly discusses DeVoto's conservation efforts and influence.

4. *Billings Gazette*, Nov. 12, 1953.

5. Earl Morris and his wife, Lucille, lived in Denver, and it is likely Willard was visiting them when he became ill.

6. *Great Falls Tribune*, Jul. 19, 1954.

7. WEF to Charlie Murray, Mar. 28, 1955, bx 831, fldr 5, Murray Papers.

8. *Eastern Montana Clarion* (Ryegate), Mar. 15, 1956.

9. Wendelanne Fraser Augunas, interview with author, Jul. 29, 2018; Mac Fraser, interview with author, Sept. 22, 2018.

10. David Hudnut's father, Rev. William H. Hudnut Jr., was the pastor of the Third Presbyterian Church in Rochester, New York, and in 1970 was pastor at the Brick Presbyterian Church on Park Avenue and 91st in Manhattan. His son, Rev. William Hudnut III served as mayor of Indianapolis for sixteen years and in 1988 was named the "Nation's Outstanding Mayor." Rev. Robert K. Hudnut was assistant pastor at Westminster Presbyterian Church in Albany in 1961 and formed a new political party in Albany called Citizens United Reform Effort (CURE). Hudnut ran against legendary mayor Erastus Corning. He lost, but his party exerted significant influence in the state's politics. He later served in churches in Minnesota and Wisconsin.

11. *Billings Gazette*, Sept. 11, 1955; Feb. 8, 1959.

12. *Billings Gazette*, Sept.11, 1955; Feb. 8, 1959; and Feb. 19, 1961.

13. WEF to Robert Frost, Aug. 7, 1956, bx 12, fldr 38, Frost-Rauner.

14. WEF to Robert Frost, Oct. 31, 1956, bx 12, fldr 38, Frost-Rauner.

15. *Billings Gazette*, Sept. 19, Sept. 28, and Oct. 5, 1956.

16. WEF to Victor Reinemer, Jan. 11, 1957, bx 832, fldr 2, Murray Papers.

17. WEF to Dr. Glyndon G. Van Deusen, Jan. 31, 1972. Van Deusen, author of a biography on William Henry Seward, was coming to Billings to speak to the Montana Association of Western Land Surveyors.

18. *Montana Standard*, Jan. 16, 1959; and *Billings Gazette*, Mar. 14, 1959.

19. *Billings Gazette*, Mar. 16, 1957.

20. WEF to Victor Reinemer, Jun. 1, 1958, bx 832, fldr 8, Murray Papers.

21. WEF to Victor Reinemer, Jul. 22, 1959, bx 831, fldr 5, Murray Papers.

22. WEF to Robert Frost, Jan. 12, 1960, bx 12, fldr 40, Frost-Rauner.

23. *Great Falls Tribune*, Feb. 19, 1960.

24. *Billings Gazette*, Apr. 29, 1960.

25. *Billings Gazette*, May 7, 1960.

26. *Billings Gazette*, Jun. 5, 1960.

27. *Billings Gazette*, Oct. 7, 1961.

28. *Billings Gazette*, Jul. 29, 1960.

29. Harrison Fagg, interview with author, Oct. 17, 2018.

30. *Billings Gazette*, Jul. 10, 1959.

31. Author phone interview with Mac Fraser, Jan. 15, 2018.

32. Jay Parini, *Robert Frost: A Life* (London: Pimlico, 2001), 412.

33. Although she was not present, Willard's sister, Jeanne Blackford, contributed a pair of argyle wool socks that she had knitted and which Frost wore that day.

34. The Frost-Udall relationship likely paved the way for the Fraser-Udall relationship.

35. *Independent Record*, Oct. 27, 1960.

36. *Missoulian*, Oct. 16, 1960; and *Billings Gazette*, Apr. 15, 1961. When newsmen asked Nutter about Dasinger and the John Birch Society, he claimed not to know anything about it but said that Dasinger was "a good solid citizen. I wish we had more like him in Montana." *Montana Standard*, Apr. 11, 1961.

37. *Billings Gazette*, Oct. 6, 1961.

38. *Billings Gazette*, Jan. 11, Jan. 19, Feb. 5, Mar. 21, Apr. 21, and May 9, 1962.

Chapter Ten

1. Although American Indians were granted U.S. citizenship in 1924, well into the twentieth century many states, counties, and hospitals denied them health care on the erroneous grounds that Indians were federal wards. Simultaneously, the Indian Health Service refused to reimburse non-reservation hospitals and clinics, citing the public health service's responsibility to aid impoverished Indians living off the reservation. For more information, see Jane Bishop, "From Hill 57 to Capitol Hill: 'Making the Sparks Fly'—Sister Providencia Tolan's Drive on Behalf of Montana's Off-Reservation Indians," *Montana The Magazine of Western History*, 43:3 (Summer 1993): 16–29; and Dana Warn, "Living Sicker, Dying Younger: Montana's Indian People Suffer from Inadequate Healthcare," NW Federation of Community Organizations and Montana Indian People's Action, October 2003.

2. *Billings Gazette*, Jan. 31, 1962.

3. *Billings Gazette*, Feb. 7, 1962.

4. *Billings Gazette*, Nov. 18, 1962.

5. *Billings Gazette*, Nov. 29, 1962.

6. *Billings Gazette*, Oct. 22 and Nov. 30, 1962.

7. *Billings Gazette*, Jan. 26, 1961.

8. *Billings Gazette*, May 11, 1962.

9. *Billings Gazette*, May 7, 1964.

10. *Billings Gazette*, Feb. 8, 1961.

11. Ibid.

12. Other articles Salisbury wrote for *U.S. News* that were inspired by his Fraser friendship included one on Western art (Apr. 19, 1967), on the Big Horn Canyon dam (Sept. 10, 1965), and the float from Polson to Perma (1965).

13. Lee Metcalf to WEF, Mar. 22, 1961, Metcalf Papers.

14. *Billings Gazette*, Jan. 19, 1962.

15. WEF to Arnold Olsen, Feb. 1, 1967, Fraser Papers.

16. *U.S. News and World Report*, Aug. 28, 1961.

17. *Billings Gazette*, Aug. 16, 1962

18. *Billings Gazette*, Sept. 5, 1962

19. *Billings Gazette*, Dec. 13 and Dec. 16, 1962.

20. Lillian Frost to Robert Frost, December 12, 1962, Frost-Rauner.

21. *Billings Gazette*, Dec. 12, 1965.

22. *Billings Gazette*, Feb. 14, 1963.

23. *Billings Gazette*, Jan. 22 and Feb. 19, 1963. The term "ward heeler" connotes the corruption of the spoils system of Tammany Hall wherein a ward politician performed illegal acts to benefit a politician and in turn received a job.

24. *Billings Gazette*, Mar. 10, 1963.

25. *Billings Gazette*, Mar. 31, 1963.

26. Ibid.

27. *Billings Gazette*, Mar. 28, 1963.

28. *Billings Gazette*, Mar. 26, 1963.

29. *Billings Gazette*, Mar. 5, 1963.

30. *Billings Gazette*, Mar. 29, 1963.

31. *Billings Gazette*, Mar. 28, 1963.

32. *Billings Gazette*, Mar. 30, 1963.

33. Harrison Fagg, interview with author, Oct. 17, 2018.

34. "Fraser to Take Over Mayor's Chair in May," *Billings Gazette*, Apr. 2, 1963.

35. Gerke to Mansfield, Jul. 28, 1964, bx 57, fldr 6, Mansfield Papers. In the letter, Gerke went on to say he was interested in heading up the Poverty Program in Montana, and that although he was running for state representative from Yellowstone County, he would drop out of the race if an important appointment came up.

36. *Billings Gazette*, Mar. 13, 1964.

37. B. K. Wheeler to Stuart Conner, Dec. 5, 1972, Fraser Papers.

38. *Billings Gazette*, Apr. 2, 1963.

39. Ibid.

40. *Billings Gazette*, Apr. 3, 1963.

41. Governor Babcock to WEF, Apr. 5, 1963, Fraser Papers.

42. *Billings Gazette*, Apr. 20, 1963.

43. *Billings Gazette*, May 1, 1963.

44. *Billings Gazette*, May 5, 1963.

Chapter Eleven

1. *Billings Gazette*, Aug. 17, 1963.

2. Stuart Conner, interview with author, Dec. 14, 2016.

3. *Missoulian*, Mar. 14, 1966.

4. *Montana Standard*, Oct. 9, 1965.

5. *Montana Standard*, Nov. 19, 1965.

6. *Great Falls Tribune*, Jan. 28, 1967.

7. *Billings Gazette*, Dec. 31, 1964.

8. *Billings Gazette*, Apr. 23, 1964.

9. WEF to Mrs. Graham, Feb. 2, 1965, Fraser Papers.

10. July 4 Proclamation, bx 1, Fraser Papers.

11. WEF to J. O. Brew, Peabody Museum, Cambridge, MA, Jul. 30, 1965, Fraser Papers.

12. Stuart Conner, interview with author, Dec. 14, 2016.

13. WEF to Smithsonian Institution, Bureau of American Ethnology, Jan. 6, 1965, Fraser Papers.

14. A self-taught archaeologist, Stuart Conner served on the Montana Historical Society board of directors, as lecturer on anthropology at the University of Montana in Missoula, and as a research associate at the Museum of the Rockies in Bozeman. In 2002, Montana State University awarded him an honorary doctorate for his work documenting archaeological sites in Montana and collecting Indigenous oral histories.

15. James Thompson, interview with author, Oct. 3, 2016.

16. WEF to Chris Angles, Mar. 22, 1970, Fraser Papers.

17. WEF to Bill Cain of Old Faithful, Yellowstone, Feb. 2, 1968, Fraser Papers.

18. *Billings Gazette*, Oct. 4, 1963.

19. Dr. Donald Harr, interview with author, Oct. 19, 2018. Dr. Harr supported Willard in other ways. He was one of many Billings doctors supporting fluoridation. He worked with Willard on one of his campaigns, and he was part of the last float trip down the Bighorn Canyon.

20. WEF to Mayor Erdmann, Jun. 23, 1965, Fraser Papers.

21. *Billings Gazette*, Nov. 19, 1964.

22. *Billings Gazette*, Apr. 4, 1967.

23. *Billings Gazette*, Oct. 21, 1967.

24. David Hudnut, interview with author, Sept. 6, 2018.

25. WEF to James Neely, May 10, 1967, Fraser Papers.

26. *Billings Gazette*, Oct. 31 and Dec. 6, 1963. Fraser's population estimate was probably on the low side. Steve Devitt, "The Billings Hispanic Community: A Contemporary Look," *Montana Magazine* (Sept. 1, 1987): 6–13, 10.

27. Billings' population surpassed fifty thousand in the 1960 census. Steve Devitt's 1987 article, "The Billings Hispanic Community," puts the Hispanic population at four thousand. More recently, in 2021, Hispanics made up 6.32 percent of Billings's population, or 6,926 people. https://www.homesnacks.com/most-hispanic-cities-in-montana.

28. https://www.bloomberg.com/new/articles/2017-02-13/how-the-bulldozer-became-an-urban-block-bluster, accessed Jan. 11, 2021.

29. Vivian A. Paladin and Jean Baucus, *Helena: An Illustrated History* (Helena: Montana Historical Society Press, 1996), 206.

30. Fraser had always been a proponent of committees. Addison Bragg once commented about Fraser's love of appointing various people to committees: "We always felt it inevitable that when the time came for Mayor Fraser to appoint a St. Patrick's Day Committee, he would name Rabbi Samuel Horowitz to serve on it. Well, this week, it did and he did." *Billings Gazette,* Mar. 12, 1966.

31. *Billings Gazette*, Feb. 12, 1964.

32. WEF to Steve Trenka, Jun. 18, 1965, Fraser Papers. This was just one of four letters from Fraser to Trenka concerning the eyesores on Trenka's property.

33. *Billings Gazette*, Apr. 3, 1965.

34. *Great Falls Tribune*, Nov. 2, 1963.

35. *Billings Gazette*, May 15, 1964.

36. *Billings Gazette*, Apr. 23, 1965.

37. *Billings Gazette*, Apr. 26, 1966.

38. Lodge Grass native Stan Lynde's "Rick O'Shay" comic strip ran in national newspapers from 1959 to 1979. He accompanied Willard on several Yellowstone float trips and occasionally stood in for Willard at official occasions. Lynde died in 2013 at eighty-one.

39. *Billings Gazette*, Dec. 10, 1963. Ralston's cabin studio, built by Ralston and his son in 1947, has been moved from its original location and is now part of the Western Heritage Center in Billings.

40. WEF to Al Edwards of Holt, Rinehart & Winston, Apr. 30, 1968, Fraser Papers.

41. For more on Montana artists Isabelle Johnson and Bill Stockton, see Michele Corriel, "Power in Place: Montana's Modern Artists Isabelle Johnson and Bill Stockton," *Montana The Magazine of Western History* 71:2 (Summer 2021): 3–27.

42. WEF letter to Billings Art Association, 1963, in "How Billings Arts Association helped start the Yellowstone Art Museum," https://www.billingsartsassociation.com/BAAhistory.html, accessed Jan. 10, 2022.

43. Ibid.

44. WEF to Patricia McCormick, Sept. 8, 1966. Fraser Papers.

45. *Billings Gazette*, Nov. 5, 1965.

46. WEF to Smithsonian, Sept. 29, 1965, Fraser Papers.

47. WEF to J. O. Brew, Aug. 4, 1966, Fraser Papers.

48. WEF to Joslyn Art Museum, Oct. 31, 1966, Fraser Papers.

49. *Reporter Dispatch* (White Plains, NY), Jan. 2, 1969.

50. Scott Carpenter to WEF, Oct. 8, 1965, Fraser Papers.

51. *Montana Standard*, Mar. 18, 1965.

52. *Billings Gazette*, Sept. 21, 1967.

53. WEF to Bill Tooley, Sept. 26, 1967, Fraser Papers.

54. *Billings Gazette*, Sept. 21, 1963.

55. WEF to Stewart Udall, Dec. 29, 1966; Jan. 3, 1967. Both letters mention seeing Udall.

56. WEF to Hunter L. Martin, Jun. 8, 1971, Fraser Papers.

57. *Billings Gazette*, Nov. 26, 1963.

58. Jacqueline Kennedy to WEF, Oct. 4, 1966, Fraser Papers. Senator Mansfield delivered the eulogy during the televised national memorial service Sunday, Nov. 24, 1963.

59. Willard was unabashedly proud of the fact that his daughter Robin was an accomplished artist. In addition to painting, Robin designed original Christmas cards each year, some of which are displayed at the Robert Frost home in Shaftsbury, Vermont. Willard prevailed upon Robin's talent to design the official city seal.

60. WEF to Robert J. Wright, Vice President, Northwest Orient Airlines, Nov. 12, 1965, Fraser Papers.

61. Ibid.

62. The conversation between Mansfield and the Johnsons is preserved at the LBJ Library and Museum. The *Paris Herald* later became the *International Herald-Tribune*.

63. *Billings Gazette*, Sept. 23, 2007.

64. Ibid.

65. *Billings Gazette*, Aug. 27, 1964.

66. WEF to Mrs. J. B. Fraser, Jan. 14, 1965, Fraser Papers.

67. *Billings Gazette*, Feb. 22, Apr. 5, and May 22, 1964.

68. *Billings Gazette*, Feb. 19, 1964.

69. *Billings Gazette*, Mar. 23, 1964.

70. James Thompson, interview with author, Jul. 19, 2019.

71. *Billings Gazette*, Jul. 18, 1964. John Self later ran for mayor against Willard and lost.

72. Margaret Jensen, "Float the Yellowstone," in *Writers under the Rims: A Yellowstone County Anthology*, eds. Sue Hart et al. (Billings, MT: Parmly Billings Library Foundation, 2001), 227.

73. WEF to Mrs. (Katie) Sid Fraser, Apr. 18, 1972, Fraser Papers.

74. Stan and Jane Lynde to WEF, n.d. (1965), Fraser Papers.

75. WEF to Richard Glendinning, Aug. 23, 1969, Fraser Papers.

76. WEF to Mrs. Anne Chamberlin of the *Saturday Evening Post*, Jul. 13, 1967, Fraser Papers.

77. WEF to Grant Salisbury, Jul. 16, 1965, Fraser Papers. Fraser refers to St. Anthony of the Desert, who went into the wilderness and was beset by and resisted various temptations including seductive women.

78. Chamberlin, who had reported on John F. Kennedy's presidential campaign for *Time*, later became "one of the wittiest and most imaginative of the Washington free-lancers." Anne Chamberlin obituary, *Washington Post*, Jan. 10, 2012.

79. WEF to A. B. Guthrie, Jul. 23, 1966, Fraser Papers.

80. WEF to Anne Chamberlin, Aug. 11, 1966, Fraser Papers.

81. *Missoulian*, Jul. 20, 1967.

Chapter Twelve

1. After being elected president of the Montana Archaeological Society, Fraser wrote to a rancher in Sidney to say that burials on his place could have scientific importance and "as President of the Montana Archaeological Society, I ask that you help preserve the burials . . . for scientific research." Even before he became president of the state society, he wrote to the Montana Highway Department to ask if they would please call a member of the Billings Archaeological Society should they uncover signs of prehistoric man. WEF to William Wyman, Sept. 29, 1966; and WEF to Montana Highway Department, Mar. 24, 1966, Fraser Papers.

2. *Billings Gazette*, May 7, 1964.

3. *Billings Gazette*, Jan. 19, 1965.

4. *Billings Gazette*, May 4, 1965.

5. *Billings Gazette*, Apr. 7, 1965.

6. *Billings Gazette*, Feb. 28, 1966.

7. *Billings Gazette*, Apr. 7, 1964.

8. A Mar. 12, 1960, *Gazette* article quoted meteorologist Herb Huennekens describing why smoke gets trapped in the valley where Billings is located. An Apr. 21, 1963, article discussed the millions of tons of coal from Colstrip that Montana Power would use in the Billings plant.

9. *Billings Gazette*, Sept. 8, 1965.

10. *Billings Gazette*, Sept. 17, 1965.

11. *Billings Gazettte*, Jun. 21, 1966.

12. *Billings Gazette*, Jun. 28, 1966

13. *Billings Gazette*, Jul. 14, 1966.

14. WEF to Grant Salisbury, Apr. 12, 1970, Fraser Papers.

15. WEF to Sister Mary Fabian, St. Vincent's, May 6, 1968, Fraser Papers.

16. Wendelanne Fraser Augunas, interview with author, Jul. 29, 2018.

17. *Billings Gazette*, Jan. 28, 1965.

18. Author interview with Stuart Conner, Jul. 2, 2019.

19. *Missoulian*, December 9, 1966.

20. *Billings Gazette*, Jun. 24 and Jun. 28, 1966.

21. Dr. Donald Harr, interview with author, Oct. 19, 2018.

22. Jim Ronquillo, interview with author, Apr. 30, 2018.

23. Harrison Fagg, interview with author, Oct. 17, 2018.

24. WEF to John West, Nov. 2, 1965, Fraser Papers.

25. WEF to Mary Stewart, Dec. 12, 1967, Fraser Papers.

26. *Billings Gazette*, Feb. 10, 1967.

27. *Billings Gazette*, Dec. 6, 1966.

28. *Billings Gazette*, Jan. 5, 1966.

29. Other Republican aldermen during Willard's first three terms included Duane Smith, Dale Madson, Charles Glenn, Dan Stockton, Eddie Leuthold, Bill Todd, Charles Yates, and Bernadine Jovanich (who defeated Wendte as an independent and then lost as a Republican).

30. *Billings Gazette*, Nov. 15, 1966.

31. WEF letter, Apr. 17, 1967, Fraser Papers.

32. James (Jim) Thompson, interview with author, Oct. 3, 2016.

33. WEF to Charles Borberg, Nov. 22, 1967.

34. *Billings Gazette*, Aug. 3, 1965.

35. WEF to Steve Trenka, Jul. 20, 1965, Fraser Papers.

36. *Billings Gazette*, Apr. 15, 1967.

37. WEF to Fr. John Dimke, Mar. 9, 1965, Fraser Papers; and *Billings Gazette*, Mar. 10, 1965.

38. *Billings Gazette*, Jun. 29 and 30, 1965.

39. WEF to Mr. Robin McNab, Secretary of Montana Livestock Association, Aug. 13, 1966, Fraser Papers.

40. WEF to Claiborne W. Brinck, Mar. 7, 1967, Fraser Papers.

41. WEF to Honorable Tim Babcock, Oct. 5, 1967, Fraser Papers.

42. David Thompson to Float participants, Aug. 12, 1965, Fraser Papers.

43. Stuart Conner, interview with author, Dec. 14, 2016.

44. *Independent Record*, Sept. 7, 1965.

45. Mac Fraser, interview with author, Jan. 15, 2019.

46. WEF to Bruce Shelton, Apr. 23, 1965, Fraser Papers.

47. Dr. Donald Harr, interview with author, Oct. 19, 2018.

48. *Billings Gazette*, Jul. 12, 1964.

49. WEF to Richard E. Morgan, Mar. 2, 1966, Fraser Papers.

Chapter Thirteen

1. WEF to Roderick Flise, Jul. 22, 1966, Fraser Papers.

2. *Billings Gazette*, Dec. 3, 1963.

3. "The Proven Science of Fluoridation," https://newsadvance.com/archives/the-proven-science-of-fluoridation, accessed Feb. 24, 2021.

4. https://www.washingtonpost.com/news/wonk/wp/2013/05/21/a-brief-history-of-America's-fluoride-wars, accessed Feb. 24, 2021.

5. *Dr. Strangelove or: How I Learned to Stop Worrying and Love the Bomb*, Stanley Kubrick, director (Columbia Pictures, 1964).

6. *Billings Gazette*, Dec. 3, 1963.

7. Ibid.

8. *Billings Gazette*, Dec. 10, 1963.

9. Several of Metcalf's letters to his constituents state that he would oppose the bill. Bx 155, fldr 8, Metcalf Papers.

10. *Billings Gazette*, Jan. 27, 1964.

11. *Billings Gazette*, Feb. 25, 1964.

12. Billings Gazette, Mar. 3, 1964.

13. *Billings Gazette*, Mar. 3, 1964.

14. *Billings Gazette*, Mar. 6, 1964.

15. *Billings Gazette*, Mar. 4, 1964.

16. *Billings Gazette*, Mar. 11, 1964

17. WEF to Professor Roger Snow, Mar. 15, 1965.

18. WEF to Mrs. George Sinnock, Apr. 20, 1965, Fraser Papers.

19. WEF to Mayor Beslanwitch, Apr. 8, 1965, Fraser Papers.

20. *Billings Gazette*, Apr. 27, 1965.

21. Ibid.

22. *Billings Gazette*, Apr. 28, 1965.

23. WEF to Miss Edith VanDyken, Jun. 6, 1965, Fraser Papers.

24. WEF to Mrs. Frances Brand, Dec. 22, 1965, Fraser Papers.

25. The prominent roles the Deiszes assumed in the fluoride wars gave them the confidence to enter future political contests, and they became spokespersons for conservative causes through the 1960s.

26. *Great Falls Tribune*, Sept. 29, 1965.

27. Francis Deisz would later be president of the Citizens Committee for Free Choice, a similar ultra-conservative group.

28. *Billings Gazette*, Aug. 19, 1966.

29. *Independent Record*, Oct. 25, 1966.

30. WEF to Prescott Frost, Sept. 29, 1966, Fraser Papers.

31. *Billings Gazette*, Oct. 10, 1966.

32. *Billings Gazette*, Oct. 8, 1966.

33. WEF to The Vatican, Sept. 13, 1966, Fraser Papers.

34. *Great Falls Tribune*, Sept. 19, 1966.

35. *Billings Gazette*, Aug. 18, 1966.

36. WEF to Chairman, Federal Communications Commission, October 7, 1966, Fraser Papers.

37. The anti-fluoride group led by the Deiszes changed its name throughout the fight, at times using "Billings Council for Free Rights" and other times "Citizens Committee for Free Choice and Pure Water."

38. *Billings Gazette*, Apr. 1, 1967.

39. *Billings Gazette*, Apr. 2, 1967.

40. *Billings Gazette*, Mar. 22, 1967.

41. *Billings Gazette*, Apr. 5, 1967.

42. *Billings Gazette*, Apr. 7, 1967.

43. *Billings Gazette*, Apr. 5, 1967. Reno's statement was the subject of Letters to the Editor and comments by councilmen such as Joe Leone in the *Gazette* on Apr. 7 and Apr. 9, 1967.

44. Dr. Donald Harr, interview with author, Oct. 19, 2018. Dr. Harr had been secretary of the Yellowstone Valley Medical Society, which paid for a pro-fluoride ad in May 1965. Francis and Leona Deisz would later lead opposition to the proposed building codes formulated by Fraser and the city council.

45. *Billings Gazette*, Apr. 17, 1967.

46. WEF to Mrs. Ethel Dinning, Dec. 8, 1967, Fraser Papers.

47. *Billings Gazette*, May 7, 1964.

48. https://www.washingtonpost.com/news/wonk/wp/2013/05/21/a-brief-history-of-America's-fluoride-wars, accessed Feb. 24, 2021.

49. "Achievements in Public Health, 1900–1999: Fluoridation of Drinking Water to Prevent Dental Cavities," https://www.cdc.gov/mmwr/preview/mmwrhtml/mm4841a1.htm, accessed Feb. 24, 2021.

50. Katherine Leitzell, "Fears Over Fluoride," *U.S. News and World Report*, Feb. 25, 2008.

51. William Heisel, "Does fluoride have lessons for the vaccine debate?" https://centerforhealth journalism.org/2016/11/10, accessed Jan. 26, 2021.

52. https://www.opb.org/news/article/portland-oregon-water-fluoridation-history-explained, accessed Feb. 25, 2021.

53. *Billings Gazette*, May 2, 1967.

Chapter Fourteen

1. Robin Fraser Hudnut, interview with author, Apr. 7, 2022.

2. Abby Ferguson, interview with author, Apr. 10, 2017.

3. WEF to Police Chief Bevins, Aug. 10, 1965, Fraser Papers.

4. WEF to Mr. Martin Mendoza, Oct. 23, 1967, Fraser Papers.

5. Unfortunately, the collection contains few letters from Fraser's first term.

6. *Billings Gazette*, Feb. 25 and May 27, 1964.

7. WEF to Phil Burke, Monitor Radio, Apr. 28, 1966, Fraser Papers.

8. WEF to George Ciampa, *Los Angeles Times* travel editor, Feb. 2, 1972, Fraser Papers.

9. WEF to Mrs. Earl Morris, Mar. 22, 1965, Fraser Papers.

10. WEF to *Redbook*, Nov. 27, 1967, Fraser Papers.

11. WEF to League of Women Voters, Oct. 19, 1969, Fraser Papers.

12. WEF to editor of *TIME*, Apr. 10, 1972, Fraser Papers.

13. *Billings Gazette*, Jul. 23, 1964.

14. James Thompson, interview with author, Oct. 3, 2016.

15. WEF to Mrs. A. O. Pemberton, May 26, 1965, Fraser Papers.

16. WEF to Georg Crane, Advisor for Cultural Affairs, Norwegian Embassy, Oct. 30, 1968, Fraser Papers.

17. WEF to League of Women Voters, Oct. 19, 1969, Fraser Papers.

18. WEF to Lillian Frost, Nov. 22, 1967, Fraser Papers.

19. James Thompson, interview with author, Oct. 3, 2016.

20. WEF to Sam Guilly, Aug. 12, 1971, Fraser Papers.

21. WEF to Burton K. Wheeler, Mar. 2, 1972, Fraser Papers. Wheeler died in 1975 at age ninety-two.

22. WEF to Grant Salisbury, Nov. 15, 1968, Fraser Papers.

23. WEF to John B. Fraser, Mar. 20, 1970, Fraser Papers.

24. "Dred Scott case: the Supreme Court decision," www.pbs.org/wgbh/aia/part4/4h2933.html, accessed Feb. 5, 2022.

25. WEF to Mrs. Robert Becker, Feb. 7, 1970, Fraser Papers.

26. Jim also recalled another set of the South Side's residents, the local prostitutes. "Everyone knew the ladies of the evening: Della Mae, Purty Mary, Big Mary, French Mamie. French Mamie had two white Pekinese dogs and when we went to school in the morning, she would be out in her white nightgown, behind the white picket fence of her yard, walking her two white dogs. She was a nice lady."

27. James Ronquillo, interview with author, Apr. 30, 2018. Laurie Mercier's essay, "Mexican-Americans of the Yellowstone Valley," in *Montana Legacy*, eds. Harry W. Fritz, Mary Murphy, and Robert R. Swartout Jr. (Helena: Montana Historical Society Press, 2002), discusses the history of the Mexican American community in depth.

28. WEF to Rev. Robert Hudnut, Apr. 4, 1967, Fraser Papers. Delsie's obituary in the Jan. 20, 1967, *Billings Gazette*.

29. Ibid.

30. History.com editors, "Jubal Early," History.com (A&E Television Networks, Nov. 9, 2009), https://www.history.com/topics/american-civil-war/jubal-a-early is a summary of Early's involvement in the war. The Time-Life volumes on the Civil War, *Rebels Resurgent*, *The Shenandoah in Flames*, and *Gettysburg* are additional resources of information on Early.

31. Harrison Fagg, interview with author, Oct. 17, 2018. Kittleson served at Our Lady of Guadalupe parish on the South Side in 1953–1954. When Kittleson died in an automobile accident in December 1962, Fraser wrote a long tribute to the *Gazette*, titled "Poet-Priest of the Prairie."

32. WEF to Mrs. Eva Grabow, Mar. 18, 1965, Fraser Papers.

33. WEF to Robert Gest, Sept. 12, 1965, Fraser Papers. At the time, Arthur Goldberg and Abe Fortas were Supreme Court justices.

34. WEF to Clarence Adams, Apr. 24, 1968, Fraser Papers.

35. WEF to Mrs. Richard DiMarzio, Jul. 6, 1966, Fraser Papers.

36. WEF to Mr. S. T. Herberg, Apr. 1, 1968, Fraser Papers.

37. WEF to William Baer, Aug. 17, 1965, Fraser Papers.

38. WEF to Grant Salisbury, Sept. 21, 1965, Fraser Papers.

39. WEF to Lou Calloway, Mar. 20, 1967, and to Sarah Fritjofson of the *Cody Enterprise*, Spring 1972, Fraser Papers.

40. WEF to Mr. Warren F. Vaughn, Aug. 18, 1965, Fraser Papers.

41. WEF to Police Chief Beven, Nov. 2, 1967, Fraser Papers.

42. WEF to Sheriff Jim Meeks, Jan. 3, 1972, Fraser Papers.

43. WEF to Chief Beven, Jun. 10, 1966, Fraser Papers.

44. WEF to Mr. and Mrs. Wade Taylor, Mar. 12, 1970, Fraser Papers.

45. WEF to mayor of Billings, Missouri, May 11, 1967, Fraser Papers.

46. WEF to U.S. Department of Health, Education, and Welfare, Oct. 1, 1965.

47. WEF to Manager, Skyview Terrace, Feb. 20, 1967, Fraser Papers.

48. WEF to Art Bazata, May 22, 1967, Fraser Papers.

49. WEF to Edward P. Morgan, Jun. 4, 1971, Fraser Papers.

50. WEF to Joe Montgomery, Mar. 27, 1972, Fraser Papers.

51. WEF to Jeanne Blackford, May 22, 1972, Fraser Papers.

52. WEF to Professor Roger Snow, Mar. 15, 1965, Fraser Papers.

53. WEF to Elisabeth Conolly, Feb. 7, 1967, Fraser Papers.

54. WEF to Grant Salisbury, Jun. 14, 1970, Fraser Papers.

55. WEF to Miss Frances Elge, Jun. 4, 1971, Fraser Papers. Born in 1906, Francis Elge was a pioneering Montana attorney, one of the first female county attorneys in the state, and later served as an Indian probate judge for the Department of Interior. For more on Elge, see Annie Hanshew, "Men Were My Friends, but Women Were My Cause": The Career and Feminism of Frances Elge, Montana Women's History Matters, 2014, https://montanawomenshistory.org/men-were-my-friends-but-women-were-my-cause-the-career-and-feminism-of-frances-elge/.

56. Editor-in-Chief, Houghton Mifflin to WEF, Apr. 10, 1972, Fraser Papers.

57. WEF to Houghton Mifflin, Apr. 1972, Fraser Papers.

58. Richard Glendinning to WEF, Mar. 2, 1970, Fraser Papers. Glendinning was part of the legendary Sarasota writers' luncheons. This "cast" may have been a portion of that group.

59. WEF to Arnold Huston, 1970, bx 3, Fraser Papers.

Chapter Fifteen

1. Stuart Conner, interview with author, Dec. 14, 2016.

2. WEF to KOYN-TV, Laurel, 1967, Fraser Papers. KOYN radio is now KBLG.

3. WEF to the Editor, *U.S. Municipal News*, May 26, 1971, Fraser Papers.

4. Stuart Conner, interview with author, Dec. 14, 2016.

5. Michelle Murphy, citing Old Coyote, in "Where There Is Rock Writing," *Montana Outdoors* 41:3 (May–June 2010): 36.

6. Ann Kooistra-Manning, "Pictograph Cave State Park," *Montana The Magazine of Western History* 51:4 (Winter 2001): 80.

7. Stuart Conner, interview with author, Dec. 14, 2016.

8. *Billings Gazette*, Apr. 1, 2012.

9. *Billings Gazette*, Nov. 9 and Nov. 14, 1963.

10. *Billings Gazette*, Jan. 9, 1964.

11. *Independent Record*, Nov. 12, 1963.

12. WEF memo to city council, Jan. 13, 1964, Fraser Papers.

13. *Billings Gazette*, Jul. 15, 1964.

14. Billings Gazette, Aug. 20, 1965.

15. Montana has fifty-five state parks as of 2020.

16. In a Sept. 15, 1971, letter to Charles Beveridge, Fraser says the bulk of the artifacts are at the School of Mines (now Montana Technological University).

17. In 2003, physical evidence of a Lewis and Clark camp was found at Travelers' Rest in western Montana. For more information about that site, see https://www.travelersrest.org/.

18. *Billings Gazette*, Aug. 17, 1963; and WEF to Mike Mansfield, Aug. 10, 1965.

19. *Billings Gazette*, Apr. 8, 1965; and WEF to George Hertzog, National Park Service, Mar. 22, 1965, Fraser Papers.

20. *Billings Gazette*, Jul. 20, 1965.

21. *Billings Gazette*, Jul. 11, 1966.

22. Evan S. Connell's *Son of the Morning Star: Custer and the Little Bighorn* (San Francisco: North Point Press, 1984) was one of the first popular books to question Custer's heroic image.

23. WEF to *TIME*, Dec. 18, 1970.

24. WEF to William Edgar Paxton, May 11, 1965, Fraser Papers. Custer's remains lie in the cemetery at West Point, NY. Libbie lies at his feet.

25. WEF to Board of Geographic Names, Feb. 19, 1968, Fraser Papers.

26. "Controversy Over Memorial to Winners at Little Bighorn," *New York Times*, Aug. 24, 1997.

27. This is undoubtedly where Fraser met Anne Chamberlin of the *Post*, a meeting that paved the way to her covering the Yellowstone Float trip and their subsequent correspondence.

28. WEF to President Johnson, Jul. 21, 1965, Fraser Papers.

29. WEF to President Johnson, Feb. 21, 1967, Fraser Papers.

30. WEF to Grant Salisbury, May 8, 1967, Fraser Papers.

31. *Billings Gazette*, Jun. 2, 1966.

32. *Billings Gazette*, Jun. 13, 1966.

33. Ibid.

34. WEF to Department of Interior, Review and Correction Board of the Department of the Army, Jan. (n.d.), 1967, Fraser Papers.

35. WEF to Chet Shore, May (n.d.), 1967, Fraser Papers.

36. WEF to Hon. Al Edwards, president of Holt, Rinehart and Winston, Mar. 16, 1970, Fraser Papers.

37. Fraser accepted the election in a letter to G. Edward Budde on Jun. 23, 1965.

38. Budde was a prominent guest at the 1966 dedication of Pompeys Pillar and corresponded with Fraser for several years.

39. WEF to G. Edward Budde, Jun. 8, 1965, Fraser Papers.

40. *Billings Gazette*, Feb. 10, Jul. 3, Jul. 11, and Jul. 17, 1966

41. *Billings Gazette*, May 25, 1968.

42. *Billings Gazette*, Sept. 16, 1964.

43. WEF to Tom Dale, Mar. 21, 1968, Fraser Papers.

44. In 1970, roughly 82 percent of tribal members spoke the Apsáalooke language as their first language; by the mid-1990s, that number had dropped to fewer than half, with less than a quarter of the Crow Tribe's children speaking the language. John G. Watts, "The Fragile Grandparent," in *Visions of an Enduring People*, 3rd ed., eds. Walter C. Fleming and John G. Watts (Dubuque, IA: Kendall/Hunt Publishing, 2009), 351.

45. A copy of the speech in the Crow language is in box 1 of the Fraser Papers. It includes handwritten pronunciation guides alongside the text. The translator was Ray Gordon of Summer Institute of Linguistics. William Medicine Trail is named as the informant.

46. WEF to Mrs. Julian Lowe, Aug. 14, 1968, Fraser Papers.

47. WEF to Henry Cox, Dec. 29, 1966, Fraser Papers.

48. D'Alesandro is the brother of Congresswoman Nancy Pelosi, who later became Speaker of the House.

49. Thomas D'Alesandro III to WEF, June (n.d.), 1971, Fraser Papers. When D'Alesandro died in 2019 at the age of ninety, his obituary in national papers cited his handling of the 1968 riots as well as the enactment of a Baltimore civil rights bill and providing programs and schools for city youth.

50. *Billings Gazette*, Aug. 30, 1968.

51. *Great Falls Tribune*, Oct. 16 and Jun. 8, 1967.

52. *Billings Gazette*, Jul. 27, 1967.

53. James Thompson, interview with author, Jul. 19, 2019.

54. *Billings Gazette*, Nov. 28, 1971.

55. Addison Bragg interview by Mark Tokarski, for *Piece of Mind with Mark Tokarski*, a collaboration of Community 7 Television, the City of Billings television, and Yellowstone Public Radio, 1982. The interview forms part of the "Remembering Mayor Willard Fraser" events that took place ten years after Fraser's death. http://www.comm7tv.com.

56. Mac Fraser, interview with author, Jan. 15, 2018; Paul Jakab, interview with author, Jul. 15, 2020.

57. Ibid.

58. WEF to William Cordingly, Jun. 4, 1971, Fraser Papers.

59. WEF to Robert Aasheim, Feb. 16, 1967, Fraser Papers.

60. WEF to Tom Anding, Mar. 1967, Fraser Papers.

61. WEF to Carling Malouf, Feb. 17, 1967, Fraser Papers.

62. WEF to Garth Brookes, Jun. 22, 1971, Fraser Papers.

63. WEF to S. T. Herberg, Dec. 8, 1971, Fraser Papers.

64. WEF to Grant Salisbury, Apr. 12, 1970, Fraser Papers.

65. WEF to Mrs. Eleanor Nafts, Apr. 13, 1965, Fraser Papers.

66. James (Jim) Thompson and John Bohlinger, interviews with author, Jul. 17, 2017.

67. WEF to Paul Jakab, Mar. 9, 1970, Fraser Papers.

Chapter Sixteen

1. *Billings Gazette*, Aug. 15, 1965. This was a favorite Fraser phrase to refer to those who protested progress.

2. *Billings Gazette*, Dec. 4, 1964.

3. *Billings Gazette*, Mar. 21, 1967.

4. *Billings Gazette*, Apr. 16, 1968; July 25, 1970.

5. WEF to Robin Fraser Hudnut, Mar. 1970, Fraser Papers.

6. WEF to Wade Fleming, Apr. 20, 1972, Fraser Papers.

7. WEF to Randi Hood in Glasgow, Feb. 15, 1965, Fraser Papers.

8. WEF to Stephanie Hauser, Nov. 15, 1968, Fraser Papers.

9. *Billings Gazette*, Feb. 7, 1969.

10. *Billings Gazette*, Mar. 18, 1970.

11. *Billings Gazette*, Mar. 29, 1970.

12. WEF to Cathy McCall, Apr. 4, 1972, Fraser Papers.

13. After Fraser's death, the *Montana Standard* published a brief article that the Butte newspaper claimed the *Billings Gazette* had been too "staid" to publish when it occurred. Fraser had noticed that the urinals in the men's restroom at the Billings Airport were too high for young boys to use, so he requested that the airport install a urinal closer to the floor in order to accommodate young boys. The *Standard* article ended with "Willard Fraser was a man of compassion." *Montana Standard*, Sept. 26, 1972.

14. WEF to Campfire Girls, Feb. 16, 1965, Fraser Papers.

15. WEF to Miss Susan Wilson of Agnes Scott College, Feb. 28, 1967, Fraser Papers.

16. John Bohlinger, interview with author, Jul. 14, 2017.

17. Abby Ferguson, interview with author, Apr. 10, 2017.

18. WEF to Julian Low, Aug. 18, 1971, Fraser Papers.

19. WEF to William McNamer, Jun. 1, 1970, Fraser Papers.

20. Facebook Group, "You know you're from Billings, Montana if . . . ," accessed Sept. 23, 2019, https://www.facebook.com/groups/157498974325938/.

21. WEF to Senior Class President of Dawson County High School, Dec. 21, 1967, Fraser Papers.

22. Sally Fraser Moskol, interview with author, Oct. 22, 2017.

23. WEF to Michael Fraser, Jul. 30, 1968, Fraser Papers.

24. Mac Fraser, interviews with author, Jan. 15 and Sept. 22, 2018.

25. Ted Cross, interview with author, Jul. 10, 2019.

26. WEF to David Hudnut Jr., Jul. 3, 1968, Fraser Papers.

27. WEF to Marjorie Hudnut, undated but in 1967, Fraser papers. This conclusion was not a recently arrived one for Fraser. A year earlier he had written to Lillian Frost, "I just had dinner with Charles Bannon, Secretary of Agriculture under Truman, and he and I agree that Truman is the greatest of the greats as far as Presidents are concerned." WEF to Lillian Frost, Sept. 29, 1966, Fraser Papers.

28. Marc C. Johnson, *Political Hell-Raiser: The Life and Times of Senator Burton K. Wheeler of Montana* (Norman: Univ. of Oklahoma Press, 2019), 235, 246, 363, 364. The Feb. 10, 1951, letter was to Wheeler's rival, Senator James Murray. Wheeler and Truman had been Senate colleagues on the Interstate Commerce Committee when they worked to investigate railroad financing. Although the resulting bill was called the Wheeler-Lea Act, Truman tended to refer to it as the Wheeler-Truman Act.

29. WEF to Robin Hudnut, Jul. 28, 1972, Fraser Papers.

30. Author telephone interview with David Hudnut Jr., Sept. 6, 2018.

31. Email exchange between the author and Russell Davidson, Sept. 26, 2019.

32. Bob Brown interview with Fred Van Valkenburg, Jun. 23, 2009, https://scholarworks.umt.edu/brown/69. Fred Van Valkenburg is a politician from Montana. He served in the state senate, among other public service. Since 2005, former Montana legislator Bob Brown has conducted oral history interviews with seventy-eight political figures in Montana, now held as the Bob Brown Oral History Interviews, OH 396, Archives and Special Collections, Mansfield Library, University of Montana–Missoula.

33. Facebook Group, "You Know You're from Billings if…," Sept. 23, 2019.

34. Author phone interview with Paul Jakab, Jul. 15, 2020.

35. WEF to Rick Damont, an Olympic contestant, Sept. 11, 1972, Fraser Papers.

36. WEF to Daniel Walks, Mar. 13, 1972, Fraser Papers.

37. Dartmouth was founded in 1769 to educate

Native Americans. The first Crow tribal members to graduate from college were three young women who graduated in 1937 from Linfield College in Oregon. While the number of Apsáalooke students attending college grew over the next thirty years, in general a low percentage of these students completed their degrees. When Bill Yellowtail graduated in 1972, he was said to be the first Indian graduate in twenty-five years.

38. WEF to Grant Salisbury, May 25, 1966, Fraser Papers.

39. WEF to Paul O'Hare, Superintendent, Jan. 10, 1968, Fraser Papers. O'Hare was superintendent of School District #2. News articles indicate more than beer was involved.

40. WEF to John Sloan Dickey, Jun. 1, 1967, Fraser Papers.

41. WEF to John Sloan Dickey, Aug. 30, 1967, Fraser Papers.

42. WEF to Mr. Alfred Tucker, Aug. 18, 1965, Fraser Papers. This letter is identical to the one he wrote to Capt. Robert Gest at Glasgow Air Force Base a week earlier.

43. WEF to Mr. Wayne Lubenow, Jun. 9, 1971, Fraser Papers.

44. Lee K. Andrews, an ex-North Dakotan, started North Dakota Days in 1967 to celebrate the many people from North Dakota who lived in Billings. For more than a decade, the two-day affair attracted from five hundred to more than a thousand participants in Pioneer Park.

45. *Billings Gazette*, Jul. 28, 1967.

46. WEF to Paul Jakab, Apr. 15, 1970, Fraser Papers.

47. WEF to Grant Salisbury, Jan. 14, 1969, Fraser Papers.

48. WEF to Senator Mike Mansfield, Nov. 8, 1971, Fraser Papers.

49. WEF to Dennis Joyce, May 8, 1968, Fraser Papers.

50. WEF to Robert Smith, Aug. 27, 1971, Fraser Papers.

51. WEF to Gerhard Pidino, Aug. 1, 1968, Fraser Papers.

52. Letter to the Editor by Phil Scott, *Chicago Daily News*, Jan. 18, 1972.

53. *American Observer and Weekly News Review*, Oct. 13, 1968. The *Observer* was a newspaper for high school students.

Chapter Seventeen

1. *The 1960s: The Decade When Everything Changed*, reissue of *LIFE*'s Classic Edition, vol. 19, no. 1 (Jan. 4, 2019).

2. After Alabama governor George Wallace was shot and paralyzed during a Maryland political rally in May 1972, Fraser wrote to a friend, "I was in Washington last week where it was really hot in every way. I was there during the shooting of Wallace. . . . What a violent people we Americans are." Wallace, an outspoken segregationist, had received publicity for his racist rhetoric and his willingness to insult groups and individuals with such terms as "little pinkos," "punks," and "pointy headed intellectuals." He was best known, however, for his declaration, "Segregation now, segregation forever." In his abhorrence of the assassination attempt on Wallace, Fraser continued, "I am no Wallace fan, as it always seems to me that he preaches hate, hate, hate, but just the same, this is a heck of a way to handle a problem." WEF to Mrs. S. T. Herberg, May 24, 1972, Fraser Papers.

3. WEF Proclamation to the Press, Jun. 7, 1968, Fraser Papers.

4. WEF to Grant Salisbury, Aug. 14, 1972, Fraser Papers.

5. Diem was assassinated in 1963 shortly before President Kennedy's assassination.

6. *Billings Gazette*, by Robert E. Miller, editor of Helena's *Independent Record*, Jul. 8, 1964.

7. WEF to "To a Young Friend," Sept. 9, 1971, Fraser Papers.

8. WEF to Corporal Hubbell, Aug. 22, 1966, Fraser Papers.

9. *Billings Gazette* Mar. 28 and Aug. 14, 1968.

10. WEF to Roma Wilhoit, Dec. 8, 1966, Fraser Papers.

11. Background information on Mansfield's position before and during the Vietnam War comes from Gregory A. Olson, *Mansfield and Vietnam: A Study in Rhetorical Adaptation* (East Lansing: Michigan State Univ. Press, 2012); Don Oberdorfer, *Senator Mansfield: The Extraordinary Life of a Great American Statesman and Diplomat* (Washington, DC: Smithsonian Books, 2003); and Fredrik Logevall, *Embers of War: The Fall of an Empire and the Making of America's Vietnam* (New York: Random House Trade Paperbacks, 2014).

12. Olson, *Mansfield and Vietnam*, 148, 150.

13. *Billings Gazette*, May 15, 1966.

14. WEF to Student Mayor and Council, Apr. 1, 1968, Fraser Papers.

15. WEF memo to Department Heads, Aug. 25, 1967, Fraser Papers.

16. *Billings Gazette*, Apr. 22, 1968.

17. WEF to S. T. Herberg, Apr. 1, 1968, Fraser Papers.

18. WEF to "Dear Sir," Mar. 14, 1968, Fraser Papers.

19. WEF to Rev. Robert Hudnut, Nov. 15, 1968; and WEF to L. A. Kikolorik [undated], Fraser Papers. The statement about not weeping or wailing over an obituary reflects Fraser's willingness to adapt quotable quotes such as Clarence Darrow's "I have never killed a man but I have read many obituaries with great pleasure." Darrow, in turn, was quoting Mark Twain.

20. WEF to Grant Salisbury, Aug. 14, 1972, Fraser Papers.

21. *Billings Gazette*, Mar. 14, 1968.

22. When Mansfield tabled a move to debate the war on the Senate floor on March 1, 1966, McCarthy declared he was clearly in the service of the Johnson administration. Olson, *Mansfield and Vietnam*, 175.

23. *Billings Gazette*, *New York Times* article by Roy Reed, Oct. 8 and Nov. 19, 1967.

24. *Billings Gazette*, Aug. 26, 2018.

25. WEF to Mr. Kim Hart, Sept. 5, 1968, Fraser Papers.

26. WEF to Hon. Robert McCann, Dec. 7, 1969, Fraser Papers.

27. WEF, "To a Young Friend," Sept. 9, 1971, Fraser Papers.

28. WEF to Grant Salisbury, Jun. 8, 1970, Fraser Papers.

29. WEF to Grant Salisbury, Apr. 12, 1970, Fraser Papers.

30. *Billings Gazette*, Mar. 9, 1970.

31. *Billings Gazette*, Jun. 29, 1971.

32. *Billings Gazette*, Apr. 23, 1969.

33. *Billings Gazette*, Oct. 7 and Nov. 15, 1969.

34. *Billings Gazette*, Jul. 18, 1970.

35. *Billings Gazette*, Sept. 4, 1970.

36. WEF "To a Young Friend," Sept. 9, 1971, Fraser Papers.

37. Muskie and Fraser had met personally several times, most recently when Muskie held a press conference in Billings two months before Muskie's *60 Minutes* interview.

38. WEF to Senator Edmund T. Muskie, Jan. 20, 1972, Fraser Papers.

39. WEF to Grant Salisbury, May 8, 1970, Fraser Papers.

40. Robin remembers her father commenting during this time, "Every now and then, the country's leaders go crazy." Robin Fraser Hudnut, email to author, Apr. 19, 2022.

41. WEF to Grant Salisbury, Jul. 17, 1972, Fraser Papers.

42. Ibid.

43. WEF to Mr. and Mrs. Don Holland, Jan. 2, 1970, Fraser Papers.

44. WEF to Veterans Council, American Legion, Billings, Sept. 2, 1971, Fraser Papers.

Chapter Eighteen

1. At the time of Bobby Fraser's death, Willard had been financing Bobby's education at Montana State University.

2. WEF to Jeanne Blackford, Dec. 11, 1967.

3. WEF to Charlie Borberg, Nov. 22, 1967.

4. *Great Falls Tribune*, Aug. 29, 1968.

5. *Billings Gazette*, Aug. 27, 1967.

6. *Great Falls Tribune*, Sept. 22, 1967.

7. *Great Falls Tribune*, Jun. 11, 1967.

8. *Great Falls Tribune*, Oct. 4, 1968

9. Fraser's views on Kennedy are apparent in a letter to Teno Roncello, Apr. 11, 1968, Fraser Papers.

10. WEF to Donald Gay, May 24, 1968, Fraser Papers.

11. Author phone interview with Stuart Conner, Oct. 2, 2018.

12. *Missoulian*, Feb. 14, 1968.

13. (Butte) *Montana Standard*, Apr. 25, 1968.

14. *Kalispell Daily Inter Lake*, Jun. 3, 1967. Also reported in Butte's *Montana Standard* and the *Billings Gazette*.

15. *Helena Independent Record*, Apr. 26, 1968. George D. Remington was the editor of the *Independent Record* at the time.

16. *Great Falls Tribune*, Jun. 1, 1968.

17. *Billings Gazette*, May 18, 1968.

18. The *Great Falls Tribune*, always favorably predisposed to Fraser, covered his candidacy on May 3, May 18, June 2, and June 3, 1968.

19. Author phone interview with Stuart Conner, Oct. 2, 2018.

20. Riddick had also run for governor in the 1960 primary, and like Billings' Mike Kuchera, he had made a name for himself by running for political office and losing. He formed a party with the challenging name of Puritan Ethic and Epic, Magneto-hydrodynamics-Puritan Epic-Prohibition Party and ran for president from that party in 1976 at the age of seventy-nine, running again in 1980 and 1984. Decades earlier, Riddick instructed future President Franklin D. Roosevelt in an aviation preparatory school in Rochester, New York. He served in both World War I and II and lived in Phillipsburg, Montana, after the war, until 1985, when he moved to Annapolis, Maryland. The *New York Times* carried his obituary in 1988.

21. *Helena Independent Record*, Jun. 7, 1968.

22. *Helena Independent Record*, Jun. 18, 1968.

23. *Billings Gazette*, Jun. 11, 1968.

24. Fraser believed in patronizing classy hotels—the Willard in Washington, D.C., the Harvey in Helena, the Florence in Missoula, and the Hilton in New York.

25. WEF to Charles Borberg, Jul. 22, 1968, Fraser Papers.

26. *Billings Gazette*, Jun. 14, 1968.

27. Darrell Ehrlick, "Then Comes the Fall: The Rise, Fall, Resurrection and Legacy of Billings Mayor Willard Fraser," *Magic City Magazine* 15:1 (Mar. 2017): 55–61, 57. Ehrlick refers to an article in the *Chicago Tribune* of Jun. 18, 1968, by Bob Nolte, which refers to Fraser as the "Montana Fireball."

28. *Billings Gazette*, Jun. 18, 1968.

29. *Billings Gazette*, Jun. 24, 1968.

30. *Billings Gazette*, Jul. 7, 1968.

31. *Billings Gazette*, Jun. 25 and Jul. 7, 1968.

32. *Great Falls Tribune*, Aug. 29, 1968; and *Billings Gazette*, Sept. 4, 1968.

33. WEF to Mr. and Mrs. Phil Scott, Jul. 23, 1968, Fraser Papers.

34. *Billings Gazette*, Jul. 13, 1968.

35. WEF to Fr. Peter J. Powell, Aug. 14, 1968, Fraser Papers. Fr. Powell was an author and the founder and first director of St. Augustine's Center for American Indians in Chicago.

36. *Montana Standard*, Jul. 25, 1968.

37. WEF to Grant Salisbury, Dec. 7, 1968, Fraser Papers.

38. *Billings Gazette*, Jul. 30, 1968.

39. *Billings Gazette*, Aug. 1, 1968.

40. Wendelanne Fraser Augunas, interview with author, Jul. 29, 2018.

41. WEF to George Pinkerton, Oct. 2, 1968, Fraser Papers.

42. *Billings Gazette*, Sept. 29, 1968.

43. WEF to Mrs. Lloyd Sorenson, Apr. 15, 1969, Fraser Papers.

44. In Leona Deisz's later years, she waged campaigns against city zoning, sex education, and sensitivity training in schools.

45. *Billings Gazette*, Mar. 19, 1969.

46. *Billings Gazette*, Apr. 12, 1969.

47. WEF to Fr. Eugene Hruska, Aug. 30, 1968, Fraser Papers. Fr. Hruska was an assistant at Holy Rosary parish and a teacher at Billings Central Catholic High School from 1958 to 1966. He became principal at Great Falls Central High School in 1966 and went from there to the parish in Forsyth, Montana, in 1968.

48. *Billings Gazette*, Sept. 25, 1968.

49. WEF to Clarence Nybo, Oct. 3, 1968, Fraser Papers.

50. WEF to Lesley Frost Ballantine, Oct. 30, 1968, Fraser Papers.

51. WEF to Lesley Frost Ballantine, Oct. 24, 1968, Fraser Papers.

52. WEF to Tim Babcock, governor, Oct. 1, 1968, Fraser Papers.

53. WEF to Grant Salisbury, Oct. 31, 1968, Fraser Papers.

54. Grant Salisbury to WEF, Nov. 4, 1968, Fraser Papers.

55. WEF to Grant Salisbury, Nov. 15, 1968, Fraser Papers.

56. WEF to Dwayne Clodfelter of California, Jan. 4, 1967, Fraser Papers.

57. WEF to Charlie Borberg, Jul. 22, 1968, Fraser Papers.

58. Presentation by Chuck Johnson, "Modern Revolution and Counter-Revolution in Montana," Oct. 9, 2018, Montana Club, Helena, MT.

59. *Billings Gazette*, Nov. 14, 1967.

60. *Billings Gazette*, Oct. 20, 1967.

61. *Billings Gazette*, Dec. 6, 1968.

62. WEF to Grant Salisbury, Dec. 7, 1968, Fraser Papers.

63. WEF to all mentioned refineries, Feb. 15, 1969, Fraser Papers.

64. WEF to Dwayne Clodfelter, Dec. 31, 1968, Fraser Papers.

65. Ibid.

66. *Billings Gazette*, Mar. 12, 1969.

67. WEF to Hal Stearns, Mar. 17, 1969, Fraser Papers.

68. *Billings Gazette*, Jun. 8, 1969.

69. *Billings Gazette*, Feb. 9, 1969.

70. *Billings Gazette*, Mar. 18, 1969.

71. WEF to Richard Shoup, mayor of Missoula, Apr. 2, 1969, Fraser Papers.

72. Paul Jakab, interview with author, Sept. 18, 2020.

73. James Thompson, interview with author, Oct. 3, 2016.

74. *Billings Gazette*, Apr. 4, 1969.

75. James Thompson, interview with author, Apr. 6, 2017.

76. *Billings Gazette*, Apr. 8, 1969.

77. *Billings Gazette*, Apr. 8 and Apr. 9, 1969.

78. Grant Salisbury to WEF, Apr. 21, 1969, Fraser Papers.

79. WEF to Mrs. Betty Maguire, Apr. 30, 1969, Fraser Papers.

80. WEF to Joseph Swindehurst, Apr. 10, 1969, Fraser Papers.

81. WEF to Charles Scheels, Apr. 25, 1969, Fraser Papers.

82. WEF to Robert Michael, Apr. 16, 1969, Fraser Papers.

83. WEF to City Council, Apr. 30, 1969, Fraser Papers.

84. *Billings Gazette*, May 2, 1969. That amount was a 1961 loan to address issues in the building that the federal government had requested. However, very soon after this, the General Services Administration commenced with plans to build the federal building in Billings and move the Bureau of Indian Affairs into it. As noted in an earlier chapter, Fraser fought this, to no avail. The BIA moved out of his building into the federal building in early April 1965 (*Gazette*, Mar. 4 and Apr. 6, 1965). Fraser became delinquent on his loan payments in May 1965. He claimed, with justification it seems, that the BIA's departure from the building destroyed the source of income necessary to make payments on the loan for the repairs the government had requested (*Gazette*, May 2, 1969).

85. *Billings Gazette*, Apr. 30, 1969.

86. *Billings Gazette*, Apr. 23 and Apr, 26, 1969.

87. *Billings Gazette*, Apr. 25, 1969.

Chapter Nineteen

1. *Billings Gazette*, Jun. 7 and Jun. 11, 1969.

2. *Billings Gazette*, Jul. 25, 1970.

3. WEF to Hon. M. Goldstein, Mar. 27, 1970, Fraser Papers.

4. *Billings Gazette*, Nov. 25, 1969.

5. *Billings Gazette*, Jan. 20, 1971.

6. *Billings Gazette*, Jun. 8, 1969.

7. Popovich wrote a now out-of-print book on artist J. K. Ralston, *The Voice of the Curlew: J. K. Ralston's Story of His Life* (Billings, MT: J. K. Ralston Studio Corporation, 1986). The book is dedicated to the memory of seven people, one of whom is Willard Fraser.

8. WEF to Helen Peterson, Aug. 6, 1969, Fraser Papers. Helen Peterson was the publisher-editor of the *Hardin Tribune Herald* and a contributor to the *Billings Gazette*, which published her in-depth articles on Crow culture and history, especially before and during the annual Crow Fair. She was adopted into the Crow Tribe with the name Akiichiwee'ichebia (Good Story Woman).

9. From this point on, Rosell was actively involved in Montana film. Over the next decade, six feature films and many commercials were shot on the Rosells' ER Ranch. Brian D'Ambrosio, *Shot in Montana: A History of Big Sky Cinema* (Helena, MT: Riverbend Publishing, 2016), 99. This is a comprehensive summary of movies filmed in Montana. The book gives more ink to Earl Rosell, who came to see himself as "the P.T. Barnum of the local movie trade," than to Willard Fraser.

10. Email to author from Wendelanne Fraser Augunas, Jul. 2, 2018.

11. *Billings Gazette*, Oct. 5, 1970.

12. John Butkovich, National General Pictures Corporation to WEF, Dec. 22, 1970, Fraser Papers.

13. WEF to Grant Salisbury, Dec. 20, 1970, Fraser Papers. Don Nunley was made a member of the Crow Tribe as part of the day's events, as Stuart Millar had been in October 1969 when Henry Old Coyote and Ellsworth Little Eye officiated (*Gazette*, Oct. 6, 1969).

14. Kimberly Lindbergs, *Little Big Man* (review), 2014. https://www.loc.gov/static/programs/

national-film-preservation-board/documents/
little_big_man.pdf.

15. *Little Big Man* continues to be appreciated in Montana for its historically significant positive portrayal of Native Americans. On Oct. 11, 2021, Art House Cinema and the Babcock Theatre hosted a showing of the film in honor of Indigenous People's Day.

16. *Billings Gazette*, Feb. 20, 1971. Willard also mentions this in a letter to Stuart Millar.

17. Prior to *Little Big Man*, a handful of Hollywood films had been filmed in the state, but none for at least a decade.

18. *Billings Gazette*, Jun. 8, 1969.

19. WEF to Brandt & Brandt, NYC, Dec. 1969, Fraser Papers. Box 33 in Fraser's papers contains nearly a dozen articles Willard wrote on various subjects.

20. *Billings Gazette*, Aug. 22, 1970.

21. WEF to Letters to the Editor, *Billings Gazette*, Mar. 17, 1970.

22. *Billings Gazette*, Mar. 17 and Sept. 29, 1970.

23. *Billing Gazette*, Sept. 22, 1971. The Concerned Citizens for a Better Billings continued to try to prevent further development on the Rims, but expensive houses continued to be constructed. However, the city, with the assistance of federal grants, did move to buy some Rimrock land acreage.

24. Samuel Herley, South Dakota Oral History Center, University of South Dakota, Mitchell, SD, email to author, Nov. 25, 2019.

25. WEF to Paul Jakab, Apr. 15, 1970, Fraser Papers.

26. WEF to Stuart Millar, Sept. 11, 1970, Fraser Papers.

27. WEF to Joe Cash, Sept. 30, 1970, Fraser Papers.

28. Mrs. Minnie Ellen Fritzler to Editor, *Billings Gazette*, Jul. 28, 1971, Fraser Papers.

29. Fritzler's handwritten note on the letter said that Susie Yellowtail had told her to get Willard involved. Willard's handwritten note on the letter stated that Fritzler was a Crow Indian lady whose granddaughter was the new baby in *Little Big Man*.

30. WEF to Grant Salisbury, Dec. 20, 1970, Fraser Papers.

31. The article, "The King's Chapel and the King's Court," is discussed at https://religionandpolitics.org/2015/07/07/the-

kings-chapel-and-the-kings-court-richard-nixon-billy-graham-and-white-house-church-services/.

32. WEF to Reinhold Niebuhr, Aug. 10, 1969, Fraser Papers. Niebuhr, a prominent philosopher and theologian, attracted posthumous attention during the Obama presidency when Obama stated Niebuhr was his favorite philosopher.

33. WEF to Jerry Willard Marriott of Honor America Day, Jul. 1, 1971, Fraser Papers.

34. WEF to *TIME*, Jun. 8, 1970, Fraser Papers.

35. *Billings Gazette*, Jan. 24, 1970.

36. Willard's office building was demolished in 1991.

37. Undated letter, apparently to his lawyer, but certainly in 1969, Fraser Papers.

38. WEF to Jeanne and Ben Blackford, Jun. 28, 1970, Fraser Papers.

39. WEF to Mrs. Joseph Jenkins, Sept. 26, 1970, Fraser Papers.

40. WEF to Dr. Larry Thompson, Jan. 30, 1967, Fraser Papers.

41. WEF to James Kennedy, Dec. 23, 1968, Fraser Papers.

42. WEF to Lesley Frost Ballantine, Sept. 12, 1970, Fraser Papers.

43. Lesley Frost Ballantine, in "Letters," *The New York Times*, Sept. 27, 1970. Nytimes.com/1970/09/27/archives/letters-90424022.html.

44. WEF to Louis Untermeyer, Sept. 12, 1970, Fraser Papers.

45. WEF to Judson Jerome, May 17, 1971, Fraser Papers.

46. WEF to Mrs. Joseph Jenkins, Sept. 26, 1970, Fraser Papers.

47. Jay Parini, *Robert Frost: A Life* (London: Pimlico, 2001), 452–55.

48. Jonathan Miles, reviewer, "FALL OF FROST: By Brian Hall. 340 Pp. Viking," in *The New York Times Book Review* (May 11, 2008): 14 ff.

49. Peter Stanlis, *Robert Frost: The Poet as Philosopher* (Wilmington, DE: ISI Books, 2007), 400; and Peter J. Stanlis, "Rehabilitating Robert Frost: The Unity of His Literary, Cultural, Political Thought," *The Imaginative Conservative*, Jul. 26, 2016, https://theimaginativeconservative.org/2012/04/rehabilitating-robert-frost-unity-of.html.

50. Stanlis, *Robert Frost: The Poet as Philosopher*, 11.

51. Other essays in the book discussed Will

James, Ernest Hemingway, and Ollie Warren, a
Billings madam.

52. WEF to William Sutton, May 19, 1971. Sutton
wrote to Willard on Jun. 7, 1971; Mar. 14, 1972; and
Mar. 29, 1972.

53. WEF to Mrs. Frank Wilson, Dec. 18, 1970,
Fraser Papers.

54. WEF to Paul Jakab, Dec. 18, 1970, and to Ted
Freestone, Dec. 18, 1970, Fraser Papers.

55. WEF to Hal Stearns, Mar. 21, 1970, Fraser
Papers.

56. WEF to Agricultural Experiment Division,
Mar. 25, 1970, Fraser Papers.

57. *Billings Gazette*, Nov. 22, 1970.

58. *Billings Gazette*, May 10, 1970.

59. The Rye situation received regular coverage
in the *Gazette* (Jul. 7, 8, 10, 30; Aug. 11, 28; and
Sept. 14, 1970).

60. *Billings Gazette*, Aug. 19, 1970.

61. *Billings Gazette*, Jan. 5, 1971.

62. Stuart Millar to WEF, Feb. 26, 1971, Fraser
Papers.

63. The Crow Tribe's ad appears in the *Billings Gazette*, Mar. 29, 1971. Fraser quote from an
Apr. 10, 1971 speech, bx 1, Fraser Papers.

64. *Billings Gazette*, Mar. 28. 1971.

65. Bohlinger's campaign skills served him well
when he, too, entered politics and served in Montana's legislature and as lieutenant governor from
2005 to 2013. James Thompson said of his friend,
"He's never lost an election." James Thompson,
interview with author, Apr. 6, 2017.

66. John Bohlinger, interview with author,
Jul. 17, 2017.

67. *Billings Gazette*, Apr. 11, 1971.

68. *Billings Gazette*, Mar. 30, 1971.

69. *Billings Gazette*, Apr. 23, 1971.

70. *Billings Gazette*, Mar. 25, 1971.

71. *Billings Gazette*, Apr. 4, 1971.

72. *Great Falls Tribune*, Apr. 5 and Apr. 10, 1971.

73. *Independent Record*, May 2, 1971.

74. *Billings Gazette*, Apr. 6, 1971.

75. *Billings Gazette*, May 4, 1971.

76. WEF to Jack Ironside, May 13, 1971, Fraser
Papers.

77. WEF to Mr. Harry Hornblower, May 17,
1971, Fraser Papers. Henry (Harry) Hornblower
II was part of the prominent and wealthy investment family. Harry was also an intellectual with
an interest in American history and archaeology, a

profile similar to Willard's. Perhaps Fraser became
acquainted with him through his archaeology
friend, J. O. Brew, of Harvard's Peabody Museum.
Harry Hornblower founded the Plimoth Plantation, a museum devoted to preserving the culture
of the Native Americans and English in the 1600s.

Chapter Twenty

1. *Billings Gazette*, Apr. 8, 1971. (Epigraph from
same source.)

2. WEF, May 7, 1971, Fraser Papers.

3. WEF to Mrs. Julian Low, Aug. 18, 1971, Fraser
Papers.

4. WEF to Robin Hudnut, Nov. 18, 1971, Fraser
Papers.

5. Galusha died of exposure Mar. 31, 1971, on
a snowmobile trip in the Beartooth Mountain
Range. The fifteen snowmobilers were trapped by
a severe winter storm with heavy snow, seventy
mph winds, and a chill factor of eighty degrees
below zero. The group had to abandon their
snowmobiles and take overnight refuge in a snow
trench. Galusha died at 6:45 the following morning. The remaining fourteen survived.

6. *Billings Gazette*, Dec. 7, 1971.

7. Willard was fond of pointing out that
George Washington shared the birthday with
Buffalo Bill.

8. *Billings Gazette*, Mar. 2, 1972.

9. WEF, letter, Mar. 7, 1972, Fraser Papers.

10. Billings Gazette, Jun. 30, 1971.

11. *Billings Gazette*, Aug. 12, 1971.

12. WEF to Dr. George Rollings, Jan. 19, 1972,
Fraser Papers.

13. *Billings Gazette*, Aug. 10, 1971.

14. *Billings Gazette*, Aug. 24, 1971. Clawson's title
was a play on *Jesus Christ Superstar*, which Fraser
took the young cyclists to see.

15. *Billings Gazette*, Oct. 6, 1971.

16. *Billings Gazette*, Nov. 28, 1971.

17. John Bohlinger, interview with author,
Jul. 17, 2017.

18. *Billings Gazette*, Dec. 20, 1971.

19. WEF to Bruce Nelson, Apr. 6, 1972, Fraser
Papers.

20. *Billings Gazette*, Feb. 8 and Feb. 10, 1972.

21. As Billings president of the National Coalition on the Crisis in Education, Leona Deisz
worked to stop sex education and sensitivity

training in schools. She headed the Montana Movement of "Woman Power—American Style," a national movement seeking to reverse U.S. Supreme Court decisions on such issues as licensed pornography, prayer, and Bible reading in schools, and Communists in schools and defense plants. Deisz was also chairman of the local branches of the National Association to Keep and Bear Arms and a group called Citizens Against Mansfield. She claimed, "Mansfield is attempting to abolish the Second Amendment to the Constitution" and that "Mansfield is in trouble." Because he had sponsored a 1968 gun-control act after the assassinations of Martin Luther King and Robert F. Kennedy, Mansfield lost some Montana support. However vocal, Deisz was not successful in truncating Mansfield's career.

22. WEF to Chief Dunbar, Dec. 5, 1971, Fraser Papers.

23. WEF to Leona Deisz, Jan. 26, 1972, Fraser Papers.

24. *Billings Gazette*, May 4, 1972.

25. *Billings Gazette*, May 1, 1972.

26. *Great Falls Tribune*, Sept. 17, 1972.

27. *Billings Gazette*, Nov. 6, 1972

28. Leona Diesz died in 1996 at age sixty.

29. *Billings Gazette*, Mar. 28, 1972.

30. *Billings Gazette*, Jan. 8, 1972.

31. WEF to Jack Clark, Jan. 8, 1972, Fraser Papers.

32. WEF to Merle Hoeft, Jan. 14, 1972, Fraser Papers.

33. WEF to Clergymen of Billings, Jan. 16, 1972, Fraser Papers.

34. WEF to Cal Taggert, Aug. 22, 1972, Fraser Papers.

35. WEF to Walter Ferguson, Apr. 17, 1972, Fraser Papers.

36. Afterward, he wrote to his sister about the time spent on the Blackford yacht: "That was a great voyage on *Flicka* and a real rest" (WEF to Jeanne Blackford, May 22, 1972, Fraser Papers). Jeanne Fraser Blackford died in 2010 at age ninety-five. The "raiding the treasury" is in a letter from WEF to Ben Blackford, Apr. 28, 1972. It was during this trip to Washington that George Wallace was shot.

37. *Billings Gazette*, Jun. 25, 1972.

38. *Billings Gazette*, Jun. 18, 1972.

39. *Billings Gazette*, Sept. 21, 1972.

40. *Great Falls Tribune*, Sept. 17, 1972.

41. Abby Ferguson, memorandum, May 15, 1972, Fraser Papers.

42. WEF to State Conservation Office, Mar. 6, 1972, Fraser Papers.

43. *Billings Gazette*, Mar. 29, 1972.

44. WEF to Robert Hudnut, Sept. 8, 1972, Fraser Papers.

45. WEF memo to "Hake," Sept. 11, 1972, Fraser Papers.

46. WEF to Billings Police Department Security Officers, Sept. 18, 1972, Fraser Papers. On the same day, Willard wrote to Rafael Elimaen in Tel Aviv and sent him a copy of *Black Elk Speaks*, bragging, "Yellowstone Park is in our backyard, and I am going up there tomorrow with the wife of President Nixon to tuck in the bears and turn off the geysers." This jovial note was probably the last letter Willard Fraser wrote.

47. *Billings Gazette*, Sept. 20, 1972.

48. Addison Bragg interview, "Remembering Mayor Willard Fraser," *Piece of Mind with Mark Tokarski*, Community 7 Television, Billings, MT, 1982.

49. Nps.gov/parkhistory/online_books/nps/second_world_conference.pdf. Accessed Mar. 20, 2022.

50. Fran Calton, interview with author, Oct. 21, 2017.

51. *Daily Tribune-Examiner* (Dillon, MT), Sept. 21, 1972.

52. Marjorie Hudnut Renner, email to author, Aug. 31, 2021.

53. Marjorie Hudnut Renner, email to author, Jun. 21, 2020.

54. *Billings Gazette*, Sept. 24, 1972.

55. Stuart Conner to Dr. J. O. Brew, Oct. 18, 1972, Fraser Papers.

56. *Missoulian*, Sept. 22, 1972.

57. J. O. Brew to Stuart Conner, Oct. 30, 1972, Fraser Papers.

58. Senator Mansfield to Sadie Fraser, Oct. 10, 1972.

59. Congressional Record, Oct. 5, 1972.

60. *Billings Gazette*, Nov. 9, 1972.

61. Sadie Fraser died in 1975 at age eighty-eight.

62. Harrison Fagg, interview with author, Oct. 17, 2018.

A Reckoning

1. Addison Bragg interview, "Remembering Mayor Willard Fraser," *Piece of Mind with Mark Tokarski*, Community 7 Television, Billings, MT, 1982.

2. Sept. 1964 Proclamation, Fraser Papers.

3. Burton K. Wheeler to Stuart Conner, Dec. 5, 1972, Fraser Papers. Wheeler died in 1975 at age ninety-two.

4. *Billings Gazette*, Jun. 22, 1999.

5. Hal Stearns, eulogy to Willard E. Fraser, Sept. 23, 1972.

6. The original Clean Air Act became law in 1963, but many of the law's provisions were not defined or codified until after 1970. Emissions standards, for example, were developed after 1970, when many of the hazardous compounds were still being identified and their toxicity calculated.

7. WEF to Mel Ruder, May 10, 1965, Fraser Papers.

8. Darrell Ehrlick, "The Legacy of Billings' Greatest Mayor," *Magic* magazine, vol. 15, no. 3 (Aug/Sept 2017): 47.

9. WEF to "Hake," Dec. 29, 1971, Fraser Clipping File, Billings Public Library, Billings, MT.

10. *Billings Gazette*, Apr. 11, 1969, in discussing Fraser's civic pride mentioned he was responsible for naming these parks through the Park Commission.

11. Willard's generosity his love of fun and was remembered by city clerk Lois Schuster when she retired in 1978 after serving under seven mayors. Of those, she recalled, Willard had "the most flair." After he returned from a conference in Hawaii one year, he brought seven muumuus, one for each of the women working in City Hall. One day they all wore them to work, Willard wore a bright flowered shirt, and they had pineapple for lunch. *Billings Gazette*, Aug. 30, 1978.

12. Robert Smith, "The Fraser Papers" (introduction to the Mayor Willard E. Fraser Collection), Montana State University–Billings, n.d.

13. *Billings Gazette*, May 31, 1974.

14. *Billings Gazette*, June 21, 1982.

15. *Billings Gazette*, May 16, 1982.

16. *Billings Gazette*, Jul. 13, 1975; Jul. 6, 1981.

17. *Billings Gazette*, Feb. 14, 1993.

18. *Billings Gazette*, June 22, 1999.

19. *Billings Gazette*, Sept. 15, 1976.

20. Willard Fraser clipping file, Billings Public Library.

21. Mac Fraser, interview with author, Dec. 4, 2017.

Index

Page numbers in italic refer to illustrations.

Adreon, (William) Clark Sr., 161, 213, *214*, 217, *218*
Adreon, (William) Clark Jr., 213, *218*
African Americans, 64, 197, 199, 220
air pollution, 119, 166–168, 220, 223–224, 227, 238, 252–253, 259–260, 264, 266–267, 296, 299, 310
Air Pollution Advisory Board (Air Pollution Control Board), 148, 253, 299, 310
Air Pollution Commission, 264, 296
airport, 134–135, 142, 154, 156–157, 220, 223, 249, 264, 268, 300–301, 303
Albin, Berthold Richard (B. R.), ix, 21–22, 30, 45, 58–63, *62*, 67, 74, 76, 78, 80–81, 91, 125, 296
Albin, Jane. *See* Jane Fraser
Albin, Mary Louise. *See* Mary Louise Fraser
"America," 49, 55, 195, 305
America First Committee, 80–81, 83–84
American Indian. *See* Native American
American Indian Research Project, 274
Amherst College, x, 3, 33–35, 155–156
Amherst, Massachusetts, 26, 41–42, 45, 51
Anaconda (Copper) Company, 27, 44, 66, 75, 298
Anderson, Forrest, 255, 257, 263, 265, 298
Anderson, LeRoy, 109, 120, 124, 257
anti-Communist, 177, 243
anti-German, 26, 28
anti-Semite (anti-Semitism), 69, 80–82
Applegate, Irva Mae, *136*
Apsáalooke: language, 219; legal rights, 108; nation, 16; people, 15; tribe, 14; veteran, 226. *See also* Crow

archaeological: colleagues, 74; digs, 34; expedition, 56; experiences, 35; knowledge, 38; meeting, 168; site, 211; study, 38; training, 33; work, 13, 40, 209
archaeology, 33, 35, 111, 153, 208, 214, 274
Army Corps of Engineers, 106, 112
art, 32, 122, 144, 151–153, 210
assassination of: Medgar Evers, 241; Bobby Kennedy, 241; John F. Kennedy, 156; Martin Luther King Jr., 241; Malcolm X, 241
asthma (asthmatic), 4, 13, 23–24, 33, 36, 48, 57, 68, 71, 83, 85, 89, 91, 97, 111, 119, 121, 125, 160, 166, 168, 182, 223, 228, 235, 266, 279, 303
Auger, Guillaume, 95–96, 290

Babcock, Albert L. (A. L.), 16, *18*, 19, 59
Babcock, L. C., *18*
Babcock, Tim, 129, 141, 154–156, *155*, 165, 173, 216, 256, 257, 262–263, 301, 305
Babcock-Fraser Company, *18*
bagpipe (pipe), 6, 161, 188, 287, 300
Baker, Donald, 166, 222, 291, 293, 313
Ballantine, Lesley Frost, 27, 53–54, 56–57, 64, 69, 83, 121, *136*, 136–137, 230, 262, 281, 290,
Bartlett, Forrest, 36–37
Bartlett, John, 35–36, 38, 52, 68
Bartlett, Margaret, 35–36, 38, 52, 68
Battin, James, 129, 170, 222, 264
Beaumont, Phillip (Braids on Top), 259, 275
beauty contests, 228
Beslanwitch, John, 160
Beven, John (Police Chief), 148, 191, 201, 223

bicycle (bike), 1, 19, 24, *226*, 226–227, 229, 233,
 269, 279, 282, 285, *286*, 292, 299, *304*, 308,
 312–315, *314*
Bighorn Canyon, 112, 173, 219
Bighorn Canyon National Recreation Area, 112,
 262
Bighorn River, 106, 111–112, 164, 173
Billings American Indian Council, 220, 272
Billings Archaeological Society, 146, 209–210, 212
Billings Art Association, 152, 160, 210
Billings Citizens for Fluoridation, 179, 183–185
Billings Public Library. *See* Parmly Library
Billings Sugar Company. *See* Great West Sugar
 Company
Billings Transit Authority, 292
Billings United Chinese Relief Committee, 80
Billings Women's Club, 21, 21, 113
Billings, Frederick, 15
Billings, Germany, 158, 282–283
Billings, Montana: air quality (*see* air pollution);
 bus system, 166, 211, 279, 299; city key, 156–158,
 158, 294, 301; city seal, 4, 156, *190*; downtown,
 16–17, 59, *59*, 64, 101, 133, 149, 150, 169, 237;
 history of, 14–17, 20–21; parks, 150, 225, 234,
 311, 312, 313; population of, 15, 64, 98, 139, 145,
 288; sewer system, 118, 169–170, 261; streets,
 135, 140, 150, 170, 191, 203, 225, 294, 299; water
 system, 104, 126, 139, 180, 292, 310
Black Mesa (Arizona), 38
Blackford, Ben 116, 121–123, 132, 234, 297
Blackford, Jeanne Fraser, 21, 59, 88, 116, 121–123,
 124, 297
Bleeding Kansas, 10, 12
Bobby Burns Day, *206*, 297
Bohlinger, John, ix, 224, 228, *284*, *285*, 284–285,
 292, 312
Bonner, John, 103, 105–107, *110*, 111
Borberg, Charlie, 32, 57, 80, 86, 111, 160, 171, 173,
 252, 263, 310
Boys' Club (Boys' and Girls' Club), 225, 229,
 312–313
Bragg, Addison, 132, 138, 143, 157–158, 160, 175, 223,
 227, 293, 303–306, *307*, 309, 312
Bread Loaf School of English, 73, 114
Brew, Joe (J. O.), 35, 153, 211, 306
Broken Flute Cave (Arizona), 35
Brooks, Chester, 210
Brose, Fred, 28
Brown, Dick, *159*
Brown, John, 9, 10, 12, 132

Brown, Rockwood Jr., 210
Budde, G. Edward (Gus), 216–218
building codes, 260–264, 265, 295, 299
Bull Tail, Alice, 275
Bureau of Indian Affairs, 101, 133, 306
Bureau of Land Management, 213
Bureau of Reclamation, 106, 109, 112

Calamity Jane Reservoir, 297, 299, 310
Calton, Cal, 303
Calton, Fran, ix, 303
Canan, Debbie, *159*
Canyon de Chelly (Arizona), 33–35, 40
Cavanagh, Jerome, 220
Cave Commission, 210, *211*, 212
Chamberlin, Anne, 162–163
Chapel, William, 291
Cheyenne (Northern Cheyenne): children, 279;
 elders, *200*; people 272, 305; pow wow singers,
 313; tribal council, 216; tribal members, 270,
 271, 272, 275; tribe, 131, 199, 208, 223, 272;
 victory, 214
Chief Plenty Coups, 14, 151, 268
Chief Plenty Coups State Park, 268
childbed fever. *See* puerperal fever
"Choose Something Like a Star," 56, 116
Citizens Committee for Free Choice and Pure
 Water, 183, 185, 295. *See also* Council for Free
 Rights and Pure Water
Citizens for Orderly Growth, 295
City Federation of Women's Clubs, 114
City Planning Committee, 149
Civil Rights Act, 241
Civil War, 8–11, 195–196, 198
Clark, Wilson, 210
Clavadetscher, Carl, 126, 130–131, 137, 160
Clawson, Roger, 1, 143, 221, 287, 292, 306, 312
Conner, Stuart (Stu), ix, 35, 111, 134, 137, 140–141,
 143, *146*, 147, 150, 168, 173, 207–209, *209*, 211–
 212, 217, 223, 234, 254, 256, 270, 274, 305–306,
 307, 310
Continental Oil Company, 264, 296
Corette power plant, 166, 167, 296
Council for Free Rights and Pure Water, 182. *See
 also* Citizens Committee for Free Rights and
 Pure Water
Cousins, Norman, 205
Cross, Frank, 57, 102, 137, 231, 306, *307*
Cross, Ted, 160, 231
Crow: Agency, 157, 219, 270; chairman, 109, 111,

270, 303; chief, 108; cultural practices, 275; elders, 208; Fair, 219, 223, 275; flute player, 313; funeral, 275; homeland, 14; horsemen, 271; Indians, 217; language, 277; leader, 289; Nation, 284, 305; people, 108, 131, 200, 217, 235–236, 274, 275, 277, 296, 303, 304; pow wow singers, 303; Reservation, 14, 108, 208, 212, 219, 270, 275; students, 259; sun dance, 275; tribal council, 111, 216, 284, 303; tribal members, 215, 259, 270–272, 274–275; Tribe, 108–109, 111, 112, 131, 173, 236, 304; veteran, 220, 226, 296, 305; wedding, 275, 276; woman, 131; women, 304; youth, 235. *See also* Apsáalooke
Cummins, John, 274
Custer Battlefield, 157, 214
Custer National Cemetery, 216
Custer, George Armstrong, 159, 214, 216, 272–273, 275
Custer, Libbie, 214–215

D'Alesandro, Thomas, 220
D'Ewart, Wesley, 102–105, 109, 111, 119
Daley, Richard J., 221, 246, 258
dams, 47–48, 106–107, 109, 112–113, 126
Darrow, George, 273
Dartmouth College, x, 3, 235–237
Daylight Saving Time, 144, 175
Davis, Jean, 236
Deisz, Francis, 180–183, 185–186
Deisz, Leona, 180–181, 181, 186, 260–261, 265–266, 285, 294–296
Department of Housing and Urban Development (HUD), 170, 260
DeVoto, Bernard, 71, 109, 119
Dibble, Ernie, 151
Dimke, John, 172, 199
Dix, Howard, 144, 221
Dixon, Joe, 28, 75
Dunaway, Faye, 265, 270
Dunbar, Gerald, 268, 294, 306

"Easter '44," 90
Eastern Montana College, 3, 61, 116, 140, 179, 210, 236, 238, 244, 247–248, 260, 268, 275, 291, 305, 310–312
education, 19, 30, 31, 86, 97, 114, 140, 230, 235–236, 239, 275, 309
8th Infantry Division, 85–86, 88–89, 91–92, 94, 100
Eighth Medical Battalion, 85–86, 88

Eisenhower, Dwight D., 88, 111, 124–125, 277
elections, 42–44, 67, 69–70, 73, 75, 78–79, 100, 102–105, 108, 111, 118–121, 124–129, 135, 137–142, 164, 165–166, 175, 179, 182–183, 185–186, 196, 245, 250, 253–257, 263–266, 284–285, 287, 295
Elge, Frances, 205
England, 47, 71, 80, 89–91, 94
environment, 4–5, 113, 168, 178, 227, 234, 285
environmental: awareness, 145; concerns, 107, 174, 263; impacts, 109; issues, 119, 310; legislation, 168; potential, 273; problem, 166, 173; safety, 311; situation, 172
Erdmann, Marian, 144–145, 148, 204, 221
Erickson, John, 43, 75
Erickson, Leif, 100, 105

Fagg, Harrison, ix, 128, 139, 169, 308
federal building, 133–135, 142, 278
Felt, Dolly, 151, 268
Ferguson, Abby, ix, 189, 228, 299
Fillner, Russell, 159, 291
First Congregational Church (Billings), 15, 21, 28, 156, 277, 305
Fisher, Sherry R., 162
Fitzgerald, Bob, 151
Fitzgerald, M. Brooks, 151
Five Finger Lake project, 299, 310
Fjare, Orvin, 120, 146, 217, 243
Flathead River float, 191
fluoridation, 176–188, 219, 260, 295; opposition to, 177–187, 183
Foote, Don, 212, 213, 217, 270
Foote, Stella, 212, 213, 270, 273
Ford, Gerald, 80
Ford, Sam, 79
Fort Benton, 110, 112, 164, 204
Fort Berthold (Indian Reservation), 109
Fort Peck, 47, 76, 112, 164, 306
Fort Peck Dam, 47, 76
Fowler investigation, 66
Fox Theater (Alberta Bair Theatre), 272
Fox, William, 290–291
France, 47, 85, 91–92, 94–95, 282, 290, 298
Fraser Realty Company, 101
Fraser building, 76, 101–102, 105, 133, 267, 278
Fraser family, 7, 96, 124
Fraser, Bobby, 252
Fraser, J. B. (John Brown), 7, 13, 17, 19, 22–23, 32, 64–65, 96, 118, 122, 124, 125
Fraser, James H. (Jim), 7, 16–17, 18

Fraser, Jane, 21, 60

Fraser, Jerry, *96*, 118, 230, 290, 305, *307*

Fraser, John, *96*, 196, 202

Fraser, Mac, ix, 19, 22, 57, 61, 65, *96*, 118, 123, 128, 160, 223, 315

Fraser, Marjorie Frost, 2, 4, 27, 33, 36–37, *37*, 40, 45–46, *46*, 49, 55, 60, 64, 97, 159, 195, 282, 305–306

Fraser, Marvin, 45, 60, *124*, 230, 306

Fraser, Mary Louise, 21, 45, 60, 118, 230

Fraser, Robert (Bob), 60, *124*, 230

Fraser, Robin. *See* Robin Fraser Hudnut

Fraser, Ruth Jeanne. *See* Jeanne Blackford

Fraser, Sadie Gay, 4, 10–11, 13, 17–23, *20*, 32, 45, 53, 56–57, 64–65, 68, 72, 86, *96*, 97, 113–114, 118, *122*, 123, *124*, 132, 136, 149, 156, 158, 252, 258, 265, 290, 304, 306, 308

Fraser, Wendelanne (Wendy), ix, 19, 25, 122, 168, 230, 260, 270–271, 305

Fraser, William, 6, 7, 8–9

Fraser, Willard Edward: birth, 13; broken hip, 228–229, 258, 262, 278–279; death, 35, 170, 303, 304–308, 311–313; funeral, 304–306, *307*; education, 29–30, 31–32; employment, 24, 32–34, 38, 40–42, 44, 47, 50, 58, 69, 76–78, 92, 100–102, 266, 269, 287; hospitalized, 86, 91, 97, 119, 120, 125, 168, 205, 258, *258*, 258–259, 262, 268; illness, 4, 23,89, 91, 97, 119, 121, 123, 125–126, 223–224, 303; marriage, 2,44–47; military medals, 97, military training, 29–30, 83–84, *85*, 92–93, 100; optimism, 4, 19, 56, 92, 15, 235, 252, 255, 288; patriotism, 83, 86, 91, 195, 243, 249, 262, 305; photographs of, *vi, 12, 24, 34, 40, 46, 57, 87, 101, 110, 113, 122, 124, 135, 136, 141, 144, 151, 155, 159, 161, 162, 171, 191, 194, 200, 204, 206, 214, 218, 222, 226, 229, 232, 236, 239, 254, 258, 274, 276, 284, 286, 289, 293, 298, 301, 302, 304, 314*; tributes to: 305–308, 312–313; views on smoking, 5, 71, 118, 119, 168, 224, 227, 310; views on war, 74, 80, 82–84, 90–94, 242–251; views on women, 148–149, 204–205, 311; as visionary, 2–5, 97, 117, 141, 163, 169, 206, 208, 255, 274, 299, 310, 312

Fritzler, Minnie, 275

Frost, Carol, 27, 38, 41, 50, 53, 71, 136

Frost, Elinor, 2, 26, 27, 35, 38, 39, 41, 43, 45–47, 50–56, 63–65, *65*, 68, 71–73, 279–280, 282

Frost family, 27

Frost, Lesley. *See* Lesley Ballantine.

Frost, Lillian, 38, 41, 52–54, 56, 71, 86, 91, 136, 195

Frost, Marjorie. *See* Marjorie Fraser

Frost, Robert, 2, 27, 33–34, 36–40, *39*, 45, 47, 50–51, 53–56, 61, 66, 68, 70–74, 79–80, 82–84, 86, 92–93, 97–100, 102–103, 107, 114–116, 121–123, 126–129, 132–136, 144, 151, 156, 227, 235, 251, 263, 277, 279–282, *280*, 308

funeral, 8, 54, 60, 75, 135, 137, 148, 156, 198, 214, 237, 243, 275, *304*, 304–306; *307*

Gallegly, Dick, 265, 273

Garcia, Larry, 296–297

Gates of Hell, 151, 194

Gateway Arch (National Park), 155, 218–219

Gay family, 10, *11*, 13

Glacier National Park, 35, 46

Glasgow Air Force Base, 220–221

Glendinning, Richard, *159*, 161, 205

gravity–flow water system, 126, 139, 292, 310

Great Depression, 3, 29–31, 41, 60, 64, 68, 98, 197, 208

Great West Sugar Company, 15, 64, *167*, 197, 296

Green, Austin, *194*

gun control, 4, 310

Guthrie, A. B., 109, 136, 142, 161–162, 193, 273

Gutierrez, Bob, *159*

Hagen, Bill, 137, 141, 165

Hagen, Harold, 210

Hanel, Tom, 313

Harr, Donald, ix, 148, 169, 173, 175, 186

Hart, Ray, 21–22, 59–61, 273

Hart, Russ, 21, 60, 83

Heywood, Stanley, 277, 305, *307*, 312

Hoffman, Dustin, 205, 265, 270–271, *271*, 284

Hoover, Herbert, 42, 75, 108, 195, 205

Hoover, J. Edgar, 261

Horowitz, Samuel, 199, 268

Hudnut, David Beecher, 122–123, 128, 132, 136, 155, 160

Hudnut, David Beecher Jr., ix, 19, 64, *96*, *123*, 125, 132, *135*, 231, 233, 300

Hudnut, Marjorie. *See* Marjorie Renner

Hudnut, Rev. Dr. William, 122, 198

Hudnut, Robin Fraser, ix, 2, 4, 19, 22, 49, 51, 53–54, 56–58, 61, 63–65, 68–69, 71–73, *72*, 83–84, 86–88, 95–99, *96*, 102, 107, 113–116, *115*, 118, 121–123, *122*, *123*, 125, 127–128, 132, *135*, 136, 155–157, 189, 231–233, 250, 258, 279, 282, 288–290, *289*, 300, 305–306, 312–313, 315

Hultgren, Howard, 166, 186, 259, 265–267, 283–285, 287

Humphrey, Hubert, 65, 128, 158, 195, 205, 216, 218, 229, 253–254
Humphrey, Muriel, 158, 265

inauguration, 63, 128, 141–142, 156, 158, 287, 290
Independent Merchants Association of Montana, 58, 63–64, 66–68, 76, 78–79, 102
Indian Caves, 140, 172, 174, 192, 208, 210–212, 234, 299, 312
influenza (flu), 24–26, 182
Internal Revenue Service (Montana), 43, 50, 66
irrigation, 15, 48, 106–109, 112

Jakab, Paul, x, 223, 234–235, 266, 282, 284, 305
Jaycees, 139, 159–160
Jefferson National Expansion Memorial, 216–218
John Birch Society, 29, 129, 176
Johnson, Isabelle, 152
Johnson, Lady Bird, 155–158, 157, 265, 294, 301
Johnson, Lyndon B., 112, 128–129, 158, 181, 195, 215, 242–245, 250, 257, 263
Johnson, Roger, 34

Kansas, x, 6–10, 12–14, 17, 22, 32, 70, 100, 113, 121–122, 132, 134, 149, 203, 269
Kelly, Tom, 155
Kennedy, Robert (Bobby), 234, 241, 245, 253, 254
Kennedy, Jacqueline (Jackie), 128, 156, 205, 262
Kennedy, John F. (JFK), 128, 133–134, 151, 154–156, 155, 181, 231, 241, 253–254
Kennedy, Ted, 141
Kenoly, Delsie, 198
Kidder, Alfred, 33, 35
Kittleson, James, 199
Klindt, Henry, 160
Knight, Earle, 118, 125
Korean War, 104, 160, 251
Ku Klux Klan, 28–29

La Plata Mountains (Colorado), 33, 35
Lasko, Gene, 270
Lawrie, Helen, 41, 46, 93
Lawson, Robley, 151
League of Women Voters, 193–195
LeBar, Jeanne, 148, 284
Lee, J. Lawson, 306, 307
Lee, Kenneth, 265
Leone, Joe, 139, 181, 210, 284, 287, 291
Lewis and Clark Expedition, 109, 152, 160, 212, 217–218, 226

Lewis and Clark Trail Commission, 217–218
Lidderdale, Charles, 291
Lindbergh, Anne Morrow, 34
Lindbergh, Charles, 34, 81
Lindsay, John, 220, 253–254, 298
Lister, Florence, 33
Lister, Robert, 33
Little Big Man, 265, 270–273, 271, 275, 282, 284, 288, 289
Little Bighorn Battle reenactment, 163, 214, 215
Little Bighorn Battlefield (Custer Battlefield), 157, 214–215, 220, 270
Little Bighorn Battlefield National Monument, 214
Little Flower Church, 156
lobbying, 99, 102–103, 111, 124, 135
Lynde, Jane, 160–161, 161
Lynde, Stan, 151, 160–162, 161, 217, 226, 254, 259, 312

Mammoth Hot Springs Hotel, 303
Mansfield, Maureen, 105, 156
Mansfield, Mike, x, 79, 82–83, 103, 105–107, 110, 110–111, 127, 141, 155, 156, 158, 170, 195, 212, 216, 234, 238, 242, 242–246, 248, 257, 273, 306
Mason General Hospital (NYC), 92
May, Conna, 210
Mayo Clinic, 53–54, 56, 121, 126, 184
Mayors' Float. *See* Yellowstone River Boat Float
McCarthy, Eugene, 120, 245–246
McCarthyism, 120
McGee, Gale, 155
McGovern, George, 234, 250
McLaughlin, John, 221, 253, 266
Medicine Crow, Joe, 14, 226, 274, 275, 305, 307, 312
Melcher, John, 254
Mesa Verde National Park, 33, 35
Metcalf, Lee, 79, 82–83, 105–106, 109, 111, 124, 129, 134, 155, 158, 170, 195, 216, 254, 263, 306
Mexican American, 64, 149, 156, 197–198, 236, 296, 300, 311
Millar, Stuart, 265, 270, 284
Missouri River, 15, 47, 106, 109, 112, 153, 164, 204, 217
Montana Air Pollution Council, 270
Montana Environmental Policy Act, 270
Montana Family Security, 102
Montana Federation of Women's Clubs, 21, 149
Montana Highway Department, 123, 169, 173, 212
Montana Historical Society, x, 153, 195
Montana Institute of the Arts, 152

Montana Inter-Tribal Policy Board, 199
Montana League of Cities and Towns, 261
Montana (state) legislature, 61, 76, 102, 105, 107, 111, 117, 126, 129, 165–166, 229, 259, 264, 296
Montana Livestock Association, 172
Montana Power Company, 66, 166, 296
Montana Sedition Act, 28
Montana State University–Billings. *See* Eastern Montana College
Montana Sulfur, 296
Montana Supreme Court, 67, 100, 183, 216
Montana Water Congress, 219
Montana–Dakota Utilities, 197, 253
Montgomery, Joe, 203–204, *204*
Morris, Ann, 33, 36
Morris, Earl, 32–35, 38, 40, 43, 56, 125, 146
Morrison, Kay, 73, 136
Morrison, Ted, 73, 136
Morrow, Elizabeth (Betty) Cutter, 34, 56, 81, 97
Morrow, Dwight Jr., 32–38, *34*, 41–43, 81, 97
Morrow, Dwight Sr., 34, 81, 97
Mountview Cemetery, 170, 172, 306
MSU–Billings Library, x, 189, 191, 236, 268
Mummy Cave (Arizona) 33, 35, 40
Murray, Charles (Charlie), 100, 106–107, 121
Murray, James E., 70–71, 75, 82–83, 100, 103, 106–107, *110*, 111, 121, 129

National Council on Indian Opportunity, 257
National historic landmark, 208, 211, 213
National Park Service, 112, 173, 210, 213, 273, 303
Native American, 102, 131, 146, 197–199, 208, 211, 214–215, 219, 227, 272, 275, 304, 310–311
"Never Again Would Birds' Song Be the Same," 56, 251
Nixon, Pat, 300–301, *301*, 303, 305
Nixon, Richard, 128, 196, 250, 263, 277, 305
No Moms Bike Hike, 226, 233, 269, 279
Nordahl, Harold, 160
Northern Hotel, 1, 142, 165, 202, 227, 270–271, 285, 287, 315
Northern Ireland, 85, 88–89
Northern Pacific Railroad, 14–16, 150
Nutter, Donald, 129

O'Bryan, Deric, 35, 38, 40
Old Coyote, Barney, 220, 275
Old Coyote, Henry, *215*
Old Coyote, Lloyd, 217

Old Coyote, Mickey, 275
Olsen, Arnold, 103, 105, 124, 127, 129, 134, 155, 264
Ommundsen, George, 160
Our Lady of Guadalupe Catholic Church, 64, 268

Pacific Power and Light, 253
Palmer House (Hotel), 257–278
parade, 1, 79, 154, 189, 207–208, 219, 231, 289–290
parking tickets, 140, 154
Parmly Library, 169, 268, 290, 311
patriotism, 26, 28–29, 83, 86, 91, 195, 243, 249, 262, 277, 305
Pearl Harbor, 76, 81–83
Pease, Eloise, 275
Penn, Arthur, 265, 270, 284
Penwell, Lewis, 21, 43–44, 66, 82
Pick-Sloan Flood Control Act (Pick-Sloan Program), 48, 106, 109, 119
Pictograph Caves. *See* Indian Caves
Pictograph Caves State Park, 211
poem, 48–49, 55–56, 89–91, 116, 128, 156, 182, 195, 251, 281, 305, 308
poetry, 23, 41–42, 49, 55, 114, 128, 195, 227, 235, 251, 280
police department (Billings), 148, 153, 163, 238, 296, 300
polio, 24–26, 182, 184–185
Pompeys Pillar, 208, 212–214, 217, 226, 269
Powers, Thomas, 144, 266
prejudice, 26, 28–29, 66, 106, 108, 197–199, 237, 309, 315. *See also* racism
Price, Evan, 30–31, 45
Price, Isabella, 31
proclamations, 127, 145–146, 189
prostitution, 171
protests, 236, 248
public lands, 4, 102, 119
puerperal fever, 52–53

Quantrill Raiders, 10

racism, 130, 199. *See also* prejudice
radio: address, 78, 80–81; announcer, 137; broadcasts, 69–70; call-ins, 261; commentator, 102; interview, 247; program, 294; station, 184, 207; talk (shows), 101, 104, 180, 184, 192, 260, 296
Ralston, J. K., 137, 151–152, 218, 226, 270, 273, 301, 306, *307*, 312
Rankin, Jeanette, 78–79, 111, 149

reading (books), 2, 23–24, 116, 132, 235, 279
Reagan, Ronald, 263
Real Bird, Edison, 111, 173, 216, 270, 275
real estate, 99, 101
recreation, 137, 140, 142, 163–164, 170, 283
refineries, 16, 166, *167*, 253, 296
Renner, Marjorie Hudnut, ix–x, 98, 231, 232
Reno, James, 172, 184–186
Reynolds, George, 31–32, 41, 43
Rides Horse, Sam, 220, 272, 289
Riedl, Cornelius (Con), 165, 167, *181*, 284, 291
Rimrocks (Rims), 14–15, 24, 29, 134–135, 139, 150, 168–169, 201, 208, 273–274, 305, 310
riots, 220–221, 241
Rocky Mountain College, 116, 140, 151, 188, 237, 306
Rocky Mountain Writers' Conference, 36, 68
Ronquillo, James (Jim), x, 4, 169, 197–198
Roosevelt, Eleanor, 19
Roosevelt, Franklin Delano (FDR), 42–43, 50, 61, 63, 69–71, 75–6, 78–79, 81–82, 92, 100, 257, 277
Roosevelt, Theodore (Teddy), 203, 210, 231
Rosell, Antoinette, 270
Rosell, Earl, 270
Rowe, Tom T., 104–105, 119
Rye, Roy, 222, 283, 291

St. Vincent's Hospital, 16, 25, 52, 53, 125, 131, 229, 258, 259, 262, 263
Sales, Milton, *151*
Salisbury, Grant, 111, 133–134, 173, *191*, 192, 196, 205, 215, 245, 272
Salk vaccine, 25–26
Schoenthal, Norman, *181*, 282, 291, 305, 310
science, 21, 24, 26, 32, 182
Scott, Mrs. Phillip, 258–259
Scott, Phillip (Phil), 193, 239, 258–259
Seil, Reverend, 28
Self, John, 152, 160, 165, 180
17-Point Program for Billings's Progress, 137, *140*
Shoup, Richard, 221, 254–255, *256*, 266
Silver Dollar Bar, 197
Skid Row (Billings), 97, 197, 269, 292, 311
Small, Aaron, 137, 306, *307*
smallpox vaccination, 177
Smith College, 34, 97, 116, 121
South Side (Billings neighborhood), x, 4, 19, 64–65, 96, 99, 149, 156, 169, 197–198, 237, 305, 309
Southwest, 13, 33–35, 38, 41, 54, 56, 58, 86, 211

Spock, Benjamin, 184, 248
Stearns, Hal (Harold G.), 5, 121, 143, 217–218, 265, 282–283, 285, 305–306, 310, 312–313
Stevenson, Adlai, 110–111, 124, 205
Stewart, David, 303
Stockbridge Productions, 264–265, 270
Stockton, Bill, 151–152, 156
"Stopping by Woods on a Snowy Evening," 308
sun dance, 223, 275

Taggart, Cal S., 112, 173
Taylor, Robert, *218*
Taylor Grazing Act, 119
Teapot Dome scandal, 75
Thompson, Edward, 216
Thompson, Elizabeth, 300, *301*
Thompson, James (Jim), ix, 146, *147*, 162, 171, 185, 194–195, 223–224, 259, 266, 278, 300, 305, *307*, 312
Thompson, Lawrance, 47, 71, 136, 279–280
Toineeta, Joy Yellowtail, *274*, 275
Tooley, Chuck, 313
tourism, 137, 145, 255, 269
Trott, Charlie, 80
Truman, Harry, 103, 110, 231–232, 277
Turman, George, 306

U.S. Census Bureau, 77, 99, 100–101
U.S. Conference of Mayors, 149, 220, 252, 298
U.S. Department of Interior, 211, 300
Udall, Stewart, 109, 112, 128, 133, 155–156, 195, 213, 218, 262
University of Colorado (Boulder), 30–32, 34, 41, 146
Untermeyer, Louis, 26, 34, 54–55, 136, 281,
urban renewal, 142, 149–150, 260, 267
Urban Renewal Committee, 149–150

Vermont, 54, 56, 58, 64, 68, 73, 83, 114, 122, 280
Veterans for Wheeler, 99
Vietnam National Memorial, 251
Vietnam War, x, 3, 241–251, 263
Vietnam War Moratorium, 245
Voting Rights Act, 241

Walsh, Thomas, 28, 43, 63, 74–75
war, 3, 8–9, 26–29, 63, 71, 74, 76–77, 79–98, 100–101, 105, 150, 157, 166, 180, 187, 208–209, 242–251, 260, 285, 294, 306

War on Poverty, 241

Water Pollution Control Board, 252–253

Werner, Dr. and Mrs., *122*

Western Heritage Museum, 289

Western Progressive, 40, 44, 47, 50, 66

Wheeler, Burton K. (B. K.), 22, 27, 43, 61–63, *62*, 70–71, 74–84, *77*, 89, 91, 97, 99–101, 106, 128, 134, 138, 139, 141, 165, 195, 216, 232, 243, 257, 310

Wheeler, Lulu, *62*, *63*, 81

Whithorn, Doris, *162*

Wilber, Douglas (Doug), 230, 290, 306, *307*

Willard Fraser Memorial Bridge, 313

Wirth, Ted, 210

Women's Council of the Christian Church, 21

Women's Liberation Movement, 311

Woodenlegs, John (Johnny), 216, 275

Works Progress Administration (WPA), 61, 209, 273

World War I, 8, 26, 28–29, 243, 245, 249, 251

World War II, 3, 8, 30, 57, 70, 74, 76, 80, 85, 88, 95, 97, 105, 109, 134, 195, 209, 226, 243, 249, 251, 273, 278, 282, 290, 297, 306

Wyoming Fish and Game Department, 173

Wyoming Highway Department, 173

Yeats, William Butler, 90–91

Yellowstone Art Center (Yellowstone Art Museum), 140, 152–153, 163

Yellowstone Historical Society, 273

Yellowstone National Park, 46, 203, 219, 300, 303

Yellowstone River, 14–15, 140, 160–161, 213, 217, 227, 253

Yellowstone River Boat Float (Mayors' Float), *112*, *159*, 159–164, 205, 209, 213, 217–219, *218*, 259, 269, 283, 310, 312

Yellowstone Taxpayers Association, 166, 170

Yellowstone Valley, 3, 14, 58, 199, 249

Yellowtail Dam, 99, 106–113, 124, 126, 138, 140, 155, 173, 219, 220, 262

Yellowtail, Bill, 235

Yellowtail, Robert, 107–108, *108*

Yellowtail, Susie Walking Bear, 275, *276*

Yellowtail, Tom, 275

youth (young people), 3, 5, 18, 201, 225, 227–230, 233, 235, 237–240, 246, 248, 255, 309, 311–312

Youth Advisory Council (Youth Committee), 229, 233–234, 299

zoning, 181, 266, 294–296, 299

Lou Mandler grew up on a dryland farm in Montana's Sheridan County and maintains an interest in the family farm and all things Montana. A graduate of Montana State University, Mandler pursued a career in education. She is the author of *This Storied Land, A Montana Memoir* and two articles on Ernest Hemingway.